International Perspectives on Household Wealth

The Levy Economics Institute of Bard College

Founded in 1986, The Levy Economics Institute of Bard College is an autonomous nonprofit public policy research organization. It is nonpartisan, open to the examination of diverse points of view and dedicated to public service.

The Institute believes in the potential for economic study to improve the human condition. Its purpose is to generate viable, effective public policy responses to important economic problems. It is concerned with issues that profoundly affect the quality of life in the USA, in other highly industrialized nations and in countries with developing economies.

The Institute's present research programs include such issues as financial instability, economic growth and employment, international trade, problems associated with the distribution of income and wealth, the measurement of economic well-being, and gender equality and the economy.

The opinions expressed in this volume are those of the authors and do not necessarily represent those of the Institute, its Board of Governors or the Trustees of Bard College.

International Perspectives on Household Wealth

Edited by

Edward N. Wolff

The Levy Economics Institute and New York University, USA

IN ASSOCIATION WITH THE LEVY ECONOMICS INSTITUTE

Edward Elgar

Cheltenham, UK • Northampton, MA, USA

Published by
Edward Elgar Publishing Limited
Glensanda House
Montpellier Parade
Cheltenham
Glos GL50 1UA
UK

Edward Elgar Publishing, Inc.
136 West Street
Suite 202
Northampton
Massachusetts 01060
USA

A catalogue record for this book
is available from the British Library

ISBN-13: 978 1 84542 116 8
ISBN-10: 1 84542 116 7

Printed and bound in Great Britain by MPG Books Ltd, Bodmin, Cornwall

Contents

Contributors

Andrea Brandolini, Bank of Italy, Economic Research Department, Rome, Italy.

Luigi Cannari, Bank of Italy, Economic Research Department, Rome, Italy.

Scott Cody, Mathematica Policy Research, Inc., Washington, DC, USA.

John L. Czajka, Mathematica Policy Research, Inc., Washington, DC, USA.

Giovanni D'Alessio, Bank of Italy, Economic Research Department, Rome, Italy.

Conchita D'Ambrosio, Università di Milano-Bicocca, Milan, Italy.

Marie Drolet, Statistics Canada, Ottawa, Ontario, Canada.

Ivan Faiella, Bank of Italy, Economic Research Department, Rome, Italy.

Elena Gouskova, Economic Behavior Program, Survey Research Center, Institute for Social Research, University of Michigan, Ann Arbor, USA.

Richard Hauser, Professor of Economics, Johann Wolfgang Goethe University, Frankfurt am Main, Germany.

Markus Jäntti, Professor of Economics, Åbo Akademi University, Turku, Finland.

F. Thomas Juster, Economic Behavior Program, Survey Research Center, Institute for Social Research, University of Michigan, Ann Arbor, USA.

Daniel Kasprzyk, Mathematica Policy Research, Inc., Washington, DC, USA.

Arthur B. Kennickell, Senior Economist and Project Director Survey of Consumer Finances, Board of Governors of the Federal Reserve System, Washington, DC, USA.

N. Anders Klevmarken, Department of Economics, Uppsala University, Uppsala, Sweden.

René Morissette, Statistics Canada, Ottawa, Ontario, Canada.

Dimitri B. Papadimitriou, President, Levy Economics Institute of Bard College, Annandale-on-Hudson, NY, USA.

Seymour Spilerman, Professor of Sociology and Director, Center for the Study of Wealth and Inequality, Columbia University, New York, NY, USA.

Frank P. Stafford, Economic Behavior Program, Survey Research Center, Institute for Social Research, University of Michigan, Ann Arbor, USA.

Holger Stein, Johann Wolfgang Goethe University, Frankfurt am Main, Germany.

Florencia Torche, Department of Sociology, New York University, and Center for the Study of Wealth and Inequality, Columbia University, New York, NY, USA.

Edward N. Wolff, Professor of Economics, New York University, New York, NY, and Senior Scholar, Levy Economics Institute of Bard College, Annandale-on-Hudson, NY, USA.

Xuelin Zhang, Statistics Canada, Ottawa, Ontario, Canada.

Foreword

Dimitri B. Papadimitriou

The publication of this collection of essays is the product of a project undertaken by the Levy Economics Institute to understand better the many economic aspects of income and wealth distribution that help define the term 'economic well-being'. During the 1990s the gap in household wealth between the United States and other advanced industrialized countries increased significantly. Particularly, in the United States trends in wealth holding among various household structures have shown to be disturbingly unequal. However, as is well known, conventional measures of trends often mask conditions of higher importance. In this respect, one may question why wealth distribution in the United States is not in concert with the longest economic growth experienced during the decade of the 1990s and with expectations that a 'rising tide lifts all boats'.

The chapters in this volume assess the already established measures of wealth, propose new ones, and analyse and compare possible alternates. Conceptual or empirical studies that identify key issues related to measurement and evaluation of wealth distribution are also included, as are empirical estimates and their significance. While one may not agree with every argument and proposal made or embrace every conclusion drawn, the essays in this collection are thoughtful and perhaps some of them are provocative. They need to be read and discussed, and their implications considered.

I would like to thank our senior scholar, Edward N. Wolff, who along with our resident scholar, Ajit Zacharias, heads the Institute's research on 'The Distribution of Income and Wealth' and 'The Economics of Well-Being', and who organized the conference from which these chapters are drawn. I am grateful to the contributors for their cooperation in carrying out revisions and to Deborah Treadway and Janice Weber for copy-editing large parts of the volume, managing final details of collating the changes by authors, and overseeing all tasks of proofreading. Finally, my heartfelt thanks to the Trustees of Bard College for supporting the Institute's programmes.

Abbreviations

ADS	Assets and Debts Survey (Canada)
BLS	Bureau of Labor Statistics
BNLS	Banca Nazionale del Lavoro Survey
CPI	Consumer Price Index
CPS	Current Population Survey
DB	defined benefit pension plan
DC	defined contribution pension plan
ECHP	Eurostat's European Community Household Panel
EK Index	Esteban and Ray's modified index
ER Index	Estaban and Ray index
ESPE	European Society for Population Economics
FANA	Financial Accounts and the National Accounts (Italy)
FCSD	Finnish Central Securities Depository
FRG	Federal Republic of Germany
GDP	gross domestic product
GDR	German Democratic Republic
GEE	generalized estimating equation
GLM	generalized linear models
GSOEP	German Socio-Economic Panel
HA	Historical Archive of the Survey of Household Income and Wealth (Bank of Italy)
HUS	Swedish household panel surveys
ICS	Income and Consumption Surveys (*Einkommens-und Verbrauchsstichprobe*) of the German Federal Statistical Office
IFLC	Intergenerational Financial Linkages in Chile
IRA	individual retirement account
IRS	Internal Revenue Service
ISEI	International Socioeconomic Index
LINDA	longitudinal individual database
LIRA	locked-in retirement accounts
LWS	Luxembourg Wealth Study
MAR	(data) missing at random
MIMIC	multiple indicators, multiple causes (model)
MIB	Milan stock exchange share index

NIA	National Institute on Aging
OECD	Organization for Economic Cooperation and Development
PPP	purchasing power parity
PSID	Panel Study of Income Dynamics
PSU	primary sampling unit
Q-D	quantile-difference
RRIF	registered retirement income funds
RRSP	registered retirement savings plans
SCF	Survey of Consumer Finances
SEM	structural equation model
SFS	Survey of Financial Security (Canada)
SHIW	Survey of Household Income and Wealth (Bank of Italy)
SIPP	Survey of Income and Program Participation
SOI	Statistics of Income Division (US IRS)
SRC	Survey Research Center, University of Michigan
SUR	seemingly unrelated regression

1. International comparisons of wealth: methodological issues and a summary of findings

Edward N. Wolff

INTRODUCTION

The chapters that follow compile the latest information on household wealth in the United States, Canada, Germany, Italy, Sweden, and Finland over the 1990s and into the twenty-first century. For the United States, they also highlight trends in wealth holdings among the low-income population in the US, changes in wealth polarization, racial differences in wealth holdings, and the dynamics of portfolio choices. We find that, in general, wealth inequality has risen among these Organization for Economic Cooperation and Development (OECD) countries since the early 1980s, although Germany stands out as an exception. In the case of the US, wealth holdings have generally failed to improve among low-income families and the racial wealth gap has widened over the late 1990s.

There are now official estimates of the size distribution of household income in the United States today (as well as most other industrialized countries). The US Census Bureau conducts an annual survey in March called the Current Population Survey (CPS), which provides detailed information on individual and household earnings and income. On the basis of these data, the Census Bureau constructs its estimates of both family and household income inequality. Since the CPS surveys have been conducted in the US since 1948, a consistent time-series exists on household income distribution for the US which covers almost five decades.

Unfortunately, comparable data does not exist on the size distribution of household wealth for the US or, for that matter, for any other country in the world. Because there are no official household surveys conducted on an annual basis for this purpose, researchers in this field have had to make estimates of household wealth inequality from a variety of sources, which are sometimes inconsistent. Compounding this problem is the fact that household wealth is much more heavily concentrated in the upper percentiles of

the distribution than income. Thus, unless surveys or data sources are especially designed to cover the top wealth groups in a country, it is quite easy
to produce biased estimates of the size distribution of wealth which under-
state the true level of inequality. The net result is that estimates of household wealth distribution are more problematic than those of income
distribution.

The estimates of household wealth contained in this volume are all based
on household survey data. When comparing estimates of the size distribution of household wealth from different sources of wealth data, there are
four issues of major importance: (1) the sampling frame; (2) the assets and
liabilities included in the definition of wealth; (3) the unit of observation;
and (4) response errors.

Sample Design

The first issue is the sampling frame. Two different types of samples have
been used: (1) random or representative samples; and (2) stratified samples.
The main problem with representative samples is that, because household
wealth is extremely skewed, the very rich (the upper tail of the distribution)
are often considerably under-represented in such samples. As a result, estimates of both the mean level of wealth and the degree of wealth inequality are liable to be considerably understated (see, for example, Wolff 1999,
for some statistical analysis of this issue).

A stratified sample, in contrast, may be designed to over-sample the rich.
In the case of the the Federal Reserve Board's Survey of Consumer
Finances (SCF), the high-income supplement is drawn from the data files
compiled by the Statistics of Income Division of the Internal Revenue
Service (see Chapters 2, 3 and 4 in this volume). For the 1983 SCF, for
example, an income cut-off of $100 000 of adjusted gross income is used as
the criterion for inclusion in the supplemental sample. Individuals are then
randomly selected for the sample within predesignated income strata. The
advantage of the high-income supplement is that it provides a much 'richer'
sample of high income and, potentially, very wealthy families. However, the
presence of a high-income supplement creates some complications because,
in order to reflect the actual population, problems arise in 'weighting' the
high-income sample with the core representative sample (see, for example,
Kennickell and Woodburn 1999, for some of the issues involved in developing these weights in the case of the SCF).

Another issue concerns the portion of a population included in the sample.
For example, in the case of the German survey data used by Hauser and Stein
(Chapter 6), some of the surveys include only German citizens while others
include both German citizens and the resident foreign population.

Accounting Framework

Surveys also differ in the assets and liabilities included in the questionnaire or the wealth concept used. The exclusion of certain assets or
liabilities can also make an important difference in estimates of both the
level of wealth and the degree of wealth inequality. For example,
Kennickell (Chapter 2) includes the value of vehicles in his definition of
wealth whereas Wolff (Chapter 4) excludes their value. The result is that
Wolff estimates a higher degree of wealth inequality in the US than
does Kennickell, since automobiles are disproportionately held by lower-
income and middle-income families, whereas the estimate of median
(and mean) wealth is correspondingly higher in Kennickell's figures.
Moreover, trends in median wealth are noticeably different in the two sets
of results.

With regard to the Canadian data used by Morissette, Zhang and Drolet
(Chapter 5), the value of retirement accounts assets is not included in the
survey data and therefore is missing from their wealth concept. Since this
type of asset is heavily concentrated in the middle class, it will likely lead to
an upward bias in their estimate of wealth inequality. In the case of the
German data used by Hauser and Stein (Chapter 6), the value of business
equity is not included in the survey questionnaire and is therefore excluded
from the wealth definition. Since business equity is heavily concentrated
among high-wealth families, this exclusion will bias downward the estimate
of wealth inequality.

Unit of Observation

Estimates of household wealth, like income, are sensitive to the unit of
observation. Three are typically used in wealth data analysis: the household, the family and the individual. The family consists of individuals
who are related by marriage or by birth (or adoption in the case of children). The household unit is based on place of residence and may include
family members as well as other relations and unrelated individuals.
Households may also refer to single individuals living by themselves. In
income statistics, both mean and median income is typically higher for
families than households, while the degree of inequality is smaller. The
individual is also used as a unit of observation if wealth or income is
measured on a per capita basis or if the analysis is based on individual
data such as labour earnings or pensions. In the case of wealth, it is often
difficult (if not impossible) to divide assets and liabilities among individuals in a family or household, since the majority of assets and debts are
jointly held.

Response Error

Household surveys are questionnaires that are given to a sample of house-holds in a population. Their primary advantage is to provide considerable discretion to the interviewer about the information requested of respondents. Their major drawback is that information provided by the respondent is often inaccurate (response error) and, in many cases, the information requested is not provided at all (nonresponse problems). Studies indicate that response error and nonresponse rates are considerably higher among the wealthy than among the middle-class (see, for example, the analysis of Brandolini, Cannari, D'Alessio and Faiella in Chapter 7).

SUMMARY OF FINDINGS

In Chapter 2, Arthur Kennickell of the Board of Governors of The Federal Reserve System in Washington, DC, looks into wealth trends in the US from 1989 to 2001 (though primarily from 1998 to 2001) on the basis of the SCF. He finds that, over these years, wealth in real terms grew broadly across US families. However, characterizing distributional changes is much more complex. There is evidence both from *Forbes* data on the 400 wealthiest Americans and from the SCF, which explicitly excludes families in the *Forbes* list, that wealth grew relatively strongly at the very top of the distribution. At the same time, the share of total household wealth held by the *Forbes* wealthiest 400 also rose. However, while the point estimate of the share of total wealth held by the wealthiest 1 per cent of families as measured by the SCF also rose between 1998 and 2001, the change is not statistically significant. In 2001, the division of wealth observed in the SCF attributed about a third each to the wealthiest 1 per cent, the next wealthiest 9 per cent, and the remaining 90 per cent of the population.

Relative to everyone else, the wealth of the highest 10 per cent of the wealth distribution tends to be heavy in terms of holdings of most assets and liabilities, but it is particularly so for stocks, bonds, business assets and real estate investments. For other families, simple deposit accounts, houses and vehicles are the most important assets, and mortgages are the most important liability. Changes in shares were surprisingly few: a shift away from the wealthiest 10 per cent in the total share of stock holdings; a shift toward that group in the share of housing equity; and an increase in the share of nonmortgage debt (largely instalment debt and credit card debt) among the least wealthy half of the population. Overall, the indebtedness ratio tends to decline sharply with wealth.

The wealth of the older baby boomers – families headed by persons between the ages of 46 and 55 in 2001 – shows the expected life-cycle pattern of increase. Although that growth appears to be spread broadly, the most striking growth was at the bottom and the top of the wealth distribution. The number of inflation-adjusted millionaires in the cohort more than tripled over the 1989–2001 period. Overall, the data for the cohort suggest that the concentration of wealth rose over the period, but the rise is not statistically significant.

Kennickell also finds that the median wealth of African Americans in 1989 was only about 5 per cent of that for white non-Hispanic families and, by 2001, the fraction had risen to about 16 per cent. Differences are most striking at the two ends of the distribution of wealth. A higher fraction of African American families have net worth less than zero and a much higher fraction have wealth between zero and $1000. At the top end of the distribution, the differences are reversed with a much larger fraction of white non-Hispanics having wealth of $250 000 or more.

In Chapter 3, John L. Czajka, Scott Cody and Daniel Kasprzyk of Mathematica Policy Research, Inc., consider the question of who shared the growth of wealth in the 1990s in the US. Their particular interest is in subpopulation trends in US household wealth holdings.

They note that, following a recession in the early 1990s, the US economy experienced a broad and sustained expansion that lasted into the next decade. Estimates from the SCF indicate that the aggregate net worth of US households grew by 43 per cent in real terms between 1992 and 1998. Even after the expansion ended and the stock markets entered a period of significant decline, aggregate net worth in 2001 was still 91 per cent higher than its estimated 1992 value.

Kennickell's analysis of changes in the distribution of wealth documents the broad-based nature of the growth of wealth in the late 1990s while providing some evidence that wealth grew most strongly in the top 1 per cent of the wealth distribution. Czajk, Cody and Kasprzyk examine differences in the growth of wealth from another perspective than that of Kennickell; they use the comparative experience of subpopulations defined by family income and by characteristics that are of interest to a segment of policy analysts who use wealth data in their research. Using data from the US Census Bureau's Survey of Income and Program Participation (SIPP) as well as the SCF, they examine differential wealth holdings by age, race and Hispanic origin and how these changed over the 1990s. They then focus on nine subpopulations and present estimates of trends in wealth holdings over this period.

Their analysis of wealth trends among population subgroups lends further support to findings that the growth of wealth in the 1990s was very broad-based. Nevertheless, participation was not universal. Age differentials in net worth grew stronger over the 1990s. The pattern of change in racial differentials was more complex. Non-Hispanic whites experienced the largest gain in mean wealth and surpassed Asians in their average holdings. However, their strong advantage over all groups in median wealth did not increase, except in comparison with Asians and American Indians and Alaskan Natives, who do not appear to have seen growth in median wealth at all. Hispanic families and non-Hispanic black families also became more leveraged.

Wealth among families at all income levels grew, but segments of the wealth distribution with little wealth did not experience gains – even when their income was comparatively high. Subpopulations that include a lot of aged persons appear to have had greater growth in wealth, although this was not entirely consistent between the SCF and the SIPP. Likewise, the SIPP data suggest that families with nonaged social security beneficiaries (primarily those receiving disability insurance benefits) experienced no growth in mean net worth. However, the SCF did not support this.

Chapter 4, by myself, Edward Wolff of New York University and the Levy Economics Institute, focuses on changes in wealth inequality in the US over the 1980s and 1990s. Also based on the SCF, this chapter extends the time period of analysis of Kennickell's study in Chapter 2 to the 1983 to 2001 period.

My analysis shows that despite slow growth in income over the 1990s, there have been marked improvements in the wealth position of average families. Both mean and median wealth grew briskly in the late 1990s. The inequality of net worth levelled off even though income inequality continued to rise over this period. Indebtedness also fell substantially during the late 1990s. However, the number of households worth $1 million or more, $5 million or more, and especially $10 million or more surged during the 1990s. Moreover, the average wealth of the poorest 40 per cent declined by 44 per cent between 1983 and 2001 and, by 2001, had fallen to only $2900. All in all, the greatest gains in wealth and income were enjoyed by the upper 20 per cent, particularly the top 1 per cent, of the respective distributions.

Indebtedness also fell substantially during the late 1990s and by 2001 the overall debt–equity ratio was lower than in 1983. However, the debt–equity ratio was also much higher among the middle 60 per cent of households in 2001 at 0.32, than among the top 1 per cent, at 0.024, or the next 19 per cent at 0.089.

The concentration of investment-type assets generally remained as high in 2001 as during the previous two decades. About 90 per cent of the total value of stock shares, bonds, trusts and business equity, and about 80 per cent of nonhome real estate were held by the top 10 per cent of households. Moreover, despite the widening ownership of stock (52 per cent of households owned stock shares either directly or indirectly through mutual funds, trust funds or pension plans in 2001), the richest 10 per cent still accounted for 77 per cent of the total value of these stocks.

The racial disparity in wealth holdings, after stabilizing during most of the 1990s, widened in the years between 1998 and 2001, as the ratio of average net worth holdings dropped sharply from 0.18 to 0.14 and the ratio of median net worth dropped from 0.12 to 0.10. Moreover, the wealth of Hispanics actually declined in real terms between 1998 and 2001.

At least since 1989, wealth shifted in relative terms away from young households (under age 55) toward households in the age group 55–74. A similar pattern is found for financial wealth. The average net worth and financial wealth of households in the age group 75 and over also fell relative to the overall mean between 1989 and 2001.

Chapter 5, by René Morissette, Xuelin Zhang and Marie Drolet of Statistics Canada, looks into the evolution of wealth inequality in Canada over the years 1984 to 1999. On the basis of data from the Canadian Assets and Debts Survey of 1984 and the Survey of Financial Security of 1999, their main findings are as follows: (1) wealth inequality increased between 1984 and 1999; (2) the growth in wealth inequality was associated with substantial declines in real average and median wealth for young couples with children and for recent immigrants; (3) real median wealth and real average wealth rose much more for university graduates than among other family units; (4) real median and average wealth fell among family units in the age group 25–34 and increased among the age group 55 and over; (5) the ageing of the Canadian population over the 1984–99 period tended to reduce wealth inequality; and (6) diverging changes in permanent income explain only a small portion of the growing gap between low-wealth and high-wealth family units.

Part 2 of this book considers wealth trends in four European countries. Chapter 6, by Richard Hauser and Holger Stein of Johann Wolfgang Goethe University in Frankfurt am Main, Germany, investigates the inequality of the distribution of personal wealth in Germany over the years 1973 to 1998 and compares the changes in the size distribution of household disposable wealth in West and East Germany between 1993 and 1998. The study is based on data from the German Income and Consumption Surveys or ICS (*Einkommens- und Verbrauchsstichprobe*). The empirical findings are based on several cross-sections of the surveys which are conducted every five years by the German Federal Statistical Office. These surveys are large quota samples that exclude the very rich, the institutionalized population and, until 1993, foreign households, as well as equity in private businesses. As a result the inequality measures derived can be considered lower bounds of the estimates of their true values.

The Gini coefficients for disposable household wealth are about double the coefficients for household disposable income and about three times the coefficients for equivalent disposable income of persons. Except for 1998 net financial assets are less unequally distributed than total disposable wealth, but net housing wealth is distributed more unequally. The authors also find a slight decrease in the inequality of disposable household wealth between 1973 and 1993 followed by a slight increase until 1998.

Hauser and Stein are also able to confirm the well-known hump shape of relative average wealth holdings of age groups in the cross-section. However, by looking at the same birth cohorts in the consecutive cross-section samples, they find that the relative position of the two oldest birth cohorts deteriorates only slightly in old age. However, using disposable wealth per household member, they find that there is only a slight decrease of the relative wealth position but no reduction in the absolute levels of disposable wealth of the aged. This is contrary to the predictions of the life-cycle model. Bequests between spouses and composition effects can be reasons for this surprising result.

Looking at inequality within household age groups, they see a consistent pattern of the highest inequality occurring among the youngest age group, which then decreases until retirement age and then increases again. This result points to the importance of inheritances and gifts *inter vivos* even at young ages. Comparing West to East Germany, they find greater inequality of the wealth distribution in East Germany but lower inequality of the distribution of disposable income of household and of equivalent income of persons. They also see a strong tendency to a convergence in the distributions of wealth and income between West and East Germany.

Chapter 7, by Andrea Brandolini, Luigi Cannari, Giovanni D'Alessio and Ivan Faiella of the Bank of Italy, looks at household wealth distribution in Italy in the 1990s. The chapter first describes the composition and distribution of household wealth in Italy over the last 40 years on the basis of newly reconstructed aggregate balance sheets. The aggregate figures show that dwellings and, more generally, tangible assets are still the main component of household wealth. The share of total financial assets has fluctuated over the years, but has increased only modestly. The investment in risky assets grew considerably during the 1990s, in parallel with the stock market boom and the rapid privatization of state-owned corporations and public utilities. With the fall in share prices and rise in house prices, the portfolio composition has tilted again in the last few years towards tangible assets.

In addition, the characteristics and quality of the main statistical source on wealth distribution – the Bank of Italy's Survey of Household Income and Wealth (SHIW) – are examined together with the statistical procedures implemented to adjust for nonresponse, nonreporting and under-reporting. The distribution of household net worth is then studied using both adjusted and unadjusted data. Wealth inequality is found to have steadily risen during the 1990s. The increased concentration of financial wealth was an important factor in determining such a path.

According to the SHIW adjusted data, the average net worth of Italian households amounted to 270 000 euros at the end of 2000. From 1989 to 2000, it grew in real terms by 2.7 per cent each year, while real disposable income remained unchanged. During the same period, the elderly, the retired and people living in the North experienced the highest increase in mean net worth.

Asset holdings vary considerably across the wealth distribution. At the bottom, consumer durables account for the largest fraction of net worth. In the middle classes, a very high proportion of assets is held in real estate, particularly the principal residence. Businesses and risky financial assets are most frequent among the richest. While the ownership of equities and mutual funds spread across all classes during the 1990s, their amount came to account for a large proportion of portfolios only among the very wealthy.

The distribution of wealth is much more unequal than the distribution of income. In 2000, the Gini index was 0.61 for net worth, compared with 0.37 for disposable income; it was 0.60 for tangible assets, and a much higher 0.81 for financial assets.

Wealth inequality declined from 1989 to 1991 and then rose considerably in the rest of the 1990s. The increase was driven by large gains at the very top of the distribution. Their decompositions of inequality indices show that a large part of the widening of the household wealth distribution was due to financial assets, which have both augmented their weight in portfolios and become more heavily concentrated. This evidence suggests that the stock market boom of the 1990s was an important factor behind the recent growth of wealth inequality.

Chapter 8, by N. Anders Klevmarken of Uppsala University in Sweden, investigates household wealth trends in Sweden over the 1990s. Influenced by a major tax reform in the beginning of the 1990s and by the exceptional boom in the stock market at the end of this decade, both the level and the inequality of the wealth of Swedish households have increased. The large baby-boom cohorts of the 1940s have been successful in accumulating wealth and they also have large claims on the public pension system. The implicit wealth in the form of these claims dominates private wealth in most Swedish households and, in this chapter, it is argued that private life-cycle savings have been small in Sweden. Most of these savings have been done though the public pension systems. However, concern about the future viability of the pension systems has probably increased private life-cycle savings in the 1990s.

At the end of the 1990s median household net wealth was about 700 000 crowns while the mean was above 1 million. Compared to the United States, the Swedish median wealth is somewhat higher while the mean is only about half of that of the US. Although the Swedish distribution of wealth is unequal relative to the distribution of income, it is much less unequal than that of the United States.

In the 1990s household median wealth in Sweden increased by about 30 per cent in real terms. Part of this increase came from increased savings after the tax reform in the beginning of the 1990s. The Swedish savings rate peaked at about 12 to 13 per cent in 1993/94 but dropped back down below 5 per cent in 1998/99. Savings in private pension policies have increased, but it is hard to know to what extent these savings are new or a reallocation of portfolios. Part of the increase in wealth can also be attributed to the exceptional increase in the stock market. Because stocks and shares are a large part of the portfolio only among the wealthy, however, the influence of the stock market on median wealth is not large. The increase in the value of stocks and shares is the major explanation for the increase in inequality of wealth during this period. More important for ordinary people than stock prices is the value of one- and two-family houses, which increased by only a modest 3 per cent in real terms during the 1990s. However, there were large regional differences, with house price increases higher in the three biggest cities, particularly Stockholm. This differential also contributed to increased regional inequality in wealth and probably also to the increase in overall wealth inequality.

The final chapter in Part 2, written by Markus Jäntti of Åbo Akademi University in Finland, examines trends in the distribution of income and wealth in Finland using Finnish Wealth Surveys from 1987 to 1998. The inequality of both disposable income and gross wealth has increased substantially over the time period covered, as has the dependence of income on wealth, as measured by the conditional nonparametric mean curve. Regression models based on the Gamma distribution suggest that the bulk of the increased inequality stems from increases in residual dispersion; bivariate analysis suggests that the residual correlation of income and wealth has also increased.

Jäntti's analysis demonstrates that: (1) the inequality of income has increased substantially in Finland from 1987 to 1998; (2) this increase was accompanied by an increase in the inequality of wealth (both gross and net); and (3) these increases are only to a minor extent due to changes in observed population characteristics or the 'returns' to those characteristics. The joint distribution of income and wealth is characterized by a substantial increase in the residual correlation and in the conditional variance of wealth, given income. There are many possible explanations for this, including a substantial increase in either (the inequality of) property income (that is, returns to wealth), or in the holding of wealth that generates property income, or both. The estimated correlation coefficients between the wealth-related income components and wealth, however, have not increased between 1987 and 1998 and, while financial wealth has increased over time, it is still a fairly small part of overall household wealth. Thus, a simple story featuring the returns to property in the lead role is not sufficient to account for the observed changes in inequality.

Part III of this book covers various topics on household wealth. In Chapter 10, Florencia Torche, Queens College and Columbia University, and Seymour Spilerman of Columbia University, use data from the 2003 Survey of Intergenerational Financial Linkages in Chile (IFLC), a nationally representative household survey, to investigate intergenerational wealth linkages. Although there are no estimates of the financial value of the assets, the asset types are primary residence, financial assets, business equity, small residential property, commercial real estate and vehicle ownership.

Torche and Spilerman find that in the case of Chile parental resources have strong effects on both the living standard and asset holdings of adult children. Parental education and occupational status are most critical to living standards (as measured by consumption expenditures); parental wealth, in contrast, has the larger impact on the children's asset portfolio. Moreover, the pathway of transmission differs according to the outcome type under consideration. In the case of living standard, the parental effects are largely mediated by children's education and earnings; thus, the avenue of transmission is via parental investments in education. With respect to the asset holdings of offspring, much of the transfer is direct and takes the form of financial assistance and inheritances.

The findings with respect to home ownership are more complex. In contrast to the other indicators of asset holdings, the home acquisition process appears to be largely detached from parental resources. The authors have linked this finding to Chilean housing policy which, beginning in the 1960s and with special vigour since the late 1980s, has provided subsidized access to home ownership, as opposed to rental solutions. The fact that the acquisition of a residence under this programme does not involve costs that young couples cannot bear appears to have reduced the pressure for parental assistance.

Chapter 11, by Elena Gouskova, F. Thomas Juster and Frank Stafford of the University of Michigan, investigates the allocation and dynamics of American family portfolios over the years 1984 to 2001. Using data from the Panel Study of Income Dynamics, the authors consider two aspects of household portfolios: the span or number of asset types held and the composition of the household portfolio. They also investigate the possibility of the 'crowding-out' effect of stocks on real estate during the last 17 years, which were marked by a strong expansion of equities in the household portfolios.

The portfolio choices of households over the period 1984–2001 show some longer-term shifts toward greater span or more numerous elements in the portfolio and holdings of equities. Much of the shift through time to greater portfolio span appears to be the result of more households in the life-cycle position where more types of assets are held – the result of rising life-cycle income and wealth. The analysis suggests that part of the reason for fewer portfolio elements of African American families is related to lower income and wealth. Yet, even allowing for these differences, on balance, African American families hold one less portfolio element compared to other families in similar circumstances.

The authors find great variability in household portfolio span across demographic and life-cycle groups with the race effect being particularly pronounced. Portfolio span is shown to be strongly associated with income, wealth and education. The observed increase in the number of portfolio components over the 1984–2001 period is more likely to have arisen from changing demographic and socio-economic factors rather than from a general increase in the financial sophistication of families.

The data show portfolio composition to be extremely heterogeneous. Five identified portfolio types account for about 50 per cent of families, with the most common type – transaction account plus housing plus transportation – held by 15 to 17 per cent of households. There are a substantial number of households with a 'null' portfolio. The results of multivariate analyses indicate that the choice of portfolio type is strongly associated with income, race and education. The results also seem to support some implications of life-cycle asset allocation models. Over the period of 1984–2001, the main change in household portfolio composition was due to increased stock ownership rates.

The final chapter in the volume, by Conchita D'Ambrosio of University of Bocconi in Italy and myself, Edward Wolff of New York University, considers whether wealth is becoming more polarized in the United States. Recent work has documented a rising degree of wealth inequality in the US between 1983 and 1998. In this chapter, the authors look at another dimension of the distribution: polarization. Using techniques developed by Esteban and Ray and further extended by D'Ambrosio, the chapter examines whether a similar pattern exists with regard to trends in wealth polarization over this period.

The approach used here is a decomposition method based on counterfactual distributions, which allows one to monitor both what factors modify the entire distribution and where precisely on the distribution these factors have an effect. An index of polarization is provided as well as summary statistics of the observed movements and of distance and divergence among the estimated and the counterfactual distributions. The decomposition method is applied to US data on the distribution of wealth between 1983 and 1998 derived from the SCF.

We find that polarization between homeowners and tenants, as well as among different educational groups, continuously increased from 1983 to 1998, while polarization by income classes groups continuously decreased. In contrast, polarization by racial groups first increased from 1983 to 1989 and then declined from 1989 to 1998, while polarization by age groups followed the opposite pattern. We also find that most of the observed variation in the overall wealth density over the 1983–98 period can be attributed to changes of the within-group wealth densities rather than to changes in household characteristics over the period.

SELECTED INTERNATIONAL COMPARISONS

Tables 1.1 and 1.2 show international comparisons of both wealth levels and wealth inequality among selected OECD countries on the basis of the work contained in this volume. Bearing in mind the qualifications set out in the introduction of this chapter regarding issues of comparability in international comparisons, we can still make some broad inferences from the results contained in these two tables.

As shown in Table 1.1, the level of mean wealth is much higher in the US than in Canada, Germany or Italy. Mean wealth also grew faster in the US than Canada or Germany over the 1980s and 1990s and faster than in Italy over the 1990s.

Median wealth is also higher in the US than in Canada (the only other country with this statistic). However, the ratio in median wealth between Canada in 1999 and the US in 1998 is 0.88 – much higher than the ratio of mean wealth of 0.54. However, over the 1980s and 1990s, median wealth grew more slowly in Canada than the US.

Wealth inequality also appears to be much higher in the US than in the other three countries (see Table 1.2). The Gini coefficient for wealth in the US in 1998 is 0.82 compared to 0.73 in Canada in 1999; 0.64 in Germany in 1998; and 0.61 in Italy in 2000. Similar disparities exist with regard to the share of top wealth holders. In the US, the top 10 per cent held 71 per cent of all wealth in 1998, compared to a share of 56 per cent in Canada in 1999, 42 per cent in Germany in 1998, and 49 per cent in Italy in 2000. Moreover, the shares of wealth held by the fourth and middle quintiles as well as the bottom 40 per cent in Canada,

Germany and Italy are considerably higher than the corresponding shares in the US. By the late 1990s, Italy appeared to be the most equal of the four countries, followed by Germany, Canada, and then the US.

Table 1.1   Mean and median wealth in selected OECD countries, 1983–2001 (thousands of 2001 US dollars)[f]

Wealth definition[a]	Data source[g]	Sample	Year	Mean net worth	Median net worth
A. *United States: Kennickell*[b]					
Standard	SCF	High-income			
		Supplement	1989	260.1	
			1992	231.1	
			1995	244.8	
			1998	308.3	
			2001	398.0	
			Annual growth	3.55%	
B. *United States: Wolff*[c]					
Standard, excluding	SCF	High-income			
vehicles		Supplement	1983	231.0	59.3
			1989	264.6	63.5
			1992	257.3	54.2
			1995	237.7	53.0
			1998	293.6	65.9
			2001	380.1	73.5
			Annual growth	2.77%	1.19%
C. *Canada: Morissette et al.*[b]					
Standard, excluding	ADS				
retirement accounts	1984	Representative	1984	115.2	52.2
(RRIFs)	SFS	High-income			
	1999	Supplement	1999	157.4	57.7
			Annual growth	2.08%	0.67%
D. *Germany: Hauser and Stein*[d]					
Standard, excluding	ICS	Representative	1983	112.5	
consumer durables			1988	117.5	
and business equity			1993	146.1	
			1998	132.3	
			Annual growth	1.08%	
E. *Italy: Brandolini, et al.*[e]					
Standard, excluding	SHIW	Representative	1989	200.3	
retirement accounts			2000	269.0	
and life insurance			Annual growth	2.68%	

Notes:
a. The standard wealth definition, based on US asset and debt components, is as follows: Total assets are defined as the sum of: (1) owner-occupied housing; (2) other real estate; (3) vehicles; (4) cash and demand deposits; (5) time and savings deposits, certificates of deposit, and money market accounts; (6) government bonds, corporate bonds, foreign bonds, and other financial securities; (7) the cash surrender value of life insurance plans; (8) the value of defined contribution pension plans including IRAs, Keogh and 401(k) plans; (9) corporate stock and mutual funds; (10) net equity in unincorporated businesses; and (11) net equity in trust funds. Total liabilities are the sum of: (1) mortgage debt; (2) consumer debt, including auto loans; and (3) other debt. Net worth equals total assets minus total liabilities.
b. Figures based on family unit.
c. Figures based on household unit.
d. Figures based on household unit; figures are for West Germany.
e. Figures based on adjusted data for household unit.
f. Figures for Canada, Germany and Italy are converted to 2001 US dollars using the Penn World Tables Purchasing Power Parities (see http://pwt.econ.upenn.edu/php_site/pwt61_ form.php).
g. Key: SCF US Survey of Consumer Finances.
         ADS Canadian Assets and Debts Survey, 1984.
         SFS Canadian Survey of Financial Security, 1999.
         ICS German Income and Consumption Survey.
         SHIW Italy's Survey of Household Income and Wealth.

Sources: For A. US, see Kennickell, Chapter 2, Tables 2.7, 2.8, 2.9 and 2.10; for B. US, see Wolff, Chapter 4, Table 4.1; for C. Canada, see Morissette et al., Chapter 5, Table 5.1; for D. Germany, see Hauser and Stein, Chapter 6, Table 6.1; for E. Italy, see Brandolini et al., Chapter 7, Table 7.6 (all in this volume).

Table 1.2   Size distribution of wealth in selected OECD countries, 1983–2001

Year	Gini coefficient	Percentage share of wealth held by:							All
		Top 1.0%	Top 5.0%	Top 10.0%	Top 20.0%	4th 20.0%	3rd 20.0%	Bottom 40.0%	
A. *United States: Kennickell*[a]									
1989		30.3	54.4	67.4					
1992		30.2	54.6	67.2					
1995		34.6	55.9	67.8					
1998		33.9	57.2	68.6					
2001		32.7	57.7	68.8					
B. *United States: Wolff*[b]									
1983	0.799	33.8	56.1	68.2	81.3	12.6	5.2	0.9	100.0
1989	0.832	37.4	58.9	70.6	83.5	12.3	4.8	−0.7	100.0
1992	0.823	37.2	60.0	71.8	83.8	11.5	4.4	0.4	100.0
1995	0.828	38.5	60.3	71.8	83.9	11.4	4.5	0.2	100.0
1998	0.822	38.1	59.4	71.0	83.4	11.9	4.5	0.2	100.0
2001	0.826	33.4	59.2	71.5	84.4	11.3	3.9	0.3	100.0

Table 1.2　(continued)

Year	Gini coefficient	Percentage share of wealth held by:							All
		Top 1.0%	Top 5.0%	Top 10.0%	Top 20.0%	4th 20.0%	3rd 20.0%	Bottom 40.0%	
C. *Canada: Morissette et al.*[c]									
1984	0.691			51.8	69.3	19.7	9.1	1.8	98.1
1999	0.727			55.7	73.1	18.4	7.5	1.1	99.0
D. *Germany: Hauser and Stein*[d]									
1973	0.748			(NA)[f]	78.0	13.5	5.7	2.8	97.2
1983	0.701			48.8	70.1	23.5	5.5	0.9	99.1
1988	0.668			45.0	66.9	24.7	7.4	1.0	99.0
1993	0.622			40.8	61.0	26.3	10.4	2.3	97.7
1998	0.640			41.9	63.0	25.9	9.5	1.6	98.4
E. *Italy: Brandolini et al.*[e]									
1989	0.553	10.6	27.3	40.2	57.9				
1995	0.573	10.7	29.0	42.1	59.5				
2000	0.613	17.2	36.4	48.5	63.8				

Notes:
For details on data sources and methods, see notes to Table 1.1.
a.　Figures based on family unit.
b.　Figures based on household unit.
c.　Figures based on family unit. Rows may not sum to unity because of rounding error.
d.　Figures based on household unit. 1973, 1983 and 1988 include only German households, while 1993 and 1998 encompass the total resident population (including foreigners). The rows may not sum to unity because of rounding error.
e.　Figures are based on adjusted data for household unit.
f.　NA = not available.

Sources:　For A. US, see Kennickell, Chapter 2, Table 2.5; for B. US, see Wolff, Chapter 4, Table 4.2; for C. Canada, see Morissette et al., Chapter 5, Tables 5.3 and 5.5; for D. Germany, see Hauser and Stein, Chapter 6, Table 6.3 and 6.4; for E. Italy, see Brandolini et al., Chapter 7, Table 7.6 (all in this volume).

REFERENCES

Kennickell, A.B. and R.L. Woodburn (1999), 'Consistent weight design for the 1989, 1992, and 1995 SCFs, and the distribution of wealth', *Review of Income and Wealth*, **45**(2), June, 193–216.
Wolff, Edward N. (1999), 'The size distribution of wealth in the United States: a comparison among recent household surveys', in James P. Smith and Robert J. Willis (eds), *Wealth, Work, and Health: Innovations in Measurement in the Social Sciences*, Ann Arbor, MI: University of Michigan Press, pp. 209–32.

PART I

Wealth Changes in North America

2. A rolling tide: changes in the distribution of wealth in the US, 1989–2001

Arthur B. Kennickell*

INTRODUCTION

This chapter examines changes in the distribution of the wealth of US families over the years from 1989 to 2001, a period when economic conditions moved from a cyclical high point to recession and recovery, through a long expansion, and finally to the beginning of another recession.[1] Over this time, a variety of factors – technical progress, changes in tastes and expectations, shifts in international trade, among others – often dramatically altered the relative returns on assets and, thus, the value of those assets. Of particular note, advances in information technology, and especially the widespread implementation of such technology, deeply affected the way that work was done as well as the way people acquired and shared information. Although there is the strong *ex post* appearance of a bubble in asset prices that began to deflate in 2001, particularly in technology-related stocks, household wealth at the end of 2001, as measured in Federal Reserve Board's Flow of Funds Accounts of the United States, stood at more than twice the level in 1989, and in inflation-adjusted terms, it was almost 50 per cent higher.

There is a perception, which is sustained by data (see, for example, Petska et al. 2002), that income inequality increased over this time. There were frequent reports of vast increases in wealth, especially in the case of 'Internet millionaires', and some reports later in the period about the decline of some of those fortunes. Although growth in ownership of corporate equities exposed increasingly many families to the fluctuations of that market, for most families a principal residence or a vehicle remained the most important asset by far. Thus, what happened away from the more publicized part of the wealth spectrum is harder to guess a priori.

Unlike the case of income, where at least two good high-frequency sources of data are available on a regular basis, IRS data from individual tax returns and data from the March supplement to the Current Population Survey (CPS) compiled by the US Census Bureau for the Bureau of Labor Statistics, data on wealth are much more limited. This chapter uses data from the triennial Survey of Consumer Finances (SCF) along with information from *Forbes* to describe changes in the distribution of wealth.

The first section of the chapter examines the changes at the very highest level of wealth, using *Forbes* data; in addition to a review of the cross-section patterns in the data, this section also looks at some dynamics. The next section uses SCF data, which explicitly exclude the *Forbes* group, to characterize shifts for the rest of the population. The next three sections look in detail at subgroups of the population: families with negative wealth, the age cohort that was aged 46 to 55 in 2001, and African American families. A summary ends the chapter.

ESTIMATES OF WEALTH USING *FORBES* DATA

Every year since 1982 *Forbes* has published information on what staff of that magazine estimate to be the wealthiest 400 people in the US.[2] Because members of the '*Forbes* 400' are personally identified, changes in the wealth of the group are more likely to have a disproportionately large influence on popular perceptions of changes in the distribution of wealth overall than the great mass of other people who are less wealthy.

The *Forbes* data show strong growth in real terms across a variety of dimensions from 1989 to 2001, but there are some striking differences within the period and across different groups (Table 2.1).[3] From 1989 to 1995, overall mean wealth of the group was fairly flat, as was the level of wealth at most of the ranks of the distribution of this population up to around the top 50. The top 50 showed substantial growth in wealth over this period. From 1995 to 1999, the whole distribution shifted up, but it shifted most strongly at the top. The highest value rose 428 per cent while the 10th value rose 265 per cent; at the same time, the cut-off value for membership in the group rose 69 per cent. After 1999, the top end led the way to a general downturn in 2001 that continued into 2002. Nonetheless, even at the end of the period, the entire distribution was distinctly above the levels of 1989. From 1989 to 2001, the total wealth of the *Forbes* 400 as a proportion of an estimate of total individual wealth (the wealth of the *Forbes* 400 plus the total wealth estimated by the SCF for the rest of the population) ranged from 1.5 per cent in 1989 to a high of 2.5 per cent in 1998 to 2.2 per cent in 2001 (Table 2.2).

Underlying the overall growth in the whole distribution of the wealth of the *Forbes* group was a considerable amount of churning, although there

Table 2.1   Forbes *400, wealth by rank and average wealth, 1989, 1992, 1995, 1998, 2000, 2001 and 2002 (millions of 2001 dollars)*

	Year							
	1989	1992	1995	1998	1999	2000	2001	2002
Wealth by **Forbes rank**								
1	7 106	7 746	17 002	63 214	89 716	64 318	54 000	42 361
10	3 417	4 303	4 940	11 907	17 943	17 356	17 500	11 723
50	1 736	1 537	2 068	3 139	4 222	4 798	3 900	3 152
100	957	984	1 034	1 840	2 533	2 654	2 000	1 773
200	615	584	689	1 028	1 267	1 531	1 200	1 084
300	478	430	500	731	897	1 000	875	763
400	376	326	391	541	660	740	600	542
Avg. wealth	921	937	1 025	1 997	2 731	3 057	2 366	2 148
Memo items:								
Number of billionaires	97	92	107	205	278	301	266	205

Sources: Author's calculations based on data from October issues of *Forbes*.

Table 2.2   *Wealth of* Forbes *400 as per cent of total wealth, 1989, 1992, 1995, 1998 and 2001*

Year	% total wealth[a]
1989	1.5
1992	1.7
1995	1.7
1998	2.5
2001	2.2

Note: a. As measured by: total *Forbes* 400 wealth + total SCF wealth.

Sources: Author's calculations based on *Forbes* data and the SCF.

was also substantial persistence. Of the 400 people in the 2001 list, 230 were not anywhere in the 1989 list (Table 2.3). Over this long a period, such movement may be somewhat less surprising, but even between 1998 and 2001 nearly a quarter of the people on the list were replaced by others. Although some of the movement is explained by the transmission of wealth through inheritance, the number of such instances appear to be small: only

Table 2.3   Forbes *400 wealth rank in 2001 by rank in 1989, 1992, 1995 and 1998 (number of families)*

Year/rank	Not in 2001	2001 rank				All groups
		1–100	101–200	201–300	301–400	
1989 rank						
Not in 1989	0	32	66	62	70	230
1–100	34	45	5	8	8	100
101–200	55	17	10	12	6	100
201–300	70	4	8	9	9	100
301–400	71	2	11	9	7	100
All groups[a]	230	100	100	100	100	630
1992 rank						
Not in 1992	0	21	61	62	66	210
1–100	28	55	8	7	2	100
101–200	44	15	15	15	11	100
201–300	57	7	13	11	12	100
301–400	81	2	3	5	9	100
All groups[a]	210	100	100	100	100	610
1995 rank						
Not in 1995	0	12	46	44	51	153
1–100	18	67	10	3	2	100
101–200	29	12	26	23	10	100
201–300	45	7	7	20	21	100
301–400	61	2	11	10	16	100
All groups[a]	153	100	100	100	100	553
1998 group						
Not in 1998	0	4	20	31	40	95
1–100	7	81	7	5	0	100
101–200	4	13	53	28	2	100
201–300	27	1	15	26	31	100
301–400	57	1	5	10	27	100
All groups[a]	95	100	100	100	100	495

Note: a. The 'all groups' categories include all cases in either 2001 or the classification year.

Sources: Author's calculations based on *Forbes* data and the SCF.

about 20 members of the 1989 list, who did not appear in the 2001 list, appear to be explained in this way, while others may have died and fragmented their wealth into pieces smaller than the *Forbes* cut-off. Persistence of individuals in the list was highest for people who were in the highest 100. Of the people in the top 100 of the 2001 list, 45 were included in the same group in 1989 and 23 others were in higher ranks of the list. Of the lowest 100 in 1989, only 29 were still somewhere in the list for 2001.

ESTIMATES OF WEALTH USING SCF DATA

The SCF is designed to measure wealth.[4] The survey questions cover the household balance sheet in detail. Through use of statistical records derived from tax returns, the survey sample design allows for more efficient and less biased estimates of wealth than are generally feasible through simpler designs, such as multistage area-probability designs. Since 1983 the survey has been conducted on a triennial basis by the Federal Reserve Board in cooperation with the Department of the Treasury. Following a major redesign in 1989, the methodology has been largely fixed. Many wealth estimates turn critically on the measurement of the upper tail of the wealth distribution and that measurement may be sensitive to the technical assumptions necessary to make the measurement. Thus, the analysis here is restricted to the 1989–2001 surveys.

Over the period from 1989 to 2001, the SCF data show that the distribution of wealth shifted up broadly in real terms (Table 2.4) – another way of saying that, in absolute terms, there were fewer poor families and more families who were wealthier.[5] The proportion of families with net worth less than $250 000 declined from 79.1 per cent in 1989 to 73.2 per cent in 2001; the proportion of families with negative net worth fell only slightly, but the proportion in all but one of the other wealth groups in the table below $250 000 fell. The proportion of families in all higher groups rose, and the rise was particularly striking for the group with $1 million or more of wealth.

The survey indicates that in the period considered, roughly a third of total wealth was held by each of the following: the highest 1 per cent of the wealth distribution, the next highest 9 per cent, and the remaining 90 per cent (Table 2.5). Within the lowest 90 per cent, wealth was also concentrated; the lowest 50 per cent of the distribution held only about 3 per cent of the total. Although the wealth distribution generally rose over the 1989 to 2001 period, simple measures of wealth concentration fail to show consistent patterns. Moreover, few changes in groups' shares are statistically significant. For example, the wealth share of the top 1 per cent of the wealth distribution moved from about 30 per cent in both 1989 and 1992 to about 35 per cent in 1995, and it tapered down to 33 per cent by 2001; none of the changes are statistically significant according to the estimation methodology used to compute standard errors for the SCF.[6]

Table 2.4   Distribution of families over wealth groups, 1989, 1992, 1995, 1998 and 2001

Net worth (2001 dollars)	Survey year				
	1989 %	1992 %	1995 %	1998 %	2001 %
<$0	7.3	7.2	7.1	8.0	6.9
	0.6	*0.4*	*0.4*	*0.4*	*0.3*
$0–$999	8.0	6.3	5.2	5.8	5.4
	0.6	*0.4*	*0.3*	*0.4*	*0.3*
$1000–$2499	3.5	3.8	2.6	2.5	2.4
	0.4	*0.3*	*0.2*	*0.2*	*0.2*
$2500–$4999	4.2	3.6	3.5	3.1	3.5
	0.5	*0.3*	*0.3*	*0.3*	*0.3*
$5000–$9999	4.1	4.9	5.6	5.0	4.7
	0.4	*0.4*	*0.4*	*0.3*	*0.3*
$10 000–$24 999	8.6	9.5	9.4	8.1	8.1
	0.6	*0.4*	*0.5*	*0.5*	*0.4*
$25 000–$49 999	9.6	10.8	10.4	9.7	9.2
	0.5	*0.6*	*0.6*	*0.5*	*0.5*
$50 000–$99 999	13.6	14.6	16.0	13.2	12.8
	0.6	*0.5*	*0.5*	*0.6*	*0.5*
$100 000–$249 999	20.2	21.6	22.1	21.6	19.2
	1.0	*0.8*	*0.7*	*0.8*	*0.6*
$250 000–$500 000	11.0	9.3	9.3	12.0	13.0
	0.7	*0.6*	*0.3*	*0.7*	*0.6*
$500 000–$999 999	5.4	4.6	5.1	6.0	7.8
	0.5	*0.3*	*0.2*	*0.5*	*0.6*
≥$1 million	4.7	3.8	3.6	4.9	7.0
	1.2	*0.2*	*0.2*	*0.3*	*0.4*
All families	100.0	100.0	100.0	100.0	100.0
	0.0	*0.0*	*0.0*	*0.0*	*0.0*

Note: Standard errors with respect to imputation and sampling are given in italics.

Sources: Author's calculations based on the SCF.

However attractive summary measures of wealth change may be for some purposes, such measures may obscure more complicated changes. An alternative is to look more directly at the changes across the entire distribution of wealth; quantile-difference (Q-D) plots are one means of doing so.[7] Briefly, a Q-D plot displays the difference in the level of two distributions

Table 2.5   *Net worth distributed by net worth groups, 1989, 1992, 1995,*
            1998 and 2001 (per cent)

Year	Net worth percentile group				
	0–49.9	50–89.9	90–94.9	95–98.9	99–100
1989	2.7	29.9	13.0	24.1	30.3
	0.4	*1.8*	*1.6*	*2.3*	*2.3*
1992	3.3	29.7	12.6	24.4	30.2
	0.2	*1.1*	*0.7*	*1.3*	*1.4*
1995	3.6	28.6	11.9	21.3	34.6
	0.2	*0.7*	*0.6*	*0.9*	*1.3*
1998	3.0	28.4	11.4	23.3	33.9
	0.2	*0.9*	*0.6*	*1.2*	*1.5*
2001	2.8	27.4	12.1	25.0	32.7
	0.1	*0.7*	*0.7*	*1.1*	*1.4*

Note: Standard errors with respect to imputation and sampling are given in italics.

Sources: Author's calculations based on the SCF.

at common percentile points; for example, the value given at the 50th percentile is the difference in the medians of two distributions.

Figures 2.1–2.4 show the Q-D plots of inflation-adjusted changes in the level of wealth for each of the pairs of surveys in sequence: 1992 minus 1989, 1995 minus 1992, 1998 minus 1995, and 2001 minus 1998.[8] To integrate over all of these changes, Figure 2.5 shows the change from 1989 to 2001. The pairs of dots clustered around the central line of the plots represent 95 per cent confidence intervals for selected percentiles.

Between 1989 and 1992, wealth tended to decline by progressively larger amounts for the groups above about the 35th percentile of the wealth distribution, and wealth rose slightly for the next lowest 20 per cent; the next lowest 10 per cent had zero or small wealth in both periods, and the remaining lowest group had its negative net worth increase in absolute value. Change over this period reflects the effects of recession on asset values. From 1992 to 1995, the range of increases spread up to about the 75th percentile; above that point there was an alternating mixture of gains and losses. Over the succeeding three years to 1998, the data show a pattern of approximately log-linear increases in the level of wealth from about the 30th to the 95th percentile; for the group above the 95th percentile, the increase was even faster. From 1998 to 2001, the range of increase begins at about the 10th percentile, and the peak at the top is steeper; the negative net worth of the group at the very bottom of the distribution declined in

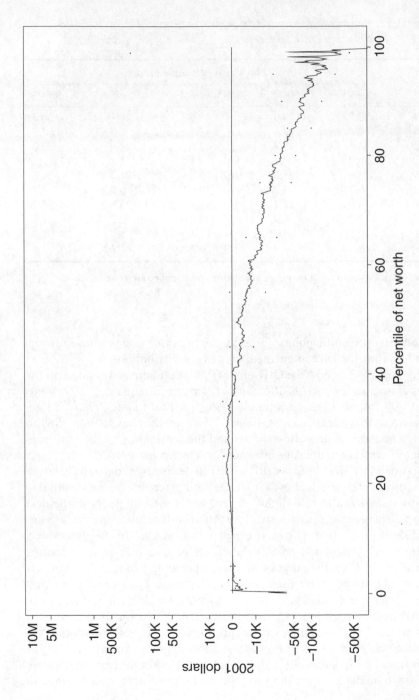

Figure 2.1 *Quantile-difference plot of wealth: 1992 minus 1989 wealth*

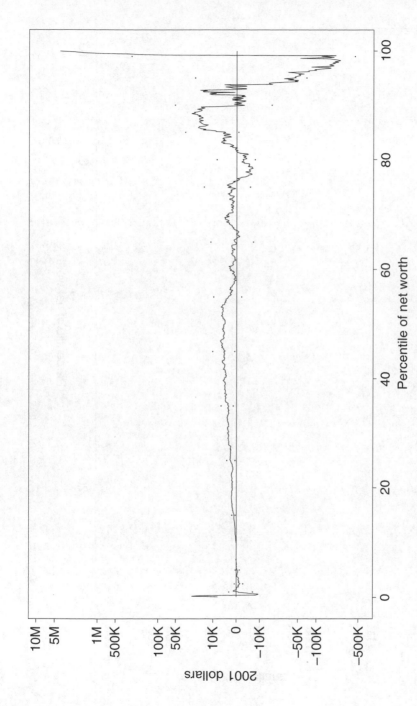

Figure 2.2 Quantile-difference plot of wealth: 1995 minus 1992 wealth

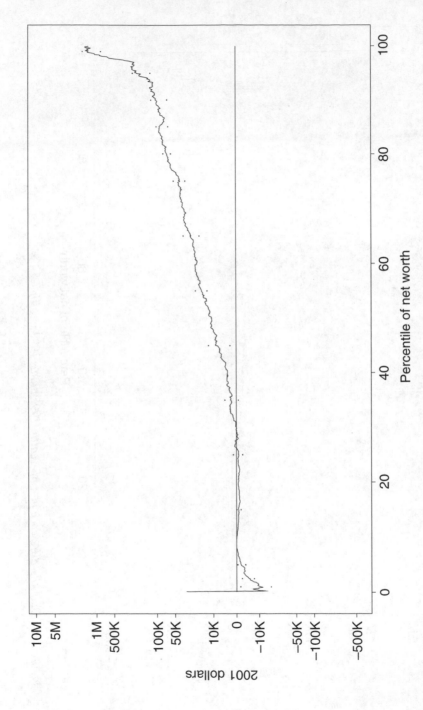

Figure 2.3   Quantile-difference plot of wealth: 1998 minus 1995 wealth

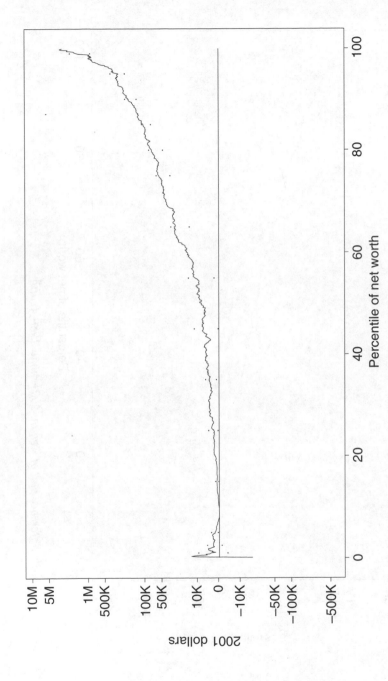

Figure 2.4 Quantile-difference plot of wealth: 2001 minus 1998 wealth

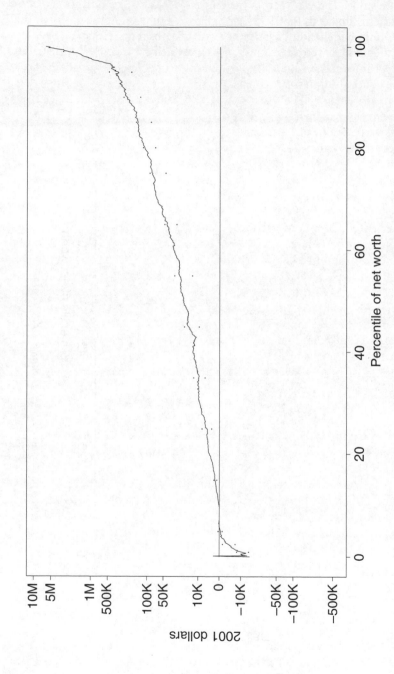

Figure 2.5   Quantile-difference plot of wealth: 2001 minus 1989 wealth

absolute value. The view across the entire 1989–2001 period shows a general pattern similar to the 1998–2001 change, but overall, the group at the very bottom had greater negative net worth in absolute terms.

Although there were large differences in wealth gains across the distribution, such information alone is not sufficient to characterize the shifts in the relative concentration of wealth across the distribution. For wealth shares of groups to change, their growth rates must differ. Figures 2.6–2.10 show the wealth changes given in Figures 2.1–2.5 normalized as a per cent of the level of wealth value at each percentile in the earlier year. Thus, the figures show the growth rates of wealth across the wealth distribution.

Because of the prevalence of negative and zero wealth values among the lowest quintile of the wealth distribution, that group is more difficult to characterize in terms of percentage changes than groups higher in the spectrum of wealth. Within the lowest 20 per cent in each of the growth rate figures, there is a region where the percentage changes are very large in absolute value or so large as to be beyond the range of the figure; because wealth is zero or nonzero and very small in absolute value in this part of the distribution, small level changes yield percentage changes for this group far beyond the range of other groups.[9] For the group below the interval where no values are displayed, the denominator values are negative; thus, for this group positive level changes (for example, lower absolute values of negative net worth) correspond to negative percentage changes and vice versa.

Percentage declines in wealth from 1989 to 1992 are substantially more even across the top half of the distribution than the level changes. The data also show progressively larger proportional growth for the part of the group below about the 30th percentile than is discernable from the level changes. The corresponding data from 1992 to 1995 show little consistent change in the top half of the distribution other than a region of increase above the 80th percentile and a region of decrease above the 90th. As in the 1989 to 2001 data, lower points in the distribution tended to have larger percentage changes. Over the next three years to 1998, percentage increases were substantial but fairly even in the top half of the distribution, with a spike upward around the 95th percentile; the part of the group below the middle had progressively smaller changes, with the changes becoming negative at about the 30th percentile. From 1998 to 2001, the highest 80 per cent of the distribution (roughly, those with wealth above $5000) saw the largest percentage gains at the two ends of that group, with the lowest growth occurring around the median. Integrating over the entire 1989 to 2001 period, the data also show strongest growth at the top and bottom of the group, with fairly even growth across the middle.

The portfolio choices of individual families, and the differential effects of variation in the market pricing of those choices, underlie many of the

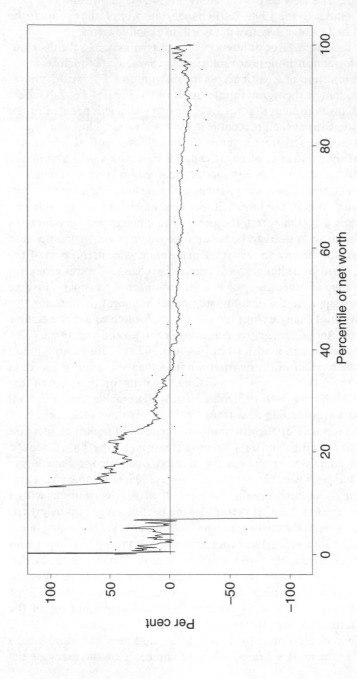

Note: In 2001 dollars.

Figure 2.6 Relative quantile-difference plot of wealth: 1992 minus 1989 wealth, as a per cent of 1989

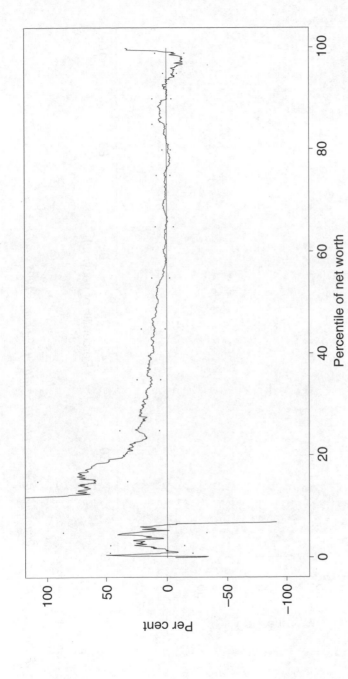

Note: In 2001 dollars.

Figure 2.7   Relative quantile-difference plot of wealth: 1995 minus 1992 wealth, as a per cent of 1992

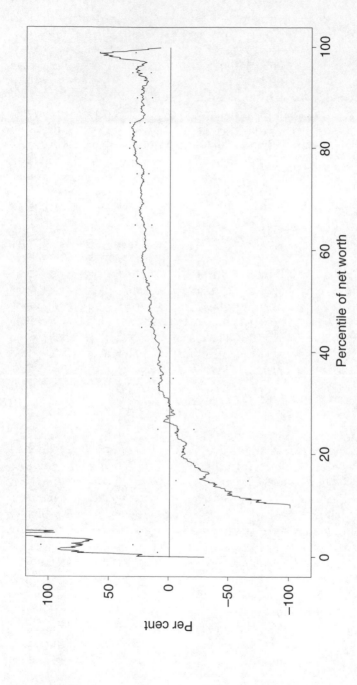

Note: In 2001 dollars.

Figure 2.8   Relative quantile-difference plot of wealth: 1998 minus 1995 wealth, as a per cent of 1995

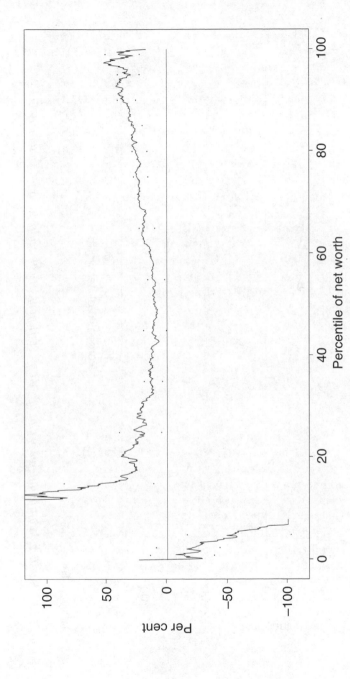

Note: In 2001 dollars.

Figure 2.9   Relative quantile-difference plot of wealth: 2001 minus 1998, as a per cent of 1998

35

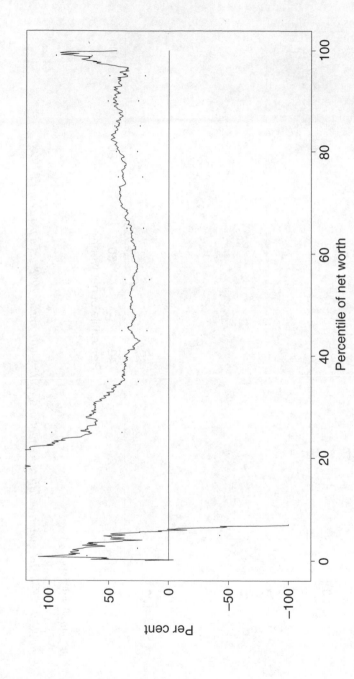

Note: In 2001 dollars.

Figure 2.10   Relative quantile-difference plot of wealth: 2001 minus 1989 wealth, as a per cent of 1989

wealth patterns seen over the 1989 to 2001 period as seen in Tables 2.6–2.10. (For definitions of wealth components, see Appendix Table 2A.1.) Several stylized facts characterize portfolio holdings across the wealth distribution during this time. The highest decile of the wealth distribution holds a disproportionately large fraction of most assets and liabilities, but the share is particularly large for direct holdings of bonds, direct and indirect holdings of corporate stocks, and equity in privately held businesses and real estate investments; holdings of these assets are even more concentrated among the wealthiest 1 per cent. The amount of outstanding debts and the value of vehicles, though still disproportionately concentrated in this decile, are notably less so.

For the group with net worth greater than the median but smaller than the value at the 90th percentile, no item is as concentrated as is the case for the wealthier group. However, a few items are held in about the same proportion or more than their population share: certificates of deposit, savings bonds, vehicles, principal residences and mortgages. The group holds substantial, but smaller shares of most other items except bonds, directly held stocks and businesses.

The remaining half of the distribution below the median holds very disproportionately small shares of all items except for outstanding balances on credit cards and instalment loans. Vehicles are the only asset for which the group holds more than a quarter of the total value. The shares of principal residences and associated mortgages are not negligible, but, because the level of debt is so large relative to the value of the asset, they hold much less than 10 per cent of total net equity in a principal residence (HOUSES minus MRTHEL in Tables 2.6–2.10).

Over the time considered here, the most striking finding is how little groups' shares varied. Only three changes seem noteworthy. After remaining fairly flat until 1998, the share of both directly- and indirectly-held stock owned by the highest 10 per cent of the wealth distribution declined in 2001, and the difference was captured by the next highest 40 per cent of the distribution. The data also show a tendency for the share of principal residences (and, somewhat more strongly, home equity) held by the highest 10 per cent of the wealth distribution to rise. Finally, the data show a strong rise from 1989 to 1992 in the share of nonmortgage debt held by the lower half of the wealth distribution, with a tendency for this share to decline in the later years.

Another way of looking at the data is to examine portfolio shares within the wealth percentile groups. The combination of business and investment real estate equity rises as a share of assets across the percentile groups; the portfolio share of the highest 1 per cent of the wealth distribution was 40 per cent in 2001, a share that had been substantially higher in earlier survey years (Table 2.11). The proportion of assets attributable to direct

Table 2.6   Net worth and components, distributed by net worth groups, 1989

| | Wealth percentile group | | | | | | | | | | | |
| | All families | | 0–50 | | 50–90 | | 90–95 | | 95–99 | | 99–100 | |
	Amount[a]	Share	Amount[a]	Share	Amount[a]	Share	Amount[a]	Share	Amount[a]	Share	Amount[a]	Share
NETWORTH[b]	24 186.2	100.0	641.5	2.7	7236.2	29.9	3167.4	13.0	5833.4	24.1	7307.7	30.3
	1943.2	*0.0*	*87.1*	*0.4*	*384.6*	*1.8*	*580.2*	*1.6*	*933.0*	*2.3*	*741.4*	*2.3*
ASSET	27 615.4	100.0	1515.2	5.5	8948.5	32.4	3499.5	12.6	6160.0	22.3	7492.2	27.2
	2036.5	*0.0*	*57.7*	*0.4*	*438.4*	*1.8*	*647.9*	*1.6*	*937.0*	*2.1*	*787.0*	*2.1*
FIN	8522.0	100.0	340.6	4.0	2337.1	27.4	1162.5	13.6	2265.3	26.5	2416.5	28.4
	714.2	*0.0*	*56.5*	*0.7*	*179.5*	*1.8*	*160.3*	*1.4*	*367.9*	*2.8*	*356.0*	*3.4*
LIQ	1584.9	100.0	95.9	6.1	507.9	32.1	208.7	13.2	338.7	21.4	433.6	27.2
	149.6	*0.0*	*5.3*	*0.7*	*40.7*	*3.7*	*27.0*	*2.2*	*96.0*	*5.7*	*177.6*	*9.1*
CDS	841.4	100.0	34.5	4.1	368.1	43.8	139.6	16.6	214.2	25.3	84.9	10.2
	76.2	*0.0*	*5.4*	*0.7*	*34.7*	*4.0*	*22.3*	*2.7*	*68.7*	*6.2*	*36.4*	*4.1*
SAVBND	125.8	100.0	8.4	6.7	60.0	47.6	23.7	19.1	24.6	19.3	9.1	7.3
	19.1	*0.0*	*1.5*	*1.7*	*10.3*	*7.4*	*9.6*	*6.9*	*11.6*	*6.6*	*5.2*	*4.3*
BOND	842.9	100.0	2.7	0.3	65.4	7.8	93.6	11.0	245.6	29.1	435.6	51.8
	176.6	*0.0*	*1.2*	*0.1*	*11.9*	*1.8*	*36.3*	*3.7*	*70.3*	*6.2*	*139.8*	*8.3*
STOCKS	1298.3	100.0	16.3	1.3	204.6	15.8	133.5	10.2	405.3	31.3	538.6	41.5
	172.6	*0.0*	*4.2*	*0.4*	*23.1*	*2.3*	*51.8*	*3.3*	*81.0*	*5.7*	*127.9*	*6.6*
NMMF	456.8	100.0	4.2	0.9	69.5	15.3	73.9	16.2	153.6	33.6	155.7	34.1
	75.6	*0.0*	*2.4*	*0.5*	*15.9*	*4.1*	*20.6*	*4.5*	*50.2*	*8.4*	*55.8*	*9.0*
RETQLIQ	1807.9	100.0	107.8	6.0	683.6	37.9	271.7	15.1	478.5	26.3	266.3	14.8
	206.9	*0.0*	*53.4*	*2.7*	*69.3*	*3.0*	*40.8*	*2.2*	*119.1*	*4.2*	*61.8*	*3.1*
CASHLI	506.4	100.0	44.6	8.8	216.5	42.8	81.0	16.0	83.0	16.4	81.3	16.0
	52.3	*0.0*	*6.2*	*1.7*	*22.2*	*4.2*	*15.4*	*3.0*	*20.8*	*3.4*	*32.9*	*5.2*

OTHMA	628.8	100.0	2.5	0.4	84.1	13.3	73.9	11.4	179.9	29.4	288.5	45.5
	139.9	*0.0*	*1.0*	*0.2*	*21.1*	*3.0*	*51.2*	*7.2*	*93.8*	*13.6*	*108.9*	*10.9*
OTHFIN	428.7	100.0	23.7	5.6	77.5	18.3	62.9	14.9	141.8	32.9	122.9	28.4
	95.8	*0.0*	*4.2*	*1.5*	*13.5*	*4.3*	*23.6*	*5.4*	*57.9*	*7.8*	*48.0*	*7.5*
NFIN	19 093.5	100.0	1174.6	6.2	6611.5	34.7	2337.0	12.2	3894.7	20.4	5075.7	26.6
	1460.0	*0.0*	*60.6*	*0.5*	*276.9*	*2.1*	*518.9*	*2.0*	*663.3*	*2.3*	*637.9*	*2.3*
VEHIC	1056.3	100.0	270.5	25.6	513.9	48.7	100.4	9.5	110.0	10.4	61.4	5.8
	43.8	*0.0*	*10.3*	*1.3*	*20.7*	*2.2*	*11.9*	*1.1*	*16.6*	*1.4*	*36.5*	*2.9*
HOUSES	8682.6	100.0	859.7	9.9	4818.7	55.5	1113.1	12.8	1316.7	15.2	574.4	6.6
	392.6	*0.0*	*46.9*	*0.7*	*177.4*	*2.3*	*134.5*	*1.2*	*229.8*	*2.1*	*107.2*	*1.0*
ORESRE	1552.0	100.0	40.4	2.6	471.3	30.4	309.9	19.9	432.4	27.9	298.0	19.3
	160.7	*0.0*	*8.9*	*0.6*	*58.7*	*3.1*	*71.2*	*3.4*	*87.9*	*4.3*	*56.4*	*3.4*
NRESRE	2112.7	100.0	-43.9	-2.1	243.8	11.6	205.3	9.6	545.4	25.9	1162.0	55.1
	394.3	*0.0*	*64.3*	*3.5*	*30.0*	*2.1*	*100.6*	*4.0*	*119.1*	*4.6*	*287.3*	*6.2*
BUS	5174.5	100.0	26.7	0.5	453.1	8.8	538.1	10.2	1400.3	27.1	2756.3	53.4
	750.8	*0.0*	*9.7*	*0.2*	*69.7*	*1.2*	*282.3*	*4.2*	*353.3*	*4.6*	*425.9*	*5.8*
OTHNFIN	515.4	100.0	21.2	4.1	110.6	21.5	70.2	13.6	89.8	17.4	223.6	43.4
	77.4	*0.0*	*4.1*	*0.9*	*13.3*	*3.9*	*21.8*	*4.2*	*32.9*	*5.6*	*69.0*	*8.4*
DEBT	3429.2	100.0	873.7	25.5	1712.4	49.9	332.1	9.7	326.5	9.5	184.5	5.4
	172.9	*0.0*	*111.2*	*2.8*	*90.6*	*2.4*	*80.6*	*2.1*	*52.5*	*1.6*	*73.8*	*2.0*
MRTHEL	2295.6	100.0	487.7	21.2	1316.4	57.3	227.0	9.9	198.3	8.7	66.2	2.9
	107.7	*0.0*	*36.3*	*1.7*	*74.7*	*2.4*	*49.3*	*1.9*	*39.9*	*1.7*	*39.5*	*1.6*
RESDBT	342.8	100.0	96.9	28.3	85.0	24.8	55.4	16.0	65.4	19.1	40.2	11.8
	96.3	*0.0*	*90.2*	*16.0*	*15.1*	*6.2*	*20.9*	*6.4*	*17.1*	*6.5*	*11.2*	*4.3*
INSTALL	557.7	100.0	230.0	41.2	242.5	43.5	30.7	5.5	34.0	6.1	20.5	3.7
	39.4	*0.0*	*12.2*	*3.0*	*16.8*	*3.0*	*8.0*	*1.4*	*9.2*	*1.6*	*32.3*	*4.8*
OTHLOC	61.9	100.0	4.6	7.7	6.6	10.9	7.4	11.6	5.2	8.6	38.0	61.3
	23.1	*0.0*	*0.9*	*4.3*	*2.5*	*6.9*	*5.6*	*7.9*	*3.8*	*8.9*	*20.8*	*16.7*

Table 2.6 (continued)

							Wealth percentile group						
	All families		0–50		50–90		90–95		95–99		99–100	
	Amount[a]	Share	Amount[a]	Share	Amount[a]	Share	Amount[a]	Share	Amount[a]	Share	Amount[a]	Share
CCBAL	94.0	100.0	40.2	42.8	46.1	49.0	4.8	5.0	2.6	2.8	0.3	0.3
	5.1	*0.0*	*3.1*	*3.0*	*3.8*	*3.2*	*2.1*	*2.2*	*0.9*	*0.9*	*0.2*	*0.2*
ODEBT	77.3	100.0	14.3	18.6	15.8	20.4	6.9	8.6	21.0	27.5	19.3	25.0
	15.0	*0.0*	*4.8*	*6.6*	*4.1*	*5.7*	*7.4*	*8.5*	*9.1*	*10.7*	*11.7*	*11.1*
Memo items:												
EQUITY	2424.5	100.0	38.6	1.6	500.7	20.7	288.0	11.7	715.1	29.6	882.1	36.4
	273.0	*0.0*	*6.0*	*0.3*	*50.4*	*2.1*	*93.1*	*2.8*	*109.5*	*4.3*	*166.2*	*4.5*
INCOME	5247.5	100.0	1279.7	24.4	2133.5	40.7	468.7	8.9	645.8	12.3	719.7	13.7
	205.9	*0.0*	*34.4*	*1.1*	*78.8*	*1.5*	*70.6*	*1.2*	*92.4*	*1.7*	*139.2*	*2.3*
# observations	3143.0		1074.0		1088.0		211.0		350.0		420.0	
# families (millons)	93.0		46.5		37.2		4.7		3.7		1.0	
Min. NW (thousands)	Negative		Negative		64.6		487.6		847.2		3141.6	

Notes:
Standard errors of the estimates are in italics below each estimate.
a. In billions of 2001 dollars.
b. See Appendix Table 2A.1 for definitions of wealth components.

Sources: Author's calculations based on the SCF.

Table 2.7 Net worth and components, distributed by net worth groups, 1992

| | | | Wealth percentile group | | | | | | | | | |
| | All families | | 0–50 | | 50–90 | | 90–95 | | 95–99 | | 99–100 | |
	Amount[a]	Share	Amount[a]	Share	Amount[a]	Share	Amount[a]	Share	Amount[a]	Share	Amount[a]	Share
NETWORTH[b]	22 164.4	100.0	724.9	3.3	6571.7	29.7	2782.0	12.6	5400.0	24.4	6685.8	30.2
	655.2	*0.0*	*40.3*	*0.2*	*185.6*	*1.1*	*164.4*	*0.7*	*337.8*	*1.3*	*444.8*	*1.4*
ASSET	25 918.4	100.0	1690.2	6.5	8322.6	32.1	3122.3	12.0	5864.8	22.6	6918.5	26.7
	690.8	*0.0*	*58.5*	*0.3*	*229.8*	*1.1*	*182.3*	*0.7*	*359.5*	*1.2*	*456.7*	*1.3*
FIN	8174.8	100.0	277.4	3.4	2319.0	28.4	1188.9	14.5	2230.5	27.3	2158.9	26.4
	237.4	*0.0*	*12.7*	*0.2*	*99.6*	*1.4*	*83.4*	*1.0*	*160.7*	*1.7*	*171.8*	*1.7*
LIQ	1425.4	100.0	92.6	6.5	495.8	34.8	196.1	13.8	325.2	22.8	315.6	22.1
	58.0	*0.0*	*4.8*	*0.4*	*30.3*	*2.2*	*18.7*	*1.3*	*37.2*	*2.4*	*47.0*	*2.7*
CDS	655.1	100.0	25.0	3.8	312.5	47.7	161.5	24.7	100.4	15.3	55.7	8.5
	47.1	*0.0*	*3.8*	*0.6*	*29.3*	*4.4*	*25.9*	*3.5*	*16.4*	*2.4*	*28.0*	*3.8*
SAVBND	93.0	100.0	9.3	10.0	43.8	47.1	16.0	17.2	15.5	16.6	8.4	9.0
	8.6	*0.0*	*1.4*	*1.8*	*4.6*	*4.7*	*5.8*	*5.4*	*3.6*	*3.6*	*3.0*	*3.1*
BOND	687.7	100.0	2.0	0.3	43.4	6.3	76.1	11.1	208.7	30.3	357.4	52.0
	69.4	*0.0*	*1.0*	*0.1*	*7.9*	*1.4*	*20.7*	*3.0*	*40.2*	*5.0*	*55.3*	*5.1*
STOCKS	1344.6	100.0	11.1	0.8	154.5	11.5	121.9	9.1	400.3	29.7	656.9	48.9
	107.7	*0.0*	*1.7*	*0.2*	*14.2*	*1.5*	*19.9*	*1.4*	*69.8*	*4.1*	*76.2*	*3.9*
NMMF	622.9	100.0	8.0	1.3	144.9	23.3	96.6	15.6	212.1	34.0	161.4	25.8
	65.4	*0.0*	*1.7*	*0.3*	*17.6*	*3.2*	*18.8*	*3.4*	*43.6*	*4.8*	*30.8*	*3.7*
RETQLIQ	2095.3	100.0	68.4	3.3	745.6	35.6	360.3	17.2	621.2	29.6	299.8	14.3
	109.0	*0.0*	*6.1*	*0.3*	*40.8*	*2.5*	*33.8*	*1.4*	*67.4*	*2.6*	*71.0*	*2.9*
CASHLI	499.2	100.0	41.3	8.3	237.9	47.7	60.4	12.1	123.1	24.6	36.6	7.3
	49.9	*0.0*	*3.0*	*1.2*	*21.9*	*4.7*	*13.3*	*2.6*	*39.5*	*6.0*	*5.3*	*1.1*

Table 2.7 (continued)

	All families Amount[a]	All families Share	0–50 Amount[a]	0–50 Share	50–90 Amount[a]	50–90 Share	90–95 Amount[a]	90–95 Share	95–99 Amount[a]	95–99 Share	99–100 Amount[a]	99–100 Share
OTHMA	444.2	100.0	3.4	0.8	67.1	15.1	66.6	15.0	135.2	30.4	172.0	38.7
	61.0	*0.0*	*1.7*	*0.4*	*12.1*	*2.5*	*16.3*	*3.7*	*34.8*	*5.4*	*40.7*	*5.2*
OTHFIN	307.3	100.0	16.5	5.4	73.6	23.9	33.3	10.8	88.9	29.0	95.0	30.9
	36.5	*0.0*	*1.9*	*1.0*	*11.9*	*3.6*	*10.9*	*3.4*	*25.3*	*6.9*	*22.2*	*5.7*
NFIN	17 743.5	100.0	1412.7	8.0	6003.6	33.8	1933.3	10.9	3634.3	20.5	4759.6	26.8
	565.1	*0.0*	*52.9*	*0.4*	*167.0*	*1.3*	*131.0*	*0.7*	*258.6*	*1.2*	*404.3*	*1.6*
VEHIC	1008.5	100.0	274.6	27.2	480.7	47.7	91.1	9.0	111.6	11.1	50.6	5.0
	21.0	*0.0*	*8.9*	*1.0*	*15.8*	*1.2*	*7.8*	*0.7*	*8.6*	*0.7*	*6.1*	*0.6*
HOUSES	8331.7	100.0	1036.9	12.4	4399.0	52.8	1016.4	12.2	1286.2	15.4	593.1	7.1
	184.0	*0.0*	*45.4*	*0.6*	*130.5*	*1.4*	*80.7*	*0.9*	*98.3*	*1.0*	*70.5*	*0.8*
ORESRE	1500.9	100.0	49.4	3.3	407.7	27.2	277.2	18.5	419.0	27.9	347.6	23.2
	83.1	*0.0*	*9.2*	*0.6*	*35.9*	*2.3*	*39.1*	*2.5*	*46.8*	*2.5*	*47.6*	*2.6*
NNRESRE	1930.5	100.0	5.0	0.3	210.2	10.9	161.1	8.3	483.4	25.0	1070.7	55.5
	211.2	*0.0*	*9.5*	*0.5*	*20.9*	*1.3*	*32.9*	*1.6*	*77.4*	*3.1*	*162.9*	*3.6*
BUS	4677.5	100.0	33.5	0.7	418.0	9.0	367.3	7.9	1261.7	27.0	2597.0	55.5
	372.3	*0.0*	*6.5*	*0.2*	*37.4*	*1.0*	*59.3*	*1.2*	*160.3*	*3.0*	*286.6*	*3.1*
OTHNFIN	294.4	100.0	13.4	4.5	87.8	29.8	20.2	6.9	72.5	24.7	100.5	34.1
	31.5	*0.0*	*2.0*	*0.8*	*13.8*	*4.0*	*5.2*	*1.7*	*17.5*	*5.1*	*20.2*	*5.2*
DEBT	3753.9	100.0	965.2	25.7	1750.9	46.6	340.2	9.1	464.8	12.4	232.7	6.2
	109.2	*0.0*	*50.2*	*1.3*	*75.6*	*1.6*	*40.0*	*1.0*	*44.8*	*1.1*	*25.6*	*0.6*
MRTHEL	2699.1	100.0	626.2	23.2	1413.1	52.4	240.4	8.9	318.5	11.8	101.0	3.7
	83.6	*0.0*	*38.1*	*1.4*	*64.3*	*2.0*	*33.8*	*1.2*	*34.6*	*1.2*	*13.6*	*0.5*

RESDBT	388.5 *36.0*	100.0 *0.0*	36.1 *13.8*	9.3 *3.2*	107.1 *17.3*	27.6 *4.0*	72.7 *17.6*	18.7 *4.1*	101.2 *17.1*	26.0 *3.6*	71.4 *12.8*	18.4 *3.0*
INSTALL	423.8 *23.9*	100.0 *0.0*	225.7 *21.3*	53.2 *2.5*	150.1 *7.9*	35.4 *1.8*	13.1 *2.5*	3.1 *0.6*	23.5 *4.3*	5.6 *1.0*	11.4 *2.5*	2.7 *0.6*
OTHLOC	31.2 *7.5*	100.0 *0.0*	2.3 *0.4*	7.4 *2.0*	8.1 *3.3*	26.0 *9.0*	3.3 *2.7*	10.6 *8.0*	1.7 *1.0*	5.2 *3.1*	15.9 *6.0*	50.8 *11.3*
CCBAL	119.9 *5.7*	100.0 *0.0*	57.1 *3.3*	47.6 *2.1*	51.9 *3.6*	43.3 *2.1*	5.8 *2.3*	4.8 *1.8*	4.0 *0.8*	3.3 *0.6*	1.1 *0.4*	0.9 *0.4*
ODEBT	91.3 *12.7*	100.0 *0.0*	17.7 *3.9*	19.4 *4.9*	20.6 *4.0*	22.6 *4.9*	4.9 *1.8*	5.3 *1.9*	16.0 *5.2*	17.5 *5.4*	32.0 *10.3*	35.1 *8.1*
Memo items:												
EQUITY	2752.4 *157.2*	100.0 *0.0*	47.0 *4.1*	1.7 *0.2*	575.7 *29.5*	20.9 *1.7*	319.1 *37.3*	11.6 *1.2*	835.1 *111.0*	30.3 *3.0*	975.5 *95.9*	35.5 *2.6*
INCOME	4751.7 *64.6*	100.0 *0.0*	1334.7 *32.6*	28.1 *0.7*	187.9 *61.6*	41.8 *1.2*	425.5 *31.3*	9.0 *0.6*	600.4 *36.6*	12.6 *0.7*	403.2 *36.3*	8.5 *0.7*
# observations	3906			1415		1156	242		449		644	
# families (millions)	95.9			47.9		38.4	4.8		3.9		1.0	
Min. NW (thousands)	Negative			Negative		60.3	429.4		795.8		2978.8	

Notes:
Standard errors of the estimates are in italics below each estimate.
a. In billions of 2001 dollars.
b. See Appendix Table 2A.1 for definitions of wealth components.

Sources: Author's calculations based on the SCF.

Table 2.8 Net worth and components, distributed by net worth groups, 1995

| | All families | | Wealth percentile group | | | | | | | | | |
| | | | 0–50 | | 50–90 | | 90–95 | | 95–99 | | 99–100 | |
	Amount[a]	Share	Amount[a]	Share	Amount[a]	Share	Amount[a]	Share	Amount[a]	Share	Amount[a]	Share
NETWORTH[b]	24238.6	100.0	868.7	3.6	6940.1	28.6	2877.7	11.9	5164.8	21.3	8387.3	34.6
	596.6	*0.0*	*30.9*	*0.2*	*141.4*	*0.7*	*151.0*	*0.6*	*249.0*	*0.9*	*456.2*	*1.3*
ASSET	28389.9	100.0	2130.7	7.5	8845.4	31.2	3234.9	11.4	5538.9	19.5	8640.0	30.4
	608.8	*0.0*	*68.5*	*0.3*	*175.8*	*0.7*	*169.5*	*0.6*	*263.4*	*0.8*	*460.7*	*1.2*
FIN	10422.5	100.0	382.7	3.7	2649.1	25.4	1421.5	13.6	2528.0	24.3	3441.2	33.0
	382.4	*0.0*	*14.6*	*0.2*	*70.5*	*0.9*	*107.6*	*0.9*	*145.9*	*1.2*	*299.4*	*1.9*
LIQ	1452.6	100.0	98.9	6.8	439.2	30.3	160.0	11.0	255.4	17.6	499.1	34.3
	123.0	*0.0*	*4.8*	*0.6*	*19.1*	*2.3*	*15.5*	*1.3*	*30.7*	*2.0*	*111.2*	*4.7*
CDS	587.3	100.0	21.5	3.7	226.3	38.5	95.9	16.3	153.5	26.1	90.1	15.4
	45.9	*0.0*	*3.3*	*0.6*	*25.5*	*3.7*	*23.7*	*3.7*	*26.0*	*3.6*	*23.2*	*3.9*
SAVBND	137.5	100.0	10.2	7.4	65.6	47.7	26.8	19.5	27.7	20.1	7.2	5.3
	11.6	*0.0*	*1.2*	*0.9*	*6.2*	*4.5*	*6.2*	*3.7*	*7.3*	*4.3*	*2.6*	*1.8*
BOND	653.0	100.0	1.3	0.2	32.9	5.0	44.2	6.8	119.6	18.3	455.1	69.7
	75.5	*0.0*	*0.8*	*0.1*	*6.8*	*1.1*	*10.2*	*1.5*	*27.2*	*3.9*	*68.4*	*4.5*
STOCKS	1628.7	100.0	13.1	0.8	144.8	8.9	110.3	6.8	450.6	27.7	909.9	55.9
	135.8	*0.0*	*2.0*	*0.1*	*13.1*	*1.0*	*23.9*	*1.3*	*68.8*	*4.2*	*125.7*	*4.6*
NMMF	1321.7	100.0	10.2	0.8	209.8	15.9	157.9	11.9	404.2	30.7	539.6	40.7
	172.8	*0.0*	*2.2*	*0.2*	*20.4*	*2.3*	*21.8*	*1.7*	*54.8*	*4.6*	*156.6*	*6.5*
RETQLIQ	2932.0	100.0	143.3	4.9	993.1	33.9	600.4	20.5	732.6	25.0	462.6	15.8
	127.0	*0.0*	*8.2*	*0.3*	*45.4*	*1.5*	*64.6*	*1.9*	*78.9*	*2.5*	*77.3*	*2.3*
CASHLI	750.2	100.0	59.3	7.9	359.0	47.9	106.5	14.2	94.2	12.5	131.2	17.5
	45.4	*0.0*	*4.6*	*0.7*	*24.4*	*2.9*	*18.4*	*2.6*	*30.6*	*3.7*	*27.0*	*3.0*

OTHMA	610.7	100.0	8.3	1.4	75.9	12.5	69.3	11.3	188.3	30.8	268.9	44.0
	74.9	*0.0*	*2.6*	*0.4*	*11.3*	*2.2*	*20.1*	*3.2*	*35.9*	*5.1*	*62.8*	*6.1*
OTHFIN	48.8	100.0	16.7	4.8	102.3	29.3	50.2	14.5	102.0	29.2	77.6	22.3
	44.2	*0.0*	*2.0*	*0.8*	*13.2*	*3.9*	*15.9*	*4.7*	*41.1*	*8.2*	*14.5*	*4.1*
NFIN	17 967.4	100.0	1748.0	9.7	6196.3	34.5	1813.4	10.1	3010.9	16.8	5198.8	28.9
	379.7	*0.0*	*59.5*	*0.4*	*141.6*	*0.9*	*98.1*	*0.5*	*165.9*	*0.8*	*308.5*	*1.3*
VEHIC	1280.6	100.0	378.4	29.6	615.2	48.0	114.5	8.9	113.5	8.9	58.9	4.6
	19.9	*0.0*	*10.9*	*0.9*	*16.8*	*1.0*	*7.3*	*0.5*	*7.6*	*0.6*	*6.9*	*0.5*
HOUSES	8526.6	100.0	1261.7	14.8	4558.1	53.5	970.3	11.4	1131.7	13.3	604.9	7.1
	123.7	*0.0*	*52.0*	*0.6*	*104.5*	*0.9*	*55.8*	*0.6*	*58.3*	*0.6*	*42.6*	*0.5*
ORESRE	1432.4	100.0	54.4	3.8	361.6	25.2	279.4	19.5	399.8	27.9	337.2	23.5
	81.4	*0.0*	*7.8*	*0.5*	*27.9*	*1.6*	*41.0*	*2.4*	*37.6*	*2.2*	*39.6*	*2.1*
NRESRE	1420.7	100.0	7.6	0.5	185.1	13.0	152.6	10.7	441.2	31.1	634.2	44.6
	104.0	*0.0*	*5.7*	*0.4*	*21.4*	*1.6*	*31.6*	*2.1*	*53.5*	*3.3*	*82.0*	*3.8*
BUS	4891.8	100.0	29.0	0.6	380.3	7.8	257.1	5.3	828.0	16.9	3397.3	69.5
	302.2	*0.0*	*5.1*	*0.1*	*35.6*	*0.8*	*41.6*	*0.8*	*111.7*	*2.1*	*266.8*	*2.4*
OTHNFIN	415.4	100.0	16.9	4.1	96.0	23.1	39.5	9.5	96.6	23.3	166.4	40.0
	40.3	*0.0*	*2.0*	*0.7*	*12.6*	*3.5*	*7.0*	*1.9*	*19.8*	*4.2*	*32.6*	*5.3*
DEBT	4151.3	100.0	1262.0	30.4	1905.3	45.9	357.2	8.6	374.1	9.0	252.7	6.1
	73.8	*0.0*	*48.6*	*1.0*	*60.5*	*1.2*	*32.7*	*0.8*	*31.1*	*0.7*	*30.9*	*0.7*
MRTHEL	3033.3	100.0	856.4	28.2	1530.4	50.5	241.0	7.9	274.6	9.1	130.9	4.3
	62.7	*0.0*	*42.3*	*1.3*	*49.7*	*1.3*	*22.6*	*0.7*	*24.4*	*0.8*	*13.6*	*0.4*
RESDBT	319.6	100.0	29.6	9.2	92.5	28.9	76.6	24.0	65.4	20.5	55.6	17.4
	28.4	*0.0*	*8.7*	*2.5*	*10.3*	*3.4*	*21.9*	*5.6*	*11.4*	*3.4*	*10.9*	*3.1*
INSTALL	494.6	100.0	266.2	53.8	178.8	36.1	21.3	4.3	18.7	3.8	9.7	2.0
	15.4	*0.0*	*12.5*	*1.7*	*9.3*	*1.6*	*3.1*	*0.6*	*3.9*	*0.8*	*3.9*	*0.8*
OTHLOC	23.8	100.0	5.4	22.7	4.9	20.8	1.9	8.1	1.8	7.5	9.8	41.0
	4.5	*0.0*	*1.2*	*5.1*	*1.8*	*6.6*	*0.6*	*2.6*	*0.9*	*3.3*	*3.5*	*8.8*

Table 2.8   (continued)

	All families		0–50		50–90		90–95		95–99		99–100	
	Amount[a]	Share	Amount[a]	Share	Amount[a]	Share	Amount[a]	Share	Amount[a]	Share	Amount[a]	Share
CCBAL	161.7	100.0	75.5	46.7	74.7	46.2	6.7	4.2	4.0	2.5	0.7	0.4
	5.9	*0.0*	*3.8*	*1.9*	*4.5*	*1.9*	*1.1*	*0.7*	*0.7*	*0.4*	*0.2*	*0.1*
ODEBT	118.3	100.0	29.0	24.7	24.1	20.3	9.7	8.2	9.6	8.3	46.0	38.6
	21.7	*0.0*	*4.0*	*5.3*	*6.9*	*5.1*	*3.4*	*2.8*	*6.7*	*5.9*	*18.4*	*10.3*
Memo items:												
EQUITY	4154.9	100.0	90.9	2.2	746.6	18.0	492.1	11.8	1248.6	30.1	1576.8	37.9
	197.0	*0.0*	*6.7*	*0.2*	*35.2*	*1.0*	*47.0*	*1.1*	*97.3*	*2.2*	*167.3*	*2.8*
INCOME	5105.8	100.0	1425.5	27.9	2073.2	40.6	464.7	9.1	555.0	10.9	587.4	11.5
	80.3	*0.0*	*31.4*	*0.7*	*51.1*	*0.9*	*34.8*	*0.7*	*34.1*	*0.6*	*54.6*	*1.0*
# observations	4299		1548		1290		292		504		665	
# families (millions)	99.0		49.5		39.6		5.0		4.0		1.0	
Min. NW (thousands)	Negative		Negative		67.0		448.8		778.9		2963.1	

Notes:
Standard errors of the estimates are in italics below each estimate.
a.   In billions of 2001 dollars.
b.   See Appendix Table 2A.1 for definitions of wealth components.

Sources: Author's calculations based on the SCF.

Table 2.9 *Net worth and components, distributed by net worth groups, 1998*

	All families		0–50		50–90		90–95		95–99		99–100	
	Amount[a]	Share	Amount[a]	Share	Amount[a]	Share	Amount[a]	Share	Amount[a]	Share	Amount[a]	Share
						Wealth percentile group						
NETWORTH[b]	31 629.6	100.0	950.1	3.0	8975.9	28.4	3603.9	11.4	7382.0	23.3	10 717.8	33.9
	1030.8	*0.0*	*52.0*	*0.2*	*360.8*	*0.9*	*217.7*	*0.6*	*538.2*	*1.2*	*572.5*	*1.5*
ASSET	36 871.3	100.0	2464.7	6.7	11 341.6	30.8	4031.7	10.9	8019.4	21.7	11 013.9	29.9
	1065.4	*0.0*	*85.0*	*0.3*	*406.7*	*0.9*	*243.8*	*0.6*	*563.1*	*1.2*	*584.9*	*1.4*
FIN	15 023.5	100.0	470.6	3.1	3972.0	26.4	1873.2	12.5	3906.8	26.0	4800.9	32.0
	595.8	*0.0*	*21.9*	*0.2*	*206.3*	*1.1*	*151.9*	*0.9*	*350.0*	*1.8*	*361.5*	*2.0*
LIQ	1702.5	100.0	117.5	6.9	634.5	37.3	226.7	13.3	369.2	21.7	354.6	20.8
	86.8	*0.0*	*5.7*	*0.4*	*43.6*	*2.6*	*66.2*	*3.5*	*41.1*	*2.5*	*53.7*	*2.7*
CDS	643.6	100.0	28.8	4.5	334.3	51.9	91.1	14.2	112.2	17.4	77.3	12.0
	60.2	*0.0*	*3.6*	*0.7*	*32.7*	*4.0*	*19.0*	*2.7*	*35.1*	*4.2*	*19.3*	*2.7*
SAVBND	101.5	100.0	7.6	7.5	61.3	60.4	13.6	13.4	11.3	11.1	7.7	7.6
	8.9	*0.0*	*1.3*	*1.1*	*7.4*	*4.1*	*2.7*	*2.9*	*2.6*	*2.4*	*2.8*	*2.5*
BOND	646.4	100.0	0.5	0.1	41.1	6.4	40.2	6.2	192.7	29.7	371.9	57.6
	62.0	*0.0*	*0.2*	*0.0*	*10.0*	*1.4*	*20.2*	*3.0*	*53.3*	*7.6*	*56.1*	*6.6*
STOCK	3407.6	100.0	18.8	0.6	348.4	10.2	256.2	7.5	881.4	25.9	1902.9	55.9
	217.0	*0.0*	*2.9*	*0.1*	*40.0*	*1.1*	*48.9*	*1.4*	*122.0*	*3.2*	*187.9*	*3.4*
NMMF	1858.4	100.0	25.0	1.3	435.5	23.4	285.5	15.4	616.8	33.2	495.6	26.7
	144.3	*0.0*	*3.5*	*0.2*	*39.6*	*2.4*	*53.7*	*2.7*	*78.9*	*3.5*	*90.0*	*3.8*
RETQLIQ	4123.2	100.0	179.6	4.4	1512.5	36.7	615.7	14.9	1077.4	26.1	738.0	17.9
	203.6	*0.0*	*13.7*	*0.4*	*84.3*	*1.7*	*60.8*	*1.4*	*120.3*	*2.3*	*121.0*	*2.6*
CASHLI	951.5	100.0	59.6	6.3	404.8	42.5	210.0	22.1	180.2	18.9	96.8	10.2
	71.1	*0.0*	*4.6*	*0.7*	*50.3*	*4.5*	*42.8*	*4.2*	*44.2*	*3.8*	*16.7*	*1.9*

Table 2.9 (continued)

	All families		0–50		50–90		90–95		95–99		99–100	
	Amount[a]	Share	Amount[a]	Share	Amount[a]	Share	Amount[a]	Share	Amount[a]	Share	Amount[a]	Share
OTHMA	1338.7	100.0	12.6	0.9	121.1	9.1	108.0	8.0	414.8	31.0	682.2	51.0
	141.6	*0.0*	*5.0*	*0.4*	*18.0*	*1.8*	*23.3*	*1.7*	*83.3*	*5.2*	*108.7*	*5.4*
OTHFIN	250.2	100.0	20.6	8.2	78.6	31.4	26.3	10.5	50.9	20.3	73.8	29.5
	27.8	*0.0*	*4.0*	*1.7*	*16.0*	*5.8*	*10.0*	*4.0*	*14.2*	*5.0*	*17.5*	*5.7*
NFIN	21 847.8	100.0	1994.1	9.1	7369.6	33.7	2158.5	9.9	4112.6	18.8	6213.0	28.4
	664.2	*0.0*	*74.6*	*0.4*	*235.9*	*1.1*	*145.9*	*0.6*	*292.8*	*1.1*	*438.1*	*1.5*
VEHIC	1407.8	100.0	387.1	27.5	670.8	47.6	127.5	9.1	136.0	9.7	86.3	6.1
	26.1	*0.0*	*9.4*	*0.8*	*22.8*	*1.1*	*10.2*	*0.7*	*12.6*	*0.8*	*10.2*	*0.7*
HOUSES	10 255.8	100.0	1464.3	14.3	5253.1	51.2	1176.6	11.5	1546.1	15.1	815.7	8.0
	207.7	*0.0*	*66.0*	*0.6*	*162.5*	*1.2*	*91.1*	*0.8*	*101.2*	*0.9*	*81.6*	*0.8*
ORESRE	1854.6	100.0	76.0	4.1	585.7	31.6	281.6	15.2	531.8	28.6	379.5	20.5
	123.5	*0.0*	*12.9*	*0.7*	*53.7*	*2.3*	*36.4*	*1.9*	*71.0*	*2.8*	*51.9*	*2.3*
NNRESRE	1685.7	100.0	12.4	0.7	252.7	15.0	164.3	9.7	476.8	28.3	779.5	46.3
	152.8	*0.0*	*3.3*	*0.2*	*30.2*	*1.9*	*22.2*	*1.4*	*78.5*	*3.8*	*118.6*	*4.2*
BUS	6262.2	100.0	32.9	0.5	515.6	8.2	365.7	5.8	1317.8	21.0	4030.3	64.4
	464.6	*0.0*	*5.4*	*0.1*	*48.4*	*0.9*	*47.2*	*0.7*	*180.3*	*2.3*	*370.1*	*2.7*
OTHNFIN	381.6	100.0	21.3	5.6	91.7	24.0	42.9	11.2	104.0	27.3	121.7	31.9
	35.9	*0.0*	*3.1*	*0.9*	*12.3*	*3.0*	*12.3*	*3.1*	*17.1*	*3.7*	*25.6*	*4.7*
DEBT	5241.8	100.0	1514.6	28.9	2365.7	45.1	427.8	8.2	637.5	12.2	296.1	5.6
	129.0	*0.0*	*75.8*	*1.3*	*86.0*	*1.3*	*43.7*	*0.8*	*51.1*	*0.9*	*35.1*	*0.7*
MRTHEL	3739.4	100.0	981.2	26.2	1856.5	49.6	308.3	8.2	435.1	11.6	158.4	4.2
	95.8	*0.0*	*53.9*	*1.4*	*77.2*	*1.6*	*30.7*	*0.8*	*37.2*	*0.9*	*23.2*	*0.6*

Wealth percentile group

RESDBT	403.6	100.0	47.9	11.9	143.3	35.5	47.2	11.7	105.8	26.2	59.4	14.7
	35.6	*0.0*	*10.7*	*2.4*	*22.0*	*3.8*	*12.4*	*2.9*	*17.4*	*3.6*	*11.9*	*2.9*
INSTALL	682.6	100.0	332.8	48.8	248.0	36.3	42.8	6.3	39.1	5.7	19.9	2.9
	21.5	*0.0*	*14.7*	*1.8*	*13.4*	*1.7*	*7.9*	*1.1*	*7.5*	*1.1*	*6.6*	*0.9*
OTHLOC	17.5	100.0	4.4	25.1	3.3	19.0	1.5	8.7	3.5	19.7	4.8	27.6
	3.1	*0.0*	*0.6*	*4.5*	*1.0*	*5.2*	*0.7*	*3.8*	*1.3*	*6.5*	*2.6*	*9.8*
CCBAL	202.8	100.0	106.3	52.4	76.8	37.9	8.8	4.4	9.5	4.7	1.3	0.7
	8.1	*0.0*	*6.9*	*2.2*	*4.3*	*2.1*	*2.0*	*1.0*	*2.4*	*1.2*	*0.7*	*0.4*
ODEBT	195.8	100.0	42.0	21.2	37.8	19.4	19.2	9.8	44.5	22.8	52.3	26.7
	45.1	*0.0*	*38.2*	*13.4*	*9.8*	*5.4*	*9.2*	*4.6*	*13.7*	*6.8*	*17.1*	*7.7*
Memo items:												
EQUITY	8077.1	100.0	145.2	1.8	1641.6	20.3	874.0	10.8	2281.9	28.2	3134.4	38.8
	391.6	*0.0*	*11.6*	*0.2*	*96.4*	*1.1*	*84.0*	*1.1*	*241.4*	*2.4*	*275.7*	*2.6*
INCOME	5937.2	100.0	1512.9	25.5	2439.8	41.1	462.6	7.8	791.6	13.3	730.3	12.3
	120.7	*0.0*	*32.7*	*0.7*	*67.8*	*0.9*	*33.3*	*0.5*	*66.7*	*1.0*	*68.4*	*1.0*
# observations	4309		1645		1280		248		500		636	
# families (millions)	102.6		51.3		41.0		5.1		4.1		1.0	
Min. NW (thousands)	Negative		Negative		80.2		537.3		953.7		4029.4	

Notes:
Standard errors of the estimates are in italics below each estimate.
a. In billions of 2001 dollars.
b. See Appendix Table 2A.1 for definitions of wealth components.

Sources: Author's calculations based on the SCF.

Table 2.10 *Net worth and components, distributed by net worth groups, 2001*

| | All families | | Wealth percentile group | | | | | | | | | |
| | | | 0–50 | | 50–90 | | 90–95 | | 95–99 | | 99–100 | |
	Amount[a]	Share	Amount[a]	Share	Amount[a]	Share	Amount[a]	Share	Amount[a]	Share	Amount[a]	Share
NETWORTH[b]	42 389.2	100.0	1175.7	2.8	11 603.3	27.4	5139.9	12.1	10 615.2	25.0	13 855.2	32.7
	712.1	*0.0*	*38.1*	*0.1*	*274.4*	*0.7*	*309.0*	*0.7*	*463.9*	*1.1*	*766.1*	*1.4*
ASSET	48 205.3	100.0	2682.8	5.6	14 391.7	29.9	5641.3	11.7	11 288.3	23.4	14 201.2	29.5
	733.2	*0.0*	*78.4*	*0.2*	*325.9*	*0.8*	*341.1*	*0.7*	*489.6*	*1.0*	*785.7*	*1.3*
FIN	20 344.8	100.0	512.0	2.5	5160	25.4	2860.5	14.1	5410.4	26.6	6401.8	31.5
	556.1	*0.0*	*20.2*	*0.1*	*173.6*	*1.0*	*202.9*	*0.9*	*320.3*	*1.5*	*493.9*	*1.9*
LIQ	2380.6	100.0	142.6	6.0	778.6	32.7	316.1	13.3	520.5	21.9	622.9	26.2
	112.1	*0.0*	*6.7*	*0.4*	*35.3*	*1.8*	*39.9*	*1.6*	*46.9*	*1.9*	*97.5*	*3.2*
CDS	624.8	100.0	26.6	4.3	334.1	53.5	108.3	17.3	116.8	18.7	39.0	6.2
	49.3	*0.0*	*4.3*	*0.7*	*31.6*	*3.8*	*26.4*	*3.7*	*24.5*	*3.2*	*11.8*	*1.7*
SAVBND	139.8	100.0	5.7	4.1	63.5	45.5	14	10.1	30.5	21.9	25.9	18.5
	23.9	*0.0*	*1.2*	*1.2*	*10.7*	*8.0*	*4.1*	*3.2*	*16.1*	*8.5*	*13.3*	*8.5*
BOND	924.1	100.0	2.3	0.3	36.6	4.0	81.1	8.8	209.3	22.7	594.8	64.3
	108.4	*0.0*	*1.3*	*0.1*	*11.6*	*1.3*	*33.5*	*3.5*	*42.6*	*4.2*	*98.1*	*5.6*
STOCKS	4378.9	100.0	22.1	0.5	498.4	11.4	434.7	9.9	1106.0	25.3	2317.9	52.9
	287.1	*0.0*	*2.9*	*0.1*	*47.8*	*1.3*	*76.1*	*1.7*	*116.1*	*2.8*	*273.3*	*3.4*
NMMF	2477.8	100.0	23.1	0.9	507.4	20.5	444.2	17.9	807.6	32.6	695.4	28.1
	155.2	*0.0*	*3.3*	*0.1*	*27.1*	*1.5*	*55.5*	*2.0*	*93.9*	*3.3*	*124.1*	*4.0*
RETQLIQ	5720.3	100.0	187.4	3.3	2081.4	36.4	1005.5	17.6	1667.4	29.1	778.6	13.6
	215.4	*0.0*	*10.2*	*0.2*	*98.2*	*1.7*	*89.3*	*1.4*	*158.3*	*2.2*	*108*	*1.8*
CASHLI	1077.7	100.0	78.0	7.2	501.5	46.5	167.7	15.6	193.7	17.9	136.8	12.7
	61.4	*0.0*	*8.0*	*0.8*	*43.7*	*3.3*	*37.5*	*3.3*	*41.3*	*3.5*	*25.8*	*2.3*

OTHMA	2208.2	100.0	7.3	0.3	287.8	13	267.1	12.1	622.0	28.3	1024.0	46.2
	221.0	*0.0*	*2.7*	*0.1*	*60.8*	*2.6*	*49.1*	*2.5*	*128.9*	*6.2*	*223.8*	*7.2*
OTHFIN	412.4	100.0	17	4.1	70.7	17.1	21.8	5.3	136.5	33.1	166.5	40.4
	61.5	*0.0*	*2.1*	*0.8*	*12.7*	*3.3*	*5.2*	*1.5*	*33.1*	*6.4*	*46.4*	*7.4*
NFIN	27 860.5	100.0	2170.7	7.8	9231.7	33.1	2780.8	10.0	5877.9	21.1	7799.4	28.0
	626.7	*0.0*	*70.5*	*0.3*	*247.2*	*1.0*	*201.6*	*0.7*	*317.1*	*1.2*	*604.5*	*1.7*
VEHIC	1656.2	100.0	462.6	27.9	799.6	48.3	156.9	9.5	153.2	9.3	83.9	5.1
	24.0	*0.0*	*12.2*	*0.7*	*16.5*	*0.8*	*12.5*	*0.7*	*10.0*	*0.6*	*8.0*	*0.5*
HOUSES	13 063.6	100.0	1602.6	12.3	6612.9	50.6	1587.8	12.2	2087	16	1173.2	9.0
	220.2	*0.0*	*63*	*0.5*	*179.4*	*1.1*	*128.4*	*1.0*	*114*	*0.8*	*114*	*0.8*
ORESRE	2256.5	100.0	42.2	1.9	605.5	26.8	264.1	11.7	689.1	30.5	655.7	29.1
	127.3	*0.0*	*5.9*	*0.3*	*47*	*2.4*	*45.7*	*1.9*	*78.7*	*2.8*	*81.1*	*2.9*
NNRESRE	2280.3	100.0	13.2	0.6	329.5	14.5	206.4	9.1	801.9	35.2	929.3	40.7
	192.2	*0.0*	*3.9*	*0.2*	*54.1*	*2.5*	*33.6*	*1.6*	*94.8*	*3.8*	*159.4*	*4.6*
BUS	8148.5	100.0	29.2	0.4	803.4	9.9	534.8	6.6	2029.8	24.9	4751.2	58.3
	518.4	*0.0*	*4.3*	*0.1*	*69.6*	*1.0*	*78.4*	*1.0*	*222.5*	*2.7*	*491.8*	*3.1*
OTHNFIN	455.4	100.0	20.9	4.6	80.8	17.7	30.8	6.7	116.9	25.7	206.2	45.2
	73.7	*0.0*	*2.7*	*0.8*	*9.4*	*2.9*	*12.0*	*2.6*	*29.9*	*5.7*	*64.4*	*7.6*
DEBT	5816	100.0	1507.1	25.9	2788.4	47.9	501.4	8.6	673.1	11.6	346.0	5.9
	119.3	*0.0*	*61.7*	*1.1*	*108.3*	*1.5*	*55.3*	*0.9*	*53*	*0.9*	*40.8*	*0.7*
MRTHEL	4370.8	100.0	1025.6	23.5	2257.9	51.7	399.3	9.1	484.6	11.1	203.4	4.7
	108.1	*0.0*	*52.8*	*1.2*	*96.7*	*1.6*	*47.1*	*1.1*	*40*	*0.9*	*27.9*	*0.6*
RESDBT	370.2	100.0	15.5	4.2	149	40.3	38.6	10.4	104.2	28.1	62.9	17
	27.4	*0.0*	*3.4*	*0.9*	*16.4*	*4.0*	*9.4*	*2.4*	*18.4*	*4.2*	*15.3*	*3.8*
INSTALL	714.0	100.0	343	48	267.8	37.5	41.0	5.7	36.8	5.2	25.4	3.6
	30.5	*0.0*	*15.6*	*1.8*	*13.1*	*1.7*	*12.3*	*1.6*	*11.8*	*1.6*	*8.4*	*1.1*
OTHLOC	29.8	100.0	4.1	13.8	7.0	23.6	1.5	5.0	8.5	28.5	8.7	29.1
	8.1	*0.0*	*1.2*	*5.6*	*2.7*	*10.4*	*1.0*	*3.9*	*5.8*	*14*	*4.6*	*12.3*
CCBAL	195.7	100.0	97.4	49.8	81.5	41.6	6.3	3.2	9.5	4.9	1.1	0.5
	8.2	*0.0*	*4.9*	*2.1*	*4.8*	*2.0*	*1.4*	*0.7*	*4.6*	*2.2*	*0.3*	*0.2*

Table 2.10 (continued)

	All families		0–50		Wealth percentile group 50–90		90–95		95–99		99–100	
	Amount[a]	Share	Amount[a]	Share	Amount[a]	Share	Amount[a]	Share	Amount[a]	Share	Amount[a]	Share
ODEBT	135.5	100.0	21.5	15.9	25.3	18.7	14.8	10.9	29.4	21.7	44.5	32.8
	15.5	*0.0*	*3.2*	*2.6*	*4.5*	*3.9*	*4.9*	*3.4*	*8.5*	*5.3*	*11.4*	*6.0*
Memo items:												
EQUITY	11 348.1	100.0	162.2	1.4	2459.3	21.7	1632.3	14.4	3285.7	29	3808.6	33.6
	422.2	*0.0*	*9.8*	*0.1*	*113.5*	*1.2*	*143.1*	*1.2*	*234.4*	*1.9*	*364.3*	*2.4*
INCOME	7400.8	100.0	1695.4	22.9	216.5	38.1	680.4	9.2	1134.2	15.3	1074.3	14.5
	204.9	*0.0*	*35.7*	*0.8*	*75.1*	*1.2*	*59.3*	*0.8*	*79.3*	*1.0*	*182.7*	*2.1*
# observations	4449		1719		1314		253		499		664	
# families (millions)	106.5		53.2		42.6		5.3		4.3		1.1	
Min. NW (thousands)	Negative		Negative		87.5		745.5		1307.1		5865.0	

Notes:
Standard errors of the estimates are in italics below each estimate.
a. In billions of 2001 dollars.
b. See Appendix Table 2A.1 for definitions of wealth components.

Sources: Author's calculations based on the SCF.

Table 2.11   Assets and liabilities as a share of total assets, by percentile groups of distribution of wealth, 1989 and 2001 (per cent)

	All families		0–50		50–95		90–95		95–99		99–100	
	1989	2001	1989	2001	1989	2001	1989	2001	1989	2001	1989	2001
NETWORTH[a]	87.6	87.9	42.3	43.8	80.9	80.6	90.5	91.1	94.7	94.0	97.5	97.6
ASSET	100.0	100.0	100.0	100.0	100.0	100.0	100.0	100.0	100.0	100.0	100.0	100.0
FIN	30.9	42.2	22.5	19.1	26.1	35.9	33.2	50.7	36.8	47.9	32.3	45.1
LIQ	5.7	4.9	6.3	5.3	5.7	5.4	6.0	5.6	5.5	4.6	5.8	4.4
CDS	3.0	1.3	2.3	1.0	4.1	2.3	4.0	1.9	3.5	1.0	1.1	0.3
SAVBND	0.5	0.3	0.6	0.2	0.7	0.4	0.7	0.2	0.4	0.3	0.1	0.2
BOND	3.1	1.9	0.2	0.1	0.7	0.3	2.7	1.4	4.0	1.9	5.8	4.2
STOCKS	4.7	9.1	1.1	0.8	2.3	3.5	3.8	7.7	6.6	9.8	7.2	16.3
NMMF	1.7	5.1	0.3	0.9	0.8	3.5	2.1	7.9	2.5	7.2	2.1	4.9
RETQLIQ	6.5	11.9	7.1	7.0	7.6	14.5	7.8	17.8	7.8	14.8	3.6	5.5
CASHLI	1.8	2.2	2.9	2.9	2.4	3.5	2.3	3.0	1.3	1.7	1.1	1.0
OTHMA	2.3	4.6	0.2	0.3	0.9	2.0	2.1	4.7	2.9	5.5	3.9	7.2
OTHFIN	1.6	0.9	1.6	0.6	0.9	0.5	1.8	0.4	2.3	1.2	1.6	1.2
NFIN	69.1	57.8	77.5	80.9	73.9	64.1	66.8	49.3	63.2	52.1	67.7	54.9
VEHIC	3.8	3.4	17.9	17.2	5.7	5.6	2.9	2.8	1.8	1.4	0.8	0.6
HOUSES	31.4	27.1	56.7	59.7	53.8	45.9	31.8	28.1	21.4	18.5	7.7	8.3
ORESRE	5.6	4.7	2.7	1.6	5.3	4.2	8.9	4.7	7.0	6.1	4.0	4.6
NNRESRE	7.7	4.7	−2.9	0.5	2.7	2.3	5.9	3.7	8.9	7.1	15.5	6.5
BUS	18.7	16.9	1.8	1.1	5.1	5.6	15.4	9.5	22.7	18.0	36.8	33.5
OTHNFIN	1.9	0.9	1.4	0.8	1.2	0.6	2.0	0.5	1.5	1.0	3.0	1.5
DEBT	12.4	12.1	57.7	56.2	19.1	19.4	9.5	8.9	5.3	6.0	2.5	2.4
MRTHEL	8.3	9.1	32.2	38.2	14.7	15.7	6.5	7.1	3.2	4.3	0.9	1.4

Table 2.11   (continued)

	All families		0–50		50–95		90–95		95–99		99–100	
	1989	2001	1989	2001	1989	2001	1989	2001	1989	2001	1989	2001
RESDBT	1.2	0.8	6.4	0.6	0.9	1.0	1.6	0.7	1.1	0.9	0.5	0.4
INSTALL	2.0	1.5	15.2	12.8	2.7	1.9	0.9	0.7	0.6	0.3	0.3	0.2
OTHLOC	0.2	0.1	0.3	0.2	0.1	0.0	0.2	0.0	0.1	0.1	0.5	0.1
CCBAL	0.3	0.4	2.7	3.6	0.5	0.6	0.1	0.1	0.0	0.1	0.0	0.0
ODEBT	0.3	0.3	0.9	0.8	0.2	0.2	0.2	0.3	0.3	0.3	0.3	0.3
Memo item:												
EQUITY	8.8	23.5	2.5	6.0	5.6	17.1	8.2	28.9	11.6	29.1	11.8	26.8

Note: a. See Appendix Table 2A.1 for definitions of wealth components.

Sources: Author's calculations based on the SCF.

54

and indirect stock holdings has increased markedly over time for all the percentile groups. For the group with wealth in the 50th to 90th percentiles of the wealth distribution, the portfolio share of such stocks rose from about 5.6 per cent in 1989 to 17 per cent in 2001; the share of such stocks is higher for the top of the distribution than for the lower part, but the disproportion is not as great as for business and investment real estate equity; for the highest 10 per cent of the wealth distribution, the declining share of businesses over time was approximately offset by the rising share of such stocks.

The value of a principal residence accounted for about 60 per cent of the assets of the lower half of the wealth distribution over the surveys considered, but it accounted for increasingly less for higher percentile groups. The asset share of vehicles fell more sharply over the wealth groups; in 2001, vehicles accounted for 17.2 per cent of the assets of the lower half of the wealth distribution but only 5.6 per cent of the assets of the next highest 40 per cent of the wealth distribution and less than 1 per cent of the assets of the wealthiest 1 per cent.

The most equal asset share across all the percentile groups is financial assets other than direct and indirect stock. In 2001 the share ranged from 13 per cent for the lower half of the distribution to 21.8 per cent for the group between the 90th and 95th percentiles of the wealth distribution.

Debt as a share of assets varies very widely across the wealth distribution. The lower half of the wealth distribution is by far the most leveraged; debt as a proportion of their assets was 56.2 per cent over the 1989 to 2001 period. For the next highest 40 per cent of the wealth distribution, the leverage rate drops to 18.8 per cent. For the highest 1 per cent of the wealth distribution, the ratio is under 3 per cent. Across all groups, the leverage rate showed no consistent pattern across the 1989–2001 period.

NEGATIVE NET WORTH

In 2001, 6.9 per cent of families had negative net worth – only slightly lower than the 7.3 per cent level in 1989. Because the general characteristics of the group with negative wealth changed relatively little over the period considered in this chapter, the discussion here focuses on the most recent SCF cross-section. For families with negative net worth in 2001, the median wealth value was minus $5100 (Table 2.12). Although this group had the lowest levels of wealth, a substantial part of the group had non-negligible assets – the median value was $7600. Across the asset distribution, the group with net worth less than minus $5000 had more than twice the assets of the part of the group with new worth closer to zero; however, the poorer group had far more debt as well. Families with negative net worth were much less

Table 2.12 *Percentiles values of net worth, by distributions of net worth, assets and debt, families with negative net worth and all families, 2001 (2001 dollars)*

Percentiles	Families with negative net worth			All families
	All <0	Negative $5000 or less (NW ≤ –5K)	Negative greater than negative $5000 (NW > –5K)	
Net worth				
10	−27.5	−33.6	−3.9	0.1
25	−13.4	−24.0	−2.6	12.7
50	−5.1	−13.2	−1.3	86.1
75	−1.3	−8.4	−0.4	283.0
90	−0.4	−6.0	−0.2	734.4
Asset				
10	0.0	0.5	0.0	4.1
25	1.2	3.5	0.1	27.6
50	7.6	11.5	5.2	136.0
75	19.6	28.5	14.2	358.7
90	69.1	83.8	43.0	815.4
Debt				
10	1.1	10.0	0.4	0.0
25	5.8	16.3	1.6	0.0
50	16.3	28.0	7.0	14.5
75	38.9	62.2	15.7	78.3
90	83.0	122.4	46.4	145.2

Sources: Author's calculations based on the SCF.

likely to have most types of assets than were all families (Table 2.13). Among financial assets, ownership was notable only for transaction accounts (79.7 per cent of families with negative wealth) and retirement accounts (23.5 per cent); among nonfinancial assets, ownership was notable only for vehicles (64.7 per cent) and principal residences (16.4 per cent).

The proximate cause of negative net worth is that the value of debt exceeds the value of assets. Thus, all families with negative net worth have some type of debt. Two types of debt were much more common among this group than among the population as a whole – instalment debt and credit card debt – and they were even more common among families with net worth less than minus $5000. Education loans and vehicle loans accounted for a very large part of the prevalence of instalment debt. Instalment

Table 2.13 *Ownership of various assets and liabilities, families with*
negative net worth and all families, 2001 (per cent)

	Families with negative net worth			All families
	All (NW<0)	Negative $5000 or less (NW≤–5K)	Negative greater than negative $5000 (NW>–5K)	
NET WORTH[a]	100.0	100.0	100.0	100.0
ASSET	90.7	96.1	85.2	96.7
FIN	83.9	91.9	75.8	93.1
LIQ	79.7	86.4	72.8	91.0
CDS	0.5	1.0	0.0	15.7
SAVBND	8.0	9.8	6.1	16.7
BOND	0.0	0.0	0.0	3.0
STOCKS	7.6	9.8	5.3	21.3
NMMF	5.8	11.0	0.6	17.7
RETQLIQ	23.5	27.3	19.6	52.2
CASHLI	6.7	6.3	7.1	28.0
OTHMA	0.0	0.0	0.0	6.7
OTHFIN	9.1	8.3	9.9	9.3
NFIN	70.3	79.4	61.0	90.7
VEHIC	64.7	74.4	54.8	84.8
HOUSES	16.4	19.1	13.6	67.7
ORESRE	1.0	0.7	1.2	11.4
NNRESRE	0.0	0.0	0.0	8.3
BUS	2.5	2.9	2.1	11.9
OTHFIN	9.1	8.3	9.9	9.3
DEBT	100.0	100.0	100.0	75.1
MRTHEL	15.5	17.3	13.6	44.6
RESDBT	0.8	0.5	1.0	4.7
INSTALL	78.2	87.5	68.7	45.1
CCBAL	71.4	74.4	68.3	44.4
OTHLOC	3.8	4.0	3.6	1.6
ODEBT	16.4	19.9	12.8	7.2
Memo items:				
EQUITY	41.4	47.5	35.3	34.9
Vehicle loan	41.4	11.8	21.2	7.2
Education loan	44.3	62.9	25.3	6.9
Only debt is credit card debt	12.3	5.0	19.8	7.7

Note: a. See Appendix Table 2A.1 for definitions of wealth components.

Sources: Author's calculations based on the SCF.

Table 2.14   *Distribution of debt, families with negative net worth and all families, 2001 (per cent)*

	Families with negative net worth			All families
	All (NW<0)	Negative $5000 or less (NW ≤ −5K)	Negative greater than negative $5000 (NW > −5K)	
DEBT[a]	100.0	100.0	100.0	100.0
MRTHEL	32.1	28.3	42.4	75.1
RESDBT	1.2	0.5	3.1	6.4
INSTALL	48.1	52.6	35.9	12.3
CCBAL	13.2	11.8	17.0	3.4
OTHLOC	0.7	0.9	0.2	0.5
ODEBT	4.6	5.9	1.4	2.3
Memo items:				
Education loan	25.3	30.6	11.0	2.9
Vehicle loan	14.3	11.8	21.2	7.2
Asset value < debt				
House<mortgage	6.6	8.9	4.2	1.0
Vehicles<loans	13.3	12.8	13.9	2.9

Note: a. See Appendix Table 2A.1 for definitions of wealth components.

Sources: Author's calculations based on the SCF.

debt accounted for almost half of the value of the group's debt, and the greatest part of the instalment debt was education loans and vehicle loans (Table 2.14). Unmeasured human capital would tend to offset the former. Of the whole group, 13.3 per cent had vehicle debt exceeding the value of their vehicles; some of this disproportion may be explained by depreciation of the vehicles, but some part is also likely to be an artifact of the method used to value the vehicles in the SCF.[10] Although a relatively small fraction of the group were homeowners, mortgage debt accounted for nearly a third of the total debt of the group; the fraction was much larger for families with relatively small absolute levels of negative net worth. While only 16.4 per cent of the group with negative wealth were homeowners, 40.2 per cent of these homeowners had housing debt exceeding the value of a principal residence. Although credit card debt as a share of the total debt of the group was relatively small, 12.3 per cent of the group had only credit card debt; for the part of the group with negative net worth between zero and minus $5000, the share was nearly one-fifth.

The group with negative wealth differs from the overall population in terms of a number of key demographic characteristics. Consistent with the expectations of the life-cycle hypothesis, families with negative net worth in 2001 were much younger than the population as a whole, with 58 per cent in the under-35 age group (Table 2.15). The disproportion of very young families was particularly large for the group with wealth of less than minus $5000. Those with negative net worth overall were more likely to have less than a high school education or its equivalent and they were somewhat less likely to have any college experience. However, the group with larger absolute negative wealth differed from the group closer to zero: the former was notably more likely than the overall population to have college experience while the latter was much less likely to have college experience. As a whole, the group was substantially more likely to be working than the full population but less likely to be self-employed. As one would expect from the age difference, a smaller fraction of the negative wealth group was retired or disabled. The proportion of families who were neither working nor retired (a group largely unemployed or out of the labour force) was more than twice as large in the group with negative net worth as in the whole population. The relative youth of the negative wealth group explains part of the relative concentration of the group in the lowest 40 per cent of the overall income distribution. The concentration was particularly strong for the group with relatively modest absolute negative wealth; over 40 per cent of this group had incomes among the lowest 20 per cent of all families. The negative wealth group contained a larger fraction of nonwhite and Hispanic families than the population as a whole, but the contrast was particularly sharp for the group with wealth between zero and minus $5000; nearly half of this group were minorities, compared with only about a quarter of the whole population as measured in the SCF.[11] The negative wealth group was relatively concentrated in the southern and western regions.

WEALTH OF THE OLDER BABY BOOMERS

The changes in wealth discussed so far are only changes in distributions, not changes for individuals. Life-cycle factors alone suggest that there should have been considerable movement within the wealth distribution as a result of saving for educational expenses and retirement, and dissaving to pay for those expenses. At the same time, differential returns on assets and differential growth of income to support saving would drive mobility across the distribution. The earlier discussion of the *Forbes* 400 indicates that differential returns are probably a very large factor in mobility for people

Table 2.15　Distribution of families across various groups in 2001: families with negative net worth, net worth of negative $5000 or less, negative net worth greater than negative $5000, and all families (per cent)

	Families with negative net worth			All families
	All (NW<0)	Negative $5000 or less (NW<−5K)	Negative greater than negative $5000 (NW>−5K)	
Age of head (years)				
Less than 35	58.0	62.7	53.1	22.7
35–44	20.3	22.5	18.0	22.3
45–54	12.8	11.3	14.2	20.6
55–64	3.8	3.4	4.2	13.3
65–74	2.3	0.0	4.7	10.7
75 or more	2.9	0.0	5.9	10.4
Education of head				
No high school diploma	19.4	13.1	25.9	16.0
High school diploma	30.6	25.4	36.0	31.7
Some college	23.6	24.2	23.1	18.3
College degree	26.3	37.3	15.1	34.0
Work status of head				
Working for someone else	72.4	73.8	71.1	60.9
Self-employed	6.6	10.0	3.0	11.7
Retired/disabled	11.5	5.8	17.3	22.9
Other not working	9.6	10.5	8.6	4.5
Percentiles of income				
Less than 20	35.2	28.1	42.5	20.0
20–39.9	30.2	28.8	31.6	20.0
40–59.9	22.4	28.2	16.6	20.0
60–79.9	10.9	12.4	9.3	20.0
80–89.9	1.3	2.5	0.0	10.0
90–100	0.0	0.0	0.0	10.0
Race or ethnicity				
White non-Hispanic	62.3	72.3	52.0	76.2
Non-white or Hispanic	37.8	27.7	48.0	23.8

Table 2.15   (continued)

	Families with negative net worth			All families
	All (NW<0)	Negative $5000 or less (NW< −5K)	Negative greater than negative $5000 (NW> −5K)	
Region				
Northeast	16.8	13.3	20.4	19.0
North central	18.7	21.1	16.2	23.0
South	38.1	38.9	37.3	36.2
West	26.4	26.7	26.1	21.8

Sources: Author's calculations based on the SCF.

who already have considerable assets. Unfortunately, the SCF does not have a panel dimension over the time considered in this chapter that would allow one to characterize wealth mobility. Earlier work by Kennickell and Starr-McCluer (1997) using a 1983–89 SCF panel indicates that, during that period, most movement was within the broad middle of the wealth distribution; the most stable group was the lowest quartile (about 71 per cent were in the group in both 1983 and 1989), and the second most stable was the highest 1 per cent (about 51 per cent were in the group in both years). Hurst et al. (1998) provide similar evidence using data from the 1984–94 waves of the Panel Study on Income Dynamics, collected by the Institute for Social Research at the University of Michigan.

Despite the lack of panel structure in the SCF, it is possible to follow age cohorts over time, at least under the assumption that membership in the cohort is fixed. Death, immigration and changes in living arrangements may be serious problems in this type of analysis. For example, individuals in older families are more likely to die. Immigration seems to be more of an issue for relatively young families than for older ones. Changes in living arrangements – marriage, divorce, living in secondary household units, living outside a standard household (for example, a dormitory or barracks) – are also relatively more common among younger people. For these reasons, the analysis here focuses on the cohort aged 46 to 55 in 2001 (34 to 43 in 1989), a group that encompasses most of the older part of the baby-boom generation. Families headed by persons in this age range accounted for about 20 per cent of all families in 2001.

With some notable interruptions in 1992, the wealth level of this cohort trended broadly upward during the 1989–2001 period (Table 2.16). At the

Table 2.16   Distribution of cohort aged 46 to 55 in 2001, by wealth groups, 1989–2001 (per cent)

Net worth (2001 dollars)	Survey year[a]				
	1989[a]	1992	1995	1998	2001[a]
<$0	9.5	4.9	4.7	5.3	4.1
$0–$999	6.7	4.8	3.7	4.1	3.8
$1000–$2499	2.5	4.4	1.5	1.0	1.2
$2500–$4999	3.2	2.9	4.1	3.0	2.7
$5000–$9999	3.8	4.7	3.6	3.7	2.8
$10 000–$24 999	7.1	10.7	7.8	6.1	6.1
$25 000–$49 999	11.9	12.9	11.9	9.6	10.0
$50 000–$99 999	15.6	16.5	18.8	15.1	11.5
$100 000–$249 999	21.6	23.2	24.4	24.1	22.6
$250 000–$500 000	10.1	8.4	8.9	13.3	14.8
$500 000–$999 999	5.1	3.6	6.8	8.5	10.2
≥$1 million	2.9	3.0	3.7	6.1	10.1
All families	100.0	100.0	100.0	100.0	100.0

Note: a. Cohorts are aged 46 to 55 in 2001 or 34 to 43 in 1989.

Sources: Author's calculations based on the SCF.

very bottom of the distribution, the percentage of families in the cohort with negative wealth fell from 9.5 per cent in 1989 to 4.1 per cent in 2001, though the great majority of that decline occurred in 1992. At the top end, the proportion of millionaires (in 2001 dollars) more than tripled to 10.1 per cent, and the fraction with wealth between $500 000 and $1 million doubled.

The upward shift may be clearer when viewed in terms of quantiles of the wealth distribution (Table 2.17). The pattern of percentage growth over the quantiles shown was U-shaped over this time. Simply by rising to a strictly positive amount, wealth rose proportionately the most at the 10th percentile for the cohort, but as was the case for families overall at this point in the distribution, the level of wealth was very low (zero dollars in 1989 and $3000 in 2001). In contrast to the other points of the distribution of the cohort's wealth shown in Table 2.17, wealth at the 25th percentile rose consistently over the period, for a total gain of 260 per cent, though the rate of increase dropped off over the most recent three-year period. This growth substantially exceeded that at the higher percentiles, which ranged from 102.5 per cent at the median to 143.3 per cent at the 90th percentile; the dollar amounts at the higher percentiles were, of course, far larger.

As one would expect from life-cycle patterns in income and retirement

Table 2.17 Net worth (2001 dollars) and per cent change in net worth, by percentiles of net worth, cohort aged 46 to 55 in 2001, 1989–2001

Year	Percentile of net worth				
	10	25	50	75	90
1989	0.0	9.1	69.3	180.3	418.1
1992	1.1	14.1	63.1	163.7	343.7
% change 1989–92	NA	55.9	−8.9	−9.2	−17.8
1995	2.5	23.2	79.0	202.2	530.4
% change 1992–95	138.8	63.9	25.2	23.5	54.3
1998	1.9	29.8	105.6	287.3	673.4
% change 1995–98	−26.3	28.5	33.7	42.1	27.0
2001	3.0	32.7	140.3	386.7	1017.3
% change 1998–2001	63.0	9.7	32.8	34.6	51.1
% change 1989–2001	NA	260.0	102.5	114.4	143.3
Memo item:					
Cohort value as %					
of value for					
whole population					
1989	NA	119.8	107.3	89.2	82.5
1992	NA	156.9	102.9	89.6	77.8
1995	NA	201.0	119.0	108.9	120.5
1998	NA	274.9	135.4	126.3	125.2
2001	NA	256.6	162.9	136.7	138.5

Note: NA = not available.

Sources: Author's calculations based on the SCF.

saving, the cohort increased its wealth relative to that of the population as a whole in nearly every survey between 1989 and 2001, at all the points from the 25th percentile and above; the 10th percentile values for both the age cohort and the full population are so small as to make such a comparison unreliable or impossible. The disproportion in the cohort's wealth is particularly large at the median and 25th percentiles across this period; in 2001, the 25th percentile of their wealth was 256.6 per cent of that of the population as a whole, whereas the 90th percentile of the cohort's wealth was 138.5 per cent of the value for the population as a whole.

The faster growth at the bottom of the distribution of the group's wealth than at the top of the distribution suggests that the cohort's wealth may have become less concentrated over the period. However, such a conclusion

Table 2.18   Gini coefficient for net worth of cohort aged 46 to 55 in 2001, 1989–2001

Year	Gini coefficient
1989	0.74
	0.02
1992	0.75
	0.01
1995	0.75
	0.01
1998	0.76
	0.01
2001	0.78
	0.01

Note: Standard errors with respect to imputation and sampling are given in italics.

Sources: Author's calculations based on the SCF.

turns on how neighbouring parts of the distribution mirror the quantiles shown. Although limited in its descriptive ability, the Gini coefficient of wealth does provide a summary of the gains and losses across the distribution (Table 2.18). The point estimates of that statistic suggest that, from 1989 to 2001, there was a steady upward trend in wealth concentration as measured by this statistic from 0.74 in 1989 to 0.78 in 2001. However, the estimated standard errors are large relative to the size of the differences.

When concentration is broken out by wealth percentile groups (Table 2.19), the shift in wealth shares is clearest in the decline in the share of the 50th to 90th percentiles of the distribution – a pattern that shows less strongly for all age groups as a whole – and the rise in the share of the 95th to 99th percentile group. Compared to the population as a whole, wealth seems somewhat less concentrated for this cohort. However, the standard errors of the ownership shares are also quite large relative to the differences.

THE WEALTH OF AFRICAN AMERICANS

This section focuses on changes in the wealth of African Americans between 1989 and 2001, using white non-Hispanic families as a comparison group. Although the raw sample numbers of African Americans in the SCF (Table 2.20) are not sufficient to allow a very detailed decomposition of differences, the samples are sufficient for a range of comparisons.

Table 2.19   Net worth distributed by net worth groups, cohort aged
46 to 55 in 2001, 1989–2001 (per cent)

Year	Percentile group				
	0–49.9	50–89.9	90–94.9	95–98.9	99–100
1989	2.6	36.0	13.9	21.5	26.0
	2.2	*3.7*	*2.4*	*4.0*	*5.0*
1992	4.6	31.2	11.5	23.2	29.5
	0.6	*2.3*	*1.3*	*3.0*	*4.5*
1995	5.5	30.8	12.7	20.7	30.3
	0.4	*1.8*	*1.6*	*2.9*	*3.9*
1998	4.7	30.2	11.6	23.0	30.4
	0.5	*2.0*	*1.5*	*3.2*	*4.1*
2001	4.2	29.1	12.0	26.5	28.2
	0.3	*1.8*	*1.4*	*2.4*	*3.3*

Note: Standard errors with respect to imputation and sampling are given in italics.

Sources: Author's calculations based on the SCF.

Table 2.20   African American and non-Hispanic white respondents to the
SCF, 1989–2001

Year	Number of respondents	
	African Americans	White non-Hispanics
1989	308	2558
1992	358	3147
1995	380	3562
1998	414	3502
2001	462	3587

Sources: Author's calculations based on the SCF.

Median wealth of white non-Hispanics was 18.5 times that of African Americans in 1989 (Table 2.21); that multiple dropped sharply to 7.1 in 1992 and was 6.4 in 2001, a bit up from 1998. At the same time, mean wealth of white non-Hispanics ranged between about five and six times the mean wealth of African Americans. From 1989, the growth rate of the African American median was above that for white non-Hispanics until 2001 when the rate for the former dropped a few percentage points below the latter. Over this period differences in the growth rates of the means were mixed.

Table 2.21   Median and mean net worth, African Americans and white non-Hispanics, 1989–2001

| | Median (2001 dollars) | | | | | | Mean (2001 dollars) | | | | | |
| | African Americans | | White non-Hispanics | | Ratio: WNH/AA | | African Americans | | White non-Hispanics | | Ratio: WNH/AA |
	Level	% change	Level	% change			Level	% change	Level	% change	
1989	5.3	–	97.8	–	18.5		57.0	–	317.6	–	5.6
1992	12.2	130.2	86.3	–11.8	7.1		59.4	4.2	275.5	–13.3	4.6
1995	12.6	3.3	88.5	2.5	7.0		51.0	–14.1	289.8	5.2	5.7
1998	16.8	33.3	103.5	16.9	6.2		69.9	37.1	365.3	26.1	5.2
2001	19.0	13.1	121.0	16.9	6.4		75.7	8.3	468.2	28.2	6.2

Sources: Author's calculations based on the SCF.

66

Underlying these relatively crude distributional indicators were more complex differences. Over all the years of data analysed here, African American families were far more likely to have wealth of $1000 or less than were white non-Hispanic families, but the difference narrowed (Table 2.22). In 1989, 37.6 per cent of African American families had net worth less than $1000, compared with 9.5 per cent of white non-Hispanic families; by 2001, the figure for African Americans had dropped to 27 per cent and the figure for white non-Hispanics was 8 per cent. At the other end of the distribution, a far larger fraction of white non-Hispanic families had wealth of at least $500 000 than was the case for African American families across the period. Both groups show the share of families in this group declining from 1989 to 1992 and then rising substantially by 2001, with faster growth for African Americans from a much lower level. Still, in 2001 the share of white non-Hispanic families with this level of wealth was 7.6 times that of African American families. Nonetheless, there was a substantial fraction of African American families over the period with 'middle class' values of net worth between $25 000 and $250 000: about 40 per cent of African American families in 2001 compared with 43 per cent of white non-Hispanic families. Although African American families are somewhat more heavily represented at the lower end of this range, it is clear from Figure 2.11 that the most striking differences are at the extremes of the wealth distribution.

A plot of the differences in the levels of the distributions for the two groups shows clearly how wide the gap is across the distribution (Figure 2.12). The 2001 data show that African Americans had much lower wealth at virtually every level including larger absolute values of negative wealth for those at the bottom end. Viewed as a percentage of the wealth of white non-Hispanics, the difference is 90 per cent or more for most of the distribution (Figure 2.13). Data for the other years of the SCF show a similar pattern.

Looking at movements across the years of data shows a mixture of gains and losses for African Americans relative to white non-Hispanics. Figure 2.14 shows a relative Q-D plot of distributional shifts between 1989 and 2001 as a percentage of 1989 levels, for African Americans and white non-Hispanics. Movements for the lowest 20 per cent of the distribution appear quite noisy, but at least over the 1989–2001 interval, the lowest 10 per cent of African American families and white non-Hispanic families saw a substantial absolute increase in their levels of negative net worth. The next highest 10 per cent have wealth values too close to zero for the changes to be meaningful.

For the groups between the 20th and 60th percentiles, the data show strong growth over this period, but particularly so for African Americans.

Table 2.22 Distribution of families over wealth groups, African Americans and white non-Hispanics, 1989–2001

Survey year										
	1989		1992		% of families 1995		1998		2001	
	AA	WNH	AA	WNH	AA	WNH	AA	WNH	AA	WNH
Net worth (2001 dollars)										
<0	12.2	5.5	10.7	6.0	13.6	5.8	12.1	6.9	11.2	5.6
$0–$999	25.4	4.0	19.0	2.9	16.6	2.5	14.7	3.8	15.8	2.4
$1000–$2499	5.3	2.7	5.5	2.9	6.8	1.8	4.0	2.0	3.8	2.0
$2500–$4999	6.7	3.2	5.7	3.3	5.5	2.9	4.0	2.5	4.9	2.6
$5000–$9999	5.6	3.5	7.6	4.2	5.6	5.0	8.1	4.0	6.0	3.8
$10 000–$24 999	4.8	9.0	11.3	9.0	10.6	9.1	12.4	7.2	11.6	7.2
$25 000–$49 999	13.2	8.8	11.9	10.4	12.8	10.0	12.5	9.3	12.0	8.7
$50 000–$99 999	12.8	13.9	12.6	15.1	16.3	16.1	12.1	13.4	16.1	12.6
$100 000–$249 999	9.8	23.4	10.9	24.8	8.9	25.2	15.5	23.8	11.8	21.4
$250 000–$500 000	3.1	13.4	3.7	11.2	2.5	11.1	3.5	14.2	4.4	15.3
≥$500 000	1.4	12.7	1.1	10.3	0.9	10.5	1.4	13.0	2.4	18.2
All of group	100.0	100.0	100.0	100.0	100.0	100.0	100.0	100.0	100.0	100.0

Sources: Author's calculations based on the SCF.

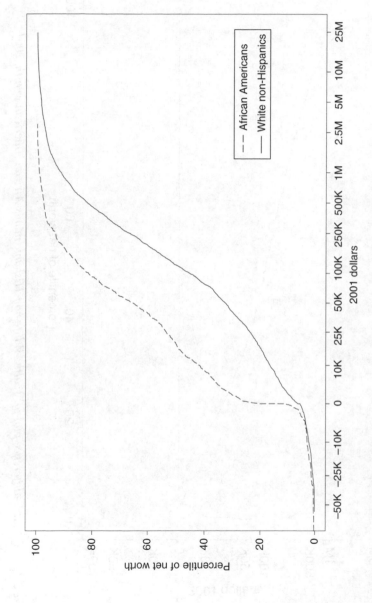

Figure 2.11 *Cumulative distribution of wealth, African Americans and white non-Hispanics, 2001*

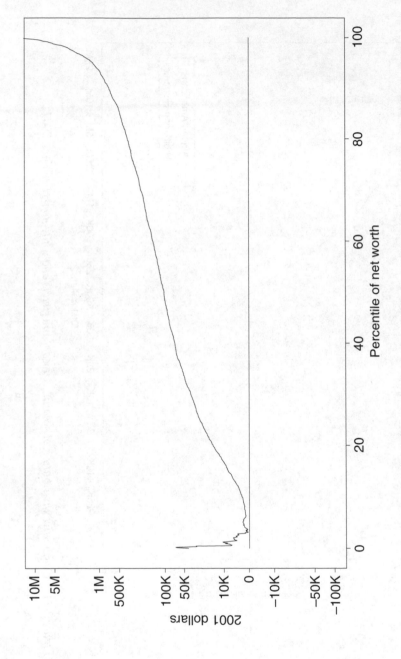

Figure 2.12   Quantile-difference plot of wealth: White non-Hispanic minus African American wealth, 2001

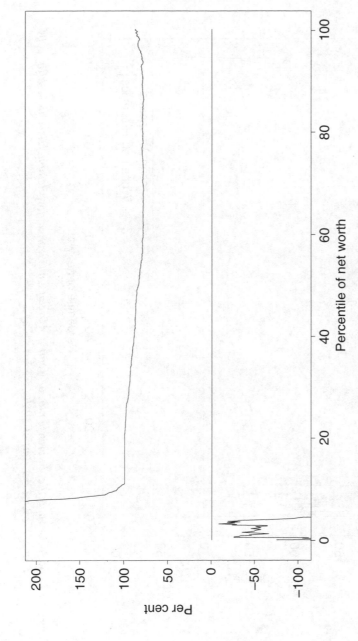

Figure 2.13   Relative quantile-difference plot of wealth: White non-Hispanic minus African American wealth, as per cent of white non-Hispanic wealth

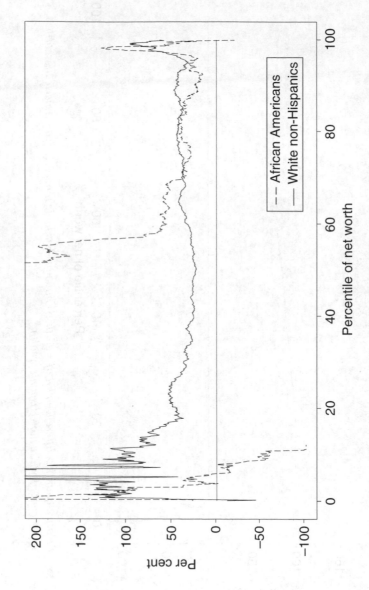

Figure 2.14 Relative quantile-difference plot of wealth: African American and white non-Hispanic wealth: 2001 minus 1989, as per cent of 1989

Within the period (not shown), this group of African Americans showed a substantial growth rate from 1989 to 1992 compared to a decline for white non-Hispanics; little movement for either group from 1992 to 1995; and a substantially larger growth rate from 1995 to 1998. More recently, the 1998–2001 data show that the growth rate for the upper half of this per-centile group of African Americans fell to approximately the same rate as that of white non-Hispanics, but the lower half largely saw losses; for all except the very top of the wealthiest 40 per cent of African Americans, the growth rate was far below that of white non-Hispanics (Figure 2.15). These data also make clear the hazard in using the median as an indicator of overall change; from 1998 to 2001, the growth at the median for African Americans was below that for white non-Hispanics, but the rates were much more similar in nearby percentiles.

An important driver of increases for African Americans over the 1989–2001 period was simply increased ownership of assets (Table 2.23). In 1989, 76.7 per cent of such families owned any asset and, in 2001, the figure was 89.5 per cent; in contrast, the figure for white non-Hispanics was already close to 100 per cent in both years. The most notable increase in ownership for African Americans was in direct and indirect holdings of publicly traded stocks – the rate more than tripled over the period. There were also notable increases in their holdings of liquid assets, retirement accounts and vehicles, and these increases were greater than those for white non-Hispanics. Both groups saw about a 5 per cent increase in their home ownership rates. However, with the exception of a miscellaneous category of financial assets, the ownership rates on all other types of assets among African Americans remained below those for white non-Hispanics.

The prevalence of debt among African Americans rose to nearly the level for white non-Hispanics in 2001, and growth in prevalence since 1989 was strongest for mortgages and credit card balances. In both 1989 and 2001, African Americans were notably more likely than white non-Hispanics to have credit card debt.

When the portfolio holdings of each group are viewed as a proportion of their total wealth, some differences are even sharper (Table 2.24). Relative to the case for white non-Hispanics, the assets of African Americans in 2001 were more heavily weighted toward nonfinancial assets, with notably larger portfolio shares for principal residences and vehicles and a notably lower share for businesses. Among financial assets, the portfolio share of direct and indirect holdings of publicly traded stocks for African Americans was about half the level for white non-Hispanics. African Americans were also much more highly leveraged; their total debt amounted to 29.6 per cent of their assets, while the debt of white non-Hispanic families was only 11.1 per cent of their assets. About two-thirds of the leverage of African Americans was

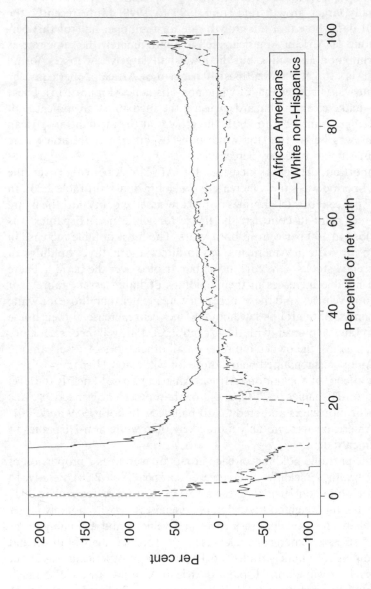

Figure 2.15   *Relative quantile-difference plot of wealth: African American and white non-Hispanic wealth: 2001 minus 1998, as per cent of 1998*

Table 2.23   *Ownership of various components of net worth, African Americans and white non-Hispanics, 1989 and 2001 (per cent)*

	African Americans		White non-Hispanics	
	1989	2001	1989	2001
NETWORTH[a]	100.0	100.0	100.0	100.0
ASSET	76.7	89.5	98.4	99.0
FIN	63.3	84.6	95.0	96.5
LIQ	56.4	81.0	92.4	94.9
CDS	3.7	6.5	25.0	18.5
SAVBND	9.8	10.3	28.0	19.5
BOND	0.5	0.5	7.2	3.8
STOCKS	3.6	9.6	21.0	24.5
NMMF	0.7	7.8	9.4	20.9
RETQLIQ	17.1	38.9	43.4	56.9
CASHLI	24.0	28.6	40.0	29.8
OTHMA	1.6	2.1	4.6	8.2
OTHFIN	10.0	9.9	14.5	9.2
NFIN	66.6	76.5	94.0	94.7
VEHIC	56.9	69.9	89.2	89.1
HOUSES	42.4	47.4	70.5	74.1
ORESRE	7.6	6.4	14.9	12.9
NNRESRE	4.8	5.0	12.8	9.6
BUS	4.8	3.0	13.7	14.0
OTHNFIN	5.1	2.2	14.7	9.0
DEBT	65.1	74.0	73.2	75.8
MRTHEL	24.8	36.5	43.0	47.6
RESDBT	2.7	2.3	5.9	5.4
INSTALL	47.4	47.2	49.3	45.3
OTHLOC	2.8	1.0	3.0	1.7
CCBAL	33.4	52.1	41.4	43.3
ODEBT	3.4	4.9	7.2	7.4
Memo item:				
EQUITY	10.6	34.2	38.3	57.5

Note: a. See Appendix Table 2A.1 for definitions of wealth components.

Sources: Author's calculations based on the SCF.

Table 2.24   Wealth holdings, African Americans and white non-Hispanics, 2001

	African Americans		White non-Hispanics	
	Amount[a]	% assets	Amount[a]	% assets
ASSET[b]	1493.3	100.0	44 373.3	100.0
FIN	496.7	33.3	19 222.0	43.3
LIQ	71.2	4.8	2211.2	5.0
CDS	13.2	0.9	582.8	1.3
SAVBND	4.4	0.3	132.6	0.3
BOND	0.5	0.0	917.5	2.1
STOCKS	45.3	3.0	4241.5	9.6
NMMF	36.3	2.4	2387.1	5.4
RETQLIQ	169.4	11.3	5317.2	12.0
CASHLI	95.8	6.4	924.9	2.1
OTHMA	38.0	2.5	2130.8	4.8
OTHFIN	22.6	1.5	376.4	0.8
NFIN	996.6	66.7	25 151.3	56.7
VEHIC	130.2	8.7	1409.0	3.2
HOUSES	630.9	42.2	11 508.0	25.9
ORESRE	90.1	6.0	2060.1	4.6
NNRESRE	93.5	6.3	2083.6	4.7
BUS	41.1	2.8	7653.0	17.2
OTHNFIN	10.7	0.7	437.6	1.0
DEBT	442.4	29.6	4912.70	11.1
MRTHEL	311.2	20.8	3711.6	8.4
RESDBT	20.6	1.4	322.4	0.7
INSTALL	82.7	5.5	569.2	1.3
OTHLOC	1.8	0.1	27.6	0.1
CCBAL	22.4	1.5	154.1	0.3
ODEBT	3.6	0.2	127.8	0.3
Memo item:				
EQUITY	203.2	13.6	10 852.10	24.5

Notes:
a.   Billions of 2001 dollars.
b.   See Appendix Table 2A.1 for definitions of wealth components.

Sources: Author's calculations based on the SCF.

explained by mortgage borrowing. Although the frequency of credit card debt was high for the group, it amounted to only 1.5 per cent of total assets.

One might well argue that aggregate portfolio shares are so influenced by very large values of assets held by a small number of families that they give a distorted impression of more 'typical' families. Excluding the wealthiest and poorest 10 per cent of the distribution of wealth in each group is one way of testing the sensitivity of the share estimates (Table 2.25). For both racial groups, the most striking changes under this constraint are a large increase in the share of principal residences and a decline in the share of direct and indirect holdings of publicly traded stocks. Moreover, residences remain a much larger share of the assets of African Americans than is the case for white non-Hispanics. The share of businesses for white non-Hispanics falls sharply, but it still remains well above that for African Americans.

In light of the other evidence presented, it is not surprising that African Americans hold less than their population share of every asset and liability considered here (Table 2.26). In 2001, the population and ownership shares were close only for instalment debt and credit card debt; cash value life insurance and vehicles were the only assets where the ownership share was more than half the population share.

As noted above, a large fraction of African Americans had zero or negative wealth over the period considered here. The fact that this proportion is so much higher than is the case among white non-Hispanics implies that wealth among African Americans is more concentrated in this simple sense among African Americans. In addition, the data indicate that some assets – for example, principal residences and businesses – are relatively more concentrated by at least some measures than is the case among white non-Hispanics. Point estimates of the Gini coefficient of wealth calculated for African Americans alone indicate that the wealth of African Americans in 1989 may have been more concentrated by this measure than was the case among white non-Hispanics, but that from 1995 to 2001, the direction of difference was reversed (Table 2.27). However, according to the estimated standard errors, none of these differences are significant.

Estimates of the concentration of wealth among various percentile groups for the two groups shows some interesting patterns, but the standard errors of the estimates for African Americans are very large (Table 2.28). The large standard error is a reflection both of the relatively small number of African American respondents and, particularly, of the small number of very wealthy African American families in the SCF. However, the stability of the patterns over time suggests that those patterns reflect more than random variation. The point estimates show a tendency for the wealthiest 1 per cent of African Americans to own a smaller fraction of the group's

*Table 2.25   Wealth holdings, central 80 per cent of wealth distribution,
African Americans and white non-Hispanics, 2001*

	African Americans		White non-Hispanics	
	Amount[a]	% assets	Amount[a]	% assets
ASSET[b]	716.7	100.0	16 213.3	100.0
FIN	173.6	24.2	5862.3	36.2
LIQ	32.7	4.6	886.0	5.5
CDS	7.3	1.0	368.2	2.3
SAVBND	3.2	0.4	64.8	0.4
BOND	0.2	0.0	61.8	0.4
STOCKS	4.9	0.7	567.5	3.5
NMMF	8.6	1.2	617.8	3.8
RETQLIQ	69.6	9.7	2345.2	14.5
CASHLI	42.7	6.0	518.4	3.2
OTHMA	2.5	0.3	352.0	2.2
OTHFIN	1.8	0.3	80.5	0.5
NFIN	543.2	75.8	10 351.0	63.8
VEHIC	91.7	12.8	1044.7	6.4
HOUSES	416.4	58.1	7383.9	45.5
ORESRE	23.2	3.2	605.6	3.7
NNRESRE	6.8	0.9	363.1	2.2
BUS	4.8	0.7	852.2	5.3
OTHNFIN	0.3	0.0	101.4	0.6
DEBT	308.5	43.0	3444.6	21.2
MRTHEL	232.8	32.5	2749.7	17.0
RESDBT	11.2	1.6	141.9	0.9
INSTALL	48.5	6.8	392.7	2.4
OTHLOC	0.2	0.0	8.9	0.1
CCBAL	14.9	2.1	114.8	0.7
ODEBT	0.9	0.1	36.7	0.2
Memo item:				
EQUITY	5.1	7.1	2840.8	17.5

Notes:
a.   Billions of 2001 dollars.
b.   See Appendix Table 2A.1 for definitions of wealth components.

Sources: Author's calculations based on the SCF.

Table 2.26   Share of net worth and components, African Americans and white non-Hispanics, 1989 and 2001 (per cent)

	African Americans		White non-Hispanics	
	1989 %	2001 %	1989 %	2001 %
NETWORTH	2.8	2.5	91.4	93.1
ASSET[a]	3.1	3.1	90.3	92.1
FIN	2.1	2.4	94.5	94.5
LIQ	2.8	3.0	92.0	92.9
CDS	1.4	2.1	95.8	93.3
SAVBND	3.2	3.2	92.8	94.9
BOND	0.2	0.1	98.0	99.3
STOCKS	0.1	1.0	98.2	97.0
NMMF	0.8	1.5	98.0	96.3
RETQLIQ	2.9	3.0	92.3	93.0
CASHLI	4.0	8.9	90.0	85.8
OTHMA	0.7	1.7	98.9	96.5
OTHFIN	8.9	5.5	88.4	91.3
NFIN	3.5	3.6	88.5	90.3
VEHIC	6.2	7.9	84.4	85.1
HOUSES	4.9	4.8	86.4	88.1
ORESRE	4.3	4.0	87.3	91.3
NNRESRE	2.7	4.1	89.9	91.4
BUS	0.7	0.5	92.2	94.0
OTHNFIN	4.9	2.4	91.4	96.1
DEBT	5.3	7.6	83.1	84.5
MRTHEL	4.8	7.1	82.9	84.9
RESDBT	2.0	5.6	87.1	87.1
INSTALL	8.9	11.6	81.0	79.7
OTHLOC	2.0	6.1	95.8	92.6
CCBAL	12.1	11.5	75.4	78.8
ODEBT	3.2	2.7	84.7	94.3
Memo item:				
EQUITY	1.1	1.8	96.7	95.7
% of families	12.7	13.0	74.8	76.2

Note: a. See Appendix Table 2A.1 for definitions of wealth components.

Sources: Author's calculations based on the SCF.

Table 2.27   Gini coefficient for net worth, African Americans and white non-Hispanics, 1989–2001

	1989	1992	1995	1998	2001
African Americans	0.80	0.77	0.75	0.75	0.76
	0.03	*0.02*	*0.03*	*0.03*	*0.03*
White non-Hispanic	0.76	0.76	0.77	0.78	0.78
	0.01	*0.01*	*0.01*	*0.01*	*0.01*

Note: Standard errors with respect to imputation and sampling are given in italics.

Sources: Author's calculations based on the SCF.

net worth than is the case for white non-Hispanics. At the other end of the wealth spectrum, the lowest 50 per cent of the distribution for African Americans holds a very small share of wealth that is far smaller than the already small share for that wealth group among white non-Hispanics. The largest difference between the racial groups appears to be in the wealth group between the 50th and 90th percentiles of the distribution: wealth is relatively more concentrated among this group for African Americans than is the case for the comparison group.

CONCLUSIONS

The value of a family's wealth is the joint outcome of the possibilities the family faced combined with the decisions they made. The period from 1989 to 2001 saw important changes in the financial services offered to families, and in other structures in the economy. Thus, it is not surprising that there were also many changes in a variety of aspects of the wealth distribution. However, given the magnitude of the economic changes, it is remarkable how narrowly defined many of the distributional changes were. This section summarizes the findings that seem most noteworthy.

From 1989 to 2001, wealth grew broadly across families. Characterizing distributional changes is much more complex and much more dependent on the specific questions asked. For example, there is evidence both from *Forbes* data on the 400 wealthiest Americans and from the SCF, which explicitly excludes families in the *Forbes* list, that wealth grew relatively strongly at the very top of the distribution. In addition, the share of total household wealth held by the *Forbes* group rose and there was an increase in concentration even in the top of that group. However, while the point estimate of the share of total wealth held by the wealthiest 1 per cent of

Table 2.28   *Net worth distributed by net worth groups, African Americans and white non-Hispanics, 1989–2001 (per cent)*

Year and Race	Percentile group				
	0–49.9	50–89.9	90–94.9	95–98.9	99–100
1989					
African American	−0.5	34.0	14.9	23.7	27.9
	0.5	*4.8*	*3.3*	*7.1*	*10.1*
White non-Hispanic	4.2	31.2	12.9	23.5	28.2
	0.5	*1.8*	*1.5*	*2.6*	*2.4*
1992					
African American	1.0	37.8	16.2	22.8	22.3
	0.3	*4.1*	*3.1*	*6.4*	*8.5*
White non-Hispanic	4.5	30.6	12.5	23.5	28.9
	0.3	*1.2*	*0.9*	*1.5*	*2.1*
1995					
African American	0.7	40.0	15.0	22.3	22.1
	0.4	*4.4*	*2.5*	*4.2*	*7.2*
White non-Hispanic	4.7	29.2	11.7	21.1	33.3
	0.2	*0.8*	*0.6*	*1.2*	*1.5*
1998					
African American	1.3	39.9	15.1	20.2	23.4
	0.4	*4.4*	*3.0*	*4.7*	*7.7*
White non-Hispanic	4.1	28.7	11.2	23.4	32.7
	0.2	*0.9*	*0.7*	*2.1*	*2.3*
2001					
African American	0.9	36.5	14.9	25.1	22.6
	0.5	*3.9*	*3.2*	*7.2*	*9.2*
White non-Hispanic	3.9	28.3	11.9	25.0	30.8
	0.2	*0.7*	*0.7*	*1.8*	*2.1*

Note: Standard errors with respect to imputation and sampling are given in italics.

Sources: Author's calculations based on the SCF.

families as measured by the SCF also rose, the change is not statistically significant. As noted in this chapter, it is possible that, despite the use of a more robust estimator of standard errors for the SCF than has been used in previous analysis of the wealth distribution, some of the simplifying assumptions necessary still may lead to inflated estimates of confidence intervals. A key stylized fact is that during this period, the division of wealth observed in the SCF attributes roughly a third each to the wealthiest 1 per cent, the next wealthiest 9 per cent, and the remainder of the population.

Relative to everyone else, the wealth of the highest 10 per cent of the wealth distribution tends to be heavy in terms of holdings of most assets and liabilities, but it is particularly so for stocks, bonds, business assets and real estate investments. For other families, simple deposit accounts, houses and vehicles are the most important assets, and mortgages are the most important liability. Changes in shares were surprisingly few: a shift away from the wealthiest 10 per cent in the total share of stock holdings; a shift toward that group in the share of housing equity; and an increase in the share of nonmortgage debt (largely instalment debt and credit card debt) among the least wealthy half of the population. Overall, leverage tends to decline sharply with wealth.

Although families with less than zero wealth are very hard to characterize in terms of distributional changes, they are a substantial fraction of the population – about 7 per cent in 2001. Credit card debt and instalment debt are much more common among this group than the population as a whole; education loans and vehicle loans are the major sources of instalment loans. The group is disproportionately young – in 2001, almost 60 per cent were headed by people age 35 and younger – which suggests that for some of the group, the condition of having negative wealth is temporary. However, there are some interesting differences between families with large absolute negative net worth and those with negative net worth closer to zero. The group with larger absolute negative wealth was more likely to have assets to offset debts, to be younger and to have some college experience.

A close analysis of the members of the *Forbes* 400 suggests that, despite substantial churning, there is still a fairly high degree of stability in terms of high-wealth status. Unfortunately, the SCF does not have panel data on the rest of the population for the period considered in this chapter. However, it is still possible to say something about changes for groups that have relatively constant characteristics. The chapter considered the case of one age cohort and the set of African American families.

The age cohort considered comprises the majority of the older baby boomers (families headed by persons between the ages of 46 and 55 in 2001). Wealth for this group shows the expected life-cycle pattern of increase. Although that growth appears to be spread broadly, the most striking growth was at the bottom and the top of the wealth distribution. The number of inflation-adjusted millionaires in the cohort more than tripled over the 1989–2001 period. Overall, the data for the cohort suggest that the concentration of wealth rose over the period, but the estimated standard errors are large relative to the size of the increases.

The last analytical section compares the wealth of African American families with that of white non-Hispanic families. The median wealth of

African Americans in 1989 was only about 5 per cent of that for white non-Hispanic families and by 2001, the fraction had risen to about 16 per cent. Differences are most striking at the two ends of the distribution of wealth. A higher fraction of African American families have net worth less than zero, and a much higher fraction have wealth between zero and $1000. At the top end of the distribution, the differences are reversed, with a much larger fraction of white non-Hispanics having wealth of $250 000 or more. However, for the group of families in the center of the distribution, there was strong growth between 1989 and 2001. Although the evidence is weak, the data suggest that wealth among African Americans is less concentrated at the top of the distribution than is the case for white non-Hispanics; wealth is relatively more concentrated in the 40 per cent of the distribution at the median and above, largely reflecting the high fraction of African Americans below the median with very low levels of wealth.

The SCF data are a very rich source of wealth data, and many more slices may be made of the data beyond the ones presented in this chapter. At least two such cuts seem potentially quite fruitful. Given the length of the period of comparable SCF cross-sections, more extended cohort analysis seems an important priority. At the same time, the deep changes in the available array of financial services suggest that there would be great value in extending the analysis of portfolio structure as well as the types of institutional relationships that support that structure.

NOTES

*   The views presented in this chapter are those of the author alone, and they do not necessarily reflect the views of the Board of Governors of the Federal Reserve System or its staff. The author wishes to thank Ryan Bledsoe and Brooke Wells for assistance with this chapter, staff at NORC for collecting the data, and the SCF respondents for generously sharing their information for research purposes. Thanks to Myron Kwast and Kevin Moore for comments. The author bears sole responsibility for any errors.

1.   In this chapter, the terms 'net worth' and 'wealth' are used interchangeably to refer to assets net of liabilities.

2.   See Canterbury and Nosari (1985) and the October 2001 issue of *Forbes*. It is not known publicly just how broad the wealth definition used by *Forbes* is. Although it seems likely that the measure does not include some common items, for example, automobiles and checking accounts (demand deposit accounts), it does seem likely that the value of such omitted items are a very small fraction of the items that are included. According to the magazine, their estimates are 'highly educated guesses' based on a variety of sources. The input data include both information that may be provided by the individuals, which is reviewed for plausibility, and publicly available data. The latter type of information may take the form of registered ownership in publicly traded corporations, records of sales of privately held firms and property, and similar types of information. Some assets, notably trusts, are very difficult to value, and misestimation of such assets may introduce error. Often distinctions must be made about the 'true' owner of assets that have a complex distribution over members of a family, and this process may also introduce error. As a check,

the *Forbes* estimates are reviewed by a panel of outside experts in a number of financial and business areas. Unfortunately, it is impossible to judge the consistency of the *Forbes* methodology over time on the basis of the limited documentation available.

3.   All dollar figures reported in this chapter were adjusted to 2001 dollar terms using the 'current methods' price index series developed by the Bureau of Labor Statistics. To the degree that it is possible to do so, this index extrapolates backwards the methodological improvements that have been made to the official Consumer Price Index.

4.   See Kennickell (2000a) for an overview of the methodology of the SCF and Aizcorbe et al. (2003) for a summary of recent data from the survey. The target population for the SCF specifically excludes individuals who are included in the *Forbes* list; it is assumed that such individuals would be so unlikely to participate in the SCF that it would not be efficient to expend effort to interview them. The wealth measure used here nets a wide variety of assets (notably including designated retirement assets) and nonfinancial assets (notably including the value of vehicles) against a broad measure of directly-held debt. One omission, a valuation of defined-benefit pension rights, may be important over the period considered here. Over this time, account-type pension arrangements that would be included in the asset measure used here grew to some degree at the expense of defined-benefit plans. For one attempt to incorporate a measure of defined-benefit wealth (and social security wealth) into net worth, see Kennickell and Sundén (1997).

5.   Some of the SCF data used here have previously been used to look at questions of wealth distribution by Weicher (1996), Wolff (1996), Kennickell and Woodburn (1992 and 1999) and Kennickell (2001).

6.   Because of the complexity of the SCF sample design, it is not feasible to apply the most common procedures for variance estimation. Instead, a bootstrap procedure is used (see Kennickell 2000b). In this approach, a large number of pseudo-samples are drawn with replacement from the full set of completed cases, and each of these replicate samples is weighted using the same apparatus applied to weight the full set of cases. The replicate selections are made in a structured but random way that is intended to reflect important sources of variation in the original sample design. In making these selections, a degree of approximation is required. Close investigation of earlier versions of the replicate samples, those used in Kennickell (2001) to evaluate earlier estimates of wealth changes, revealed that the selection of those samples was introducing imbalances that would not have been allowed in an actual SCF. Although the standard errors reported in this chapter are based on a revision of the methodology that attempts to correct for those imbalances, other imbalances that artificially inflate variability may remain. At the same time, there may also be important sources of variability that are understated. Nonetheless, the estimation methodology applied in this chapter reflects the best information available at this time for evaluating the meaningfulness of comparisons between SCF estimates.

7.   See Kennickell (2002) for a more detailed discussion of such graphs.

8.   In order to display the enormous range of differences without overly compressing relative variation in some parts of the wealth distribution, the vertical axis is scaled using the inverse hyperbolic sine transformation with a scale parameter of 0.0001. Close to zero, the transformation is approximately linear; at larger absolute values, it is approximately logarithmic.

9.   When the denominator was actually zero, $1 was substituted for zero as a denominator to make division possible.

10. For most vehicles, the SCF respondents are asked the model year, make and model of each vehicle. That information is used to match the vehicle to a market value obtained from NADA. Because some vehicles may carry expensive options that are not reflected in the basic description of the vehicle, the value attributed to such vehicles would be biased downward. For vehicles such as motorhomes, boats and aeroplanes, respondents are asked to provide a value directly.

11. In the SCF, the racial and ethnic identification of respondents is determined based on a single question that allows multiple responses using as categories 'White', 'Black/African American', 'Hispanic/Latino', 'Asian', 'American Indian/Alaska Native', 'Native Hawaiian/

Other Pacific Islander' and an open-ended category that was subsequently classified in a formal coding operation. The open-ended category almost always yielded responses that could have been coded directly into another of the categories provided. Respondents were asked to list first the category with which they identify most strongly. A very small number of respondents gave more than one answer and taking account of additional responses has a very small effect on most analyses. Only the first three categories contain sufficient numbers of observations to make separately classified analysis statistically meaningful. Although the 'White' and 'Black/African American' categories appear to yield good population estimates over time, the 'Hispanic/Latino' classification does not appear as stable when compared to estimates from the Current Population Survey (CPS) of the US Bureau of the Census. The CPS takes a different approach to measurement; it asks two questions: one about racial identification and one about ethnic identification that can be used to determine whether a person fits a definition of 'Hispanic'. Comparison of SCF and CPS data suggest that people who identify as 'Hispanic/Latino' in the SCF are poorer in terms of income than people who would be classified in this way by the CPS. In a time of substantial migration of Hispanics who tend to be economically disadvantaged, using the SCF to characterize changes for all Hispanics might well lead to misleading conclusions. See Aizcorbe et al. (2003) for additional discussion of the measurement of racial and ethnic identification in the SCF.

REFERENCES

Aizcorbe, A.M., A.B. Kennickell and K.B. Moore (2003), 'Recent changes in US family finances: evidence from the 1998 and 2001 Survey of Consumer Finances', *Federal Reserve Bulletin*, **89** (January), 1–32.

Canterbury, E.R. and E.J. Nosari (1985), 'The *Forbes* four hundred: the determinants of super-wealth', *Southern Economic Journal*, **51** (April), 1073–82.

Hurst, E., Ming Ching Luoh and F.P. Stafford (1998), 'The wealth dynamics of American families', *Brookings Papers on Economic Activity*, **1**, 267–337.

Kennickell, A.B. (2000a), 'Wealth measurement in the Survey of Consumer Finances: methodology and directions for future research', working paper, Washington, DC: Board of Governors of the Federal Reserve System, www.federalreserve.gov/pubs/oss/oss 2/method.html.

Kennickell, A.B. (2000b), 'Revisions to the variance estimation procedure for the SCF', working paper, Washington, DC: Board of Governors of the Federal Reserve System, www.federalreserve.gov/pubs/oss/oss 2/method.html.

Kennickell, A.B. (2001), 'An examination of changes in the distribution of wealth from 1989 to 1998: evidence from the Survey of Consumer Finances', working paper, Washington, DC: Board of Governors of the Federal Reserve System, http://www.federalreserve.gov/pubs/oss/oss 2/method.html.

Kennickell, A.B. (2002), 'Demographic shifts in the distribution of wealth, 1992 to 1998: evidence from the Survey of Consumer Finances', paper presented at the 2002 meeting of the International Association for Research in Income and Wealth, Stockholm.

Kennickell, Arthur B. and Martha Starr-McCluer (1997), 'Household saving and portfolio change: evidence from the 1983–89 SCF panel', *Review of Income and Wealth*, **43** (December), 381–99.

Kennickell, Arthur B. and Annika E. Sundén (1997), 'Pensions, social security, and the distribution of wealth', FEDS Paper 1997-55, Washington, DC: Board of Governors of the Federal Reserve System (October).

Kennickell, A.B. and R.L. Woodburn (1992), 'Estimation of household net worth using model-based and design-based weights: evidence from the 1989 Survey of Consumer Finances', working paper, Washington, DC: Board of Governors of the Federal Reserve System, http://www.federalreserve.gov/pubs/oss/oss 2/method.html.

Kennickell, A.B. and R.L. Woodburn (1999), 'Consistent weight design for the 1989, 1992, and 1995 SCFs, and the distribution of wealth', *Review of Income and Wealth*, **45**(2) (June), 193–215.

Petska, T., M. Strudler and R. Petska (2002), 'New estimates of the distribution of individual income and taxes', working paper, Washington, DC: Internal Revenue Service, Statistics of Income Division.

Weicher, J.C. (1996), 'The distribution of wealth: increasing inequality?', Washington, DC: American Enterprise Institute for Policy Research.

Wolff, E.N. (1996), 'International comparisons of wealth inequality', *Review of Income and Wealth*, **42**(4) (December), 433–51.

APPENDIX

Table 2A.1   Definitions of wealth components

NETWORTH	ASSET-DEBT.
ASSET	FIN+NFIN.
FIN	LIQ+CDS+SAVBND+BOND+STOCKS+NMMF+ RETQLIQ+CASHLI+OTHMA+OTHFIN.
LIQ	Holdings of checking, savings, money market, and call accounts.
CDS	Holdings of certificates of deposit.
SAVBND	Holdings of savings bonds.
BOND	Direct holdings of bonds.[a]
STOCKS	Direct holdings of publicly traded stocks.[a]
NMMF	Mutual funds other than money market mutual funds.
RETQLIQ	IRAs, Keogh accounts, and other pension accounts where withdrawals or loans may be taken (such as 401(k) accounts).
CASHLI	Cash value of life insurance.
OTHMA	Equity holdings of annuities, trusts, and managed investment accounts.
OTHFIN	Value of miscellaneous financial assets (e.g., futures contracts, oil leases, royalties, etc.).
NFIN	VEHIC+HOUSES+ORESRE+BUS+OTHNFIN.
VEHIC	Market value of all personally owned automobiles, trucks, motor homes, campers, motorcycles, boats, airplanes, helicopters, and miscellaneous vehicles.
HOUSES	Market value of principal residences.
ORESRE	Market value of residential real estate other than principal residences.
NNRESRE	Net equity in real estate other than HOUSES and ORESRE.
BUS	Net equity in closely held businesses.
OTHNFIN	Value of miscellaneous nonfinancial assets (e.g., antiques, artwork, etc.).
DEBT	MRTHEL+INSTALL+OTHLOC+CCBAL+ODEBT.
MRTHEL	Amount outstanding on mortgages and home equity lines of credit secured by principal residences.
RESDBT	Amount outstanding on mortgages secured by residential real estate other than a principal residence.
INSTALL	Amount outstanding on instalment debt.
OTHLOC	Amount outstanding on lines of credit other than home equity lines of credit.
CCBAL	Amount outstanding on credit cards.

Table 2A.1   (continued)

ODEBT	Amount outstanding on miscellaneous debts (e.g., debts to family members, borrowing against insurance policies or pension accounts, margin debt, etc.).
EQUITY	Total value of direct and indirect stock holdings (included in STOCKS and RETQLIQ).[a]
INCOME	Total income for the year preceding the survey year.

Note: a. Direct holdings are those held outside of the managed assets such as mutual funds, trusts, managed investment accounts, annuities, and tax-deferred retirement accounts.

3. Who shared in the growth of wealth in the 1990s? Subpopulation trends in US household wealth holdings

John L. Czajka, Scott Cody and Daniel Kasprzyk

INTRODUCTION

Following a recession in the early 1990s, the United States economy experienced a broad and sustained expansion that lasted into the next decade. Estimates from the Federal Reserve Board's Survey of Consumer Finances (SCF) indicate that the aggregate net worth of US households grew by 43 per cent in real terms between 1992 and 1998. Even after the expansion ended and the stock markets entered a period of significant decline, aggregate net worth in 2001 was still 91 per cent higher than its estimated 1992 value.[1] Arthur Kennickell's analysis of changes in the distribution of wealth (Chapter 2) documents the broad-based nature of the growth of wealth in the 1990s while providing some evidence that wealth grew most strongly in the top 1 per cent of the wealth distribution.

This chapter examines differences in the growth of wealth from another perspective, using the comparative experience of subpopulations defined by family income and by other characteristics that are of interest to a segment of policy analysts who use wealth data in their research.[2] After describing our data sources, we examine differentials in wealth holdings by age, race and Hispanic origin, and how these changed over time. We then focus on nine subpopulations and present estimates of trends in mean and median wealth holdings and, for four of those subpopulations, we present changes in wealth holdings at selected quantile points of the wealth distribution.

DATA SOURCES

This chapter uses data from the Federal Reserve Board's Survey of Consumer Finances (SCF) and the US Census Bureau's Survey of Income and Program Participation (SIPP). We briefly describe these two data sources.

The SCF is the premier survey of wealth in the US. Designed explicitly to measure wealth, the SCF devotes several hundred questions to this topic, and its interviewers are well trained in guiding respondents through the detailed instrument. The SCF also employs very sophisticated imputation procedures to adjust for item nonresponse, which can run very high for many of the wealth questions. In this chapter we use data from the 1992 and 1998 SCF. Estimates from the earlier survey have been adjusted to the reference period of the 1998 survey.[3]

The SIPP is a longitudinal survey that collects detailed data on income, labour force activity, participation in federal and state programmes, health insurance coverage, demographic characteristics, and a variety of additional topics. SIPP panels run two to four years in duration, with interviews conducted every four months. The SIPP has collected data on wealth since its inception in 1984. Wealth data are collected at intervals of one year.

While the SCF was designed to measure wealth, the SIPP was not. The strengths of SIPP lie in other areas, including sample size, the measurement of income – particularly at the low end of the distribution – and the collection of demographic data, among a host of other characteristics that make the data useful for policy analysis. The SIPP's large sample size, which runs ten times that of the SCF over most of the wealth distribution, makes it particularly well suited to subgroup comparisons. The SIPP's limitations in measuring wealth include a substantial under-representation of high-wealth families and an understatement of their wealth. In addition, the SIPP does not measure all of the components of wealth that are captured in the SCF, and it obtains smaller rates of ownership and smaller amounts for many of the components that it does measure. Despite these limitations, as this chapter illustrates, the SIPP seems to capture particular kinds of wealth trends remarkably well. In this chapter we present wealth estimates from wave 4 of the 1992 SIPP panel, administered in early 1993, and wave 9 of the 1996 panel, administered in early 1999. SIPP dollar amounts from 1993 are adjusted to the reference period of the 1999 survey.

Both the SCF and the SIPP surveys are considered to be representative of the household population, though each collects data from a different unit of observation within the household. The SCF collects its most detailed data on the 'primary economic unit', which includes the economically dominant individual or couple and all others who are financially dependent. The estimates presented here refer to this unit of analysis. The SIPP collects wealth data from each adult member (15 years of age and older) of the sample household. With these data it is possible to construct alternative units of analysis. The SIPP estimates presented here refer to a unit of analysis that is based on US Census Bureau family concepts. For this chapter we define the SIPP family to include the household head and spouse and any children or other relatives who do not have their own spouses or children living with them.[4] Unmarried partners, who are included in the SCF unit, are not included in the SIPP unit because the US Census Bureau did not begin to identify such persons until the 1996 panel.

AGE AND RACE

The wealth holdings of American families rise steeply with the age of the family head well into the retirement years, then decline somewhat. Age is a key factor in the accumulation of wealth because it reflects the opportunities for wealth to grow. Wealth holdings also exhibit substantial variation by the race and Hispanic origin of the head, but unlike age, race is not instrumental to the accumulation of wealth. Racial differentials in wealth holdings develop and are maintained for a variety of other reasons (including, in a small way, age). The data on race and Hispanic origin in the SIPP are better than that of the SCF, which provides reason to focus on the SIPP.[5]

To what extent did families from across the age spectrum and from across races share in the growth of wealth in the 1990s? Table 3.1 reports mean and median net worth by age and by race and Hispanic origin in 1993 and 1999. While mean net worth among all families grew by 29 per cent (in constant dollars) over this six-year period, the mean net worth of families whose heads were under 65 grew at barely half that rate or less. Among families headed by persons 65–74, average wealth grew by 41 per cent, and among families headed by persons 75 and older, mean wealth grew by 55 per cent.

Median net worth did not grow at all in the SIPP, whereas, as a later table will show, it grew by 27 per cent in the SCF. We attribute this substantial discrepancy to an unexplained decline in SIPP-measured wealth in the lower half of the wealth distribution, which occurred between the 1993 and 1996 panels and altered the trend. The relationship between assets and liabilities changed as well, which may have contributed to the decline in net worth (Czajka et al. 2003). Nevertheless, the ratio of SIPP median net worth in 1999 to 1993 increased with age in the same way as mean net worth did.

The patterns that we see by age are affected, in part, by the movement of families from one age group to the next older age group. However, this is not true of differences by race and Hispanic origin. Among families with a white non-Hispanic head, mean net worth grew by 41 per cent. Among the other groups, only Hispanic families showed appreciable growth (20 per cent). Much the same pattern is evident in median net worth, with the Asian

*Table 3.1   SIPP mean and median net worth by demographic subgroup, by
year (1000s of 1999 dollars)*

Demographic characteristic	Mean net worth[a]			Median net worth[a]		
	1993	1999	Ratio 1999 to 1993	1993	1999	Ratio 1999 to 1993
All families	100.8	130	1.3	41.8	41.9	1.00
Age of head						
< 30	16.7	13.3	0.80	3.6	2.2	0.60
30 −< 40	53.8	59.0	1.10	18.1	15.5	0.86
40 −< 50	99.9	115.0	1.15	47.7	45.5	0.95
50 −< 65	155.3	179.6	1.16	92.4	82.2	0.89
65 −< 75	168.1	236.9	1.41	107.1	109.2	1.02
> = 75	135.3	209.6	1.55	82.8	97.6	1.18
Race of head						
White, non-Hispanic	110.5	156.1	1.41	51.8	61.2	1.18
Black, non-Hispanic	27.9	29.9	1.07	2.0	5.7	2.80
Hispanic	32.3	38.8	1.20	4.6	5.4	1.17
Asian or Pacific Islander	122.2	126.5	1.04	39.6	30.5	0.77
American Indian or Alaskan Native	54.9	54.6	0.99	20.5	13.9	0.68

Notes: a. Net worth is defined consistently over time. The 1999 estimate excludes 401(k)
and thrift accounts, which were not measured prior to the 1996 panel.

Sources: MPR analysis of the 1992 and 1996 SIPP panels.

or Pacific Islander and American Indian or Alaskan Native populations
(populations not distinguished in the SCF) showing declines while whites
and Hispanics showed gains. Blacks, however, showed a near tripling of
their very low median assets, matching the Hispanic median by 1999. Still,
both medians stood at only one-twelfth the white median and even substantially less than the Asian and Native American medians at that point.

Growth in mean assets showed the same age patterns as net worth.
However, the pronounced increase with age is not evident in median assets,
which show a 16 per cent growth overall (Table 3.2). The race patterns differ
somewhat from those observed with net worth. Hispanic families appear to
have experienced greater growth in both mean and median assets than
white families, but this was offset by greater growth in liabilities (Table 3.3).
Black families showed both the most substantial growth in median
assets and the greatest growth in median liabilities, although the absolute

Table 3.2   SIPP mean and median assets by demographic subgroup, by year (1000s of 1999 dollars)

Demographic characteristic	Mean assets			Median assets		
	1993	1999	Ratio 1999 to 1993	1993	1999	Ratio 1999 to 1993
All families	135.0	173	1.3	79.6	92.7	1.16
Age of head						
< 30	38.5	42.1	1.09	10.7	10.9	1.02
30 −< 40	100.5	118.7	1.18	59.5	70.1	1.18
40 −< 50	152.8	177.5	1.16	100.7	111.4	1.11
50 −< 65	193.0	229.4	1.19	126.7	130.5	1.03
65 −< 75	178.2	251.3	1.41	116.5	126.4	1.08
> = 75	138.8	215.0	1.55	86.1	101.2	1.18
Race of head						
White, non-Hispanic	146.3	203.0	1.39	93.1	113.8	1.22
Black, non-Hispanic	45.3	55.7	1.23	4.8	16.8	3.47
Hispanic	51.8	75.9	1.47	12.4	17.1	1.38
Asian or Pacific Islander	177.8	188.6	1.06	95.2	92.0	0.97
American Indian or Alaskan Native	89.5	82.6	0.92	40.1	37.4	0.93

Notes: Assets are defined consistently over time. The 1999 estimate excludes 401(k) and thrift accounts, which were not measured prior to the 1996 panel.

Sources: MPR analysis of the 1992 and 1996 SIPP panels.

magnitude of the former far exceeded that of the latter. Median liabilities, which grew by 61 per cent, have a very different age profile than assets or net worth. Median liabilities among families with a head 65 and older were zero in 1993 and did not change. In most other age groups, median liabilities grew by almost 60 to 70 per cent. Means assets grew most among families with the oldest heads, but the growth was fairly uniform among families with heads under 65.

One outcome of these different patterns for assets and liabilities is a change in leverage rates (mean liabilities as a percentage of mean assets) across subgroups over time. Leverage rates grew for families with nonaged heads, with the greatest growth occurring among families with heads under 30, whose leverage rate was over 50 per cent at the beginning of the period and grew to more than two-thirds (Table 3.4). Leverage rates also grew for black families and Hispanic families but not for any of the other groups.

Table 3.3   SIPP mean and median liabilities by demographic subgroup, by year (1000s of 1999 dollars)

Demographic characteristic	Mean liabilities			Median liabilities		
	1993	1999	Ratio 1999 to 1993	1993	1999	Ratio 1999 to 1993
All families	34.3	43.8	1.3	7.4	12.0	1.61
Age of head						
< 30	21.7	28.8	1.33	5.2	8.5	1.65
30 −< 40	46.7	59.7	1.28	20.3	31.9	1.57
40 −< 50	52.9	62.5	1.18	28.3	37.2	1.31
50 −< 65	37.7	49.8	1.32	11.3	19.0	1.69
65 −< 75	10.0	14.4	1.44	0.0	0.0	0.89
> = 75	3.5	5.4	1.56	0.0	0.0	—[a]
Race of head						
White, non-Hispanic	35.8	46.9	1.31	8.9	15.0	1.68
Black, non-Hispanic	17.4	25.8	1.48	0.7	4.0	5.42
Hispanic	19.6	37.1	1.89	1.4	5.5	4.08
Asian or Pacific Islander	55.6	62.1	1.12	8.3	20.0	2.40
American Indian or Alaskan Native	34.7	28.0	0.81	10.1	5.3	0.52

Note: a. A ratio is not reported because the value of the denominator was zero or near zero.

Sources: MPR analysis of the 1992 and 1996 SIPP panels.

SUBPOPULATIONS

We identified nine subpopulations that are of potential interest to policy analysts within the Social Security Administration and that illustrate the strengths and limitations of SIPP wealth data. These nine subpopulations are listed in Table 3.5, with the size of each as estimated from the SIPP and the SCF. The first four subpopulations are defined by income in relation to poverty and cover about 92 per cent of the total population. The remaining five subpopulations consist of families with an aged (65 or older) head or spouse; a head nearing retirement (employed and at least 55 but less than 65); a prime working-age head (30 to 60); an aged head or spouse receiving social security benefits; and a nonaged head or spouse receiving such benefits (consisting mostly of disability insurance). These last five subpopulations are not mutually exclusive.

Table 3.4   Leverage rate by demographic subgroup, by year

Demographic characteristic	1993 %	1999 %	Ratio 1999 to 1993
All families	25.4	25.3	1.00
Age of head			
<30	56.4	68.4	1.21
30 –< 40	46.5	50.3	1.08
40 –< 50	34.6	35.2	1.02
50 –< 65	19.5	21.7	1.11
65 –< 75	5.6	5.7	1.02
>= 75	2.5	2.5	1.00
Race of head			
White, non-Hispanic	24.5	23.1	0.94
Black, non-Hispanic	38.4	46.3	1.21
Hispanic	37.8	48.9	1.29
Asian or Pacific Islander	31.3	32.9	1.05
American Indian or Alaskan Native	38.8	33.9	0.87

Note: The leverage rate is the mean liabilities divided by the mean assets in each year, multiplied by 100.

Sources: MPR analysis of the 1992 and 1996 SIPP panels.

The SIPP's strength in sample size is evident in the sample counts for these subpopulations (Table 3.6). For example, in 1999 the SIPP had nearly 1800 sample families with a nonaged head or spouse receiving social security benefits, whereas the SCF had fewer than 200. Similarly, the SIPP had nearly 10 000 low-income families in 1999 compared to 1100 for the SCF.

CHANGES IN MEANS AND MEDIANS

Table 3.7 reports mean net worth by subpopulation for 1992 and 1998, based on the SCF, with six-year growth rates from both the SCF and the SIPP. (Growth rates from the two surveys cover roughly the same period of time.) Despite the fact that mean net worth for all families in the SIPP is less than half the SCF estimate of mean net worth, the six-year growth rates estimated by the two surveys are very similar: 29 per cent for the SIPP compared to 33 per cent for the SCF. We also find general similarity in the

Table 3.5 Estimated number of families in each subpopulation: SIPP and SCF (weighted estimates in 1000s)

Subpopulation	SIPP		SCF	
	1993	1999	1992	1998
All families	96 365	102 468	95 918	102 549
Low-income (< 200% of poverty)	32 958	33 427	35 956	34 788
Middle-income (200% to < 400%)	35 150	35 938	30 126	32 459
Lower high-income (400% to < 600%)	16 647	19 061	15 250	17 721
Mid high-income (600% to < 800%)	6995	7622	6976	8243
Aged head or spouse	21 269	22 538	21 354	22 330
Head nearing retirement	7628	9216	8444	8163
Prime working age head	56 325	62 330	54 424	60 980
Receiving social security benefits (aged)	19 782	21 143	19 706	20 512
Receiving social security benefits (nonaged)	5785	6199	6855	5439

Sources: MPR analysis of the 1992 and 1996 SIPP panels and the 1992 and 1998 SCF.

Table 3.6 Sample counts of families in each subpopulation: SIPP and SCF

Subpopulation	SIPP		SCF	
	1993	1999	1992	1998
All families	18 552	28 969	3906	4305
Low-income (< 200% of poverty)	6264	9907	1046	1110
Middle-income (200% to < 400%)	6769	10 026	905	1018
Lower high-income (400% to < 600%)	3258	5212	528	603
Mid high-income (600% to < 800%)	1361	2093	283	333
Aged head or spouse	4146	6877	918	915
Head nearing retirement	1485	2547	449	476
Prime working age head	10 781	17 171	2254	2598
Receiving social security benefits (aged)	3854	6452	785	787
Receiving social security benefits (nonaged)	1108	1795	222	196

Sources: MPR analysis of the 1992 and 1996 SIPP panels and the 1992 and 1998 SCF.

estimated growth rates across the nine subpopulations. The SIPP and SCF estimates of growth rates agree closely across three of the four income groups, differing only on the middle-income subpopulation, for which the SIPP finds a comparatively high growth rate (41 per cent) while the SCF

Table 3.7   Mean net worth by subpopulation (1000s of 1998 dollars)

Subpopulation characteristic	SCF 1992	SCF 1998	SCF 1998 to 1992	SIPP 1999 to 1992
All families	212.6	283.3	1.33	1.29
Low-income (< 200% of poverty)	50.4	60.7	1.20	1.23
Middle-income (200% to < 400%)	119.2	134.6	1.13	1.41
Lower high-income (400% to < 600%)	208.3	226.4	1.09	1.10
Mid high-income (600% to < 800%)	308.7	353.0	1.14	1.13
Aged head or spouse	294.3	388.5	1.32	1.45
Head nearing retirement	463.6	621.9	1.34	1.21
Prime working age head	207.1	275.5	1.33	1.20
Receiving social security benefits (aged)	282.5	368.6	1.30	1.47
Receiving social security benefits (nonaged)	176.9	202.8	1.15	0.98

Note: Net worth is defined consistently over time in each survey but differently between surveys.

Sources: MPR analysis of the 1992 and 1998 SCF and the 1992 and 1996 SIPP panels.

finds a relatively low growth rate (13 per cent). Since we would have expected above-average growth for these subpopulations, it is significant that the two surveys agree that the upper-income groups had comparatively low rates of growth of mean net worth over the six years.

The SIPP estimates for the next four subpopulations appear more plausible than the SCF estimates. The SIPP shows higher growth rates for the two older subpopulations, whereas the SCF shows uniformly average growth rates for all four subpopulations. Finally, the two surveys agree that families receiving social security benefits for a nonaged head or spouse had below-average growth rates. The SIPP estimates imply no growth overall; the SCF finds a growth rate of 15 per cent, or about half the rate for all families.

Estimates of median net worth from the SCF show an overall growth rate of 27 per cent (Table 3.8), which compares to both the SIPP and SCF estimates of growth in mean net worth. However, in contrast to mean net worth, the SCF subpopulation medians show growth rates rising with family income instead of higher growth among low and middle-income families. Families with a head nearing retirement had no growth in median net worth compared to 34 per cent in mean net worth. The most striking

Table 3.8   Median net worth by subpopulation (1000s of 1998 dollars)

Subpopulation characteristic	SCF 1992	SCF 1998	SCF 1998 to 1992	SIPP 1999 to 1993
All families	56.4	71.8	1.27	1.00
Low-income (< 200% of poverty)	12.2	10.1	0.83	0.90
Middle-income (200% to < 400%)	57.8	64.0	1.11	1.00
Lower high-income (400% to < 600%)	111.6	124.5	1.12	0.84
Mid high-income (600% to < 800%)	173.8	209.4	1.20	0.84
Aged head or spouse	103.4	136.7	1.32	1.06
Head nearing retirement	169.2	171.4	1.01	0.88
Prime working age head	58.4	75.6	1.30	0.99
Receiving social security benefits (aged)	105.2	137.4	1.31	1.08
Receiving social security benefits (nonaged)	57.2	39.0	0.68	0.72

Note: Net worth is defined consistently over time in each survey but differently between surveys.

Sources: MPR analysis of the 1992 and 1998 SCF and the 1992 and 1996 SIPP panels.

result, however, is the 32 per cent reduction in median net worth among families with a nonaged social security beneficiary. In this respect the SCF and SIPP medians agree. Elsewhere, however, the SIPP growth rates are almost consistently lower than those of the SCF and, as we have seen, the SIPP shows no growth at all in median net worth.

Estimates of change in mean assets compare closely to the estimates of change in mean net worth (Table 3.9), but median assets show somewhat different patterns. Perhaps most significantly, the SCF shows a 10 per cent rise in the median assets of families with nonaged members receiving social security benefits (Table 3.10). In other respects the results are very similar to the findings for median net worth, which is not too surprising given that assets are the positive component in net worth. The SIPP shows 16 per cent growth in median assets (only half the SCF estimate) but is nevertheless more consistent with the SCF than SIPP estimates of change in median net worth.

Estimates of change in mean liabilities are very similar across the two surveys, and the same is true of estimates of change in median liabilities (Tables 3.11 and 3.12). Both surveys show a much bigger increase in median than mean liabilities, suggesting that the greatest growth occurred lower rather than higher in the distribution. It is interesting to note, however,

Table 3.9   Mean assets by subpopulation (1000s of 1998 dollars)

Subpopulation characteristic	SCF 1992	SCF 1998	SCF 1998 to 1992	SIPP 1999 to 1993
All families	250.5	332.1	1.33	1.28
Low-income (< 200% of poverty)	62.1	74.8	1.20	1.22
Middle-income (200% to < 400%)	149.1	173.1	1.16	1.37
Lower high-income (400% to < 600%)	256.2	292.7	1.14	1.14
Mid high-income (600% to < 800%)	385.2	438.6	1.14	1.14
Aged head or spouse	307.4	405.0	1.32	1.44
Head nearing retirement	512.9	691.3	1.35	1.24
Prime working age head	260.2	341.3	1.31	1.21
Receiving social security benefits (aged)	294.4	383.5	1.30	1.47
Receiving social security benefits (nonaged)	198.7	230.0	1.16	1.03

Note: Assets are defined consistently over time in each survey but differently between surveys.

Sources: MPR analysis of the 1992 and 1998 SCF and the 1992 and 1996 SIPP panels.

Table 3.10   Median assets by subpopulation (1000s of 1998 dollars)

Subpopulation characteristic	SCF 1992	SCF 1998	SCF 1998 to 1992	SIPP 1999 to 1993
All families	87.5	116.5	1.33	1.16
Low-income (< 200% of poverty)	20.0	19.3	0.97	1.09
Middle-income (200% to < 400%)	93.8	114.0	1.22	1.15
Lower high-income (400% to < 600%)	176.6	200.9	1.14	1.01
Mid high-income (600% to < 800%)	239.9	287.3	1.20	0.96
Aged head or spouse	111.5	146.4	1.31	1.07
Head nearing retirement	196.4	207.3	1.06	0.99
Prime working age head	103.6	131.9	1.27	1.15
Receiving social security benefits (aged)	111.6	146.0	1.31	1.09
Receiving social security benefits (nonaged)	67.5	74.3	1.10	0.95

Note: Assets are defined consistently over time in each survey but differently between surveys.

Sources: MPR analysis of the 1992 and 1998 SCF and the 1992 and 1996 SIPP panels.

Table 3.11　Mean liabilities by subpopulation (1000s of 1998 dollars)

Subpopulation characteristic	SCF 1992	SCF 1998	SCF 1998 to 1992	SIPP 1999 to 1993
All families	37.9	48.8	1.29	1.28
Low-income (< 200% of poverty)	11.8	14.1	1.19	1.21
Middle-income (200% to < 400%)	30.0	38.5	1.28	1.26
Lower high-income (400% to < 600%)	47.9	66.3	1.38	1.26
Mid high-income (600% to < 800%)	76.6	85.6	1.12	1.18
Aged head or spouse	13.0	16.6	1.28	1.39
Head nearing retirement	49.3	69.4	1.41	1.38
Prime working age head	53.1	65.8	1.24	1.23
Receiving social security benefits (aged)	12.0	15.0	1.25	1.44
Receiving social security benefits (nonaged)	21.8	27.2	1.25	1.30

Sources:　MPR analysis of the 1992 and 1998 SCF and the 1992 and 1996 SIPP panels.

Table 3.12　Median liabilities by subpopulation (1000s of 1998 dollars)

Subpopulation characteristic	SCF 1992	SCF 1998	SCF 1998 to 1992	SIPP 1999 to 1993
All families	6.9	11.9	1.72	1.61
Low-income (< 200% of poverty)	0.8	0.7	0.88	1.64
Middle-income (200% to < 400%)	9.1	15.2	1.67	1.49
Lower high-income (400% to < 600%)	28.5	47.5	1.67	1.39
Mid high-income (600% to < 800%)	47.7	59.0	1.24	1.19
Aged head or spouse	0.0	0.0	_a	_a
Head nearing retirement	13.5	29.2	2.16	1.82
Prime working age head	20.4	32.0	1.57	1.39
Receiving social security benefits (aged)	0.0	0.0	_a	_a
Receiving social security benefits (nonaged)	2.0	0.0	0.00	1.09

Note:　a. A ratio is not reported because the value of the denominator was zero or near zero.

Sources:　MPR analysis of the 1992 and 1998 SCF and the 1992 and 1996 SIPP panels.

Table 3.13   Leverage rates by subpopulation

Subpopulation characteristic	SCF 1992 %	SCF 1998 %	SCF 1998 to 1992	SIPP 1999 to 1993
All families	15.1	14.7	0.97	1.00
Low-income (< 200% of poverty)	19.0	18.9	0.99	0.99
Middle-income (200% to < 400%)	20.1	22.2	1.10	0.92
Lower high-income (400% to < 600%)	18.7	22.7	1.21	1.11
Mid high-income (600% to < 800%)	19.9	19.5	0.98	1.03
Aged head or spouse	4.2	4.1	0.98	0.96
Head nearing retirement	9.6	10.0	1.04	1.11
Prime working age head	20.4	19.3	0.95	1.01
Receiving social security benefits (aged)	4.1	3.9	0.95	0.98
Receiving social security benefits (nonaged)	11.0	11.8	1.07	1.26

Sources: MPR analysis of the 1992 and 1998 SCF and the 1992 and 1996 SIPP panels.

that the one major difference between the SIPP and the SCF occurs among low-income families: the SCF finds a 12 per cent reduction in median liabilities and the SIPP finds a 64 per cent increase. Three subpopulations have median liabilities of zero, so growth in the median cannot be measured. Two of these subpopulations include aged family members while the third receives social security benefits for a nonaged member. Given the large reduction in median net worth but with the small increase in median assets, we would have expected an increase in liabilities for this last group. While this particular group showed 25 to 30 per cent growth in mean liabilities, this increase was not exceptional.

Lastly, the two surveys agree that the leverage rate for all families did not change between late 1992/early 1993 and late 1998/early 1999 (Table 3.13). The changes in leverage rates estimated by the two surveys are also very similar across the nine subpopulations. One of the two biggest differences occurs among middle-income families, where the SCF finds a 10 per cent increase and the SIPP finds an 8 per cent reduction. In addition, the SIPP finds a bigger increase in the leverage rate among families with nonaged members receiving social security benefits: 26 per cent versus 7 per cent for the SCF.

As Kennickell notes in Chapter 2, the sizable growth in net worth in the 1990s was accomplished with little change in asset ownership rates – either overall or by type. For the universe of all families, 401(k)[6] and thrift accounts showed the largest increase in ownership between 1992 and 1998, followed by stocks and mutual funds (data not shown). Ownership of other types of assets showed small increases (principal residence, for example), no change (motor vehicles), or, in some instances, declines (life insurance). On the liability side, ownership of home mortgages and vehicle loans increased a modest amount while loans from financial institutions decreased. The SIPP and the SCF tell similar stories except that the SIPP did not measure 401(k) and thrift accounts before the 1996 panel, therefore, no trend data for that asset are available. (The most notable exceptions are assets held at financial institutions for which ownership declined by 5 percentage points in the SIPP but rose by 4 percentage points in the SCF.)

Table 3.14 reports the percentages of the subpopulations owning stocks or mutual funds by year, based on the SIPP. The proportion of those owning stocks or mutual funds rose by 25 per cent among all families, and grew by a comparable amount in most subpopulations. The exceptions are in low-income families, where the increase was 64 per cent, and families receiving social security benefits for a nonaged head or spouse, where there was no change in ownership between 1993 and 1999.

On the whole, we are struck more by the similarities across the subpopulations than by the differences. This suggests that, apart from whatever may have happened at the very top of the wealth distribution, these four income groups and five additional subpopulations of policy interest shared, if not equally then at least similarly, in the growth in net worth over the 1990s.

Table 3.14   Percentage of families owning stocks or mutual funds

Subpopulation characteristic	SIPP 1993 %	SIPP 1999 %	Ratio 1999 to 1993
All families	18.9	23.6	1.25
Low-income (< 200% of poverty)	4.6	7.4	1.61
Middle-income (200% to < 400%)	17.1	21.2	1.24
Lower high-income (400% to < 600%)	32.0	35.1	1.10
Mid high-income (600% to < 800%)	41.3	46.9	1.14
Aged head or spouse	21.8	26.1	1.20
Head nearing retirement	25.4	31.9	1.26
Prime working age head	19.3	24.5	1.27
Receiving social security benefits (aged)	22.0	26.1	1.19
Receiving social security benefits (nonaged)	18.6	18.3	0.98

Sources: MPR analysis of the 1992 and 1996 SIPP panels.

CHANGES IN THE DISTRIBUTION OF NET WORTH BY INCOME

Tabulations of summary statistics such as the mean or median cannot convey how the wealth of families across the distribution may have changed if change was not uniform. Kennickell (2002 and Chapter 2 in this volume) has developed graphic displays that can depict the unevenness of growth in wealth across the entire wealth distribution. Here we follow a simpler tack, comparing quantile points of the distribution of net worth at different points in time for the four subpopulations defined by income. This analysis is based solely on SCF data.

Among low-income families, real growth in net worth occurred above but not below the 60th percentile (Table 3.15). Furthermore, growth in net worth appears to have exceeded a rate of 25 per cent at percentiles 95 and above. Among middle-income families, there was modest growth across much of the distribution – even at levels of wealth ($10 000 to $20 000) that saw no growth among low-income families. Curiously, after rising to a peak around the 95th percentile, the growth rate then fell off rapidly to less than zero.

Among lower high-income families, there was consistent growth of about 15 per cent, on average, across virtually the entire distribution; only the bottom 10 to 20 per cent were clearly excluded. We note that the level of net worth that corresponds to the 20th percentile in this distribution ($34 000 in 1992) would have been at the 65th percentile among low-income families, and even low-income families at that level of net worth experienced real growth over the 1990s. Finally, among mid high-income families, there was growth across the entire distribution. The rate of growth was highest at the bottom of the distribution – actually the highest in the entire table. This rate of growth then declined through the 40th percentile, rose through the 60th percentile, and then diminished to its lowest level in the upper tenth of the distribution.

We draw three conclusions from the changes in these percentile distributions. First, ranges of the distributions that correspond to very low levels of wealth in 1992 – below $20 000 to $30 000 – saw little if any growth between 1992 and 1998. Second, ranges of the distributions above these levels saw at least modest growth among all four income groups. Third, the biggest increases in net worth occurred among families with the most disparate combinations of income and wealth: low income with high wealth, or high income with low wealth. In fact, it is only among low-income families that we find more than modest growth at the top of the wealth distribution. Equally puzzling, families with the same level of wealth (about $300 000 to $500 000 in 1992) but with higher income did not experience nearly the same rate of growth in net worth. Low-income families with

Table 3.15 Percentiles of net worth in 1992 and growth, 1992–8, by income level

Net worth percentile	Income level				Income level			
	Low	Middle	Lower high	Mid high	Low	Middle	Lower high	Mid high
	Percentile value in 1992 ($1000s)				Ratio of 1998 to 1992			
10	−0.5	1.8	16.4	23.7	2.20[a]	0.50	0.76	1.94
20	0.0	9.1	33.7	64.4	_[b]	1.09	1.14	1.37
30	1.4	20.0	54.6	103.2	1.00	1.16	1.19	1.15
40	4.4	37.6	79.3	140.5	1.07	1.03	1.16	1.12
50	12.2	57.8	111.6	173.8	0.83	1.11	1.12	1.20
60	25.1	82.4	148.1	216.4	0.97	1.17	1.19	1.31
70	43.9	117.5	205.0	315.5	1.14	1.15	1.12	1.18
80	80.1	175.1	275.0	441.5	1.04	1.11	1.20	1.17
90	134.8	267.0	461.3	711.1	1.15	1.21	1.06	1.10
95	193.9	358.4	707.9	948.8	1.27	1.27	1.03	1.09
98	293.3	624.8	970.4	1422.9	1.55	1.08	1.16	1.10
99	465.9	995.4	1498.4	2157.7	1.41	0.95	1.07	1.08

Notes:

Percentile values in 1992 are expressed in 1998 dollars.

a. Negative value of net worth more than doubled.

b. A ratio is not reported because the value of the denominator was zero or near zero.

Sources: MPR analysis of the 1992 and 1998 SCF.

comparatively high wealth may be older than higher-income families with the same wealth, and perhaps more of their wealth was invested in the types of assets that appreciated the most during the 1990s.

CONCLUSION

Our analysis of wealth trends among population subgroups lends further support to findings that the growth of wealth in the 1990s was very broad-based. Nevertheless, participation was not universal. Age is indicative of having had the opportunity to accumulate wealth, and age differentials in net worth grew stronger over the 1990s. The pattern of change in racial differentials was more complex. Non-Hispanic whites experienced the largest gain in mean wealth and surpassed Asians in their average holdings. However, their strong advantage over all groups in median wealth did not increase, except in comparison with Asians and American Indians and Alaskan Natives, who do not appear to have grown in median wealth at all. Hispanic families and non-Hispanic black families became more leveraged.

Wealth among families at all income levels grew, but segments of the wealth distribution with little wealth did not experience gains – even when their income was comparatively high. Subpopulations that include a high number of aged persons appear to have had greater growth in wealth, although this is not entirely consistent between the SCF and the SIPP. Likewise, the SIPP suggests that families with nonaged social security beneficiaries (primarily those receiving disability insurance benefits) experienced no growth in mean net worth. However, the SCF did not support this.

NOTES

1. These estimates are from Kennickell (Chapter 2 in this volume). Note that, because the number of households was also increasing, mean net worth did not grow by the same proportion as aggregate net worth.
2. This chapter extends research that compared the wealth data collected in four surveys (Czajka et al. 2003) and was carried out under contract to the US Social Security Administration.
3. SCF interviews are conducted in the second half of the calendar year. Our adjustment assumes a September midpoint.
4. In US Census Bureau terminology, our unit of analysis is the primary family, less subfamilies, or, if the head of household is living with no other relatives, the primary individual.
5. Chapter 2 in this volume discusses limitations in the measurement of race and Hispanic origin in the SCF.
6. A 401(k) account is a type of retirement savings plan to which an employee may contribute a percentage of earnings (up to an annual maximum) from pre-tax income – often with matching contributions from the employer. Plan funds accumulate tax free until withdrawal.

REFERENCES

Czajka, J.L., J.E. Jacobson and S. Cody (2003), 'Survey estimates of wealth: a comparative analysis and review of the Survey of Income and Program Participation', Washington, DC: Mathematica Policy Research, final report.

Kennickell, A.B. (2002), 'Demographic shifts in the distribution of wealth, 1992 to 1998: evidence from the Survey of Consumer Finances', Washington, DC: Federal Reserve Board, paper presented at the 2002 meeting of the International Association for Research in Income and Wealth, Stockholm.

4. Changes in household wealth in the 1980s and 1990s in the United States

Edward N. Wolff

INTRODUCTION

The 1990s witnessed some remarkable events. The stock market boomed. On the basis of the Standard & Poor's 500 Index, stock prices surged 171 per cent between 1989 and 2001. Stock ownership spread and, by 2001 (as we shall see below), over half of US households owned stock either directly or indirectly. Real wages, after stagnating for many years, finally grew in the late 1990s. According to Bureau of Labor Statistics figures, real mean hourly earnings gained 8.3 per cent between 1995 and 2001.[1]

Most studies have looked at the distribution of well-being or its change over time in terms of income. However, family wealth is also an indicator of well-being, independent of the direct financial income it provides. There are four reasons. First, owner-occupied housing provides services directly to their owner. Second, wealth is a source of consumption, independent of the direct money income it provides, because assets can be converted directly into cash and thus provide for immediate consumption needs. Third, the availability of financial assets can provide liquidity to a family in times of economic stress, as occasioned by unemployment, sickness or family break-up. Fourth, in a representative democracy, the distribution of power is often related to the distribution of wealth.

Previous work of mine (see Wolff, 1994, 1996, 1998, 2001 and 2002a), which used the 1983, 1989, 1992, 1995 and 1998 Survey of Consumer Finances (SCF) conducted by the Federal Reserve Board of Washington, DC, presented evidence of sharply increasing household wealth inequality between 1983 and 1989, followed by a modest rise between 1989 and 1998. Both mean and median wealth holdings climbed briskly during the 1983–89 period. From 1989 to 1998, mean wealth continued to surge, while median net worth rose at a rather anaemic pace. Indeed, the only segment of the population that experienced large gains in wealth since 1983 is the richest 20 per cent of households. Moreover, despite the buoyant economy over the 1990s, overall indebtedness continued to rise among American families. Stocks and pension accounts also rose as a share of total household wealth, with offsetting declines in bank deposits, investment real estate and financial securities.

The ratio of mean wealth between African American and white families was very low in 1983, at 0.19, and barely budged during the 1990s, though median wealth among African American families did advance relative to white families. In 1983, the richest households were those headed by persons between 45 and 69 years of age, though between 1983 and 1989, wealth shifted away from this age group toward both younger and older age groups. However, the relative wealth holdings of both younger and older families fell between 1989 and 1998.

Though wealth and income are positively correlated among households, the correlation is far from perfect and there exists a large variation of wealth holdings within income class. One issue that has generated some controversy over the last few years is that the largest wealth gains from 1983 to 1989 were being received by middle-income families. From 1989 to 1998, the situation reversed and nonelderly middle-income families actually experienced the largest losses in wealth.

With the release of the 2001 SCF, I can now extend some of my earlier analysis on the ownership of household wealth to 2001. First, I discuss the measurement of household wealth and describe the data sources used for this study. The sections that follow present a range of results and analyses: results on time trends in average wealth holdings; changes in the concentration of household wealth; and the composition of household wealth. I then investigate changes in wealth holdings by race, and report on changes in the age–wealth profile, as well as on wealth by marital status. Finally, I examine wealth differences by income class, and provide details on stock ownership for different demographic groups. A summary of results and concluding remarks are provided in the final section.

DATA SOURCES AND METHODS

The data sources used for this study are the 1983, 1989, 1992, 1995, 1998 and 2001 SCF. Each survey consists of a core representative sample combined with a high-income supplement. The supplement is drawn from the data files compiled by the Statistics of Income (SOI) Division of the Internal Revenue Service (IRS). For the 1983 SCF, for example, an income cut-off of $100 000 of adjusted gross income is used as the criterion for inclusion in the supplemental sample. Individuals were randomly selected for the sample within predesignated income strata. The advantage of the high-income supplement is that it provides a much 'richer' sample of high income and, therefore, potentially very wealthy families. However, the presence of a high-income supplement creates some complications because weights must be constructed to meld the high-income supplement with the core sample.[2]

The SCF also supplies alternative sets of weights. For the 1983 SCF, I have used the 'Full Sample 1983 Composite Weights' because this set of weights provides the closest correspondence between the national balance sheet totals derived from the sample and those in the Federal Reserve Board's Flow of Funds Accounts of the United States. For the same reason, results for the 1989 SCF are based on the average of University of Michigan Survey Research Center (SRC) SRC-Design-S1 series (X40131 in the database itself) and the SRC design-based weights (X40125); results for the 1992, 1995, 1998 and 2001 SCF rely on the design-based weights (X42000) – a partially design-based weight constructed on the basis of original selection probabilities and frame information and adjusted for nonresponse.[3] In the case of the 1992 SCF, this set of weights produced major anomalies in the size distribution of income for 1991. As a result, I have modified the weights somewhat to conform to the size distribution of income as reported in the SOI (see, for details on the adjustments, Wolff 1996).

The Federal Reserve Board imputes information for missing items in the SCF. However, despite this procedure, there still remain discrepancies for several assets between the total balance sheet value computed from the survey sample and the Flow of Funds data. Consequently, the results presented below are based on my adjustments to the original asset and liability values in the surveys which aligns asset and liability totals from the survey data to the corresponding national balance sheet totals. In most cases this entails a proportional adjustment of reported values of balance sheet items in the survey data (see, for details, Wolff, 1987, 1994, 1996 and 1998).[4] It should be noted that the alignment has very little effect on the measurement of wealth inequality – both the Gini coefficient and the quantile shares. However, it is important to make these adjustments when comparing changes in mean wealth both overall and by asset type.

The principal wealth concept used here is marketable wealth (net worth), which is defined as the current value of all marketable or fungible assets less the current value of debts. Net worth is thus the difference in value between total assets and total liabilities (debt). Total assets are defined as the sum of: (1) the gross value of owner-occupied housing; (2) other real estate owned by the household; (3) cash and demand deposits; (4) time and savings deposits, certificates of deposit and money market accounts; (5) government bonds, corporate bonds, foreign bonds and other financial securities; (6) the cash surrender value of life insurance plans; (7) the cash surrender value of pension plans, including IRAs, Keogh and 401(k) plans; (8) corporate stock and mutual funds; (9) net equity in unincorporated businesses; and (10) equity in trust funds. Total liabilities are the sum of: (1) mortgage debt; (2) consumer debt, including auto loans; and (3) other debt.

This measure reflects wealth as a store of value and, therefore, a source of potential consumption. I believe that this is the concept that best reflects the level of well-being associated with a family's holdings. Thus, only assets that can be readily converted to cash (that is, 'fungible' ones) are included. Consumer durables, such as automobiles, televisions, furniture, household appliances and the like, are excluded here because these items are not easily marketed or their resale value typically far understates the value of their consumption services to the household. Also excluded is the value of future social security benefits that the family may receive upon retirement (usually referred to as 'social security wealth'), as well as the value of retirement benefits from private pension plans ('pension wealth'). Even though these funds are a source of future income to families, they are not under their direct control and cannot be marketed.[5] I also use a more restricted concept of wealth, which I call 'financial wealth'. This is defined as net worth minus net equity in owner-occupied housing. Financial wealth is a more 'liquid' concept than marketable wealth since one's home is difficult to convert into cash in the short term. It thus reflects the resources that may be immediately available for consumption or various forms of investments.

WEALTH GREW RAPIDLY DURING THE 1990S

Table 4.1 documents a robust growth in wealth during the 1990s. Median wealth (the wealth of the household in the middle of the distribution) was 16 per cent greater in 2001 than in 1989. After rising by 7 per cent between 1983 and 1989, median wealth fell by 17 per cent from 1989 to 1995, then rose by 39 per cent from 1995 to 2001. As a result, median wealth grew slightly faster between 1989 and 2001, 1.32 per cent per year, than between 1983 and 1989, at 1.13 per cent per year. Moreover, as shown in the third row of the 'Net worth' panel A, the percentage of households with zero or negative net worth increased from 15.5 per cent in 1983 to 17.9 per cent in 1989 but fell off a bit to 17.6 per cent in 2001. The share of households with net worth less than $5000 and less than $10 000 (both in 1995 dollars) also declined somewhat between 1989 and 2001.

Mean net worth also showed a sharp increase from 1983 to 1989 followed by a rather precipitous decline from 1989 to 1995 and then, buoyed largely by rising stock prices, another surge in 2001. Overall, it was 65 per cent higher in 2001 than in 1983 and 44 per cent larger than in 1989.[6] In fact, mean wealth grew quite a bit faster between 1989 and 2001, at 3.02 per cent

Table 4.1   Mean and median wealth and income, 1983–2001 (thousands of 2001 dollars)

Wealth concept	1983	1989	1992	1995	1998	2001	% change 1983–89	% change 1989–01	% change 1983–01
Net worth									
Median	59.3	63.5	54.2	53.0	65.9	73.5	7.0	15.8	23.9
Mean	231.0	264.6	257.3	237.7	293.6	380.1	14.6	43.7	64.6
% with net worth									
a. zero or negative[a]	15.5	17.9	18.0	18.5	18.0	17.6			
b. less than $5000[a]	25.4	27.6	27.2	27.8	27.2	26.6			
c. less than $10 000[a]	29.7	31.8	31.2	31.9	30.3	30.1			
Financial net worth									
Median	12.8	15.1	12.7	11.6	19.4	23.2	18.0	53.4	81.1
Mean	167.6	197.5	196.1	182.4	230.7	298.5	17.8	51.1	78.1
% with zero or negative financial wealth	25.7	26.8	28.2	28.7	25.7	25.5			
Income[b]									
Median	37.1	41.3	38.7	39.6	42.2	42.2	11.2	2.3	13.7
Mean	45.2	52.2	49.0	52.2	56.3	58.2	15.5	11.6	28.9

Notes:
a.   Constant 1995 dollars.
b.   Household income data from the Current Population Survey, US Census Bureau (available on the Internet).

Sources: Author's computations from the 1983, 1989, 1992, 1995, 1998, and 2001 SCF. The 1983 weights are the Full Sample 1983 Composite Weights; and the 1989 weights are the average of the SRC-Design-S1 series (X40131) and the SRC design-based weights (X40125). The 1992 calculations are based on the design-based weights (X42000), with my adjustments (see Wolff, 1996). The 1995 weights are the design-based weights (X42000). The 1998 and 2001 weights are partially design-based weights (X42001), which account for the systematic deviations from CPS estimates of homeownership by racial-ethnic groups. The 1983, 1989, 1992 and 1995 asset and liability entries are aligned to national balance sheet totals (see Note 2). The 1998 and 2001 asset and liability entries are based on original, unadjusted survey data.

per year, than from 1983 to 1989, at 2.27 per cent per year. Moreover, mean wealth grew almost three times as fast as the median, suggesting widening inequality of wealth over these years.

Financial wealth grew even faster than net worth during the 1990s. Median financial wealth rose by 18 per cent between 1983 and 1989, then plummeted by 24 per cent from 1989 to 1995, then surged over the next six years, for a net increase of 53 per cent between 1989 and 2001 and 81 per cent from 1983 to 2001. Between 1983 and 1995, the fraction of households with zero or negative financial wealth expanded from 25.7 to 28.7 per cent but fell back to 25.5 per cent in 2001. Mean financial wealth, after increasing by 18 per cent from 1983 to 1989, declined by 8 per cent between 1989 and 1995, and then jumped after that, for a net gain of 51 per cent between 1989 and 2001 and 78 per cent from 1983 to 2001. These increases were almost identical to those for median financial wealth. The bull market was largely responsible for the sharp growth in financial wealth between 1995 and 2001.

Median household income, based on Current Population Survey (CPS) data compiled by the US Census Bureau for the Bureau of Labor Statistics, after gaining 11 per cent between 1983 and 1989, grew by only 2.3 per cent from 1989 to 2001, for a net change of 14 per cent. In contrast, mean income rose by 16 per cent from 1983 to 1989 and by another 12 per cent from 1989 to 2001, for a total change of 30 per cent.

In sum, while household income virtually stagnated for the average American household over the 1990s, median net worth and especially median financial wealth grew strongly over this period.

WEALTH INEQUALITY SHOWS LITTLE CHANGE OVER THE 1990S

Table 4.2 also shows that wealth inequality, after rising steeply between 1983 and 1989, remained virtually unchanged from 1989 to 2001. The share of wealth held by the top 1 per cent rose by 3.6 percentage points from 1983 to 1989 and the Gini coefficient (a measure of overall inequality) increased from 0.80 to 0.83. Between 1989 and 2001, the share of the top percentile actually declined sharply, from 37.4 to 33.4 per cent, though this was almost exactly compensated for by an increase in the share of the next four per-centiles. As a result, the share of the top 5 per cent actually increased slightly, from 58.9 to 59.2 per cent, as did the share of the top quintile, from 83.5 to 84.4 per cent. The share of the fourth and middle quintiles also declined slightly, while that of the bottom 40 per cent increased somewhat, so that, overall, the Gini coefficient fell very slightly, from 0.832 to 0.826.

Table 4.2 Size distribution of wealth and income, 1983–2001

Year	Gini coefficient	Percentage share of wealth or income held by:								All
		Top 1.0%	Next 4.0%	Next 5.0%	Next 10.0%	Top 20.0%	4th 20.0%	3rd 20.0%	Bottom 40.0%	
Net worth[a]										
1983	0.799	33.8	22.3	12.1	13.1	81.3	12.6	5.2	0.9	100.0
1989	0.832	37.4	21.6	11.6	13.0	83.5	12.3	4.8	-0.7	100.0
1992	0.823	37.2	22.8	11.8	12.0	83.8	11.5	4.4	0.4	100.0
1995	0.828	38.5	21.8	11.5	12.1	83.9	11.4	4.5	0.2	100.0
1998	0.822	38.1	21.3	11.5	12.5	83.4	11.9	4.5	0.2	100.0
2001	0.826	33.4	25.8	12.3	12.9	84.4	11.3	3.9	0.3	100.0
Financial wealth[b]										
1983	0.893	42.9	25.1	12.3	11.0	91.3	7.9	1.7	-0.9	100.0
1989	0.926	46.9	23.9	11.6	11.0	93.4	7.4	1.7	-2.5	100.0
1992	0.903	45.6	25.0	11.5	10.2	92.3	7.3	1.5	-1.1	100.0
1995	0.914	47.2	24.6	11.2	10.1	93.0	6.9	1.4	-1.3	100.0
1998	0.893	47.3	21.0	11.4	11.2	90.9	8.3	1.9	-1.1	100.0
2001	0.888	39.7	27.8	12.3	11.4	91.3	7.8	1.7	-0.7	100.0
Income[c]										
1982	0.480	12.8	13.3	10.3	15.5	51.9	21.6	14.2	12.3	100.0
1988	0.521	16.6	13.3	10.4	15.2	55.6	20.6	13.2	10.7	100.0
1991	0.528	15.7	14.8	10.6	15.3	56.4	20.4	12.8	10.5	100.0
1994	0.518	14.4	14.5	10.4	15.9	55.1	20.6	13.6	10.7	100.0
1997	0.531	16.6	14.4	10.2	15.0	56.2	20.5	12.8	10.5	100.0
2000	0.562	20.0	15.2	10.0	13.5	58.6	19.0	12.3	10.1	100.0

Table 4.2 (continued)

		Addendum:		
	Total number of households (1000s)	Number of households (in 1000s) with net worth equal to or exceeding (1995 dollars):		
Year		1 million	5 million	10 million
1983	83 893	2411	247.0	66.5
1989	93 009	3024	296.6	64.9
1992	95 462	3104	277.4	41.6
1995	99 101	3015	474.1	190.4
1998	102 547	4783	755.5	239.4
2001	106 494	5892	1067.8	338.4
% change	26.9	144.4	332.3	408.9

Notes:
a. For the computation of percentile shares of net worth, households are ranked according to their net worth.
b. For percentile shares of financial wealth, households are ranked according to their financial wealth.
c. For percentile shares of income, households are ranked according to their income.

Sources: Author's computations from the 1983, 1989, 1992, 1995, 1998 and 2001 SCF.

Financial wealth is even more concentrated than net worth, with the richest 1 per cent (as ranked by financial wealth) owning 40 per cent of total household financial wealth in 2001 (compared to 33 per cent for net worth) and the top 20 per cent owning 91 per cent (compared to 84 per cent for net worth). However, the inequality of financial wealth shows a different time trend than net worth. The share of the top 1 per cent gained 4.0 percentage points and the Gini coefficient increased from 0.89 to 0.93 between 1983 and 1989 – trends mirroring those of net worth. In the ensuing 12 years, however, the share of the richest 1 per cent plummeted by 7 percentage points, the share of the top 5 per cent fell by 3 percentage points, and that of the top quintile by 2 percentage points. The share of the fourth quintile increased by 0.4 percentage points, the share of the middle quintile held its own, and that of the bottom two quintiles rose. As a result, the Gini coefficient fell from 0.93 in 1989 to 0.89 in 2001 and was actually slightly lower in 2001 than in 1983.

The top 1 per cent of families (as ranked by income and based on the SCF data) earned 20 per cent of total household income in 2000 and the top 20 per cent accounted for 59 per cent – large figures, but lower than the corresponding wealth shares. The time trend for income inequality also contrasts with those for net worth and financial wealth inequality. Income inequality increased sharply between 1982 and 1988, with the Gini coefficient rising from 0.48 to 0.52 and the share of the top 1 per cent from 12.8 to 16.6 per cent. There was then very little change between 1988 and 1997. While the share of the top 1 per cent remained at 16.6 per cent of total income, the share of the next 19 per cent increased by 0.6 percentage points and the share of the other quintiles lost, so that the Gini coefficient grew slightly, from 0.52 to 0.53. However, between 1997 and 2000, income inequality again surged, with the share of the top percentile rising by 3.4 percentage points, the shares of the other quintiles falling again, and the Gini index advancing from 0.53 to 0.56. As a result, the years from 1989 to 2001 saw almost the same degree of increase in income inequality as the 1983–89 period.[7]

Despite the stability in overall wealth inequality during the 1990s, the decade witnessed a near explosion in the number of very rich households (see Addendum to Table 4.2). The number of millionaires almost doubled between 1989 and 2001, the number of 'penta-millionaires' ($5 million or more) increased 3.5 times, and the number of 'deca-millionaires' ($10 million or more) grew more than fivefold. Much of the growth occurred between 1995 and 2001 and was directly related to the surge in stock prices.

Table 4.3 shows the absolute changes in wealth and income between 1983 and 1998. The results are even more striking. Over this period, the largest gains in relative terms were made by the wealthiest households. The top

Table 4.3 *Mean wealth holdings and income by wealth or income class, 1983–2001 (thousands of 2001 dollars)*

Variable	Top 1.0%	Next 4.0%	Next 5.0%	Next 10.0%	Top 20.0%	4th 20.0%	3rd 20.0%	Bottom 40.0%	All
Net worth[a]									
1983	7796	1289	560.8	302.8	939.3	145.2	60.3	5.1	231.0
2001	12 692	2453	937.4	490.3	1604.7	215.3	75.0	2.9	380.1
% change	62.8	90.2	67.2	61.9	70.8	48.3	24.4	-43.6	64.6
% of gain[d]	32.8	31.2	12.6	12.6	89.2	9.4	2.0	-0.6	100.0
Financial wealth[b]									
1983	6722	984	384.6	172.4	715.3	61.9	13.3	(6.9)	156.7
2001	14 075	1833	669.8	301.5	1388.4	102.7	21.5	(10.1)	298.5
% change	109.4	86.2	74.2	74.9	94.1	65.8	61.4	46.1	90.5
% of gain[d]	51.9	23.9	10.1	9.1	95.0	5.7	1.2	-0.9	101.0
Income[c]									
1982	655	169	105.1	78.9	132.2	55.2	36.1	14.7	51.0
2000	1117	224	139.7	102.3	186.8	69.3	44.3	17.9	67.2
% change	70.5	32.5	33.0	29.7	41.3	25.6	22.7	22.0	31.9
% of gain[d]	28.4	13.5	10.6	14.4	67.0	17.4	10.1	7.9	102.3

Notes:

a. For the computation of percentile shares of net worth, households are ranked according to their net worth.
b. For percentile shares of financial wealth, households are ranked according to their financial wealth.
c. For percentile shares of income, households are ranked according to their income.
d. The computation is performed by dividing the total increase in wealth of a given group by the total increase of wealth for all households over the period, under the assumption that the number of households in each group remains unchanged over the period. It should be noted that the households found in a given group (such as the top quintile) may be different in each year.

Sources: Author's computations from the 1983 and 2001 SCF.

1 per cent saw their average wealth (in 2001 dollars) rise by almost $5 million, or 63 per cent. The average wealth of the remaining part of the top quintile increased in the range of 62 to 90 per cent and the average wealth of the fourth quintile gained 48 per cent. While the middle quintile gained 24 per cent, the poorest 40 per cent lost 44 per cent. By 2001, their average wealth had fallen to $2900.

Another way of viewing this phenomenon is afforded by calculating the proportion of the total increase in real household wealth between 1983 and 2001 accruing to different wealth groups. This is computed by dividing the increase in total wealth of each percentile group by the total increase in household wealth, while holding constant the number of households in that group. If a group's wealth share remains constant over time, then the percentage of the total wealth growth received by that group will equal its share of total wealth. If a group's share of total wealth increases (or decreases) over time, then it will receive a percentage of the total wealth gain greater (or less) than its share in either year. However, it should be noted that, in these calculations, the households found in each group (say the top quintile) may be different in the two years.

The results indicate that the richest 1 per cent received about one-third of the total gain in marketable wealth over the period from 1983 to 2001. The next 4 per cent also received close to one-third of the total gain and the next 15 per cent received another quarter, so that the top quintile together accounted for 89 per cent of the total growth in wealth, while the bottom 80 per cent accounted for 11 per cent.

The pattern of results is similar for financial wealth. The average financial wealth of the richest 1 per cent more than doubled; that of the next richest 4 per cent grew by 86 per cent; and that of the next richest 15 per cent grew by about three-quarters. Altogether, the financial wealth of the top quintile gained 94 per cent. However, in the case of financial wealth, the fourth and third quintiles also showed substantial gains, of 66 and 61 per cent, respectively, and the bottom quintiles also showed positive growth. Of the total growth in financial wealth between 1983 and 2001, 52 per cent accrued to the top 1 per cent and 95 per cent to the top quintile, while the bottom 80 per cent collectively accounted for only 5 per cent.

A similar calculation using income data reveals that the greatest gains in real income over the period from 1982 to 2000 were households in the top 1 per cent of the income distribution, whose incomes grew by 71 per cent. Mean incomes increased by about a third for the next highest 9 per cent and by 30 per cent for the next highest 10 per cent. Groups in the bottom 80 per cent of the income distribution all experienced 25 per cent or less real growth in income. Of the total growth in real income between 1982 and 2000, 28 per cent was received by the top 1 per cent and 67 per cent by the top quintile, with the remaining 33 per cent distributed among the bottom 80 per cent.

These results indicate rather dramatically that, despite the stability of inequality of net worth and the decrease of financial wealth inequality during the 1990s, the growth in the economy during the period from 1983 to 2001 was concentrated in a surprisingly small part of the population – the top 20 per cent and particularly the top 1 per cent.

STOCKS REMAIN HIGHLY CONCENTRATED IN THE HANDS OF THE RICH

The portfolio composition of household wealth shows the forms in which households save. In 2001, owner-occupied housing was the most important household asset in the breakdown shown in Table 4.4, accounting for 28 per cent of total assets. However, net home equity (the value of the house minus any outstanding mortgage) amounted to only 19 per cent of total assets. Real estate, other than owner-occupied housing, comprised 10 per cent, and business equity another 17 per cent.

Demand deposits, time deposits, money market funds, CDs (certificates of deposit), and the cash surrender value of life insurance made up 9 per cent; pension accounts made up 12 per cent. Bonds and other financial securities amounted to 2 per cent; corporate stock, including mutual funds, came to 15 per cent; and trust equity to a little less than 5 per cent. Debt as a proportion of gross assets was 13 per cent, and the debt–equity ratio (the ratio of total household debt to net worth) was 0.14.

There have been some notable trends in the composition of household wealth over the period between 1983 and 2001. The first is that pension accounts rose from 1.5 to 12.3 per cent of total assets. This increase largely offset the decline in total liquid assets, from 17.4 to 8.8 per cent, so that it is reasonable to conclude that households have substituted tax-free pension accounts for taxable savings deposits.

The second trend is that gross housing wealth remained almost constant as a share of total assets over this period. Moreover, according to the SCF data, the homeownership rate (the per cent of households owning their own home, including mobile homes), after falling from 63.4 per cent in 1983 to 62.8 per cent in 1989, picked up to 67.7 per cent in 2001. However, net equity in owner-occupied housing has fallen almost continuously, from 23.8 per cent in 1983 to 18.2 per cent in 1998, though it did pick up to 18.8 per cent in 2001.

The difference between the two trends is attributable to the changing magnitude of mortgage debt on homeowner's property, which increased from 21 per cent in 1983 to 37 per cent in 1998 but then fell back to 33 per cent

Table 4.4 Composition of total household health, 1983–2001 (per cent of gross assets)

Wealth component	1983	1989	1992	1995	1998	2001
Principal residence (gross value)	30.1	30.2	29.8	30.4	29.0	28.2
Other real estate (gross value)[a]	14.9	14.0	14.7	11.0	10.0	9.8
Unincorporated business equity[b]	18.8	17.2	17.7	17.9	17.7	17.2
Liquid assets[c]	17.4	17.5	12.2	10.0	9.6	8.8
Pension accounts[d]	1.5	2.9	7.2	9.0	11.6	12.3
Financial securities[e]	4.2	3.4	5.1	3.8	1.8	2.3
Corporate stock and mutual funds	9.0	6.9	8.1	11.9	14.8	14.8
Net equity in personal trusts	2.6	3.1	2.7	3.2	3.8	4.8
Miscellaneous assets[f]	1.3	4.9	2.5	2.8	1.8	1.8
Total	100.0	100.0	100.0	100.0	100.0	100.0
Debt on principal residence	6.3	8.6	9.8	11.0	10.7	9.4
All other debt[g]	6.8	6.4	6.0	5.3	4.2	3.1
Total debt	13.1	15.0	15.7	16.3	15.0	12.5
Memo (selected ratios in %):						
Debt–equity ratio	15.1	17.6	18.7	19.4	17.6	14.3
Debt–income ratio	68.4	87.6	88.8	91.3	90.9	81.1
Net home equity–total assets[h]	23.8	21.6	20.1	19.5	18.2	18.8
Principal residence debt–house value	20.9	28.6	32.7	36.0	37.0	33.4
Stocks, directly or indirectly owned–total assets[i]	11.3	10.2	13.7	16.8	22.6	24.5

Notes:
a. In 2001, this equals the gross value of other residential real estate plus the net equity in non-residential real estate.
b. Net equity in unincorporated farm and non-farm businesses and closely-held corporations.
c. Checking accounts, savings accounts, time deposits, money market funds, certificates of deposits, and the cash surrender value of life insurance.
d. IRAs, Keogh plans, 401(k) plans, the accumulated value of defined contribution pension plans, and other retirement accounts.
e. Corporate bonds, government bonds (including savings bonds), open-market paper, and notes.
f. Gold and other precious metals, royalties, jewellery, antiques, furs, loans to friends and relatives, future contracts, and miscellaneous assets.
g. Mortgage debt on all real property except principal residence; credit card, instalment, and other consumer debt.
h. Ratio of gross value of principal residence less mortgage debt on principal residence to total assets.
i. Includes direct ownership of stock shares and indirect ownership through mutual funds, trusts, and IRAs, Keogh plans, 401(k) plans, and other retirement accounts.

Sources: Author's computations from the 1983, 1989, 1992, 1995, 1998 and 2001 SCF.

in 2001. Overall, indebtedness first increased, with the debt–equity ratio leaping from 15.1 per cent in 1983 to 19.4 per cent in 1995 before falling off to 17.6 per cent in 1998 and 14.3 per cent in 2001. Likewise, the ratio of debt to total income first surged from 68 per cent in 1983 to 91 per cent in 1995, levelled off in 1998, and then declined to 81 per cent in 2001. Moreover, as we saw above, the fraction of household recording zero or negative net worth jumped from 15.5 per cent in 1983 to 18.0 per cent in 1998 and then fell slightly to 17.6 per cent in 2001. However, if mortgage debt on principal residence is excluded, then the ratio of other debt to total assets fell off even more, from 6.8 per cent in 1983 to 3.1 per cent in 2001. One implication is that, over the 1990s, families have been using tax-sheltered mortgages and home equity loans to finance normal consumption rather than consumer loans and other forms of consumer debt.

The proportion of total assets in the form of other (nonhome) real estate fell off sharply, from 15 per cent in 1983 to 10 per cent in 2001, as did financial securities, from 4.2 to 2.3 per cent. Unincorporated business equity fell slightly as a share of gross wealth over this period. These declines were largely offset by a rise in the share of corporate stock in total assets, from 9.0 in 1983 to 14.8 per cent in 2001, reflecting the bull market in corporate equities. Still, in 2001 direct stock ownership ranked only third in total value in this breakdown, behind housing and business equity. However, if we include the value of stocks indirectly owned through mutual funds, trusts, IRAs, Keogh and 401(k) plans and other retirement accounts, then the share of total stocks owned shoots up to 25 per cent of total assets in 2001 – more than double the share in 1983.

This tabulation provides a picture of the average holdings of all families in the economy, but there are marked class differences in how middle-class families and the rich invest their wealth. As shown in Table 4.5, the richest 1 per cent of households (as ranked by wealth) invested almost 80 per cent of their savings in investment real estate, businesses, corporate stock and financial securities in 2001. Corporate stocks, either directly owned by the households or indirectly owned through mutual funds, trust accounts or various pension accounts, comprised 27 per cent by themselves. Housing accounted for only 8 per cent of their wealth, liquid assets another 6 per cent, and pension accounts another 6 per cent. Their ratio of debt to net worth was 2 per cent and their ratio of debt to income was 34 per cent.

Among the next richest 19 per cent of US households, housing comprised 27 per cent of their total assets, liquid assets another 9 per cent, and pension assets 16 per cent. Forty-six per cent of their assets took the form of investment assets – real estate, business equity, stocks and bonds – and 28 per cent was in the form of stocks directly or indirectly owned. Debt amounted to 9 per cent of their net worth and 77 per cent of their income.

Table 4.5   Composition of household wealth by wealth class, 2001
(per cent of gross assets)

Asset type	All households[a]	Top 1 %[a]	Next 19 %[a]	Middle 3 quintiles[a]
Principal residence	28.2	8.4	26.8	59.2
Liquid assets (bank deposits, money market funds, and cash surrender value of life insurance)	8.8	5.7	9.3	12.1
Pension accounts	12.3	5.5	16.5	12.7
Corporate stock, financial securities, mutual funds, and personal trusts	21.8	33.6	21.4	6.2
Unincorporated business equity	27.0	44.3	24.4	8.5
Other real estate				
Miscellaneous assets	1.8	2.6	1.7	1.2
Total assets	100.0	100.0	100.0	100.0
Memo (selected ratios in %):				
Debt/equity ratio	12.5	2.4	8.9	31.7
Debt/income ratio	81.1	33.6	76.9	100.3
All stocks/total assets[c]	24.5	27.4	27.8	12.6
Ownership rates (%)				
Principal residence	67.7	97.5	95.7	75.9
Mobile home	4.5	1.0	0.8	6.4
Other real estate	16.8	76.3	41.3	13.2
Vacation homes	5.7	35.0	13.9	4.4
Pension assets	52.2	89.3	82.7	52.9
Unincorporated business	11.9	71.9	31.9	7.9
Corporate stock, financial securities,[b] mutual funds and personal trusts	33.0	90.4	73.5	27.5
Stocks, directly or indirectly owned[c]	51.9	95.0	85.2	51.1
$5000 or more	40.6	94.8	83.3	39.1
$10 000 or more	35.9	94.1	82.0	32.7

Notes:
a.   Households are classified into wealth class according to their net worth. Brackets for 2001 are: top 1 per cent: net worth of $5 838 000 or more; next 19 per cent: net worth between $355 580 and $5 838 000; quintiles 2 to 4: net worth between $400 and $355 580.
b.   Financial securities exclude US government savings bonds in this tabulation.
c.   Includes direct ownership of stock shares and indirect ownership through mutual funds, Trusts, and IRAs, Keogh plans, 401(k) plans, and other retirement accounts.

Sources: Author's computations from the 2001 SCF.

In contrast, almost 60 per cent of the wealth of the middle three quintiles (60 per cent) of households was invested in their own home in 2001. Another 25 per cent went into monetary savings of one form or another and into pension accounts. Together, housing, liquid assets and pension assets accounted for 84 per cent of the total assets of the middle class. The remainder was about evenly split among nonhome real estate, business equity, and various financial securities and corporate stock. Stocks directly or indirectly owned amounted to only 13 per cent of their total assets. The ratio of debt to net worth was 32 per cent, much higher than for the richest 20 per cent, and their ratio of debt to income was 100 per cent, also higher than the top quintile.

Almost all households among the top 20 per cent of wealth holders owned their own home, in comparison to 76 per cent of households in the middle three quintiles. Though this homeownership rate looks large, 6 per cent of households in the middle three quintiles reported having a mobile home as their primary residence. Three-quarters of very rich households (in the top percentile) owned some other form of real estate (35 per cent owned a vacation home), compared to 41 per cent of rich households (those in the next 19 per cent of the distribution) and 13 per cent of households in the middle 60 per cent. Almost 90 per cent of the very rich owned some form of pension asset, compared to 83 per cent of the rich and 53 per cent of the middle. A somewhat startling 72 per cent of the very rich reported owning their own business. The comparable figures are 32 per cent among the rich and only 8 per cent of the middle class.

Among the very rich, 90 per cent held corporate stock, mutual funds, financial securities or a trust fund, in comparison to 74 per cent of the rich and 28 per cent of the middle. Ninety-five per cent of the very rich reported owning stock either directly or indirectly, compared to 85 per cent of the rich and 51 per cent of the middle. If we exclude small holdings of stock, then the ownership rates drop off sharply among the middle three quintiles, from 51 per cent to 39 per cent for stocks worth $5000 or more and to 33 per cent for stocks worth $10 000 or more.

Another way to portray differences between middle-class households and the rich is to compute the share of total assets of different types held by each group (see Table 4.6). In 2001 the richest 1 per cent of households held half of all outstanding stock, financial securities, trust equity and business equity, and 35 per cent of nonhome real estate. The top 10 per cent of families as a group accounted for about 90 per cent of stock shares, bonds, trusts and business equity, and about 80 per cent of nonhome real estate. Moreover, despite the fact that 52 per cent of households owned stock shares either directly or indirectly through mutual funds, trusts or various pension accounts, the richest 10 per cent of households accounted for

Table 4.6 Per cent of total assets held by wealth class, 2001

Asset type	Top 1.0%[d]	Next 9.0%[d]	Bottom 90.0%[d]	All	Share of top 10%					
					1983	1989	1992	1995	1998	2001
Investment assets										
Stocks and mutual funds	44.1	40.4	15.5	100.0	90.4	86.0	86.3	88.4	85.1	84.5
Financial securities	58.0	30.6	11.3	100.0	82.9	87.1	91.3	89.8	84.1	88.7
Trusts	46.3	40.4	13.3	100.0	95.4	87.9	87.9	88.5	90.8	86.7
Business equity	57.3	32.3	10.4	100.0	89.9	89.8	91.0	91.7	91.7	89.6
Non-home real estate	34.9	43.6	21.5	100.0	76.3	79.6	83.0	78.7	74.9	78.5
Total for group	47.8	37.7	14.5	100.0	85.6	85.7	87.6	87.5	86.2	85.5
Stocks, directly or indirectly owned[a]	33.5	43.4	23.1	100.0	89.7	80.8	78.7	81.9	78.7	76.9
Housing, liquid assets, pension assets, and debt										
Principal residence	8.9	28.0	63.0	100.0	34.2	34.0	36.0	31.7	35.2	37.0
Deposits[b]	21.7	35.5	42.8	100.0	52.9	61.5	59.7	62.3	51.0	57.2
Life insurance	12.5	33.5	54.0	100.0	33.6	44.6	45.0	44.9	52.8	46.0
Pension accounts[c]	13.3	47.0	39.6	100.0	67.5	50.5	62.3	62.3	59.8	60.4
Total for group	11.9	34.0	54.1	100.0	41.0	43.9	45.2	42.5	44.0	45.9
Total debt	5.8	20.1	74.1	100.0	31.8	29.4	37.5	28.3	27.0	25.9

Notes:

a. Includes direct ownership of stock shares and indirect ownership through mutual funds, trusts, and IRAs, Keogh plans, 401(k) plans, and other retirement accounts.

b. Includes demand deposits, savings deposits, time deposits, money market funds, and certificates of deposit.

c. IRAs, Keogh plans, 401(k) plans, the accumulated value of defined contribution pension plans, and other retirement accounts.

d. Households are classified into wealth class according to their net worth. Brackets for 2001 are: top 1 per cent: net worth of $5 838 000 or more; next 9 per cent: net worth between $714 500 and $5 838 000; bottom 90 per cent: net worth less than $714 500.

Sources: Author's computations from the 1983, 1989, 1992, 1995, 1998 and 2001 SCF.

77 per cent of the total value of these stocks, only slightly less than this group's 85 per cent share of directly owned stocks and mutual funds.

In contrast, owner-occupied housing, deposits, life insurance and pension accounts were more evenly distributed among households. The bottom 90 per cent of households accounted for 63 per cent of the value of owner-occupied housing, about half of deposits and life insurance cash value, and 40 per cent of the value of pension accounts. Debt was the most evenly distributed component of household wealth, with the bottom 90 per cent of households responsible for 74 per cent of total indebtedness.

There was relatively little change between 1983 and 2001 in the concentration of asset ownership, with three exceptions. First, the share of total stocks and mutual funds held by the richest 10 per cent of households declined from 90 to 85 per cent over this period, and their share of stocks directly or indirectly owned from 90 to 77 per cent. Second, the proportion of total pension accounts held by the top 10 per cent fell from 68 per cent in 1983 to 51 per cent in 1989, reflecting the growing use of IRAs by middle-income families, and then rebounded to 60 per cent in 2001 from the expansion of 401(k) plans and their adoption by high-income earners. Third, the share of total debt held by the top 10 per cent also fell from 32 to 26 per cent.

THE RACIAL DIVIDE GROWS IN THE LATE 1990S

Striking differences are found in the wealth holdings of different racial and ethnic groups. In Tables 4.7 and 4.8, households are divided into three groups: non-Hispanic whites, non-Hispanic African Americans and Hispanics.[8] In 2001, while the ratio of mean incomes between non-Hispanic white and non-Hispanic black households was a very low 0.48 and the ratio of median incomes was 0.57, the ratios of mean and median wealth holdings were even lower, at 0.14 and 0.10, respectively, and those of financial wealth still lower, at 0.12 and 0.03, respectively.[9] The home-ownership rate for black households was 47 per cent in 2001, less than two-thirds the rate among whites, and the percentage of black households with zero or negative net worth stood at 30.9, more than double the corresponding percentage among whites.

Between 1982 and 2000, while the average real income of non-Hispanic white households increased by 37 per cent and the median by 13 per cent, the former rose by only 23 per cent for non-Hispanic black households and the latter by 15 per cent. As a result, the ratio of mean income slipped from 0.54 in 1982 to 0.48 in 2000, while the ratio of median income rose slightly, from 0.56 to 0.57. Between 1983 and 2001, average net worth

Table 4.7   *Family income and wealth for non-Hispanic whites and non-Hispanic African Americans, 1983–2001 (thousands of 2001 dollars)*

Households[a]	Means			Medians		
	Non-Hispanic whites	Non-Hispanic African Americans	Ratio	Non-Hispanic whites	Non-Hispanic African Americans	Ratio
Income						
1982	55.4	29.8	0.54	39.0	21.7	0.56
1988	60.6	27.0	0.45	40.4	15.3	0.38
1991	60.3	30.2	0.50	37.1	21.0	0.57
1994	55.4	26.7	0.48	37.2	19.8	0.53
1997	62.8	30.9	0.49	40.2	21.7	0.54
2000	75.9	36.8	0.48	44.0	25.0	0.57
Net worth						
1983	269.9	50.8	0.19	77.7	5.2	0.07
1989	319.3	53.5	0.17	92.3	2.4	0.03
1992	309.0	57.4	0.19	77.4	13.0	0.17
1995	281.6	47.4	0.17	70.9	8.5	0.12
1998	348.7	63.3	0.18	88.7	10.9	0.12
2001	465.8	66.3	0.14	106.4	10.7	0.10
Financial wealth						
1983	198.9	25.6	0.13	21.6	0.0	0.00
1989	241.4	26.2	0.11	29.2	0.0	0.00
1992	237.9	32.7	0.14	23.8	0.2	0.01
1995	219.0	24.7	0.11	21.0	0.2	0.01
1998	276.8	40.8	0.15	40.8	1.3	0.03
2001	369.7	43.2	0.12	42.1	1.1	0.03

Table 4.7 (continued)

Households[a]	Means			Medians		
	Non-Hispanic whites	Non-Hispanic African Americans	Ratio	Non-Hispanic whites	Non-Hispanic African Americans	Ratio
Homeownership rate (%)						
1983	68.1	44.3	0.65			
1989	69.3	41.7	0.60			
1992	69.0	48.5	0.70			
1995	69.4	46.8	0.67			
1998	71.8	46.3	0.67			
2001	74.1	47.4	0.64			
% households with zero or negative net worth						
1983	11.3	34.1	3.01			
1989	12.1	40.7	3.38			
1992	13.8	31.5	2.28			
1995	15.0	31.3	2.09			
1998	14.8	27.4	2.09			
2001	13.1	30.9	2.35			

Note: a. Households are divided into four racial/ethnic groups: (i) non-Hispanic whites; (ii) non-Hispanic blacks; (iii) Hispanics; and (iv) American Indians, Asians, and others. For 1995, 1998 and 2001, the classification scheme does not explicitly indicate non-Hispanic whites and non-Hispanic blacks for the first two categories so that some Hispanics may have classified themselves as either whites or blacks.

Sources: Author's computations from the 1983, 1989, 1992, 1995, 1998 and 2001 SCF.

Table 4.8   *Family income and wealth for non-Hispanic whites and*
Hispanics, 1983–2001 (thousands of 2001 dollars)

	Means			Medians		
	Non-Hispanic whites	Hispanics	Ratio	Non-Hispanic whites	Hispanics	Ratio
Income						
1982	55.4	33.5	0.60	39.0	25.8	0.66
1988	60.6	27.6	0.46	40.4	19.4	0.48
1991	60.3	28.5	0.47	37.1	19.8	0.53
1994	55.4	35.9	0.65	37.2	25.6	0.69
1997	62.8	33.8	0.54	40.2	25.0	0.62
2000	75.9	37.6	0.50	44.0	24.0	0.55
Net worth						
1983	269.9	43.9	0.16	77.7	3.0	0.04
1989	319.3	52.6	0.16	92.3	1.9	0.02
1992	309.0	68.7	0.22	77.4	4.7	0.06
1995	281.6	59.6	0.21	70.9	5.8	0.08
1998	348.7	86.1	0.25	88.7	3.3	0.04
2001	465.8	80.1	0.17	106.4	3.0	0.03
Financial wealth						
1983	198.9	13.0	0.07	21.6	0.0	0.00
1989	241.4	25.7	0.11	29.2	0.0	0.00
1992	237.9	44.1	0.19	23.8	0.0	0.00
1995	219.0	34.0	0.16	21.0	0.0	0.00
1998	276.8	54.8	0.20	40.8	0.0	0.00
2001	369.7	51.5	0.14	42.1	0.2	0.01
Homeownership rate (%)						
1983	68.1	32.6	0.48			
1989	69.3	39.8	0.57			
1992	69.0	43.1	0.62			
1995	69.4	44.4	0.64			
1998	71.8	44.2	0.64			
2001	74.1	44.3	0.60			
% households with zero or negative net worth						
1983	11.3	40.3	3.55			
1989	12.1	39.9	3.31			
1992	13.8	41.2	2.98			
1995	15.0	38.3	2.56			
1998	14.8	36.2	2.56			
2001	13.1	35.3	2.69			

Note: See Table 4.7 for details on racial/ethnic categories.

Sources: Author's computations from the 1983, 1989, 1992, 1995, 1998 and 2001 SCF.

(in 2001 dollars) rose by a whopping 73 per cent for whites but only by 31 per cent for black households, so that the net worth ratio fell from 0.19 to 0.14. Most of the slippage occurred between 1998 and 2001, when white net worth surged by a spectacular 34 per cent and black net worth advanced by only a respectable 5 per cent. Indeed, mean net worth growth among black households was slightly higher in the 1998–2001 years, at 1.55 per cent per year, than in the preceding 15 years, at 1.47 per cent per year. The difference in the 1998–2001 period was the huge increase in household wealth among white households. In the case of median wealth, the black–white ratio first increased from 7 to 12 per cent between 1983 and 1998, and then diminished to 10 per cent in 2001. In this case, median wealth for white households grew by 20 per cent between 1998 and 2001, but declined in absolute terms by 2 per cent among black households.

Average financial wealth also increased somewhat more for black than white households between 1983 and 1998, so that the ratio rose from 13 to 15 per cent. However, between 1998 and 2001, mean financial wealth among white households also surged by 34 per cent but inched up only 6 per cent among black households, so that the ratio dwindled back to 0.12 – even lower than in 1983. The median financial wealth of non-Hispanic black households also increased, from virtually zero in 1983 to a positive $1100 in 2001, and the corresponding ratio also grew, from zero to 3 per cent.

The homeownership rate of black households grew from 44.3 to 47.4 per cent between 1983 and 2001, but relative to white households, the home-ownership rate first increased from a ratio of 0.65 in 1983 to 0.67 in 1998, then slipped to 0.64 in 2001. The change over the last three years primarily reflects a big jump of 2.3 percentage points in the white homeownership rate. In contrast, the percentage of black households reporting zero or negative net worth fell from 34.1 per cent in 1983 to 27.4 per cent in 1998 (and likewise declined relative to white households), but then retreated to 30.9 per cent in 2001 (and also rose relative to the corresponding rate for white households).[10]

The picture is quite similar for Hispanics (Table 4.8). The ratios of mean and median income between Hispanics and non-Hispanic whites in 2001 were 0.50 and 0.55, respectively – about the same as those between African American and white households. The ratio of mean net worth was 0.17 and the ratio of mean financial wealth 0.14, both slightly higher than the corresponding ratios between black and white households. However, the ratios of medians were 0.03 and 0.01, respectively, which were lower than those between blacks and whites. The Hispanic homeownership rate was 44 per cent, less than that of non-Hispanic black households, and 35 per cent of Hispanic households reported zero or negative wealth, compared to 31 per cent of African Americans.

Progress among Hispanic households over the period from 1983 to 2001 is also a mixed story. Mean household income for Hispanics advanced a bit between 1983 and 2001, while median income actually declined slightly. As a result, the ratio of mean income dropped from 60 to 50 per cent and that of median income from 66 to 55 per cent. Between 1983 and 1998, mean wealth almost doubled for Hispanic households and mean financial wealth grew more than four-fold. However, between 1989 and 2001, both declined in absolute terms. As a result, the ratio of mean net worth climbed from 16 per cent in 1983 to 25 per cent in 1998, then tumbled to 17 per cent in 2001; the ratio of mean financial wealth jumped from 7 to 20 per cent between 1983 and 1998, then fell off to 14 per cent in 2001. Median wealth among Hispanics remained largely unchanged, as did median financial wealth (at virtually zero), so that the ratio of both median wealth and median financial wealth between Hispanics and non-Hispanic whites stayed pretty much the same. On the other hand, the homeownership rate among Hispanic households surged from 33 to 44 per cent between 1983 and 2001, and the percentage with zero or negative net worth fell from 40 to 35 per cent.

What is also disturbing is that, even in 2001, the respective wealth gaps between African Americans and Hispanics on the one hand and non-Hispanic whites on the other were still much greater than the corresponding income gap. While the income ratios were of the order of 50 to 55 per cent, the wealth ratios were of the order of 12 to 17 per cent. Median financial wealth among non-Hispanic black and Hispanic households was still virtually zero in 2001, and the per cent with zero or negative net worth was around a third, in contrast to 13 per cent among non-Hispanic white households (a difference that appears to mirror the gap in poverty rates). Moreover, we may speculate that blacks and Hispanics were left out of the wealth surge of the years 1998 to 2001 because of relatively low stock ownership (see the section below entitled, 'Trends in Stock Ownership, 1983–2001' for more details).[11]

THE YOUNG ARE GETTING POORER

As shown in Table 4.9, the cross-sectional age–wealth profiles of 1983, 1989, 1992, 1995, 1998 and 2001 generally follow the predicted hump-shaped pattern of the life-cycle model (see, for example, Modigliani and Brumberg 1954). Mean wealth increases with age up to age 65 or so, and then falls off. Financial wealth has an almost identical profile, though the peak is generally somewhat higher than for net worth. Homeownership rates also have a similar profile, though the fall-off after the peak age is

Table 4.9 Age–wealth profiles and homeownership rates by age, 1983–2001

Age	1983	1989	1992	1995	1998	2001
Mean net worth (ratio to overall mean)						
Overall	1.00	1.00	1.00	1.00	1.00	1.00
Under 35	0.21	0.29	0.20	0.16	0.22	0.19
35–44	0.71	0.72	0.71	0.65	0.68	0.64
45–54	1.53	1.50	1.42	1.39	1.27	1.25
55–64	1.67	1.58	1.82	1.81	1.91	1.86
65–74	1.93	1.61	1.59	1.71	1.68	1.72
75 and over	1.05	1.26	1.20	1.32	1.12	1.20
Mean financial wealth (ratio to overall mean)						
Overall	1.00	1.00	1.00	1.00	1.00	1.00
Under 35	0.17	0.28	0.18	0.14	0.21	0.19
35–44	0.59	0.68	0.69	0.62	0.67	0.61
45–54	1.53	1.48	1.45	1.43	1.31	1.27
55–64	1.72	1.60	1.89	1.86	1.99	1.94
65–74	2.12	1.69	1.60	1.75	1.66	1.74
75 and over	1.10	1.27	1.14	1.26	1.00	1.11
Homeownership rate (%)						
Overall	63.4	62.8	64.1	64.7	66.3	67.7
Under 35	38.7	36.3	36.8	37.9	39.2	40.2
35–44	68.4	64.1	64.4	64.7	66.7	67.6
45–54	78.2	75.1	75.5	75.4	74.5	76.1
55–64	77.0	79.2	77.9	82.3	80.6	83.2
65–74	78.3	78.1	78.8	79.4	81.7	82.5
75 and over	69.4	70.2	78.1	72.5	76.9	76.2

Note: Households are classified according to the age of the householder.

Sources: Author's computations from the 1983, 1989, 1992, 1995, 1998, and 2001 SCF.

much more attenuated than for the wealth numbers. In 2001, the wealth of elderly households (age 65 and over) averaged 67 per cent higher than the nonelderly and their homeownership rate was 15 percentage points higher.

Despite the apparent similarity in the profiles, there have been notable shifts in the relative wealth holdings of age groups between 1983 and 2001. The relative wealth of the youngest age group (under 35 years of age) expanded from 21 per cent of the overall mean in 1983 to 29 per cent in 1989, plummeted to 16 per cent in 1995, but rebounded to 19 per cent in 2001; the relative wealth of households between 35 and 44 of age, after rising slightly from 71 per cent in 1983 to 72 per cent in 1989, dropped to

65 per cent in 1995 and then to 64 per cent in 2001. In contrast, the wealth of the oldest age group (age 75 and over) gained substantially, from only 5 per cent above the mean in 1983 to 32 per cent in 1995, but then fell back to 20 per cent in 2001. Results for financial wealth are very similar. The financial wealth of the youngest age group, after climbing from 17 to 28 per cent of the overall mean from 1983 to 1989, declined to 19 per cent in 2001, while that of the oldest age group rose from 10 per cent above the mean in 1983 to 26 per cent above the mean in 1995, then fell back to 11 per cent above the mean in 2001.

Changes in homeownership rates tend to mirror these trends. While the overall ownership rate increased from 63.4 to 67.7 per cent between 1983 and 2001, the share of households in the youngest age group owning their own home increased by only 1.5 percentage points. It fell from 68.4 to 67.6 per cent for those between 35 and 44 years of age, and from 78.2 to 76.1 per cent for those between 45 and 54 years of age. The three oldest age groups showed increases, particularly households ages 75 and over, whose home-ownership rate grew by almost 7 percentage points. The statistics point to a clear shifting of asset ownership away from younger towards older households between 1983 and 2001 – particularly from 1989 to 1995.

Another dimension is afforded in Table 4.10, which considers the relative wealth positions of families defined by both age and parental status. It is first of note that childless families were much wealthier than families with children. In 1983, among married couples under the age of 65, the mean net worth of the former group was twice that of the latter; the former's financial wealth was about 2.5 times greater; and their debt–equity ratio was half as great, though their homeownership rate was about the same. Among households headed by females, the relative statistics are very similar: mean wealth twice as high; mean financial wealth three times as high; a debt–equity ratio two-thirds as great; and a homeownership rate slightly higher. Moreover, in comparison to married couples age 65 and over, the relative wealth position of families with children was even lower in relative terms. Part of these differences is due to the fact that childless households are, on average, older than those with children and therefore tend to have higher incomes and to have had more time to accumulate assets. Another likely reason is that raising children absorbs financial resources and thus reduces household savings.

However, according to the calculations shown in Table 4.10, the relative position of married couples with children has improved in terms of wealth since the early 1980s. From 1983 to 2001, average net worth (in real terms) climbed by 93 per cent among married couples with children, but rose by only 46 per cent among nonelderly married couples without

Table 4.10   *Mean wealth for households with and without children, 1983 and 2001 (thousands of 2001 dollars)*

	1983	2001	% change 1983– 2001	Percentage point change 1983–2001
Net worth				
All households	231.0	380.1	64.6	
Married couples, under 65:				
a. with children	191.8	370.3	93.1	
b. without children	373.3	544.9	46.0	
Female head, under 65				
a. with children	52.2	61.2	17.3	
b. without children	112.6	158.9	41.1	
65 and over, married	552.5	813.8	47.3	
Financial wealth				
All households	167.6	298.5	78.1	
Married couple, under 65				
a. with children	122.4	289.9	136.9	
b. without children	283.3	442.2	56.1	
Female head, under 65				
a. with children	24.6	41.2	67.4	
b. without children	78.7	115.8	47.2	
65 and over, married	451.3	641.0	42.0	
Debt/equity ratio (%)				
All households	15.1	14.3		–0.8
Married couple, under 65				
a. with children	27.8	25.1		–2.7
b. without children	13.7	13.4		–0.3
Female head, under 65				
a. with children	33.6	44.4		10.8
b. without children	23.6	19.9		–3.7
65 and over, married	2.4	3.3		0.9
Homeownership rate (%)				
All households	63.4	67.7		4.3
Married couple, under 65				
a. with children	73.2	76.3		3.1
b. without children	75.3	76.1		0.8
Female head, under 65				
a. with children	39.6	38.3		–1.3
b. without children	41.5	50.8		9.3
65 and over, married	84.1	89.1		5.0

Note: Households are classified according to the presence of children in the household under the age of 18 and by age group according to the age of the householder.

Sources: Author's computations from the 1983 and 2001 SCF.

children, and by 47 per cent among elderly families. Among female heads under the age of 65, average wealth also grew, by 41 per cent for those without children, and by only 17 per cent among those with children. The results are quite similar for financial wealth, with its average value rising much more among married couples with children than among married couples without children (both elderly and nonelderly). In this case, average financial wealth rose somewhat more among female-headed families with children than among female heads without children. Still, by 2001 both average net worth and financial wealth were still considerably lower among married couples with children than among both elderly and nonelderly married couples without children, and less among families headed by females with children than families without children.

Indebtedness (relative to net worth) declined somewhat more for married couples under age 65 with children than couples under age 65 without children, while indebtedness increased somewhat for married couples age 65 and over. The debt–equity ratio actually fell among female-headed families without children, while it grew sharply among female heads with children. Still, by 2001 the debt–equity ratio was about twice as great for nonelderly married couples with children as those without children, and much higher among female heads with children than those who were childless. Indebtedness was by far the lowest among the elderly.

Between 1983 and 2001, the homeownership rate rose by 3.1 percentage points among nonelderly married couples with children and by only 0.8 percentage points among nonelderly married couples without children, and by 2001 it was actually slightly greater for the former than the latter. On the other hand, the homeownership rate fell among female-headed families under age 65 with children, but rose substantially among female-headed families under age 65 without children, so that the gap widened from 2 percentage points in 1983 to 13 percentage points in 2001. The homeownership rate was by far the highest among elderly married couples in 2001.

One may speculate why families with children have done better, in both relative and absolute terms, with regard to their wealth holdings over the period from 1983 to 2001. One reason is that in 2001 families with children tended to be older, on average, than in 1983 and to have fewer children. Another possible reason is that such families have received financial help from their parents. Elderly families, as is evident, have considerably greater financial resources than the nonelderly and it is quite likely that they have transferred wealth to their (grown) children, particularly those with children of their own, in the form of gifts and through bequests.

THE RELATION BETWEEN HOUSEHOLD INCOME AND WEALTH GAINS IS A MIXED BAG

Another perspective is afforded by looking at average wealth holdings by income class. As shown in Table 4.11, households are divided into those under age 65 and those 65 or over because the elderly tend to accumulate a large amount of wealth (see Table 4.10), but after retirement tend to have lower incomes than younger families. Lumping the two groups together might induce a spurious correlation between income and wealth gains due to age.

Wealth and income are strongly correlated, with mean wealth rising monotonically with income for each age group and in each of the five years. It is also of note that, among the nonelderly, only the top income class reported mean net worth exceeding the national average, while the top three income classes among the elderly did.

Among the nonelderly, there is a very clear relation between income level and wealth gains over the 1983–2001 period, with greater wealth gains the higher the income class. Among those in the lowest income class (under $15000), net worth actually declined in real terms. Middle-income families ($15000–$49999) enjoyed only a very modest gain in net worth; the upper middle class ($50000–$74999) saw their net worth rise by 27 per cent; and those in the top income class saw gains of 33 per cent.

The correspondence is less clear among elderly households. By far the largest wealth gains were found among the middle class ($25000–$49999), followed in turn by the lowest two income classes, upper middle income households ($50000–$74999), and lastly, by the top income class.

TRENDS IN STOCK OWNERSHIP, 1983–2001

Tables 4.12 and 4.13 report on overall stock ownership trends from 1983 to 2001. The proportion of households that owned corporate stock shares directly declined a bit between 1983 and 1989, from 13.7 to 13.1 per cent, while the share of households that owned any stocks or mutual funds plunged over these years, from 24.4 to 19.9 per cent.[12] In contrast, the share of households owning stocks and mutual funds worth $5000 or more (in 1995 dollars) was stable over this period; and, indeed, the proportion with holdings of $10000 or more and with $25000 or more actually rose over this period. These changes over the 1983–89 period might reflect the steep drop in the stock market in 1987 and the consequent exit of small fund holders during and after 1987. Yet, despite a 62 per cent real increase in stock prices (as measured by the Standard & Poor's 500 Index), stocks plus

Table 4.11 Mean household net worth by income class and age class, 1983–2001 (thousands of 2001 dollars)

Income class (1995 $)	Mean net worth						% change		
	1983	1989	1992	1995	1998	2001	1983–89	1989–2001	1983–2001
All	231.0	264.6	257.3	237.7	293.6	380.1	14.6	43.7	64.6
Age under 65	197.7	230.5	226.3	201.9	260.8	333.2	16.6	44.5	68.6
Under $15 000	36.6	24.2	30.1	37.0	34.8	31.0	−34.0	28.4	−15.2
$15 000–$24 999	57.8	83.0	51.2	58.4	45.8	62.5	43.7	−24.7	8.2
$25 000–$49 999	101.1	120.4	92.1	89.9	88.5	106.9	19.0	−11.2	5.7
$50 000–$74 999	190.9	199.6	182.2	197.0	190.9	241.8	4.5	21.2	26.7
$75 000 or over	959.8	960.8	1081.8	899.8	920.0	1277.8	0.1	33.0	33.1
Age 65 or over	370.9	387.6	367.7	365.5	414.9	555.4	4.5	43.3	49.7
Under $15 000	63.6	64.8	68.4	85.3	84.1	84.1	1.9	29.8	32.4
$15 000–$24 999	175.8	191.9	173.7	157.8	185.2	219.5	9.1	14.4	24.9
$25 000–$49 999	320.4	343.4	363.5	314.1	318.7	481.3	7.2	40.1	50.2
$50 000–$74 999	648.7	821.3	718.1	691.0	523.5	714.3	26.6	−13.0	10.1
$75 000 or over	3023.4	3144.0	3133.8	2800.4	2223.6	3048.1	4.0	−3.1	0.8

Note: Households are classified according to the age of the householder.

Sources: Authors computations from the 1983, 1989, 1992, 1995, 1998 and 2001 SCF.

Table 4.12   Per cent of households owning stock, 1983 and 1989

Stock type	1983	1989	1983–89
Direct stock holdings only	13.7	13.1	
Stocks and mutual funds			
Any holdings	24.4	19.9	
Holdings worth $5000 or more[a]	14.5	14.6	
Holdings worth $10 000 or more[a]	10.8	12.3	
Holdings worth $25 000 or more[a]	6.2	8.4	
Memo:			
Stocks plus mutual funds as % of total assets	9.0	6.9	
Percentage change in S&P 500 Index, in constant dollars over period			61.7

Note: a. In 1995 dollars.

Sources: Author's computations from the 1983 and 1989 SCF.

mutual funds as a share of total household asset actually declined from 9.0 per cent in 1983 to 6.9 per cent in 1989.

In contrast, the years 1989 to 2001 saw a substantial increase in stock ownership (see Table 4.13). The share of households with direct ownership of stock climbed from 13.1 per cent in 1989 to 21.3 per cent in 2001, while the share of households with some stock owned, either outright or indirectly through mutual funds, trusts or various pension accounts, surged from 31.7 to 51.9 per cent. Much of the increase was fuelled by the growth in pension accounts such as IRAs and Keogh and 401(k) plans. Between 1989 and 2001, the share of households owning stock through a pension account more than doubled, accounting for the bulk of the overall increase in stock ownership. Indirect ownership of stocks through mutual funds also greatly expanded over 1989–2001, from 5.9 to 16.7 per cent, as did indirect ownership through trust funds, from 1.6 to 5.1 per cent. All told, the share of households with indirect ownership of stocks more than doubled, from 23.5 per cent in 1989 to 47.7 per cent in 2001.

Despite the overall gains in stock ownership, only slightly more than half of all households had any stake in the stock market by 2001. Moreover, many of these families had only a minor stake. In 2001, while 52 per cent of households owned some stock, only 40 per cent had total stock holdings worth $5000 or more (in 1995 dollars); only 35 per cent owned $10 000 or more of stock; and only 27 per cent owned $25 000 or more of stocks. However, direct plus indirect ownership of stocks as a per cent of total

Table 4.13   Per cent of households owning stock, 1989–2001

Stock type	1989	1992	1995	1998	2001	1989–2001
Direct stock holdings only	13.1	14.8	15.2	19.2	21.3	
Indirect stock holdings only	23.5	29.3	34.8	43.4	47.7	
Through mutual funds	5.9	8.4	11.3	15.2	16.7	
Through pension accounts	19.5	24.8	29.2	37.4	41.4	
Through trust funds	1.6	1.2	1.9	2.4	5.1	
All stock holdings[a]						
Any holdings	31.7	37.2	40.4	48.2	51.9	
Stock worth $5000 or more[b]	22.6	27.3	29.5	36.3	40.1	
Stock worth $10 000 or more[b]	18.5	21.8	23.9	31.8	35.1	
Stock worth $25 000 or more[b]	10.5	13.1	16.6	24.3	27.1	
Memo:						
Direct plus indirect stocks as % of total assets	10.2	13.7	16.8			
Percentage change in S&P 500 Index, in constant dollars over period						171.4

Notes:
a.   Includes direct ownership of stock shares and indirect ownership through mutual
     funds, trusts, and IRAs, Keogh plans, 401(k) plans, and other retirement accounts.
b.   In 1995 dollars.

Sources: Author's computations from the 1989, 1992, 1995, 1998 and 2001 SCF.

household assets did more than double over these years, from 10.2 in 1989 to 24.5 in 2001. This increase may reflect in large measure the 171 per cent surge in stock prices over these years.

Stock ownership is also highly skewed by wealth and income class. As shown in Table 4.14, 95 per cent of the very rich (the top 1 per cent) reported owning stock either directly or indirectly in 2001, compared to 49 per cent of the middle quintile and 21 per cent of the poorest 20 per cent. While 94 per cent of the very rich also reported stocks worth $10 000 or more, only 31 per cent of the middle quintile and less than 3 per cent of the bottom quintile did so. The top 1 per cent of households owned 34 per cent of all stocks, the top 5 per cent over 60 per cent, the top 10 per cent over three-quarters, and the top quintile almost 90 per cent.

Stock ownership also trails off by income class (see Table 4.15). Whereas 94 per cent of households in the top 2.7 per cent of income recipients (those who earned $250 000 or more) owned stock in 2001, 49 per cent of the middle class (incomes between $25 000 and $50 000), 26 per cent of the

Table 4.14   Concentration of stock ownership by wealth class, 2001

Wealth class	% households owning stock[a] worth more than:			% stock owned	
	Zero	$4999[b]	$9999[b]	Shares	Cumulative
Top 1%	95.0	94.8	94.1	33.5	33.5
Next 4%	93.7	93.2	92.5	28.8	62.3
Next 5%	89.3	88.2	87.4	14.6	76.9
Next 10%	79.8	76.2	74.3	12.4	89.3
2nd quintile	69.0	61.3	55.1	7.8	97.1
3rd quintile	48.9	37.6	31.0	2.2	99.3
4th quintile	35.5	16.0	8.9	0.5	99.8
Bottom quintile	20.7	4.7	2.5	0.2	100.0
All	51.9	40.6	35.9	100.0	

Notes:
a.   Includes direct ownership of stock shares and indirect ownership through mutual
     funds, trusts, IRAs, Keogh plans, 401(k) plans, and other retirement accounts.
b.   In 2001 dollars.

Source: Author's computations from the 2001 SCF.

Table 4.15   Concentration of stock ownership by income class, 2001

Income level	Share of households	% households owning stock[a] worth more than:			% stock owned	
		Zero	$4999[b]	$9999[b]	Shares	Cumulative
$250 000 or more	2.7	93.9	91.5	90.5	40.6	40.6
$100 000–$249 999	11.3	88.3	84.7	80.0	27.9	68.6
$75 000–$99 999	9.3	79.8	70.0	64.3	8.9	77.4
$50 000–$74 999	17.5	73.1	56.6	49.7	11.8	89.3
$25 000–$49 999	27.7	49.2	33.0	26.7	8.3	97.6
$15 000–$24 999	14.8	25.7	14.4	11.1	1.3	98.9
Under $15 000	16.7	11.0	5.6	4.5	1.1	100.0
All	100.0	51.9	36.3	31.8	100.0	

Notes:
a.   Includes direct ownership of stock shares and indirect ownership through mutual
     funds, trusts, and IRAs, Keogh plans, 401(k) plans, and other retirement accounts.
b.   In 2001 dollars.

Source: Author's computations from the 2001 SCF.

lower middle class (incomes between $15 000 and $25 000), and only 11 per cent of poor households (income under $15 000) reported stock ownership. The comparable ownership figures for stock holdings of $10 000 or more are 91 per cent for the top 1 per cent, 27 per cent for the middle class, 11 per cent for the lower middle class, and 5 per cent for the poor. Moreover, over three-quarters of all stocks were owned by households earning $75 000 or more (the top 23 per cent), and 89 per cent by the top 40 per cent of households in terms of income.

Thus, in terms of wealth or income, substantial stock holdings have still not penetrated much beyond the reach of the rich and the upper middle class. The big winners from the stock market boom of the late 1990s have been these groups, while the middle class and the poor have not seen sizable benefits from the bull market. It is also apparent which groups benefit from the preferential tax treatment of capital gains.

Table 4.16 provides details on stock ownership among whites and African Americans in 2001. It is first of note that, while the overall ratio of net worth between blacks and whites was 0.14, the wealth ratio was somewhat higher when households are divided by income class. Interestingly, the ratio of net worth was highest among poor households (under $15 000 of income), at 0.39, and second highest among the upper middle class, at 0.35. The ratio declined to 0.28 among lower middle-income households, to 0.24 among middle-income households ($25 000 to $50 000), and then fell of to 0.20 among the rich ($75 000 or more of income).

While 58 per cent of white households owned stock, either directly or indirectly, the figure was 34 per cent for African American households. Disparities in the stock ownership rate persist even when households are classified into income class, though the difference attenuates among higher income households. On average, white households who hold stock owned more than five times as much stock as African American stockholders. Here, again, when households are separated into income class, the ratios are higher, but still relatively low, except for the lowest income class where there is virtual parity in average stockholdings. Indeed, in the top income class of $75 000 or more, the ratio of average stockholdings between black and white owners is only 19 per cent, just slightly above the overall ratio. As a result, while 25 per cent of the total assets of white households were invested in stocks in 2001, the corresponding figure for black households is only 15 per cent. These differences remain by income class though they are generally less marked than the overall discrepancy.

All in all, the greater stock ownership by white households than black households, both in terms of ownership rate and value of stocks, might help to explain the rather precipitous decline in the black–white net worth ratio between 1998 and 2001.

Table 4.16 Wealth and stock ownership by race and income class, 2001

Income class[a]	Percentage frequency distribution		Average net worth			% owning stock[b]		Average stock holdings (owners only)			Ratio of stock to total assets	
	Whites[c]	Blacks[d]	Whites[c]	Blacks[d]	Ratio	Whites[c]	Blacks[d]	Whites[c]	Blacks[d]	Ratio	Whites[c]	Blacks[d]
Under $15 000	12.8	31.2	61.2	23.7	0.39	13.7	7.3	69.5	67.7	0.97	13.8	16.7
$15 000–$24 999	13.4	18.4	114.2	31.7	0.28	30.8	19.6	43.2	10.0	0.23	10.1	4.1
$25 000–$49 999	28.7	24.6	164.7	38.7	0.24	51.8	40.4	72.1	19.4	0.27	18.8	11.6
$50 000–$74 999	18.4	14.8	288.5	101.3	0.35	74.2	67.0	109.7	35.7	0.33	23.3	14.8
$75 000 and over	26.7	10.9	1283.4	260.9	0.20	86.5	77.5	453.8	85.7	0.19	27.7	18.3
All	100.0	100.0	465.8	66.3	0.14	57.5	34.2	232.0	42.8	0.18	25.4	14.9

Notes:

a. See Table 4.7 Notes for details on racial/ethnic categories.
b. Stock ownership includes direct ownership of stock shares and indirect ownership through mutual funds, trusts, and IRAs, Keogh plans, 401(k) plans, and other retirement accounts.
c. 'Whites' refers to non-Hispanic whites only.
d. 'Blacks' refers to non-Hispanic African Americans only.

Source: Author's computations from the 2001 SCF.

Table 4.17   Stock ownership by age and income class, 2001 (%)

Income class	Under 35	35–44	45–54	55–64	65–74	75 & over	All
Frequency distribution by age and income class							
Under $15 000	19.0	9.6	11.0	14.1	22.4	35.8	16.7
$15 000–$24 999	17.4	11.3	9.6	13.0	22.6	21.7	14.8
$25 000–$49 999	31.9	27.5	25.9	28.3	24.1	25.7	27.7
$50 000–$74 999	17.9	21.3	18.9	16.9	14.6	8.9	17.5
$75 000 and over	13.8	30.3	34.6	27.7	16.3	7.9	23.2
All	100.0	100.0	100.0	100.0	100.0	100.0	100.0
Households owning stock by age and income class							
Under $15 000	15.6	11.4	9.5	9.6	10.6	7.3	11.0
$15 000–$24 999	30.5	20.2	27.0	31.5	19.1	24.8	25.7
$25 000–$49 999	46.4	50.9	46.4	52.4	51.7	51.3	49.2
$50 000–$74 999	76.7	75.3	70.8	75.0	57.3	76.8	73.1
$75 000 and over	87.5	86.5	87.1	87.2	72.0	78.5	85.6
All	48.9	59.6	59.2	57.1	39.3	34.2	51.9
Ratio of stocks to total assets by age and income class							
Under $15 000	18.3	6.4	22.9	6.4	20.9	4.1	13.1
$15 000–$24 999	10.1	5.2	14.0	8.1	10.2	8.8	9.2
$25 000–$49 999	12.1	13.8	11.8	18.2	29.4	19.0	18.3
$50 000–$74 999	8.7	17.5	21.0	29.6	24.9	30.9	22.6
$75 000 and over	26.4	20.9	27.3	27.2	25.6	40.1	26.9
All	19.3	19.2	25.2	26.0	25.0	29.3	24.5

Note: 'Stock ownership' includes direct ownership of stock shares and indirect ownership through mutual funds, trusts, and IRAs, Keogh plans, 401(k) plans, and other retirement accounts.

Table 4.17 shows stock ownership by age and income class. The per cent of households owning stock generally rises slowly or remains about constant with age until age group 55–64 and then falls off rapidly with age. The major exceptions are the lowest income class and the middle income class, with stock ownership showing very little relation with age. In contrast, the share of stocks in total assets tends to rise with age across all age classes. However, the patterns are much more erratic by age group among households in the bottom two income classes.

Table 4.18 provides another cut at stock ownership patterns: years of education and income class. In this case, the pattern is much stronger than it is in the case of age and income class. Conditional on income, stock ownership rates rise directly with years of schooling. Among the middle-income class, for example, the rate grows from 39 per cent to 64 per cent between those households with less than a high school education and households

Table 4.18   Stock ownership by education and income class, 1998 (%)

Income class	Less than 12 years	12 years	13–15 years	16 years or more	All
Frequency distribution by education and income class					
Under $15 000	41.8	17.4	11.5	4.6	16.7
$15 000–$24 999	24.7	16.8	14.9	6.8	14.8
$25 000–$49 999	20.1	35.7	32.7	20.6	27.7
$50 000–$74 999	7.3	17.6	19.7	21.8	17.5
$75 000 and over	6.1	12.4	21.2	46.1	23.2
All	100.0	100.0	100.0	100.0	100.0
Households owning stock by education and income class					
Under $15 000	4.3	11.9	18.1	31.5	11.0
$15 000–$24 999	12.3	22.2	38.7	42.3	25.7
$25 000–$49 999	38.8	44.1	49.4	63.9	49.2
$50 000–$74 999	50.9	69.4	67.6	84.3	73.1
$75 000 and over	52.5	76.6	81.6	92.1	85.6
All	19.6	43.3	54.6	78.3	51.9
Ratio of stocks to total assets by education and income class					
Under $15 000	2.1	10.4	22.6	26.0	13.1
$15 000–$24 999	4.0	7.5	8.7	17.4	9.2
$25 000–$49 999	19.6	13.0	19.5	22.4	18.3
$50 000–$74 999	6.2	15.6	20.4	28.6	22.6
$75 000 and over	8.2	20.1	22.0	28.9	26.9
All	9.2	16.0	20.5	28.3	24.5

Note: 'Stock ownership' includes direct ownership of stock shares and indirect ownership through mutual funds, trusts, and IRAs, Keogh plans, 401(k) plans, and other retirement accounts.

with 16 or more years of schooling. The same pattern generally emerges with respect to the share of stocks in total assets, which tends to rise with educational attainment. The effect is strongest in the highest income class, with the share increasing from 9 per cent among households with less than a high school education to 28 per cent among those with four years of college or more.

Table 4.19 cuts stock ownership by marital status and presence of children. Married couples under 65, both with and without children, have the highest incidence of stock ownership overall, while single mothers with children have the lowest overall. Conditional on income, these patterns generally hold, except for the highest income class, for which stock ownership rates tend to be invariant across marital class. However, no clear pattern

Table 4.19   Stock ownership by marital and parental status and income class, 1998 (%)

Income class	Married with children under 65	Married no children under 65	Female head with children under 65	Female head no children under 65	Married 65 and over	All
Frequency distribution by marital and parental class						
Under $15 000	5.5	5.3	35.3	25.0	9.2	16.7
$15 000–$24 999	8.2	8.2	25.7	20.1	21.2	14.8
$25 000–49 999	24.3	27.0	29.5	36.5	30.7	27.7
$50 000–$74 999	24.0	21.1	6.6	12.4	19.2	17.5
$75 000 and over	38.0	38.5	2.8	6.0	19.7	23.2
All	100.0	100.0	100.0	100.0	100.0	100.0
Households owning stock by marital and parental status and income class						
Under $15 000	15.7	13.2	4.3	13.1	3.5	11.0
$15 000–$24 999	14.8	24.7	22.5	46.9	16.7	25.7
$25 000–$49 999	46.8	50.0	38.8	54.6	52.9	49.2
$50 000–$74 999	75.7	70.0	64.9	83.1	61.9	73.1
$75 000 and over	87.3	86.1	79.0	96.1	75.4	85.6
All	64.8	64.1	25.3	48.7	46.8	51.9
Ratio of stocks to total assets by marital and parental status and income class						
Under $15 000	6.4	23.5	1.7	12.9	1.4	13.1
$15 000–$24 999	8.0	5.1	6.4	13.0	10.1	9.2
$25 000–$49 999	12.5	13.4	12.3	14.3	22.6	18.3
$50 000–$74 999	17.6	24.8	7.7	20.1	26.9	22.6
$75 000 and over	22.8	27.2	20.6	38.0	28.8	26.9
All	21.3	25.6	12.2	27.3	26.5	24.5

Note: 'Stock ownership' includes direct ownership of stock shares and indirect ownership through mutual funds, trusts, and IRAs, Keogh plans, 401(k) plans, and other retirement accounts.

emerges between the share of stocks in total assets and marital and parental status.

A summary table on trends in stock ownership by demographic characteristics over the years 1989 to 2001 is given in Table 4.20. The stock ownership rate rises steeply with income class in all three years. However, the largest gains in stock ownership over the years from 1989 to 2001 occurred in the three income classes ranging between $25 000 and $99 999. Non-Hispanic whites had the highest rate of stock ownership in all three years, followed closely by Asians, African Americans (except for 1989) and lastly, Hispanics. However, the greatest gain in stock ownership occurred among Asian households, followed by blacks, whites and lastly, Hispanics.

Table 4.20   *Stock ownership by group, 1989, 1998 and 2001 (% of households holding stocks)*

Category	1989	1998	2001	% change 1989–2001
All households	31.7	48.2	51.9	20.2
Income level[a]				
Under $15 000	4.2	10.6	12.5	8.3
$15 000–$24 999	16.7	29.2	30.6	14.0
$25 000–$49 999	32.3	52.0	54.5	22.2
$50 000–$74 999	48.6	70.9	74.8	26.2
$75 000–$99 999	60.4	80.7	83.5	23.1
$100 000–$249 999	81.1	89.0	88.6	7.5
$250 000 or more	79.2	93.3	96.1	16.9
Race				
Non-Hispanic whites	38.0	53.7	57.5	19.5
Non-Hispanic African Americans	10.5	29.7	34.2	23.7
Hispanics[b]	12.4	21.0	28.0	15.6
Asian and other races	17.5	46.9	51.2	33.7
Age class[c]				
Under 35	22.5	40.6	48.9	26.4
35–44	38.6	55.9	59.6	21.1
45–54	41.9	58.1	59.2	17.4
55–64	35.8	55.6	57.1	21.3
65–74	26.7	41.9	39.3	12.6
75 and over	25.6	27.6	34.2	8.6
Education[d]				
Less than 12 years	10.1	18.8	19.6	9.4
12 years	26.7	42.2	43.3	16.6
13–15 years	36.0	53.7	54.6	18.6
16 years or more	57.6	70.0	78.3	20.8

Notes: 'Stock ownership' includes direct ownership of stock shares and indirect ownership through mutual funds, trusts, and IRAs, Keogh plans, 401(k) plans, and other retirement accounts.
a.   In 1995 dollars.
b.   Hispanics can be of any race.
c.   Households are classified according to the age of the head of household.
d.   Households are classified according to the education of the head of household.

Sources: Author's computations from the 1989, 1998 and 2001 SCF.

The biggest gain in stock ownership occurred among households under the age of 35, followed by middle-aged households, and then the elderly. As a result, the pattern of stock ownership with respect to age class switched from a U-shaped profile in 1989, with a peak in the 45–54 age group, to one where ownership rates were fairly flat with respect to age up to age 65, and then dropped off sharply. There is a strong correlation between stock ownership rates and education in all three years, as well as between gains in stock ownership and education. The largest gain in stock ownership occurred among college graduates, followed by those with one to three years of college, high school graduates, and lastly, those with less than 12 years of schooling.

SUMMARY AND CONCLUDING COMMENTS

There is mostly good news provided in this report. I find that, despite slow growth in income over the 1990s, there have been marked improvements in the wealth position of average families. Both mean and median net worth and financial wealth grew briskly in the late 1990s. The inequality of net worth levelled off, while that of financial wealth showed a marked decline despite the fact that income inequality continued to rise over this period.

However, the number of households worth $1 million or more, $5 million or more, and especially $10 million or more, surged during the 1990s. Moreover, the average wealth of the poorest 40 per cent declined by 44 per cent between 1983 and 2001, and by 2001 had fallen to only $2900. All in all, the greatest gains in wealth and income were enjoyed by the upper 20 per cent, particularly the top 1 per cent, of the respective distributions. Between 1983 and 2001, the top 1 per cent received 33 per cent of the total growth in net worth, 52 per cent of the total growth in financial wealth, and 28 per cent of the total increase in income. The figures for the top 20 per cent are 89 per cent, 95 per cent and 67 per cent, respectively.

Indebtedness also fell substantially during the late 1990s and, by 2001, the overall debt–equity ratio was lower than in 1983. The proportion of households reporting zero or negative net worth, after increasing from 15.5 per cent in 1983 to 18.0 per cent in 1998, fell to 17.6 per cent in 2001. Net equity in owner-occupied housing as a share of total assets fell sharply from 23.8 per cent in 1983 to 18.2 per cent in 1998, and then rebounded somewhat to 18.8 per cent in 2001. This trend reflects rising mortgage debt on homeowners' property between 1983 and 1998, which grew from 21 to 37 per cent, before retreating to 33 per cent in 2001. The debt–equity ratio was also much higher among the middle 60 per cent of households in 2001, at 0.32, than among the top 1 per cent, at 0.024, or the next 19 per cent at 0.089.

The concentration of investment type assets generally remained as high in 2001 as during the previous two decades. About 90 per cent of the total value of stock shares, bonds, trusts and business equity, and about 80 per cent of nonhome real estate, were held by the top 10 per cent of households. Moreover, despite the widening ownership of stock (52 per cent of households owned stock shares either directly or indirectly through mutual funds, trust funds or pension plans in 2001), the richest 10 per cent still accounted for 77 per cent of the total value of these stocks.

The racial disparity in wealth holdings, after stabilizing during most of the 1990s, widened in the years between 1998 and 2001, as the ratio of average net worth holdings dropped sharply from 0.18 to 0.14 and the ratio of median net worth went from 0.12 to 0.10. With regard to mean net worth, the reason for this disparity is that white net worth gained a spectacular 34 per cent between 1998 and 2001 and black net worth advanced by only 5 per cent (a rate that was slightly greater than in previous years). In the case of median net worth, wealth for white households grew by 20 per cent between 1998 and 2001, but declined in absolute terms by 2 per cent among black households. Between 1998 and 2001, mean financial wealth among white households also surged by 34 per cent, but went up by only 6 per cent among black households, so that the ratio dwindled from 0.15 to 0.12 – even lower than in 1983. The black homeownership rate grew from 44.3 to 47.4 per cent between 1983 and 2001, but the homeownership rate relative to white households, after increasing from a ratio of 0.65 in 1983 to 0.67 in 1998, slipped back to 0.64 in 2001. The change over the last three years primarily reflected a big jump in the white homeownership rate.

Hispanic households also lost ground between 1998 and 2001 both in absolute terms and relative to non-Hispanic white households. Between 1998 and 2001, both mean and median net worth and mean financial wealth declined in absolute terms (median financial wealth increased from zero to $200). The ratio of mean net worth, after climbing from 16 per cent in 1983 to 25 per cent in 1998, collapsed to 17 per cent in 2001, and the ratio of mean financial wealth, after jumping from 7 to 20 per cent between 1983 and 1998, plummeted to 14 per cent in 2001. The homeownership rate among Hispanic households, after advancing from 33 per cent in 1983 to 44 per cent in 1995, levelled off in the ensuing six years, and the ratio of homeownership rates advanced from 48 per cent in 1983 to 64 per cent in 1995, and then dropped to 60 per cent in 2001.

Still, in 2001 the respective wealth gaps between African Americans and Hispanics on the one hand and non-Hispanic whites on the other were still much greater than the corresponding income gap. Racial (and ethnic) differences in net worth remain large even by income class, as do patterns of stock investment. A large part of the reason that both black and

Hispanic households lost ground relative to non-Hispanic white households between 1998 and 2001 is traceable to the much lower rate of stock ownership among black and Hispanic families than among non-Hispanic whites, even conditional on household income.

At least since 1989, wealth shifted in relative terms away from young households (under age 55) toward households in age group 55 to 74. A similar pattern is found for financial wealth. The average net worth and financial wealth of households in age group 75 and over also fell relative to the overall mean between 1989 and 2001. Moreover, childless couples (both nonelderly and elderly) were much wealthier than families with children. However, the relative position of married couples with children has improved substantially in terms of wealth since the early 1980s.

While the years 1983 to 1989 saw some diminution in stock holdings, the years 1989 to 2001 saw a substantial increase in stock ownership. The share of households with direct ownership of stock climbed from 13.1 to 21.3, while the share with some stock owned either outright or indirectly through mutual funds, trusts, or various pension accounts surged from 31.7 to 51.9 per cent. However, in 2001, while 52 per cent of households owned some stock, only 40 per cent had total stock holdings worth $5000 or more (in 1995 dollars), only 35 per cent owned $10 000 or more of stock, and only 27 per cent owned $25 000 or more of stocks.

Stock ownership is also highly skewed by wealth and income class. The top 1 per cent of households classified by wealth owned 34 per cent of all stocks, the top 10 per cent owned over three-quarters, and the top quintile owned almost 90 per cent. Moreover, over three-quarters of all stocks were owned by households earning $75 000 or more, and 89 per cent were owned by households with incomes of $50 000 or more.

I also find that stock ownership rates in 2001 were higher for nonelderly households (under age 65) than those of elderly households (age 65 or over). However, the value of stocks as a share of total assets rose almost directly with age. Between 1989 and 2001, the gain in the stock ownership was strongest among young households (under age 35) and weakest among elderly households. In 2001, both the stock ownership rate and stocks as a share of total assets varied directly with educational attainment, even conditional on the income level of the household. Gains in the stock ownership rate between 1989 and 2001 were also directly correlated with educational attainment.

Though the 'wealth' news generally seems very good for the years 1998 to 2001, these results must be interpreted cautiously. A large part of the story of this period is the erosion of traditional defined benefit (DB) pension plans and the substitution of defined contribution (DC) plans such as 401(k) plans for traditional DB pensions. According to standard wealth accounting methods, DC pensions are included in (standard) net worth while DB pension wealth is not. Though this topic is somewhat beyond the scope of this chapter, in related work (Wolff, forthcoming) I show that if we include DB pension wealth as well in our wealth measure, then we find virtually no growth in median wealth and an increase in wealth inequality between 1989 and 2001.

NOTES

1. These figures are based on the Bureau of Labor Statistics (BLS) hourly wage series. The source is: US Council of Economic Advisers (2004). The BLS wage figures are converted to constant dollars on the basis of the Consumer Price Index (CPI-U).
2. Three studies conducted by the Federal Reserve Board – Kennickell and Woodburn (1992) for the 1989 SCF; Kennickell et al. (1996) for the 1992 SCF; and Kennickell and Woodburn (1999) for the 1995 SCF – discuss some of the issues involved in developing these weights.
3. The 1998 and 2001 weights are actually partially design-based weights (X42001), which account for the systematic deviation from the CPS estimates of homeownership rates by racial and ethnic groups.
4. The adjustment factors by asset type and year are as follows:

Table 4.21   Adjustment factors by asset type and year

	1983 SCF	1989 SCF	1992 SCF	1995 SCF
Checking accounts	1.68			
Savings and time deposits	1.50			
All deposits		1.37	1.32	
Financial securities	1.20			
Stocks and mutual funds	1.06			
Trusts		1.66	1.41	1.45
Stocks and bonds				1.23
Nonmortgage debt	1.16			

No adjustments were made to other asset and debt components, or to the 1998 or 2001 SCF.
5. See Wolff (2002b) for recent estimates of social security and pension wealth.
6. The time trend is very similar when the unadjusted asset values are used instead of my adjusted values and when the value of vehicles is included in net worth. Similar results can also be derived from the estimates provided by Kennickell and Woodburn for 1989 and 1995 (see Kennickell and Woodburn 1999.)
7. It should be noted that the SCF data show a much higher level of income inequality than the CPS data. In the year 2000, for example, the CPS data show a share of the top 5 per cent of 22.1 per cent and a Gini coefficient of 0.462. The difference is primarily due to two factors. First, the SCF over-samples the rich (as noted above), while the CPS is a representative sample. Second, the income concepts differ between the two samples. In particular, the SCF income definition includes capital gains whereas the CPS definition does not. However, the CPS data also show a large increase of inequality between 1989 and 2000, with the share of the top 5 per cent rising from 18.9 to 22.1 per cent and the Gini coefficient from 0.431 to 0.462. Further analysis of the difference in income figures between the two surveys is beyond the scope of this chapter.

8. The residual group, American Indians and Asians, is excluded here.
9. It should be stressed that the unit of observation is the household, which includes both families (two or more related individuals living together), as well as single adults.
10. There is a large amount of variation in the income and wealth figures for both blacks and Hispanics on a year by year basis. This is probably a reflection of the small sample sizes for these two groups and the associated sampling variability as well as some changes in the wording of questions on race and ethnicity over the five surveys.
11. One important reason for the wealth gap is differences in inheritances. According to my calculations from the SCF data, in 1998 24.1 per cent of white households reported receiving an inheritance over their lifetime, compared to 11 per cent of black households, and the average bequest among white inheritors was $115 000 (present value in 1998) and only $32 000 among black inheritors. Thus, inheritances appear to play a vital role in explaining the large wealth gap, particularly in light of the fact that black families appear to save more than white families at similar income levels (see, for example, Blau and Graham 1990; Oliver and Shapiro 1997).
12. The 1983 data do not permit an estimation of indirect stock ownership, so we present the results for 1983 and 1989 separately from the other years.

REFERENCES

Blau, F.D. and J.W. Graham (1990), 'Black–white differences in wealth and asset composition', *Quarterly Journal of Economics*, **105**(2), May, 321–39.

Kennickell, A.B. and R.L. Woodburn (1992), 'Estimation of household net worth using model-based and design-based weights: evidence from the 1989 Survey of Consumer Finances', Federal Reserve Board of Washington, DC, (April), unpublished paper.

Kennickell, A.B. and R.L. Woodburn (1999), 'Consistent weight design for the 1989, 1992, and 1995 SCFs, and the distribution of wealth', *Review of Income and Wealth*, **45**(2), June, 193–216.

Kennickell, A.B., D.A. McManus and R.L. Woodburn (1996), 'Weighting design for the 1992 Survey of Consumer Finances', Federal Reserve Board of Washington, DC, (March), unpublished paper.

Modigliani, Franco and Richard Brumberg (1954), 'Utility analysis and the consumption function: an interpretation of cross-section data', in K. Kurihara (ed.), *Post-Keynesian Economics*, New Brunswick, NJ: Rutgers University Press.

Oliver, Melvin L. and Thomas M. Shapiro (1997), *Black Wealth, White Wealth*, New York: Routledge.

US Council of Economic Advisers (1994), *Economic Report of the President, 1994*, Washington, DC: United States Government Printing Office.

Wolff, E.N. (1987), 'Estimates of household wealth inequality in the United States, 1962–83', *Review of Income and Wealth*, **33**(3), September 231–56.

Wolff, E.N. (1994), 'Trends in household wealth in the United States, 1962–1983 and 1983–1989', *Review of Income and Wealth* **40**(2), June, 143–74.

Wolff, E.N. (1996), *Top Heavy: A Study of Increasing Inequality of Wealth in America*, New York: New Press.

Wolff, E.N. (1998), 'Recent trends in the size distribution of household wealth', *Journal of Economic Perspectives*, **12**(3), Summer, 131–50.

Wolff, E.N. (2001), 'Recent trends in wealth ownership, from 1983 to 1998', in Thomas M. Shapiro and Edward N. Wolff (eds), *Assets for the Poor: The Benefits of Spreading Asset Ownership*, New York: Russell Sage Foundation, pp. 34–73.

Wolff, E.N. (2002a), *Top Heavy: A Study of Increasing Inequality of Wealth in America*, updated and expanded edition, New York: New Press.

Wolff, E.N. (2002b), *Retirement Insecurity: The Income Shortfalls Awaiting the Soon-to-Retire*, Washington, DC: Economic Policy Institute.

Wolff, E.N. (forthcoming), 'The transformation of the American pension system', in Teresa Ghilarducci and John Turner (eds), *Work Options for Mature Americans*, Notre Dame, IN: University of Notre Dame Press.

5. The evolution of wealth inequality in Canada, 1984–99

René Morissette, Xuelin Zhang and Marie Drolet

INTRODUCTION

Distributional issues have attracted considerable interest since the early 1990s in Canada and in most OECD countries. In Canada, individual earnings inequality has risen since the beginning of the 1980s, at least among male workers (Morissette et al. 1994; Beach and Slotsve 1996). In contrast, inequality in family disposable income did not increase during the 1980s but rose during the 1990s (Frenette et al. 2004). Whether wealth inequality at the family level has risen over the last two decades remains unknown.

The goal of this chapter is to fill this gap. In the first section, we describe the Assets and Debts Survey of 1984 (ADS 1984) and the Survey of Financial Security of 1999 (SFS 1999), the two Canadian wealth surveys used in this study. In the next section, we document changes in average and median wealth between 1984 and 1999. We find that both average and median wealth rose between 1984 and 1999. Since older families tend to have accumulated more wealth than their younger counterparts, part of the observed increase in average wealth could simply be due to the ageing of the Canadian population. Using shift-share analysis, we find that about one-third of the growth in average wealth can be attributed to the ageing of family units.

In the third section, we show that wealth inequality increased between 1984 and 1999. The increase in wealth inequality did not occur in a context where all segments of the population enjoyed increases in wealth: median wealth fell in the bottom three deciles of the wealth distribution but rose 27 per cent or more in the top three deciles. Furthermore, only families in the tenth decile (and in some samples in the ninth decile as well) increased their share of total net worth during the period.

We then describe changes in the wealth structure. We show that both average and median wealth rose much more among family units whose major income recipient is a university graduate than among others. Furthermore, both fell among family units whose major income recipient is aged 25–34 and increased among those whose major income recipient is aged 55 and over.

In the next section, we use re-weighting methods to examine the extent to which changes in family structure, changes in the age structure, and changes in relative wealth by age and education of the major income recipient account for the growth of wealth inequality. We show that the ageing of the Canadian population tended to reduce wealth inequality. Furthermore, we implement the semi-parametric approach proposed by Dinardo et al. (1996) and answer the following question: what would wealth inequality have been in 1999 if permanent income and other attributes of family units had remained at their 1984 level *and* family units had kept the net worth observed in 1999? Our results suggest that permanent income and other family attributes – as measured with cross-sectional data – are not major factors behind the growth of wealth inequality.

In the section that follows, we confirm these findings with regression-based methods. We attempt to quantify the contribution of changes in family units' permanent income and demographics to the change in wealth inequality. We acknowledge that our ability to do so is limited by the fact that we are using cross-sectional data to explain a variable – wealth – which is best understood with longitudinal microdata. Using Oaxaca-Blinder decomposition methods, we find that neither diverging changes in permanent income nor diverging changes in socio-demographic characteristics explain a substantial portion of the growing gap between low-wealth and high-wealth family units.

Finally, we examine the extent to which some specific wealth components have contributed to the growth of wealth inequality. We show that, in a purely accounting sense, registered retirement savings plans (RRSP) have, of all wealth components, contributed the most to the increase in wealth inequality.

We conclude that, between low-wealth and high-wealth family units, differences in the number of years worked full-time, in the growth of inheritances, *inter vivos* transfers and rates of return on savings are likely to have played a major role in the growth of wealth inequality. In particular, rates of return on savings may have increased more for wealthy family units than for their poorer counterparts as a result of the booming stock market during the 1990s.

DATA AND CONCEPTS

We use the ADS 1984 and SFS 1999. ADS 1984 is a supplement to the May 1984 Survey of Consumer Finances. SFS 1999 is a distinct survey which was conducted from May to July 1999. In both cases, the sample used is based on the Labour Force Survey sampling frame and represents all families and individuals in Canada, except the following: residents of the Yukon and the Northwest Territories; members of households located on Indian reserves; full-time members of the Armed Forces; and inmates of institutions.[1] Data is obtained for all members of a family 15 years and over.

Some differences between the two surveys are worth noting. First, in ADS 1984, all information on components of assets (except housing) and debts were collected for each member of the family aged 15 years and over and then aggregated at the family level. In contrast, in SFS 1999, information on components of assets and debts were directly collected at the family level. Second, contrary to ADS 1984, SFS 1999 contained a 'high-income' supplementary sample (consisting initially of about 2000 households) which was included to improve the quality of wealth estimates. The final sample of ADS 1984 includes 14 029 family units and that of SFS 1999 includes 15 933 units. Family units include both unattached individuals and families. Wealth figures are converted into 1999 constant dollars using the Consumer Price Index as a deflator.

It is well known that the quality of wealth data is viewed as being lower than the quality of income data. This is largely because records of the current value of assets and debts are not as readily available as records of income. Also, the value of real assets (such as housing and vehicles) is judged to be of higher quality than that of financial assets.

To make the concept of wealth comparable between the two surveys, we have to exclude the value of the following items from the 1999 data, as they were not included in the 1984 survey: contents of the home, collectibles and valuables, annuities and RRIF (registered retirement income funds). We define the wealth of a family unit as the difference between the value of its total asset holdings and the amount of total debts. Our concept of wealth excludes the value of work-related pension plans and/or entitlements to future social security provided by the government in the form of Canada or Quebec Pension Plan or Old Age Security Systems. It also excludes the family's human capital measured in terms of the value of the discounted flow of future earnings for all family members.

One particularly difficult issue with wealth data is the measurement of the upper tail of the wealth distribution. Using a variety of data sources, Davies (1993) estimates that the share of total wealth held by the top 1 per cent of family units in 1984 may increase from 17 per cent (using ADS 1984) to 22–27 per cent after making appropriate adjustments. Similarly, his estimates suggest that the share of total wealth held by the top 5 per cent of family units in 1984 may increase from 38 to 41–46 per cent.

A further complication arises from the fact that we are comparing wealth at two points in time and that the degree of truncation of the wealth distribution may change over time. Assume that the true wealth distribution remains unchanged between 1984 and 1999. Extending the argument of Davies (1993, p. 160) to the analysis of changes in the wealth distribution, if no Canadian family with wealth over $10 million ever consents to an interview in 1984, and if no Canadian family with wealth over $50 million ever consents to an interview in 1999, ADS 1984 and SFS 1999 will show an (incorrect) increase in wealth inequality which could simply be due to the use of better interviewing techniques in the latter survey than in the former.[2] For these reasons, most of the analysis conducted in this chapter uses three different samples: (1) all family units (first sample); (2) all family units except those at the top 1 per cent of the wealth distribution (second sample); and (3) all family units except those at the top 5 per cent of the wealth distribution (third sample). For simplicity, we use the terms 'wealth' and 'net worth' interchangeably.

CHANGES IN AVERAGE WEALTH AND MEDIAN WEALTH

Table 5.1 shows average and median wealth for all three aforementioned samples. For all three samples, median wealth grew by roughly 10 per cent between 1984 and 1999. Average wealth rose between 28 per cent and 37 per cent. Note that excluding the top 1 per cent of family units lowers the growth rate of average wealth from 37 per cent to 31 per cent, indicating that the choice of the sample matters. The growth in median and average wealth occurred despite an increase in the percentage of family units with zero or negative wealth.[3]

Financial wealth is a second concept of wealth that is useful for analysis. By financial wealth, we mean net worth minus net equity in housing and net business equity. Put simply, we define financial wealth as the stock of wealth left to a family without selling the house and the business. Financial wealth measures the stock of liquid assets a family could use relatively quickly to finance consumption following a substantial decrease in family income. Median financial wealth increased by 27–36 per cent between 1984 and 1999 while average financial wealth rose at a much faster pace, growing at a rate of 53–92 per cent. As a result, the relative importance of financial wealth in net worth rose during the period.[4]

Table 5.3 shows that wealth increases with the age of the major income recipient, at least until 65. Part of the increase in average wealth observed between 1984 and 1999 could then be due to the ageing of family units. Shift-share analysis reveals that between 30 and 39 per cent of the growth in average wealth appears to be related to the ageing of family units. The rest is due to growth in average wealth within age groups.

Table 5.1   Average and median wealth, by family unit, 1984 and 1999

Family unit	1999 constant dollars		% change 1984–99
	1984	1999	
All family units			
Net worth			
Median	58 392	64 600	10.6
Average	128 875	176 087	36.6
% with zero or negative net worth	10.8	13.3	23.1
Financial wealth[b]			
Median	10 897	14 850	36.3
Average	34 563	66 514	92.4
% with zero or negative financial wealth	17.7	19.7	11.3
Sample size	14 029	15 933	–
Top 1% of family units excluded[a]			
Net worth			
Median	56 982	63 066	10.7
Average	107 918	140 864	30.5
Zero or negative net worth (%)	10.9	13.4	22.9
Financial wealth[b]			
Median	10 728	14 310	33.4
Average	31 371	54 274	73.0
% with zero or negative financial wealth	17.8	19.9	11.8
Sample size	13 870	15 452	–
Top 5% of family units excluded[a]			
Net worth			
Median	51 483	56 600	9.9
Average	84 315	108 116	28.2
% with zero or negative net worth	11.3	14.0	23.9
Financial wealth[b]			
Median	9 962	12 650	27.0
Average	25 423	38 783	52.6
% with zero or negative financial wealth	18.2	20.7	13.7
Sample size	13 282	14 474	–

Notes:
a. After ranking family units by ascending order of their net worth.
b. Financial wealth equals net worth minus net equity in housing and net business equity.

Sources: Assets and Debts Survey of 1984, Survey of Financial Security of 1999.

Table 5.2   Standard errors of Gini coefficients, 1984–99

Family unit	1984[b]	1999[b]	% change 1984–99
All family units			
Unit of analysis: family unit	0.691	0.727	5.2
	(0.0062)	(0.0057)	
Unit of analysis: individuals	0.678	0.723	6.6
	(0.0062)	(0.0058)	
Top 1% of family units excluded[a]			
Unit of analysis: family unit	0.646	0.675	4.4
	(0.0039)	(0.0036)	
Unit of analysis: individuals	0.635	0.674	6.2
	(0.0042)	(0.0039)	
Top 5% of family units excluded[a]			
Unit of analysis: family unit	0.605	0.637	5.4
	(0.0042)	(0.0039)	
Unit of analysis: individuals	0.597	0.642	7.5
	(0.0045)	(0.0041)	

Notes:
a.   After ranking family units by ascending order of their net worth.
b.   Standard errors are in parentheses. The standard errors for 1999 take account of the complex design of SFS 1999. The standard errors for 1984 are obtained by multiplying the standard errors of 1999 by an adjustment factor of 1.08. See text for details.

Sources: Authors' calculations from the Assets and Debts Survey of 1984 and Survey of Financial Security of 1999.

WEALTH INEQUALITY, 1984–99

Since it is unclear whether family units should be the unit of analysis used when measuring wealth inequality (Davies 1979), we consider, for each of the three samples, two different units of analysis: the family unit and the individual.[5] When individuals are the unit of analysis, wealth is divided by the number of individuals in the family.

Apart from the Gini coefficient, we use two other inequality measures: the coefficient of variation and the exponential measure. While the Gini coefficient is sensitive to changes in the middle of the wealth distribution, the coefficient of variation is sensitive to changes at the top and the exponential measure is sensitive to changes at the bottom of the distribution.

The Gini coefficient increased – between 4 per cent and 8 per cent – for all six combinations of samples and units of analysis considered (Table 5.5).

Table 5.3   *Average wealth by age of major income recipient, 1984 and 1999*

	Average wealth (1999 constant dollars)			Distribution of family units by age of major income recipient		
	(1) 1984	(2) 1999	(3) % change 1984–99	(4) 1984 %	(5) 1999 %	(6) % change 1984–99
All family units						
Age of major income recipient						
Less than 25	32 284	32 918	2.0	10.2	5.9	–4.2
25–34	69 890	67 264	–3.8	26.0	19.5	–6.5
35–44	137 608	151 915	10.4	20.2	24.7	4.5
45–54	202 422	247 751	22.4	14.7	19.6	4.9
55–64	210 290	302 856	44.0	13.1	11.9	–1.2
65 and over	140 749	211 862	50.5	15.9	18.3	2.4
Average wealth: Total	128 875	176 087	36.6	100.0	100.0	–

% of growth in
  average wealth
  (36.6% = 100)
  accounted for by
  demographic
  weights
    1984 weights   31.4
    1999 weights   29.9

Top 1% of family units excluded						
Age of major income recipient						
Less than 25	31 722	24 599	–22.5	10.3	6.0	–4.3
25–34	61 864	58 476	–5.5	26.2	19.7	–6.5
35–44	113 998	118 501	3.9	20.1	24.8	4.6
45–54	158 823	190 114	19.7	14.5	19.5	4.9
55–64	176 397	234 190	32.8	13.0	11.8	–1.2
65 and over	122 615	185 074	50.9	15.9	18.3	2.4
Average wealth: Total	107 918	140 864	30.5	100.0	100.0	–

% of growth in
  average wealth
  (30.5% = 100)
    1984 weights   35.4
    1999 weights   31.5

Table 5.3   (continued)

	Average wealth (1999 constant dollars)			Distribution of family units by age of major income recipient		
	(1)	(2)	(3)	(4)	(5)	(6)
	1984	1999	% change 1984–99	1984 %	1999 %	% change 1984–99
Top 5% of family units excluded						
Age of major income recipient						
Less than 25	24 123	16 461	–31.8	10.6	6.2	–4.4
25–34	51 388	49 404	–3.9	26.8	20.3	–6.5
35–44	93 122	97 697	4.9	20.3	25.2	4.9
45–54	125 117	141 893	13.4	14.2	18.9	4.8
55–64	129 691	167 891	29.5	12.3	11.3	–1.1
65 and over	97 023	147 156	51.7	15.8	18.1	2.3
Average wealth: Total	84 315	108 117	28.2	100.0	100.0	–
% of growth in average wealth (28.2% = 100) accounted for by demographic weights						
1984 weights 38.6						
1999 weights 34.6						

Sources: Assets and Debts Survey of 1984, Survey of Financial Security of 1999.

Using bootstrap weights, we find that the increase is always statistically significant at the 1 per cent level.[6] For the sample including all family units, the coefficient of variation increases much more (35 per cent), no doubt reflecting changes in the upper tail of the wealth distribution. For the first two samples, all three inequality measures show an increase which varies between 3 and 30 per cent. However, for the sample excluding the top 5 per cent of family units, the exponential measure decreases by 4–7 per cent. This implies that the 1999 Lorenz curve and the 1984 Lorenz curve cross in this case.

In order to make rigorous statements about changes in wealth inequality, selecting a set of inequality measures is insufficient. The real test consists in plotting Lorenz curves for both 1984 and 1999: if the 1999 Lorenz curve lies below the 1984 curve at all points of the wealth distribution, then analysts can say unambiguously that wealth inequality has risen. In contrast, if the two Lorenz curves cross, it is unclear whether wealth inequality has risen. In this

Table 5.4   Changes in wealth inequality, 1984–99

	1984	1999	% change 1984–99
Bottom 0.5% of family units excluded[a]			
Unit of analysis: family unit			
Gini	0.686	0.723	5.4
CV	2.311	3.130	35.4
Exponential	0.498	0.537	7.8
Unit of analysis: individuals			
Gini	0.673	0.719	6.8
CV	2.375	3.089	30.1
Exponential	0.486	0.534	9.9
Bottom 0.5% and top 1% of family units excluded[a]			
Unit of analysis: family unit			
Gini	0.640	0.669	4.5
CV	1.416	1.505	6.3
Exponential	0.452	0.484	7.1
Unit of analysis: individuals	0.628	0.668	6.4
Gini	1.503	1.627	8.3
CV	0.439	0.481	9.6
Exponential			
Bottom 0.5% and top 5% of family units excluded[a]			
Unit of analysis: family unit			
Gini	0.597	0.630	5.5
CV	1.153	1.239	7.5
Exponential	0.411	0.447	8.8
Unit of analysis: individuals			
Gini	0.589	0.635	7.8
CV	1.249	1.382	10.6
Exponential	0.398	0.447	12.3

Note: a. After ranking family units by ascending order of their net worth.

Sources: Assets and Debts Survey of 1984, Survey of Financial Security of 1999.

case, it is always possible to find one inequality measure which will show an increase in inequality and another which will show the opposite conclusion.

Inspection of the Lorenz curves (not shown here) for all six combinations reveals that, in general, these curves cross at the first percentile. In other words, the 1999 Lorenz curve lies below the 1984 Lorenz curve at all

Table 5.5 Changes in wealth inequality, 1984–99

	1984	1999	% change 1984–99
All family units			
Unit of analysis: family unit			
Gini	0.691	0.727	5.2
CV	2.325	3.146	35.3
Exponential	0.531	0.560	5.5
Unit of analysis: individuals			
Gini	0.678	0.723	6.6
CV	2.390	3.105	29.9
Exponential	0.501	0.541	8.0
Top 1% of family units excluded[a]			
Unit of analysis: family unit			
Gini	0.646	0.675	4.4
CV	1.429	1.517	6.2
Exponential	0.542	0.556	2.6
Unit of analysis: individuals			
Gini	0.635	0.674	6.2
CV	1.517	1.639	8.0
Exponential	0.468	0.493	5.5
Top 5% of family units excluded[a]			
Unit of analysis: family unit			
Gini	0.605	0.637	5.4
CV	1.169	1.255	7.4
Exponential	0.906	0.838	−7.4
Unit of analysis: individuals			
Gini	0.597	0.642	7.5
CV	1.266	1.397	10.3
Exponential	0.492	0.472	−3.9

Note: a. After ranking family units by ascending order of their net worth.

Sources: Assets and Debts Survey of 1984, Survey of Financial Security of 1999.

points of the wealth distribution except the first percentile. Hence, for the six combinations defined above, we cannot rigorously say that wealth inequality has risen between 1984 and 1999.

However, this ambiguity disappears when we alter slightly these six combinations, that is, when we further exclude the bottom 0.5 per cent of the wealth distribution.[7] In this case, the Lorenz curve for 1999 lies always below the Lorenz curve for 1984. As expected, all three measures of inequality now increase between 1984 and 1999 as seen in Table 5.4. Hence, when we consider 99.5 per cent, 98.5 per cent, or 94.5 per cent of family units, we can say that wealth inequality has unambiguously risen between 1984 and 1999.[8] This is the position we adopt in this chapter.[9]

For all three samples, the choice of the unit of analysis does not appear to matter: the percentage changes in inequality obtained using family units as the unit of analysis are fairly close to those obtained when individuals are considered.[10] For this reason, the rest of the analysis conducted in this chapter uses family units as the unit of analysis.

While the aforementioned inequality measures provide a summary of the changes in the wealth distribution, they are not very intuitive. A simple way to look at changes in the wealth distribution is to compare growth rates of median wealth across deciles. This exercise shows that median wealth fell in the bottom three deciles but rose at least 27 per cent in the top three deciles (Table 5.6). Hence, the increase in wealth inequality did not occur in a context where all segments of the population enjoyed increases in real wealth.

Only family units located in the upper two deciles (ninth and/or tenth decile) of the wealth distribution have increased their share of total net worth during the period (Table 5.7). For all other eight deciles, the share of total net worth has fallen. These results imply that only family units located in the upper two deciles have seen their average wealth increase faster than overall average wealth.

Wealth inequality did not rise uniformly in all types of family units. As measured by the Gini coefficient, it increased much more among nonelderly couples with children and among lone-parent families than among unattached individuals and nonelderly couples with no children (Table 5.8). Results not shown confirm that this pattern also holds when we use the coefficient of variation and the exponential measure.[11] Among nonelderly couples with children under 18, average wealth fell roughly 15 per cent in the second quintile but rose about 20 per cent in the fourth quintile and even more in the fifth quintile (Table 5.9).

CHANGES IN THE WEALTH STRUCTURE: OVERVIEW

The growth of wealth inequality occurred in conjunction with substantial changes in the wealth structure. Median wealth and average wealth evolved very differently for different family units. First, they rose much more among family units whose major income recipient is a university graduate than among other family units (Table 5.10). Second, they fell among family units whose major income recipient is aged 25–34 and increased among those whose major income recipient is aged 55–64. They

Table 5.6   Changes in median net worth, by net worth decile, 1984–99

	Median net worth (1999 constant dollars)		Change 1984–99	
	(1) 1984	(2) 1999	(3) (2)–(1)	(4) %
All family units				
Decile				
1st	−1824	−5700	−3876	–
2nd	674	101	−573	−85.0
3rd	6743	5920	−823	−12.2
4th	21 380	22 700	1320	6.2
5th	45 365	49 580	4215	9.3
6th	72 155	81 466	9311	12.9
7th	104 764	129 000	24 237	23.1
8th	147 751	192 500	44 749	30.3
9th	222 861	299 373	76 512	34.3
10th	464 376	628 100	163 724	35.3
Top 1% of family units excluded[a]				
Decile				
1st	−1839	−5900	−4061	–
2nd	615	100	−515	−83.7
3rd	6448	5550	−898	−13.9
4th	20 684	22 000	1316	6.4
5th	44 139	47 929	3790	8.6
6th	70 861	79 301	8440	11.9
7th	102 331	125 400	23 069	22.5
8th	143 298	186 025	42 728	29.8
9th	213 797	283 545	69 748	32.6
10th	407 976	559 350	151 374	37.1
Top 5% of family units excluded[a]				
Decile				
1st	−1992	−6220	−4228	–
2nd	463	50	−413	−89.2
3rd	5574	4500	−1074	−19.3
4th	17 864	19 060	1196	6.7
5th	39 388	42 597	3209	8.1
6th	65 288	72 200	6912	10.6
7th	93 028	112 600	19 572	21.0
8th	130 031	165 600	35 569	27.4
9th	183 957	242 455	58 498	31.8
10th	296 079	410 500	114 421	38.6

Note: a. After ranking family units by ascending order of their net worth.

Sources: Assets and Debts Survey of 1984, Survey of Financial Security of 1999.

Table 5.7   Shares of total net worth held, by each decile, 1984 and 1999

	(1) 1984 %	(2) 1999 %	(3) (2)–(1)
All family units			
Decile			
1st	−0.5	−0.6	−0.1
2nd	0.1	0.0	−0.1
3rd	0.5	0.4	−0.2
4th	1.7	1.3	−0.4
5th	3.5	2.8	−0.7
6th	5.6	4.7	−1.0
7th	8.2	7.4	−0.8
8th	11.5	11.0	−0.6
9th	17.5	17.4	−0.2
10th	51.8	55.7	3.9
Top 1% of family units excluded[a]			
Decile			
1st	−0.6	−0.8	−0.2
2nd	0.1	0.0	−0.1
3rd	0.6	0.4	−0.2
4th	1.9	1.6	−0.4
5th	4.1	3.4	−0.7
6th	6.6	5.7	−0.9
7th	9.5	9.0	−0.5
8th	13.4	13.3	−0.1
9th	20.1	20.7	0.6
10th	44.2	46.6	2.4
Top 5% of family units excluded[a]			
Decile			
1st	−0.7	−1.0	−0.3
2nd	0.1	0.0	−0.1
3rd	0.7	0.5	−0.2
4th	2.2	1.8	−0.4
5th	4.7	4.0	−0.7
6th	7.7	6.7	−1.0
7th	11.1	10.4	−0.7
8th	15.5	15.4	−0.1
9th	22.0	22.8	0.8
10th	36.8	39.5	2.6

Note: a. After ranking family units by ascending order of their net worth.

Sources: Assets and Debts Survey of 1984, Survey of Financial Security of 1999.

Table 5.8   Gini coefficient, by family type, 1984 and 1999

	1984	1999	% change
All family units			
Unattached individuals – elderly	0.647	0.655	1.2
Unattached individuals – nonelderly	0.853	0.868	1.8
Nonelderly couples with no children or other relatives	0.666	0.695	4.4
Nonelderly couples with children under 18[b]	0.647	0.707	9.3
Nonelderly couples with children 18 and over or other relatives[c]	0.540	0.614	13.7
Elderly couples with no children or other relatives	0.540	0.541	0.2
Lone-parent families	0.807	0.897	11.2
Other family types	0.667	0.650	−2.5
Top 1% of family units excluded[a]			
Unattached individuals – elderly	0.626	0.633	1.1
Unattached individuals – non elderly	0.840	0.852	1.4
Nonelderly couples with no children or other relatives	0.612	0.618	1.0
Nonelderly couples with children under 18[b]	0.587	0.636	8.3
Nonelderly couples with children 18 and over or other relatives[c]	0.460	0.530	15.2
Elderly couples with no children or other relatives	0.490	0.486	−0.8
Lone-parent families	0.807	0.866	7.3
Other family types	0.612	0.603	−1.5
Top 5% of family units excluded[a]			
Unattached individuals – elderly	0.598	0.599	0.2
Unattached individuals – nonelderly	0.823	0.840	2.1
Nonelderly couples with no children or other relatives	0.568	0.569	0.2
Nonelderly couples with children under 18[b]	0.535	0.591	10.5
Nonelderly couples with children 18 and over or other relatives[c]	0.385	0.461	19.7
Elderly couples with no children or other relatives	0.416	0.416	0.0
Lone-parent families	0.801	0.864	7.9
Other family types	0.560	0.553	−1.3

Notes:
a.   After ranking family units by ascending order of their net worth.
b.   The family includes at least one child of the major income earner under 18. Other relatives may also be in the family.
c.   Includes no children under 18.

Sources: Assets and Debts Survey of 1984, Survey of Financial Security of 1999.

Table 5.9   Average wealth of nonelderly couples with children under 18,
by quintile, 1984–99

	Average net worth (1999 constant dollars)		Change 1984–99	
	(1) 1984	(2) 1999	(3) (2)–(1)	(4) %
All nonelderly couples with children under 18[a] Quintile				
1st	65	−3275	−3340	–
2nd	34849	29819	−5030	−14.4
3rd	77853	80498	2645	3.4
4th	140961	170174	29213	20.7
5th	493015	703527	210512	42.7
Top 1% of nonelderly couples with children under 18 excluded[b] Quintile				
1st	−83	−3392	−3309	–
2nd	34289	29192	−5097	−14.9
3rd	76645	78806	2161	2.8
4th	137703	165624	27921	20.3
5th	383161	494398	111237	29.0
Top 5% of nonelderly couples with children under 18 excluded[b] Quintile				
1st	−708	−4013	−3305	–
2nd	31954	26815	−5139	−16.1
3rd	71845	72356	511	0.7
4th	126223	149044	22821	18.1
5th	269504	349289	79785	29.6

Notes:
a.   Couples with at least one child of the major income earner under age 18.
b.   After ranking couples with children by ascending order of their net worth.

Sources: Assets and Debts Survey of 1984, Survey of Financial Security of 1999.

Table 5.10 Wealth by characteristics of the major income recipient, all family units, 1984–99

	Median wealth			Average wealth		
	(1) 1984 (1999 constant dollars)	(2) 1999	(3) % change 1984–99	(4) 1984 (1999 constant dollars)	(5) 1999 $	(6) % change 1984–99
Education level of major income recipient						
Not a university graduate	52 807	54 100	2.4	119 344	145 279	21.7
University graduate	99 637	118 000	18.4	189 295	289 522	52.9
Age of major income recipient						
24 or younger	3073	150	−95.1	32 285	32 918	2.0
25–34	23 395	15 100	−35.5	69 890	67 264	−3.8
35–44	73 488	60 000	−18.4	137 608	151 915	10.4
45–54	123 987	115 200	−7.1	202 422	247 751	22.4
55–64	129 090	154 115	19.4	210 290	303 856	44.5
65 or older	80 789	126 000	56.0	140 749	211 863	50.5
Education/Age of major income recipient						
25–34 not a university graduate	21 196	11 100	−47.6	62 564	49 836	−20.3
25–34 university graduate	41 224	30 900	−25.0	102 119	112 088	9.8
35–54 not a university graduate	80 461	65 800	−18.2	153 211	156 045	1.8
35–54 university graduate	130 271	144 741	11.1	218 715	312 320	42.8

Immigration status of major income recipient					
Canadian-born	53 947	60 500	12.1	122 866	168 695	37.3
Immigrant, in Canada 20 years or more	120 002	171 300	42.7	194 756	285 585	46.6
Immigrant, in Canada 10–19 years	68 047	44 500	−34.6	114 357	140 782	23.1
Immigrant, in Canada less than 10 years	17 625	13 100	−25.7	90 103	75 686	−16.0
Family type						
Unattached individuals – elderly	41 380	70 000	69.2	78 674	138 107	75.5
Unattached individuals – non elderly	5 772	6 000	4.0	47 204	63 888	35.3
Couples, no children[a]	71 526	101 603	42.1	151 171	244 174	61.5
Couples, children under 18[b]	77 703	77 800	0.1	144 151	195 922	35.9
Couples, children 18 and over[c]	155 788	167 400	7.5	252 529	312 493	23.7
Elderly couples, no children[d]	121 075	177 500	46.6	198 498	280 487	41.3
Lone-parent families	1 870	3 656	95.5	38 534	63 808	65.6
Other family types	75 856	112 700	48.6	147 715	210 155	42.3

Notes:
a. Nonelderly couples with no children or other relatives.
b. Nonelderly couples with children under 18.
c. Nonelderly couples with children 18 and over or other relatives.
d. Elderly couples with no children or other relatives.

Sources: Assets and Debts Survey of 1984 and Survey of Financial Security of 1999.

rose even more among family units whose major income recipient is aged 65 and over. Third, they increased among Canadian-born family units and among foreign-born family units who have been living in Canada for 20 years or more but fell among foreign-born family units who have been living in Canada for less than ten years. Fourth, they increased faster among nonelderly couples with no children than among nonelderly couples with children under 18.

In many population subgroups, median wealth grew much more slowly than average wealth, likely reflecting an increase in inequality within population subgroups. For instance, among family units whose major income recipient is aged 25–34, median wealth fell 36 per cent while average wealth fell only 4 per cent. Similarly, nonelderly couples with children under 18 experienced essentially no change in their median wealth but enjoyed an increase of 30 per cent in their average wealth (Table 5.11).[12]

Young couples with children under 18 – those whose major income earner is aged 25–34 – experienced drastic changes. Their median and average wealth fell 30 per cent and 20 per cent, respectively.[13] This decline in net worth has had non-negligible consequences: the percentage of these couples with zero or negative wealth rose from 9.5 per cent in 1984 to 16.1 per cent in 1999. The decline in their median wealth led to a 39 per cent decrease in their net equity on principal residence, which was partly offset by an increase in their median financial wealth.[14]

Among family units whose major income recipient is aged 25–34, the decline in median wealth is unlikely to be due solely to a decrease in their real median after-tax income. The reason is that while the former dropped by 36 per cent, the latter fell by only 7 per cent.[15] However, growth rates of average wealth and average after-tax income diverge to a much lesser extent, being equal to minus 4 per cent and 1 per cent, respectively. Inheritances and *inter vivos* transfers (for example, parental financing of education or of the down payment on a house) are unlikely to be a factor since the parents of the 1999 cohort are unlikely to be poorer than those of the 1984 cohort. Other potential explanations are discussed below.

In contrast, the dramatic increase in median wealth and average wealth (56 per cent and 51 per cent, respectively) of family units whose major income recipient is at least 65 years old likely reflects a combination of factors: (1) possibly larger inheritances received by the 1999 cohort, compared to the 1984 cohort; (2) higher income from private pensions; and (3) higher income from the Canada and Quebec Pension Plans, from the Guaranteed Income Supplement, and Old Age Security.

In sum, family units headed by new entrants to the labour market – young individuals and recent immigrants – have lost ground relative to older families.[16] Furthermore, within a given age group, families headed by

Table 5.11   Wealth of nonelderly couples with children under 18, by age of major income recipient, 1984–99

	Net worth (1999 constant dollars)		
	(1) 1984	(2) 1999	(3) % change
Age of major income recipient			
25–54			
Average	149 674	194 949	30.2
Median	78 622	78 500	−0.2
% of couples with zero or negative net worth	6.2	8.5	
25–34			
Average	94 915	76 408	−19.5
Median	43 990	30 841	−29.9
% of couples with zero or negative net worth	9.5	16.0	
35–44			
Average	163 372	197 931	21.2
Median	91 123	89 500	−1.8
% of couples with zero or negative net worth	4.9	6.8	
45–54			
Average	227 809	326 831	43.5
Median	144 370	161 500	11.9
% of couples with zero or negative net worth	2.8	3.4	

Note: Nonelderly couples with at least one child of the major income recipient age 18.

Sources: Assets and Debts Survey of 1984, Survey of Financial Security of 1999.

individuals who do not have a university degree have lost ground relative to families headed by university graduates.[17]

WHY HAS WEALTH INEQUALITY INCREASED? RE-WEIGHTING METHODS

The substantial changes in family structure that Canada experienced over the last two decades may have had an impact on wealth inequality. Specifically, the growing proportion of unattached individuals and lone-parent families, which generally have lower than average wealth, could have contributed to the growth of wealth inequality. To assess the extent to which this is the case, we re-weight the 1999 data so that the relative importance of various types of family units is equal to that observed in 1984.[18] We then calculate the inequality measures resulting from this re-weighting. The results are presented in Table 5.12.

Whether changes in family structure tended to increase wealth inequality cannot be said with certainty. When all family units are considered, the impact of changes in family structure is ambiguous. Comparing columns 2 and 3 of Table 5.12, we find that applying the 1984 family structure to the 1999 data decreases the Gini coefficient and the exponential measure but increases the coefficient of variation (compared to their 1999 actual values). For the sample excluding the top 1 per cent of the wealth distribution, wealth inequality would have been lower in 1999 if the composition of

Table 5.12   *Counterfactual levels of wealth inequality in family units, based on 1984 weights, 1999*

	Actual data		1999 based on	
	(1) 1984	(2) 1999	(3) 1984 family type structure	(4) 1984 age structure
All family units				
Gini	0.691	0.727	0.724	0.750
CV	2.325	3.146	3.157	3.261
Exponential	0.531	0.560	0.558	0.590
Top 1% of family units excluded				
Gini	0.646	0.675	0.669	0.702
CV	1.429	1.517	1.498	1.613
Exponential	0.542	0.556	0.554	0.612
Top 5% of family units excluded				
Gini	0.605	0.637	0.629	0.668
CV	1.169	1.255	1.235	1.341
Exponential	0.906	0.838	0.848	1.074

Note: Family units are the unit of analysis.

Sources: Assets and Debts Survey of 1984 and Survey of Financial Security of 1999.

family units had remained the same as it was in 1984. For this sample, changes in family structure account for 14–22 per cent of the growth in wealth inequality.[19] For the sample that excludes the top 5 per cent of the wealth distribution, changes in family structure account for 25 per cent and 23 per cent of the growth in the Gini coefficient and the coefficient of variation, respectively.

The ageing of the Canadian population may also have affected wealth inequality. A priori, its impact is unclear since it is associated with a decline in the relative importance of young families, who have lower than average wealth, and an increase in the relative importance of older families, who tend to have higher than average wealth. To assess the impact of ageing, we re-weight the 1999 data with the 1984 age structure, using the six age groups defined in Table 5.3. Columns 2 and 4 of Table 5.12 show that the impact of ageing is unambiguous: had the 1984 age structure prevailed in 1999, wealth inequality would have been higher than it was in 1999. Hence, the ageing of the Canadian population tended to reduce wealth inequality.

Since median and average wealth evolved very differently across age groups and education levels, it is worth measuring the extent to which changes in the wealth structure have induced an increase in wealth inequality. In the third and fourth columns of Table 5.13, we ask what the level of wealth inequality would have been in 1999 if the structure of average wealth by age and/or education level of the major income recipient had been the same as it was in 1984. To do so, we simply re-scale the 1999 wealth values within each age/education cell j by the factor M_{j84}/M_{j99}, where M_{j84} and M_{j99} equal the average wealth of group j in 1984 and 1999, respectively.[20] Applying the 1984 wealth structure to the 1999 data generally tends to decrease the Gini coefficient (compared to its 1999 value) but generally tends to increase the coefficient of variation and the exponential measure. Thus, it is unclear whether changes in relative wealth by age and education (of the major income recipient) have contributed to the growth of wealth inequality.

The re-weighting methods used so far are fairly simple but cannot be used when explanatory variables, such as a family unit's permanent income, are continuous. Since wealth of a family depends, among other factors, on its permanent income, this is an important limitation. Fortunately, DiNardo et al. (1996) have proposed a semi-parametric approach which allows analysts to take into account the impact of continuous variables as well as of discrete variables.

In the fifth column of Table 5.13, we implement this approach. We answer the following question: what would wealth inequality have been in 1999 if permanent income and other attributes of family units had

Table 5.13   Counterfactual levels of wealth inequality in 1999

	Actual data		1999 based on		
	(1) 1984	(2) 1999	(3) 1984 Relative wealth by age	(4) 1984 Relative wealth by age and education level	(5) 1984 Family character- istics
All family units					
Gini	0.691	0.727	0.725	0.721	0.740
CV	2.325	3.146	3.207	3.161	3.244
Exponential	0.531	0.560	0.572	0.580	0.603
Top 1% of family units excluded					
Gini	0.646	0.675	0.672	0.671	0.695
CV	1.429	1.517	1.519	1.507	1.597
Exponential	0.542	0.556	0.643	0.656	0.676
Top 5% of family units excluded					
Gini	0.605	0.637	0.637	0.636	0.661
CV	1.169	1.255	1.260	1.257	1.326
Exponential	0.906	0.838	1.222	1.174	1.312

Note: Family units are the unit of analysis.

Sources: Assets and Debts Survey of 1984 and Survey of Financial Security of 1999.

remained at their 1984 level *and* family units had kept the net worth observed in 1999? The other attributes considered in this exercise are: age of major income recipient (five age groups), education level of major income recipient (two education levels), a lone-parent family indicator, family size, provincial controls and a rural–urban indicator.[21] For all three samples, our counterfactual inequality measures for 1999 are always higher than the actual inequality measures in 1999. This means that if the distribution of permanent income and other family attributes had remained at their 1984 level and family units had kept the net worth observed in 1999, wealth inequality would have been higher than it was in 1999. At the very least, this suggests that permanent income and other socio-demographic characteristics, as measured with cross-sectional data, are not major factors behind the growth of wealth inequality. In the next section, we confirm this finding using regression-based methods.

WHY HAS WEALTH INEQUALITY INCREASED? REGRESSION-BASED METHODS

In this section, we move away from the concept of inequality (where greater inequality implies that the 1999 Lorenz curve would lie below the 1984 Lorenz curve at all points of the wealth distribution) and ask the following question: why has the average wealth of low-wealth family units grown at a smaller rate than the average wealth of wealthier family units? To do so, we use regression-based methods.

Empirical Framework

We follow the methodology used by Blau and Graham (1990) to study black–white wealth differentials and apply it to the investigation of the causes of the growth in wealth inequality. First, we specify the following wealth equation:

$$lnW_{it} = \alpha_0 + Y_{it}*\beta_1 + Z_{it}*\beta_2 + u_{it} \qquad (5.1)$$

where lnW_{it} is the natural logarithm of net worth of family unit i at year t, Y_{it} is a vector of a family unit's permanent and transitory income, Z_{it} is a vector of socio-demographic characteristics which may affect a family unit's savings rate, and u_{it} is a normally distributed random term. We define a family unit's permanent income as the predicted income of this unit when the major income recipient is aged 45 and the spouse (if present) age is set equal to what his or her age would be when the major income recipient is aged 45.[22] Defining $w_{it} = lnW_{it}$, we rewrite equation (5.1) in a more compact form:

$$w_{it} = X_{it}*\beta + u_{it} \qquad (5.2)$$

where X_{it} combines the two vectors Y_{it} and Z_{it}.

Second, using the standard Oaxaca-Blinder decomposition, we note that:

$$\overline{w}_{99}^j - \overline{w}_{84}^j = \hat{\beta}_{99} * (\overline{X}_{99}^j - \overline{X}_{84}^j) + \overline{X}_{84}^j * (\hat{\beta}_{99}^j - \hat{\beta}_{84}^j) \qquad (5.3)$$

Equation (5.3) indicates that the change in average log wealth between 1984 and 1999 for family units of group j (for example, low-wealth family units) is the sum of two components. The first component on the right of (5.3) is the part of the growth in wealth of this group attributable to changes over time in the mean characteristics of the group. The second component is the part due to differences in the returns to these characteristics as well as differences in the constant terms. Applying (5.3) to both low-wealth and high-wealth family units, the difference between the growth rate of wealth of high-wealth family units (h) and the growth rate of wealth of low-wealth family units (l) can be expressed as follows:

$$(\overline{w}_{99}^h - \overline{w}_{84}^h) - (\overline{w}_{99}^l - \overline{w}_{84}^l)$$
$$= (\hat{\beta}_{99}^h * (\overline{X}_{99}^h - \overline{X}_{84}^h) - \hat{\beta}_{99}^l * (\overline{X}_{99}^l - \overline{X}_{84}^l)) \qquad (5.4)$$
$$+ (\overline{X}_{84}^h * (\hat{\beta}_{99}^h - \hat{\beta}_{84}^h) - \overline{X}_{84}^l * (\hat{\beta}_{99}^l - \hat{\beta}_{84}^l))$$

The first line of equation (5.4) is the difference between the change over time in average log wealth of high-wealth family units and that of low-wealth family units. The component on the second line of (5.4) is the portion of this difference due to changes in relative mean characteristics across groups of family units, that is, relative changes in the composition of the population, weighted at group-specific 1999 coefficients. This component allows us to measure the degree to which differences in the growth of permanent or transitory income (or other socio-demographic characteristics) account for the growth in the wealth gap between low-wealth and high-wealth family units. The second component, defined on the third line of the equation (5.4), is the change due to variation in the relative returns to these characteristics across groups of family units, weighted by group-specific 1984 means of the explanatory variables. Equation (5.4) can also be rewritten in an equivalent way by weighting the second line of (5.4) at group-specific 1984 coefficients and the third line of (5.4) at group-specific 1999 means of the explanatory variables.

To perform this decomposition, we estimate equation (5.1) separately for low-wealth and high-wealth family units and for each of the years 1984 and 1999. The dependent variable we first select is the natural logarithm of net worth of a family unit. The explanatory variables in the wealth regressions include permanent income, transitory income, age of major income recipient (five age groups), education level of major income recipient (two education levels), a lone-parent family indicator, family size, provincial controls and a rural–urban indicator.[23] Low-wealth family units are defined as those located between the 15th and the 50th percentile of the wealth distribution. High-wealth family units are defined in two different ways: (1) those located between the 50th and the 85th percentile; and (2) those located between the 60th and the 95th percentile of the wealth distribution. The decomposition of equation (5.4) is performed using the two types of weighting schemes defined in the previous paragraph.

It is important to acknowledge that the lack of longitudinal data prior to 1984 for family units selected in ADS 1984 and prior to 1999 for those selected in SFS 1999 limit our ability to estimate family units' permanent income. As pointed out by Altonji et al. (2000), much of the variation in permanent income may be within the socio-demographic cells included in the income regression used to calculate permanent income. Furthermore, our measure of permanent income is based solely on family units' current income (and demographics) and, as such, does not capture the number of years members of a family unit have been working full-time in the labour market. Thus, if members of young families have been getting full-time jobs later in their lives in the 1990s than their counterparts did in the 1980s, the former group will have accumulated less money than the latter when they reach, say, age 30. Although this may be an important factor behind the growth of wealth inequality, it will not be captured in our wealth regressions.[24]

Estimation Results

Table 5.14 shows the average values of the variables used in the log wealth regressions. Between 1984 and 1999, average log wealth of family units located in the 15th–50th percentile dropped by minus 0.128 while average log wealth of those located in the 50th–85th (60th–95th) percentile increased by 0.210 (0.264).

For low-wealth family units as well as for both definitions of high-wealth family units, permanent income is higher than actual (after-tax) income. As expected, transitory income is, on average, very close to zero.

Between 1984 and 1999, permanent income has dropped slightly for low-wealth family units but has increased for high-wealth family units. Hence, this difference in changes in permanent income may potentially explain part of the growth in the wealth gap between high-wealth family units and low-wealth family units.

The percentage of young family units – for example, those whose major income recipient is less than 30 years old – has dropped much more among low-wealth family units (from 35 to 21 per cent) than among their high-wealth counterparts (from 10 to 5 per cent for family units located in the 50–85th percentile, from 8 per cent to 3 per cent for family units located in the 60–95th percentile. Since the average wealth of young family units is below the overall average, these diverging changes in the relative import-ance of young family units may tend to reduce the wealth gap. However, the percentage of older family units – for example, those whose major income recipient is at least 65 years old – has risen by at least 5 percentage points among high-wealth family units but has remained virtually unchanged among low-wealth family units. This diverging pattern tends to increase the wealth gap. As a result, the effect of the changes in the age composition of low-wealth and high-wealth units on the growth in the wealth gap is unclear.

Table 5.14   Descriptive statistics, variables included in the log wealth regressions, 1984 and 1999

	15th–50th percentile		50th–85th percentile		60th–95th percentile	
	1984	1999	1984	1999	1984	1999
Explanatory variables in the wealth regression						
Actual income[a]	30.394	31.509	43.929	46.289	49.326	50.815
Permanent income ($000)	35.847	34.744	50.908	54.408	56.290	58.902
Transitory income ($000)	7.48E-08	−1.57E-08	2.31E-07	2.08E-07	4.86E-08	−1.72E-07
Fraction of family units whose major income recipient is aged:						
Less than 30	0.348	0.211	0.097	0.046	0.077	0.030
30–44	0.338	0.407	0.353	0.340	0.323	0.294
45–54	0.091	0.156	0.185	0.233	0.215	0.246
55–64	0.076	0.079	0.171	0.137	0.195	0.170
65 and over	0.148	0.147	0.195	0.245	0.191	0.260
Fraction of family units whose major income recipient is:						
Not a university graduate	0.889	0.826	0.857	0.781	0.833	0.744
A university graduate	0.111	0.174	0.143	0.219	0.167	0.256
Fraction of family units who are:						
Not lone-parent families	0.964	0.948	0.981	0.982	0.983	0.987
Lone-parent families	0.036	0.052	0.019	0.018	0.017	0.013
Family size	2.384	2.254	2.922	2.655	2.997	2.701

Fraction of family units living in:						
Newfoundland	0.022	0.021	0.021	0.015	0.015	0.009
Prince-Edward-Island	0.004	0.005	0.005	0.004	0.004	0.004
Nova Scotia	0.034	0.034	0.036	0.032	0.029	0.026
New Brunswick	0.033	0.029	0.025	0.026	0.019	0.018
Quebec	0.294	0.294	0.252	0.245	0.216	0.212
Ontario	0.319	0.330	0.380	0.375	0.403	0.409
Manitoba	0.039	0.040	0.044	0.039	0.045	0.035
Saskatchewan	0.036	0.031	0.037	0.036	0.041	0.035
Alberta	0.104	0.089	0.077	0.102	0.083	0.104
British Columbia	0.115	0.127	0.122	0.125	0.145	0.147
Fraction of family units living in:						
Rural areas	0.145	0.156	0.177	0.195	0.166	0.180
Urban areas	0.855	0.844	0.823	0.805	0.834	0.820
Wealth						
Average wealth (1999 constant $)	21 386	22 652	121 670	153 684	188 469	250 223
Average log wealth	9.453	9.325	11.643	11.853	12.050	12.314
Sample size	4863	5252	5049	5499	4974	5509

Note: a. Not an explanatory variable in the wealth regression. See text for the definition of permanent and transitory income.

Sources: Assets and Debts Survey of 1984, Survey of Financial Security of 1999.

Increases in educational attainment are very similar across groups of family units. The percentage of major income recipients with a university degree has risen by 6 percentage points (from 11 to 17 per cent) among low-wealth family units and by 7 to 9 percentage points among high-wealth family units. Hence, education is unlikely to be a major factor behind the growth in the wealth gap. Similarly, the percentage of lone-parent families has risen very slightly (from 4 to 5 per cent) among low-wealth family units and has remained virtually unchanged among high-wealth family units. As a result, changes in the relative importance of lone-parent families are also unlikely to play a substantial role.

The same conclusion can be reached for family size, province and urban–rural status: there are no substantially diverging patterns for these three variables. Hence, our expectations are that changes in permanent income and in age composition may play a role in explaining the growing wealth gap while changes in other demographic characteristics are unlikely to do so.

Table 5.15 confirms these expectations. Whatever definition of high-wealth family unit is considered and whatever weighting scheme is used, education, lone-parent status, family size, province, and urban–rural status explain virtually none of the growth in the wealth gap.[25] Differences in the growth of permanent income do play a role but their impact is very limited: they only explain between 9 and 15 per cent of the growth in the wealth gap. Unsurprisingly, transitory income has no impact. The effect of permanent income is offset by the fact that differences in changes in age composition across groups tended to reduce the wealth gap. The consequence is that, taken together, all explanatory variables explain virtually none of the growth in the wealth gap.

The conclusion is that neither diverging changes in permanent income nor diverging changes in socio-demographic characteristics – as measured with cross-sectional data – explain a significant portion of the growing gap between low-wealth and high-wealth family units.[26] This suggests that differences across groups in the growth of inheritances, *inter vivos* transfers, past rates of return and/or in the number of years spent working full-time are likely to have contributed to the growth in the wealth gap between low-wealth and high-wealth family units.

AN ACCOUNTING EXPLANATION FOR THE GROWTH OF WEALTH INEQUALITY

In any given year t, the Gini coefficient of wealth (G_t) is the sum of the contributions of each wealth component k to overall inequality (C_{kt}):

Table 5.15   *Decomposition of the growing gap between wealthy and low-wealth family units, 1984–99*

Average log wealth	1984	1999	Change 1984–99
15th–50th percentile	9.453	9.325	−0.128
50th–85th percentile	11.643	11.853	0.210
Difference in changes over time	–	–	0.338
15th–50th percentile	9.453	9.325	−0.128
60th–95th percentile	12.050	12.314	0.264
Difference in changes over time	–	–	0.392

Decomposition of
difference in changes
over time

	(0.338 = 100.0)		(0.392 = 100.0)	
	Weighting scheme 1	Weighting scheme 2	Weighting scheme 1	Weighting scheme 2
Percentage explained by:				
Permanent income	15.2	9.8	12.6	8.6
Transitory income	0.0	0.0	0.0	0.0
Age	−14.8	−10.3	−15.1	−10.4
Education	−1.5	−1.9	−0.1	−1.4
Lone-parent status	−0.1	1.8	−0.2	1.5
Family size	−1.9	0.2	−1.0	0.7
Province	2.9	1.6	2.7	1.6
Urban/rural status	−1.8	−1.3	−1.4	−0.8
Total explained	−2.0	−0.1	−2.5	−0.2
Percentage unexplained	102.0	100.1	102.5	100.2
Difference in changes over time	100.0	100.0	100.0	100.0

Sources: Authors' calculations from the Assets and Debts Survey of 1984 and the Survey of Financial Security of 1999.

$$Gt = \Sigma \; C_{kt} \qquad (5.5)$$

In the case of the Gini coefficient, the contribution of each wealth component k to overall inequality equals (Lerman and Yitzhaki 1985):

$$C_{kt} = G_{kt} * S_{kt} * R_{kt} \qquad (5.6)$$

where G_{kt} is the Gini coefficient of wealth component k in year t, S_{kt} is the share of component k in total net worth and R_{kt} is the 'Gini correlation' between the component k and the overall net worth.[27] Equation (5.6) implies that wealth component k will contribute greatly to overall wealth inequality when: (1) this wealth component is unequally distributed (the higher G_{kt} is); (2) the relative importance of this wealth component in overall net worth is large (the greater S_{kt} is); and (3) this wealth component is highly correlated with overall net worth is (the greater R_{kt} is). For instance, since the share of housing (vehicles) in overall net worth is high (low), we expect – other things being equal – housing (vehicles) to have a relatively large (small) contribution to overall inequality in a given year.

Combining equations (5.5) and (5.6), the change in the Gini coefficient between 1984 and 1999 can be expressed as the sum of the changes in the contribution of each component:

$$G_{99} - G_{84} = (\Sigma \ G_{k99} * S_{k99} * R_{k99}) - (\Sigma \ G_{k84} * S_{k84} * R_{k84}) \qquad (5.7)$$

It is important to understand that the decomposition of the change in the Gini coefficient performed in equation (5.7) is a purely accounting exercise. For instance, equation (5.7) may reveal that part of the growth in inequality observed between 1984 and 1999 is accounted for by an increase in the contribution C_{kt} of stocks to overall inequality. If this increase in the contribution of stocks is, for instance, due to an increase in the relative importance of stocks in overall net worth (S_{kt}) or to an increase in inequality in the stocks distribution (G_{kt}), equation (5.8) does not tell us why the relative importance of stocks has increased nor why the distribution of stocks has become more unequal.

In Table 5.16, we use the sample consisting of all family units and look at the contribution C_{kt} of each wealth component to overall inequality in a given year.[28] Information on G_{kt}, S_{kt} and R_{kt} is also presented. Three points are worth noting regarding these last three variables.

First, of all wealth components representing at least 5 per cent of net worth, principal residence and vehicles are the two most equally distributed wealth components, exhibiting a Gini coefficient ranging between 0.605 and 0.635, depending on the year considered (Table 5.14, column 2). In contrast, (1) stocks, bonds and mutual funds; (2) real estate other than principal residence; and (3) business equity, are the three most unequally distributed wealth components, with Gini coefficients ranging between 0.916 and 0.985. Second, principal residence is by far the most important wealth component, accounting for 49–51 per cent of net worth (Table 5.16, column 3). Third, the Gini correlation is the highest for business equity (between 0.928 and 0.933), indicating that the ranking of family units by business equity is very

Table 5.16   *Overall wealth inequality by wealth component, all family units, 1984 and 1999*

	(1) Gt	(2) Gkt	(3) Skt	(4) Rkt	(5) Ckt (2)*(3)*(4)	(6) Ckt/Gt %
1984: Wealth component						
Assets						
Deposits, non-RRSP	–	0.773	0.114	0.741	0.065	9.5
Stocks, bonds and mutual funds, non-RRSP	–	0.916	0.061	0.791	0.044	6.4
RRSPs / LIRAs[a]	–	0.889	0.044	0.755	0.029	4.3
Other investments or financial assets, non-RRSP	–	0.970	0.028	0.773	0.021	3.0
Principal residence	–	0.629	0.494	0.798	0.248	35.9
Real estate other than principal residence	–	0.920	0.115	0.742	0.078	11.3
Vehicles	–	0.610	0.065	0.525	0.021	3.0
Other assets	–	0.987	0.002	0.586	0.001	0.2
Business equity	–	0.963	0.246	0.933	0.221	32.0
Debts						
Mortgage on principal residence	–	0.833	0.100	0.250	0.021	−3.0
Other debt	–	0.832	0.069	0.306	0.018	−2.5
Total	0.691	–	–	–	–	100.0
1999: Wealth component						
Assets						
Deposits, non-RRSP	–	0.825	0.075	0.747	0.046	6.3
Stocks, bonds and mutual funds, non-RRSP	–	0.948	0.109	0.902	0.093	12.9
RRSPs / LIRAs	–	0.823	0.159	0.827	0.109	14.9
Other investments or financial assets, non-RRSP	–	0.966	0.020	0.761	0.014	2.0
Principal residence	–	0.605	0.513	0.805	0.250	34.4
Real estate other than principal residence	–	0.931	0.109	0.773	0.079	10.8
Vehicles	–	0.635	0.058	0.590	0.022	3.0
Other assets	–	0.990	0.004	0.885	0.004	0.5
Business equity	–	0.985	0.165	0.928	0.151	20.7

Table 5.16   (continued)

	(1) Gt	(2) Gkt	(3) Skt	(4) Rkt	(5) Ckt (2)*(3)*(4)	(6) Ckt/Gt %
Debts						
Mortgage on principal residence	–	0.794	0.141	0.224	0.025	−3.5
Other debt	–	0.792	0.072	0.268	0.015	−2.1
Total	0.727	–	–	–	–	100.0

Note: a. Locked-in retirement accounts.

Sources: Authors' calculations from the Assets and Debts Survey of 1984 and the Survey of Financial Security of 1999.

close to the ranking of family units by net worth (Table 5.16, column 4). Conversely, among all assets, the Gini correlation is the lowest for vehicles: it ranges between 0.525 and 0.590. This means that the ranking of family units by value of vehicles conveys less information about the ranking of family units by net worth, compared to business equity.[29]

Dramatic shifts in the relative importance of wealth components took place between 1984 and 1999. The share of RRSPs in wealth increased from 4 to 16 per cent, reflecting the growing popularity of this financial asset in family units' portfolio.[30] Similarly, the share of stocks, bonds and mutual funds rose from 6 to 11 per cent. The share of mortgage on principal residence rose from 10 to 14 per cent, probably due in part to the easier access to mortgage loans provided by financial institutions between 1984 and 1999.[31] These changes were accompanied by a marked decrease in the relative importance of business equity (from 25 to 17 per cent) and a more moderate decrease in the relative importance of deposits (from 11 to 8 per cent).[32]

In a given year, which wealth components contribute the most to wealth inequality? Both in 1984 and 1999, principal residence has by far the biggest contribution to overall inequality. It accounts for 34–36 per cent of overall inequality (Table 5.16, column 6). While the contribution of principal residence remained stable between 1984 and 1999, this was not the case for other wealth components. The contribution of RRSPs to overall inequality rose from 4 to 15 per cent. The contribution of stocks, bonds and mutual funds increased from 6 to 13 per cent. In contrast, the contribution of business equity dropped dramatically, showing a decline from 32 to 21 per cent. The contribution of deposits also fell (from 10 to 6 per cent).[33]

While the growing contribution of RRSPs, stocks, bonds and mutual funds to overall inequality comes as no surprise, the markedly decreasing contribution of business equity is, at first, puzzling.

The puzzle can be resolved. First, note that the decline in the contribution of business equity to overall inequality is, in an accounting sense, entirely explained by the decrease in the relative importance of business equity in net worth (from 25 to 17 per cent).[34] Second, note that the bulk of the decrease in the relative importance of business equity in net worth is explained by the fact that the average business equity for family units who have a business dropped from $224 000 in 1984 to $156 000 in 1999.[35]

Third, shift-share analysis shows that this decrease in the average business equity of family units with a business is entirely explained by the fact that the distribution of businesses moved towards very small firms. More precisely, the percentage of businesses with net equity ranging between $0 and $10 000 rose from 20 per cent in 1984 to 49 per cent in 1999 while the relative importance of businesses with net equity of $100 000–$500 000 dropped from 29 to 17 per cent (Table 5.17). This increase in self-employment in very small businesses occurred in a period where self-employment without paid help grew tremendously.[36] This suggests that the move towards self-employed jobs without paid help and with very small assets, for example, self-employed persons operating a consulting business with a microcomputer and some other electronic equipment at home, is at the heart of the decrease in the relative importance of business equity, and thus, this is an important factor behind the decrease in the contribution of business equity to overall inequality.

Since the contribution of RRSPs and stocks, bonds and mutual funds to overall inequality has increased between 1984 and 1999 while the contribution of business equity and deposits has fallen, we expect these four wealth components to be the major factors accounting for the growth in wealth inequality during the period.

Using equation (5.7), we confirm this conjecture. Between 1984 and 1999, the Gini coefficient of wealth increased by 0.036 (Table 5.18, column 1). The two most important contributors to the growth of wealth inequality were RRSPs (0.079) and stocks, bonds and mutual funds (0.049), which tended to increase the Gini by 0.128 (0.079 + 0.049). The effect of these two factors was partially offset by business equity and deposits: business equity tended to reduce the Gini by 0.071 while deposits tended to reduce the Gini by 0.019. Principal residence explained virtually none of the growth in wealth inequality.

Thus, when we consider all family units, the growth of wealth inequality can be explained, in an accounting sense, mainly by the growing contribution of RRSPs and stocks, bonds and mutual funds to overall inequality,

*Table 5.17   Percentage distribution of family units, by net equity classes,
1984 and 1999*

	1984 %	1999 %	% Change 1984–99
Distribution			
Net equity classes (1999 constant $)			
x<0	0.4	1.0	0.6
(0<x<10 000)	20.2	48.6	28.4
(10 000<=x<20 000)	9.7	7.3	−2.4
(20 000<=x<30 000)	4.7	5.4	0.7
(30 000<=x<40 000)	7.7	3.1	−4.6
(40 000<=x<50 000)	3.6	2.1	−1.5
(50 000<=x<60 000)	2.5	3.4	0.9
(60 000<=x<70 000)	3.3	1.8	−1.4
(70 000<=x<80 000)	4.0	1.6	−2.4
(80 000<=x<90 000)	1.3	1.1	−0.3
(90 000<=x<100 000)	2.7	0.8	−1.9
(100 000<=x<500 000)	28.6	16.9	−11.7
(500 000<=x<1 000 000)	7.7	3.8	−3.9
x>=1 000 000	3.8	3.1	−0.7
Total	100.0	100.0	–

Shift-share analysis

Average business equity for family units with a business (1999 constant $):	224 086	155 610
(*a*) *Hypothetical* average business equity in 1999 based on 1984 class-specific weights	–[a]	231 206
(*b*) *Hypothetical* average business equity in 1984 based on 1999 class-specific weights	146 358	–[a]

Fraction of the decline in average business
equity accounted for by changes in the
distribution of businesses by net equity classes:
(a) 1984 class-specific weights:
   (231 206 – 155 610)/(224 086 – 155 610) = 110.4%
(b) 1999 class-specific weights:
   (224 086 – 146 358)/(224 086 – 155 610) = 113.5%

Notes:
Family units with non-zero business equity only.
a.   Statistic not defined for the year in which it appears.

Sources: Assets and Debts Survey of 1984, Survey of Financial Security of 1999.

Table 5.18   Decomposition of the change in Gini coefficient by wealth component, 1984–99

Contribution of each wealth component to the change in Gini coefficient	(1) All family units	(2) Top 1% of family units excluded	(3) Top 5% of family units excluded
Wealth component			
Assets			
Deposits, non-RRSP	−0.019	−0.016	−0.024
Stocks, bonds and mutual funds, non-RRSP	0.049	0.024	0.006
RRSPs / LIRAs	0.079	0.084	0.076
Other investments or financial assets, non-RRSP	−0.006	−0.006	−0.002
Principal residence	0.001	0.011	0.020
Real estate other than principal residence	0.000	−0.004	−0.008
Vehicles	0.001	0.002	0.001
Other assets	0.002	0.000	0.000
Business equity	−0.071	−0.060	−0.024
Debts			
Mortgage on principal residence	−0.004	−0.008	−0.011
Other debt	0.002	0.001	−0.002
Change in Gini coefficient between 1984 and 1999[a]	0.036	0.029	0.032

Note: a. The sum of contributions of wealth components may not add to the change in Gini coefficient due to rounding.

Sources: Authors' calculations from the Assets and Debts Survey of 1984 and the Survey of Financial Security of 1999.

which is partially offset by the declining contribution of business equity and deposits.[37]

This qualitative conclusion holds when we exclude the top 1 per cent of family units (Table 5.18, column 2).[38] However, it must be altered when we exclude the top 5 per cent of family units. In this case, RRSPs remain the most important contributor to the growth of wealth inequality but stocks, bonds and mutual funds no longer have a major impact.[39] Business equity and deposits remain the two most important factors tending to decrease wealth inequality.

SUMMARY AND CONCLUSION

This chapter has documented the evolution of wealth inequality in Canada between 1984 and 1999. The main findings can be summarized as follows:

1. Wealth inequality has increased between 1984 and 1999.
2. The growth in wealth inequality has been associated with substantial declines in average and median wealth for some groups, such as young couples with children and recent immigrants.
3. Only the tenth (and for some samples, the ninth) decile has increased its share of total net worth between 1984 and 1999.
4. Wealth inequality increased more among nonelderly couples with children and among lone-parent families than among unattached individuals and nonelderly couples with no children.
5. Median wealth and average wealth rose much more among family units whose major income recipient is a university graduate than among other family units; they both fell among family units whose major income recipient is aged 25–34 and increased among those whose major income recipient is aged 55 and over.
6. The ageing of the Canadian population over the 1984–99 period has tended to increase average wealth and to reduce wealth inequality.
7. When all family units are considered, changes in family structure – for example, the growing proportion of lone-parent families and unattached individuals – have an ambiguous impact on wealth inequality. However, when the top 1 per cent of family units are excluded, changes in family structure account for 14 to 22 per cent of the growth in wealth inequality.
8. Changes in relative average wealth by age and education level of the major income recipient have an ambiguous effect on wealth inequality.
9. Whether wealth is specified in logarithms or levels, regression-based methods suggest that changes in families' permanent after-tax income account for little of the growth in the wealth gap between low-wealth and high-wealth family units.
10. In a purely accounting (and not causal) sense, RRSPs have, of all wealth components, contributed the most to the increase in wealth inequality.

Several factors may have contributed to the growth of wealth inequality. First, the increase in the length of time young individuals stay in school before entering the labour market in a full-time job (decreasing the number of years over which they have had significant incomes) and the greater debt load of students probably account for part of the decrease in their median wealth (Morissette 2002b).[40] Second, the booming stock market of the

1990s has likely contributed to the rapid revaluation of financial assets observed in Canada over the last decade. Since financial assets are held predominantly by families at the top of the wealth distribution, this revaluation is likely to have contributed to the growth of wealth inequality.[41] Third, easier access to credit and/or changes in preferences may have induced some low-wealth families to accumulate more debt in order to finance consumption expenditures, thereby decreasing their net worth. Fourth, increases in contributions to RRSPs made by families in the middle of the wealth distribution could have widened the gap between them and poorer families if these greater contributions induced an increase in their savings rate. Fifth, differences between low-wealth and high-wealth family units in the growth of inheritances and *inter vivos* transfers may also have played a role. These factors cannot be quantified with existing data sets.

The growing proportion of young couples with children who have zero or negative wealth suggests that a non-negligible fraction of today's young families may be vulnerable to negative shocks; that is, families that have no accumulated savings that can provide liquidity in periods of economic stress. Whether the picture one gets of vulnerable families changes when considering wealth instead of income is a question which deserves further research.

NOTES

1. Institutions such as penal institutions, mental hospitals, sanatoriums, orphanages and seniors' residences.
2. Weighting procedures cannot correct this problem since no family with wealth over $10 ($50) million would be observed in the sample.
3. Using the sample that includes all family units (first sample), the percentage of family units with zero or negative net worth increased from 11 per cent in 1984 to 13 per cent in 1999. Similar increases are observed for the two other samples.
4. The share of average financial wealth in net worth rose from: (1) 27 to 38 per cent; (2) 29 to 39 per cent; (3) 30 to 36 per cent for the first, second and third sample, respectively.
5. When using family units as the unit of analysis, an unattached individual with a net worth of $49 000 will be given a lower rank in the wealth distribution than a family of four with a net worth of $50 000. A different conclusion would be reached if individuals were the unit of analysis – in other words, if wealth was divided by the number of individuals in the family.
6. We are not able to create bootstrap samples properly for the 1984 survey because we have only the final weights. The construction of bootstrap samples should use the original weights and other information on the details of the sample which are no longer available for the 1984 survey. While bootstrapping with the available information is do-able, it would probably underestimate the true level of sampling error. We overcome this problem by noting that since the sample size for the 1984 survey was a little smaller than the 1999 survey, we can assume that the sampling error in the 1984 survey is at least equal to and likely a little larger than for the 1999 survey. The standard errors for average wealth were published for the 1984 survey and can be compared to standard errors for

comparable wealth estimates in the 1999 survey. This allows us to compare the difference between the sampling error levels in the two surveys and create an adjustment factor if it appears necessary to estimate a higher sampling error for the 1984 survey. Hence, we use the 1999 survey (bootstrap) sampling error levels to estimate roughly the error levels in the 1984 surveys. While this method is very crude, it is easy to implement and reflects the view that our ability to estimate sampling errors in the 1984 survey more precisely is limited. The adjustment factor is 1.08, indicating the standard error for average wealth in 1984 is 8 per cent higher than its counterpart in 1999 (measured in 1984 constant dollars). To provide conservative significance tests, we assume that the adjustment factor is 2.0 (a doubling of the standard error in 1984). Even with these conservative assumptions, we find that the increase in the Gini coefficient is always significant at the 1 per cent level as seen in Table 5.2.

7.   We refer here to the bottom 0.5 per cent of the wealth distribution of family units.
8.   For all six combinations, the increases in the Gini coefficient observed between 1984 and 1999 when we further exclude the bottom 0.5 per cent of the wealth distribution exceed by at most 0.3 of a percentage point the increases reported in the third column of Table 5.5.
9.   One could argue that the growth in wealth inequality documented in this chapter is spurious, that it simply reflects the fact that financial assets – which are predominantly held by the rich – are better reported in 1999 than they were in 1984. We address this issue in Morissette et al. (2002). We compare estimates of financial assets derived from the wealth surveys used in this chapter with estimates derived from National Accounts. We show that, compared to National Accounts' estimates, financial assets are less under-reported in SFS 1999 than they were in ADS 1984. However, most of the increase in the Gini coefficient measured in this chapter remains after implementing either proportional corrections or nonlinear corrections which assume a greater degree of underreporting among wealthy families than among their poorer counterparts. Therefore, we conclude that the growth in wealth inequality documented in this chapter is unlikely to be spurious.
10. The only exceptions occur for the exponential measure which produces more pronounced relative differences in growth rates (between family units and individuals) for the samples excluding the top 1 per cent and the top 5 per cent of family units.
11. Among elderly couples with no children or other relatives, inequality rose little except when we use the coefficient of variation and consider the sample of all family units.
12. Couples with children under 18 are defined as couples with at least one child of the major income earner under age 18.
13. The bootstrap standard error of median wealth in 1999 equals 2666.69. Even if we assume that the standard error of median wealth in 1984 is twice as high, the difference between median wealth in 1999 and median wealth in 1984 is statistically significant at the 5 per cent level.
14. Median net equity on principal residence fell from $26054 in 1984 to $16000 in 1999. Median financial wealth rose from $7157 in 1984 to $8000 in 1999.
15. This statement must be made with caution since changes in wealth depend, among other things, on changes in the set of annual after-tax incomes received in the past, not only on changes in current after-tax income measured by cross-sectional data. In other words while current after-tax income dropped by 7 per cent, cumulative after-tax income could have dropped by more than 7 per cent.
16. Morissette (2002a) combines wealth data with income data and shows that between 1984 and 1999, recent immigrants have become much more vulnerable to income losses and unexpected expenditures. In 1984, of all persons living in immigrant families arrived less than 10 years ago, 16 per cent were living on low incomes and would have remained in low income even if they had liquidated all their financial assets and added the proceeds to their after-tax income. This fraction rose to 26 per cent in 1999. The corresponding numbers for all individuals living in Canada were 10 per cent both in 1984 and 1999, compared to at least 42 per cent for persons living in female lone-parent families.
17. Since there is evidence that financial assets are better reported in 1999 than in 1984 (Morissette et al. 2002), the growth rates of wealth observed for groups with growing

wealth must be interpreted with caution. They likely represent an upper bound for the true growth rates of wealth of these groups.

18.   We use 14 categories to define various types of family units.

19.   The coefficient of variation one would have observed in 1999 if the 1984 family structure had prevailed equals 1.498, rather than 1.517. Hence, in this case, 22 per cent [(1.517 – 1.498)/(1.517 – 1.429)] of the growth in the coefficient of variation can be accounted for by changes in family structure.

20.   When doing so, we hold constant wealth inequality within age–education cells but allow average wealth to change for the whole population.

21.   We define a family unit's permanent income as the predicted income of this unit when the major income recipient is aged 45 and the spouse (if present) age is set equal to what his or her age would be when the major income recipient is aged 45. See next section for further details.

      To implement this approach, we first pool the 1984 and 1999 data. Second, we estimate a logit model where the dependent variable equals 1 if a family unit with a given level of permanent income and other given attributes is observed in 1984, 0 if it is observed in 1999. Third, we re-weight the 1999 data by the factor $(P_{i84}/P_{i99})*(K_{99}/K_{84})$, where P_{i84} and P_{i99} are the probability of family i being observed in 1984 and 1999, respectively, K_{99} and K_{84} are the sum of weights for 1999 and 1984, respectively. Fourth, after reweighting the 1999 data, we calculate the counterfactual inequality measures. The explanatory variables used in the logit model include permanent income and other attributes defined above.

22.   Since current income may not be a very good proxy for the lifetime or permanent income upon which savings decisions are based, we follow Blau and Graham (1990) and estimate wealth regressions with measures of permanent and transitory income. To estimate permanent income, we first regress after-tax family income on: (1) a vector of age dummy variables for the major income recipient (less than 30, 30–44, 45–54, 55–64 and 65 and over); (2) education of the major income recipient (not a university graduate, university graduate); (3) a variable distinguishing singles from couples and classifying couples by age and education level of the spouse (male neither married nor living common-law, female neither married nor living common-law and 12 types of couples: six age categories for the age of the spouse times two categories for the education of the spouse); (4) provincial controls; and (5) urban–rural status. Permanent income is set equal to predicted income evaluated at age of major income recipient equal to 45 (the spouse's age is set equal to what his or her age would be when the major income recipient was 45). Transitory income is defined as the difference between observed income and predicted income evaluated at the actual age of the major income recipient and of his or her spouse. Altonji et al. (2000) take advantage of the longitudinal nature of the Panel Study of Income Dynamics (PSID) and estimate permanent income using panel data regressions.

23.   Education is included as a potential factor that may affect a family's savings rate. Changes in the coding of the education variable between 1984 and 1999 imply that only the two following educational categories are consistent over time: individuals with less than a university degree and university graduates. The lone-parent family indicator is used to capture the negative impact of child care expenditures on lone-parent families' savings rate. For a given level of income, larger family size likely increases consumption expenditures and decreases a family's savings rate. Provincial and urban–rural controls are intended to capture differences in wealth associated with differences in cost of living. Controls for inheritances, *inter vivos* transfers and past rates of return on savings are not included in the wealth equation since ADS 1984 and SFS 1999 contain no information on these variables.

24.   This potential decrease in the number of years worked full-time could be offset by the fact that the longer time spent by youth living at their parents' home in the 1990s (compared to the 1980s) may allow them to accumulate more money than if they had left home earlier.

25.   Detailed regression results are presented in Appendix 3 of Morissette et al. (2002).

26.   This conclusion holds when we use the level of wealth as the dependent variable and compare wealth changes of family units located in the bottom half of the wealth

distribution to those of family units located between the 60th and 95th percentile. See Morissette et al. (2002) for details.

27. R_{kt} equals the ratio of the covariance of wealth component k with cumulative distribution of overall net worth to the covariance of wealth component k with the cumulative distribution of component k. It equals 1 whenever the ranking of family units on the particular component is identical to the ranking of family units on overall net worth.

28. See Appendix 4 of Morissette et al. (2002) for the results regarding the two other samples excluding the top 1 per cent and the top 5 per cent of family units, respectively.

29. Almost all of these qualitative conclusions hold for the two other samples. The only exception is that the Gini correlation for business equity, while among the highest across wealth components, is not always the highest in the two other samples, especially in the sample excluding the top 5 per cent of family units.

30. The Income Tax Act raised the dollar limit on contributions to RRSPs from $5500 in 1984 to $13 500 in 1999 (for individuals without a registered pension plan). This is likely to have contributed to the growing popularity of RRSPs. The growing importance of self-employed individuals, who rely on RRSPs and other financial assets to build retirement savings, may also have contributed to the growing popularity of RRSPs.

31. This easier access to mortgage loans is also consistent with the fact that inequality in mortgage on principal residence decreased from 0.833 to 0.794 during the period.

32. These qualitative conclusions hold when we exclude the top 1 per cent of family units. However, when we exclude the top 5 per cent of family units, the relative importance of stocks, bonds and mutual funds rises only marginally and the relative importance of deposits falls more than the relative importance of business equity.

33. These qualitative conclusions hold when we exclude the top 1 per cent of family units. However, when we exclude the top 5 per cent of family units, the contribution of stocks, bonds and mutual funds rises only marginally.

34. The Gini coefficient for business equity rose slightly between 1984 and 1999 (from 0.963 to 0.985) while the Gini correlation for business equity remained virtually unchanged (0.933 in 1984 and 0.928 in 1999).

35. Between 1984 and 1999, average wealth rose from $128 875 to $176 087. Average business equity for all family units dropped from $31 743 to $29 028. This decrease occurred despite the fact that the proportion of family units with a business rose from 14.2 to 18.7 per cent during the period. Hence, all of the drop in average business equity is due to the fact that average business equity for family units with a business dropped from $224 086 to $155 610. Had average business equity for family units with a business remained unchanged at $224 086, average business equity for all family units would have been equal to $41 904 ($224 086 × 18.7%) and would have represented 24 per cent ($41 904 ÷ $176 087) of net worth. Under these conditions, the relative importance of business equity in net worth would have dropped only from 25 to 24 per cent, rather than from 25 to 17 per cent. Hence, the bulk of the decrease in the relative importance of business equity in net worth is explained by the fact that the average business equity for family units with a business dropped from $224 086 in 1984 to $155 610 in 1999.

36. ADS 1984 and SFS 1999 indicate that, between 1984 and 1999, the number of family units having a business with a net equity of $0–$10 000 rose by roughly 850 000. This is consistent with the fact that, during the same period, the number of self-employed individuals without paid help grew by roughly 760 000.

37. In the late 1980s, pension legislation was revised to allow people leaving their employer pension plan to remove the money from the plan and put it in a locked-in RRSP (called a locked-in retirement account or LIRA). In 1984, this money would more likely have been left in the plan. Since we do not have estimates of employer pension plan assets for 1984, we would ideally like to exclude LIRAs from our concept of wealth when using 1999 data. Unfortunately, data editing suggested that many respondents did not have a clear idea of the distinction between LIRAs and RRSPs in 1999. Accordingly, it was decided to include LIRAs with RRSPs in the SFS data set. To check whether the finding that RRSPs have, of all wealth components, contributed the most to the increase in wealth inequality, is robust, we also calculated imputed values for LIRAs and excluded

these values from the concept of wealth in 1999. In this case, the Gini coefficient of wealth increased by 0.037. The two most important contributors to the growth of wealth inequality were still RRSPs (0.072) and stocks, bonds and mutual funds (0.051), which tended to increase the Gini by 0.123 (0.072 + 0.051). Once again, the effect of these two factors was partially offset by business equity and deposits: business equity tended to reduce the Gini by 0.069 while deposits tended to reduce the Gini by 0.019. Principal residence explained virtually none of the growth in wealth inequality. Thus, excluding LIRAs from the 1999 data does not affect our conclusion regarding the importance of RRSPs.

38. Between 1984 and 1999, the Gini coefficient of wealth increased by 0.029 for this sample. RRSPs and stocks, bonds and mutual funds tended to increase the Gini by 0.084 and 0.024, respectively. Business equity tended to reduce the Gini by 0.060 while deposits tended to reduce the Gini by 0.015. Principal residence had some effect (0.011) but this was mainly offset by the equalizing impact of mortgage on principal residence (–0.008).

39. Principal residence was the second most important contributor to the growth of wealth inequality but its impact was partially offset by the equalizing effect of mortgage on principal residence.

40. The fact that young individuals get married later – thereby benefiting later from the economies of scale associated with cohabitation – could also be a factor. However, it might be offset by the fact that some young individuals stay with their parents for a longer period and/or use other forms of cohabitation. Similarly, the downward shift in the age–earnings profile of young men, documented by Beaudry and Green (2000), may have tended to reduce real wealth of young males but its impact may have been partly offset by the growing number of dual-earner couples among young families.

41. This is what we mean when we argue that differences – between low-wealth and high-wealth family units – in the growth of rates of return on savings are likely to have played a role in the growth of wealth inequality.

REFERENCES

Altonji, J., U. Dorazelski and L. Segal (2000), 'The role of permanent income and demographics in black–white differences in wealth', Northwestern University, working paper.

Beach, C.M. and G.A. Slotsve (1996), *Are We Becoming Two Societies?*, Toronto, Canada: C.D. Howe Institute.

Beaudry, P. and D. Green (2000), 'Cohort patterns in Canadian earnings: assessing the role of skill premia in inequality trends', *Canadian Journal of Economics*, **33**(4), 907–36.

Blau, F. and J. Graham (1990), 'Black–white differences in wealth and asset composition', *Quarterly Journal of Economics*, **105**(2), 321–39.

Davies, J.B. (1979), 'On the size distribution of wealth in Canada', *Review of Income and Wealth*, **25** (September), 237–59.

Davies, J.B. (1993), 'The distribution of wealth in Canada', in Edward Wolff (ed.), *Research in Economic Inequality*, Greenwich, CT: JAI Press, pp. 159–80.

DiNardo, J., N.M. Fortin and T. Lemieux (1996), 'Labor market institutions and the distribution of wages, 1973–1993: a semi-parametric approach', *Econometrica*, **64**(5), 1001–44.

Frenette, M., D. Green and G. Picot (2004), 'Rising income inequality amid the economic recovery of the 1990s: an exploration of three data sources', Statistics Canada, Analytical Studies Branch Research Paper No. 219.

Lerman, R. and S. Yitzhaki (1985), 'Income inequality effects by income source: a new approach and applications to the United States', *Review of Economic Statistics*, **67**, 151–6.

Morissette, R. (2002a), 'Families on the financial edge', *Perspectives on Labour and Income*, **14**(3), 9–20, Statistics Canada.

Morissette, R. (2002b), 'Cumulative earnings among young workers', *Perspectives on Labour and Income*, **14**(4), 33–40, Statistics Canada.

Morissette, R., J. Myles and G. Picot (1994), 'Earnings inequality and the distribution of working time in Canada', *Canadian Business Economics*, **2**(3), 3–16.

Morissette, R., X. Zhang and M. Drolet (2002), 'The evolution of wealth inequality in Canada, 1984–1999', Statistics Canada, Analytical Studies Branch Research Paper No. 187.

PART II

Wealth Inequality in European Countries

6. Inequality of the distribution of personal wealth in Germany, 1973–98

Richard Hauser and Holger Stein*

INTRODUCTION

In their comprehensive survey of the distribution of wealth, Davies and Shorrocks (2000)[1] generalize some facts about personal wealth holdings known for various countries:

1. The distribution of wealth is more unequal than that of income, and has a long upper tail.
2. Many households never accumulate much private wealth, even in rich countries.
3. Wealth inequality has been on a downward trend for most of the past century but with interruptions and reversals.
4. Financial assets are less unequally distributed than non-financial assets, at least when owner-occupied housing is the major component of non-financial assets.
5. The distribution of inherited wealth is much more unequal than that of wealth in general.
6. The age–wealth pattern is much less pronounced than predicted by the life cycle hypothesis.[2]

In this survey, information about the distribution of wealth in Germany is very scarce; only two studies are cited, Börsch-Supan (1994), referring to 1983 and Burkhauser et al. (1997)[3] referring to 1988. Davies and Shorrocks (2000, Table 1, p. 637) neglected some earlier studies written in German, presumably due to language problems. An overview of earlier studies can be found in Ring (2000, pp. 200–252). Our chapter presents cross-sectional results for the period from 1973 to 1998 based on the Income and Consumption Surveys (ICS) (*Einkommens- und Verbrauchsstichprobe*) of the German Federal Statistical Office.[4] We examine whether the summary of facts given by Davies and Shorrocks can be corroborated for Germany. Additionally, we analyse more closely the extent to which the changes resulting from the reunification of Germany reflect in the distribution of personal wealth (for example, the change of the East German economic system from a socialist economy, with a dominance of state ownership of enterprises, land and housing, to a Western-type welfare state).

We restrict the analysis to the conventional concept of marketable household wealth, which, following the terminology used by Wolff (1991), we call 'household disposable wealth'.[5] This is a concept of net wealth that results from deducting the sum of liabilities from the sum of assets. The unit of measurement is either the household and its disposable wealth or the person with disposable wealth calculated per household member.

First, we describe the main characteristics of our data sources and briefly report some aggregate figures of household wealth as estimated by the Deutsche Bundesbank, which include wealth holdings of nonprofit organizations. The next three sections are restricted to West Germany for which we can construct a time series from 1973 to 1998. We present measures of the level and the overall trend in the inequality of household disposable wealth and household disposable income, as well as trends in the equivalent disposable income of individuals. Then we deal with inequality in the distribution of financial assets and housing as the two main components of disposable wealth for the vast majority of households. In the next section, we look at the average disposable wealth of age groups and its dispersion. Additionally, we construct two pseudo cohorts to distinguish between age and cohort effects. Following a brief introduction to the main institutional changes that accompanied German reunification, we analyse the distribution of disposable wealth and its components in East Germany in the final section. We conclude by arguing that wealth inequality may increase further because of the current retrenchment policy.

MICRODATA AND WEALTH HOLDINGS OF THE HOUSEHOLD SECTOR

The ICS has been conducted at five-year intervals from 1962/63. It is a quota sample of between 45000 and 60000 households who participate voluntarily.[6] At first it centred mainly on demographic characteristics and on income and expenditure. Later on it also included the assets of private households. The ICS places a great burden on the sample households because they have to participate in several interviews and keep track of all members' incomes and expenditures for up to a year. Since participation rates differ, the Federal Statistical Office adjusts the survey weights to the marginal distributions of a mandatory random 1 per cent sample of the resident population in Germany, the so-called Micro Census (*Mikrozensus*). Additionally, top coding is applied.[7] The institutionalized population and the homeless are excluded. Households with a foreign head have been included only since 1993, but it is assumed that only the better-integrated foreigners are represented. In 1973 and in 1983, tax values of equity in private businesses were reported and had to be adjusted to market value. Marketable stocks are included in financial assets. The ICS of 1993 and 1998 contain the market prices of houses and land as estimated by the owners. However, for previous years only much lower tax values were given and, as a result, had to be adjusted to market values. For scientific analyses only random subsamples of between 80 and 98 per cent of the total sample are available. It is also well known that assets are usually under-reported in surveys. These shortcomings of the ICS lead to a downward bias in the measured inequality of disposable household wealth and, to some extent, also limit comparability over time.

From the ICS we can calculate grossed-up values of the total disposable wealth of private households as well as the disposable wealth per household and per household member. Table 6.1 presents the results.

From 1983 to 1998, total disposable wealth increased from 1626 billion euros in West Germany to 4251 billion[8] euros in united Germany. This means an average growth rate of around 6.6 per cent per year. This increase is due in part to the reunification of Germany. If we restrict the analysis to West Germany, the increase is from 1626 to 3910 billion euros, a growth rate of around 6 per cent. During this period the number of households changed considerably. Therefore, the increase in disposable wealth per household was only from 72 100 to 130 500 euros – a growth rate of 4 per cent. If we again restrict the view to West Germany, the rate of growth of disposable household wealth per household was 3.2 per cent. As we will explain later, disposable wealth per household is much higher in West Germany than in East Germany. In 1993 the West German average was about 3.3 times as high as the East German average, but by 1998 this ratio had been reduced to 2.6.

To check the reliability of the grossed-up figures for the disposable wealth of German households, one might compare these figures with the respective figures of the national balance sheets. However, because the German Federal Statistical Office has never produced national balance sheets for total German wealth disaggregated by sectors, such a comparison is not possible. The Deutsche Bundesbank published estimates of aggregate wealth for several sectors and for broad categories of assets, but since the figures for the household sector include net wealth holdings of all nonprofit organizations, such as churches, labour unions and foundations,

Table 6.1 *Disposable wealth of private households in Germany, based on the ICS, 1983–98[a] (recalculated in euros)[b]*

	1983	1988	1993	1998
		(billions of euros)		
Total disposable wealth[c] of households				
West Germany	1626	1984	3662	3910
East Germany	NA[d]	NA	257	341
united Germany	NA	NA	3919	4251
Disposable wealth[c] per household				
West Germany	72 100	82 900	126 600	130 500
East Germany	NA	NA	38 400	50 000
united Germany	NA	NA	110 100	115 600
Disposable wealth[c] per person				
West Germany	30 900	37 300	56 200	60 300
East Germany	NA	NA	16 500	22 800
united Germany	NA	NA	48 500	53 300

Notes:
a. For details on the ICS, see appendix Tables 6A.1 and 6A.2.
b. Figures recalculated at the official exchange rate 1 euro = 1.95583 Deutschmarks.
c. Disposable wealth includes gross monetary assets (including quoted shares) and gross housing wealth less consumer debts and debts for housing construction. Consumer durables and equity in private businesses are not included. Mierheim and Wicke (1978, p. 199) estimated equity of private businesses together with quoted shares to be about 10 per cent of gross total assets.
d. NA = not available.

Source: Authors' calculations.

comparability is limited. Furthermore, the reference years of the estimates of the Deutsche Bundesbank do not correspond to the survey years. Table 6.2 shows what is known for Germany.

These figures from the Deutsche Bundesbank allow us to calculate by simple interpolation rough estimates of the total disposable wealth holdings of private households that correspond to the reference years of the surveys. If consumer durables are left out and, in addition, 5 per cent of wealth is deducted as a rough estimate of the wealth of nonprofit organizations, the resulting figures are comparable to the grossed-up figures from the surveys (because equity in private businesses is neither included in the figures of the Deutsche Bundesbank nor in the grossed-up totals from the

Table 6.2   *Disposable wealth of the household sector in Germany from 1980 to 1997[a] (recalculated in euros)[b]*

	1980	1990[c]	1993[c]	1997[c]
		(billions of euros)		
Property wealth[d]	1228	2598	3096	3626
Consumer durables[e]	315	574	715	827
Monetary wealth[f]	754	1573	2011	2646
Gross wealth	2297	4745	5822	7099
Debts[g]	314	548	687	917
Disposable wealth	1983	4197	5135	6182

Notes:
a.   Figures include wealth of nonprofit organizations.
b.   Figures recalculated at the official exchange rate 1 euro = 1.95583 Deutschmarks.
c.   Figures for 1990, 1993 and 1997 refer to unified Germany.
d.   Housing (replacement costs less depreciation) and real estate; Equity in private businesses is excluded.
e.   Evaluated at replacement costs less depreciation.
f.   Includes securities evaluated at current prices and traded shares.
g.   Includes consumer debts and debts for housing construction.

Sources: Deutsche Bundesbank (1993, p. 31) and Deutsche Bundesbank (1999, p. 43).

surveys). Moreover, the Deutsche Bundesbank figure for 1990 must be reduced by another 10 per cent because it refers to united Germany. These estimates in billions of euros are: 2038 (1983), 2795 (1988), 4200 (1993) and 5087 (1998). Comparing these estimates with the respective figures in Table 6.1, one finds that the ICS figures are between 7 and 29 per cent lower. Keeping in mind that the top income – and wealthiest group – is excluded from the survey and that some assets are under-reported, this can be considered an acceptable approximation.[9]

INEQUALITY OF DISPOSABLE WEALTH ACROSS HOUSEHOLDS IN WEST GERMANY FROM 1973 TO 1998

Table 6.3 presents time series of Gini coefficients for household disposable wealth, household disposable income, and equivalent disposable income of individuals. In Germany, the Gini coefficients for household disposable wealth range from 75 to 62 per cent. This range lies within the wider range from 79 per cent (USA) to 52 per cent (Japan) as reported by Davies and Shorrocks (2000, Table 1, p. 637), referring to the mid-1980s.

Table 6.3 Distribution of disposable wealth and disposable income across households and equivalent disposable income across persons in West Germany, 1973–98 (Gini coefficients in per cent)[a]

Coverage of population	German households only			Resident population including foreigners	
	1973	1983	1988	1993	1998
Household disposable wealth	74.8[1]	70.1[2] 68.3[3]	66.8[4]	62.2[4]	64.0[4]
Household disposable income	30.1[5]	32.7[5]	32.9[5]	33.3[5]	33.5[5]
Equivalent disposable income of persons	24.8[5]	25.0[5]	25.3[5]	26.9[5]	27.2[5]

Note: a. Gini coefficients were calculated by setting negative disposable wealth holdings of certain households to zero.

Sources:
1. Mierheim and Wicke (1978), 58–9.
2. Schlomann (1992), 136–9.
3. Stein (2004), Table 3.19, p. 210. This figure was derived by excluding equity in private businesses and by reducing the multiplier for correcting the tax value of housing to market prices.
4. Hauser (2003), Table 7.1; taken from Stein (2004), Table 3.19, p. 210.
5. Hauser (2003), Table A.1. p. 25. To derive equivalent income of persons the original OECD equivalence scale was used which assigns a weight of 1.0 to the first adult of a household, weights of 0.7 to additional members who are 15 years or older, and weights of 0.5 to younger children.

We presume, however, that these estimates for Germany – with the exception of the result for 1973 – are lower bounds of the estimates of the true values because the ICS does not capture households with very high incomes, most of which also belong to the group of the wealthiest.[10,11]

Comparing the Gini coefficients for disposable wealth and household disposable income, one finds that this measure is much lower for income inequality than for wealth inequality, with a value of mostly less than one-half. When one looks at the Gini coefficient for equivalent disposable income of persons, this measure is approximately one-fifth lower than that for household disposable income in all years, a typical fact shown in many studies of income distribution. For Germany, this corroborates the findings summarized by Davies and Shorrocks as to the level of inequality of household disposable wealth and household disposable income. We also presume a long tail of the wealth distribution in Germany, but cannot

Table 6.4   Distribution of household disposable wealth in West Germany, 1973–98 based on various ICS (decile shares in per cent)

Coverage of population	German households only			Resident population including foreigners	
	1973[1]	1983[2]	1988[3]	1993[3]	1998[3]
1st decile		−0.3	−0.8	−0.3	−0.4
2nd decile	0.8	0.1	0.1	0.3	0.1
3rd decile		0.4	0.5	0.7	0.6
4th decile	2.0	0.7	1.2	1.6	1.3
5th decile		1.5	2.4	3.3	3.0
6th decile	5.7	4.0	5.0	7.1	6.5
7th decile		9.0	9.6	11.2	10.7
8th decile	13.5	14.5	15.1	15.1	15.2
9th decile		21.3	21.9	20.2	21.1
10th decile	78.0	48.8	45.0	40.8	41.9
Total	100.0	100.0	100.0	100.0	100.0

Note: For details on the ICS, see appendix Tables 6A.1 and 6A.2.

Sources:
1.   Mierheim and Wicke (1978), pp. 58–9; only quintile shares available.
2.   Schlomann (1992), pp. 136–9.
3.   Hauser and Stein (2001), pp. 112, 124.

give precise quantitative results (see, for example, Schupp and Wager 2003).

Another way of looking at the inequality of disposable wealth is to ascertain the share of the top 1 per cent, top 5 per cent and top 10 per cent of households in terms of total disposable net wealth. This is the strategy often used to characterize trends in wealth inequality because only tax figures for the wealthy households are available in some countries (Wolff 1996; Davies and Shorrocks 2000). Obviously, these measures focus attention on a small segment of the population, which may be of interest from a certain political point of view. These measures, however, do not capture the wealth distribution across the entire population, which is also important, especially in Germany, where policies promoting the spread of wealth holdings among the middle classes have been in place for decades (Ring 2000, pp. 297–360). Decile share distributions contain information for both views. Table 6.4 presents the decile share distributions for West Germany from 1973 to 1998.

The lowest decile shows negative disposable net wealth. Since the value of consumer durables is not included, consumer loans are obviously higher than available financial assets. More generally, we can observe that the lowest four deciles possess only a negligible share of total disposable net wealth. This corroborates one of the findings reported for other countries by Davies and Shorrocks. The middle group consists of the fifth and sixth decile, of which both have shares of total disposable net wealth that are still far below their respective population shares. One has to go up to the seventh decile to see the first one in which the share of total disposable net wealth corresponds approximately to its population share. With the top three deciles, the share of total disposable net wealth exceeds their population share. The lion's share of wealth, however, belongs to the top decile. Again, keeping in mind that the top group of wealth holders is not fully covered by the ICS – except for the year of 1973 – these figures must be considered lower bounds of the estimates of their true shares, which, in reality, may be slightly over one-half of the total disposable net wealth in West Germany.[12]

Comparing these results for West Germany with figures for several other countries in the mid-1980s that are reported in Wolff (1996), Table 6.5 shows that the shares of the two bottom quintiles are extremely low everywhere. Slight differences may be due to the inclusion of some consumer durables in some countries.

In West Germany the share of the third quintile is lowest while the share of the fourth quintile is highest. There seems to be a broader upper middle class of wealth holders in Germany than in other countries. This presumption is corroborated by the data on the shares of the top quintiles. The share of the top quintile is lower in Germany and in Canada than in the United States and in Sweden, with Australia somewhere in the middle. This can

Table 6.5   Size distribution of household wealth in selected countries, based on household survey data, mid-80s (quintile shares)

Country	West Germany 1983[1]	USA 1983[2]	Canada 1984[2]	Australia 1986[2]	Sweden 1986[2]
1st quintile	−0.2	0	0	0	NA[a]
2nd quintile	1.1	2	2	0	NA
3rd quintile	5.5	6	9	7.1	NA
4th quintile	23.5	13	20	20.8	NA
5th quintile	70.1	80	69	72.0	75

Note: a. NA = not available.

Sources:
1. Schlomann (1992), pp. 136–9.
2. Wolff (1996), Table 4, p. 447. For details about the country surveys from which these figures are derived, see the footnotes to Wolff's table.

only be a tentative conclusion, however, since in Germany the share of the top quintile is biased downwards as mentioned above.

Looking at the development of the Gini coefficients in Table 6.3, first row, and the shares of the ninth and tenth deciles in Table 6.4, one could ascertain a trend of decreasing wealth inequality in West Germany for the two decades from 1973 to 1993. Such a tendency was also found for several other countries, at least for the 1970s (Wolff 1996; Davies and Shorrocks 2000). There are, however, several limitations to an interpretation of these figures at face value because they are not strictly comparable. Mierheim and Wicke (1978) adjusted their figures for the first reference year, 1973, to national totals. (See Table 6.3, first row, first column). They also estimated the number and the average disposable wealth of households of the top income group that were neglected in the ICS, and combined them with the survey results. As a result, a complete picture of wealth inequality in Germany is constructed.[13] Such extensive adjustments were not made for the other years.

In Table 6.3 (first row, second column, first line), the Gini coefficient for 1983 for household disposable wealth was calculated by Schlomann to include the value of stocks and equity in private businesses, but neglects the wealth holdings of the top wealth holders not covered by the ICS.[14] This is only a partial correction and makes it not strictly comparable to either the figures for 1973 or for 1988 to 1993. To ensure better comparability with the following years, the Gini coefficient for 1983 for household disposable wealth (Table 6.3, first row, second column, second line) was recalculated by Stein to include only the value of tradable stocks while excluding the equity of private businesses.

The figures for 1983 in Table 6.3, (first row, second line) and for 1988, first row, also neglect the wealthiest. Since it can be assumed that equity in private businesses is concentrated in the tenth decile (Table 6.4), both these facts contribute to a downward bias of the Gini coefficients in these years. Between 1988 and 1993 two structural changes occurred: the extension of the ICS to foreign households living in West Germany and the inclusion of all households living in East Germany, due to the reunification of the Federal Republic of Germany with the former German Democratic Republic. In West Germany, foreigners made up around 9 per cent of the resident population. Although there are indications that only the better-integrated foreigners participated in the surveys, it can be assumed that most of them belonged to the lower wealth deciles.[15] This means that the values of the Gini coefficients – if restricted to the German households – would be somewhat lower than their values for the resident population as shown in Table 6.3, first row.

In determining the trend in wealth inequality, the theoretical question pursued determines whether the total resident population in each year is taken as the relevant group, or only a subset of it is. We prefer to look at the resident population because, in a period of globalization, one can no longer abstract from migration. Therefore, we consider the Gini coefficients for 1983 and 1988, which excluded foreigners, as slightly biased downward, in addition to the other biases mentioned.[16]

Given the available evidence and taking all these arguments into consideration, we can corroborate only a slight tendency of decreasing inequality of household disposable wealth from 1983 to 1993. This trend was reversed from 1993 to 1998. We also presume a slight decrease in wealth inequality between 1973 and 1983, but its magnitude cannot be determined.

INEQUALITY OF THE DISTRIBUTION OF NET FINANCIAL ASSETS AND NET HOUSING WEALTH ACROSS HOUSEHOLDS IN WEST GERMANY FROM 1983 TO 1998

When consumer durables and equity in private businesses are disregarded, the total disposable household net wealth can be split up into net financial assets and net housing wealth. 'Net' means that consumer debts are deducted from the gross sum of financial assets and housing debts are deducted from the gross value of housing and real estate. It is interesting to note that the share of net financial assets in total disposable net wealth was about one-quarter, rising from 22.1 per cent in 1983 to 27.6 per cent in 1998. Correspondingly, the share of the net value of housing wealth decreased during this period from 77.9 per cent to 72.4 per cent, despite the fact that the ownership rate for housing wealth increased from 45.5 per cent in 1983 to 49.1 per cent in 1998 after a high of 50.7 per cent in 1993.[17] Thus the ownership rate for houses in Germany is far lower than for financial assets of all kinds, which may be over 90 per cent, even though many households own only small amounts.

For these two broad categories of household wealth, we can also ask what the level of inequality is, and whether this period was characterized by a trend in inequality. Table 6.6 shows the results.

Table 6.6 shows that net financial wealth is less unequally distributed than total disposable net wealth except in the last year of our series, 1998. This lower concentration of financial assets could be expected since households with low disposable wealth usually keep their assets in the form of bank accounts, savings accounts with banks or savings and loan institutions, or in life insurance policies. Since the prices of apartments and houses in Germany are rather high compared to average disposable income and banks usually finance no more than 75 per cent of the price of a house, buyers need a large amount of capital for a down payment to acquire

Table 6.6   Distribution of net financial wealth and net housing wealth across households in West Germany from 1983 to 1998 (Gini coefficients in %)

	1983	1988	1993	1998
Net financial wealth	62.1	63.5	60.6	65.3
Net housing wealth	76.2	74.0	69.1	70.4
Total disposable wealth	68.3	66.8	62.2	64.0

Note: Calculations are based on various ICS. For details see Appendix Tables 6A.1 and 6A.2.

Source: Stein (2004), Table 3.19, p. 210.

property. This is the main reason why ownership rates of housing are low compared to other countries. Therefore, it is not surprising that net housing wealth is more unequally distributed than total disposable wealth.

There was, however, a noticeable trend toward decreasing inequality of net housing wealth from 1983 to 1993, which was reversed after 1993. Inequality of net financial wealth fluctuated. One has to bear in mind, however, that the stock market boom had already started in 1998 but had not yet reached its peak. This picture corresponds with the mixed results reported by Davies and Shorrocks (2000, p. 607) with respect to the inequality of monetary asset holdings observed in other countries.

INEQUALITY OF WEALTH HOLDINGS BETWEEN AND WITHIN AGE GROUPS[18]

The simple life-cycle model predicts that personal disposable wealth at the beginning of working life of each birth cohort is zero for all members of a birth cohort, which also implies complete equality.[19] In the course of working life, wealth is accumulated according to the opportunities and willingness to save from unequally distributed earned incomes. Personal disposable wealth is highest at retirement age, and inequality of the distribution of personal wealth is also highest. During the retirement period, disposable wealth is steadily reduced to finance consumption and, therefore, inequality of wealth holdings may also decrease. At the time of death, personal disposable wealth is again reduced to zero and equality of wealth holdings is restored. To come closer to reality, many factors have to be integrated into this simple life-cycle model. At the individual level, the first factor includes the distribution of earnings and its determinants; the second factor includes the rates of return for accumulated wealth and capital gains or losses. Moving from the individual to the family level, marriage and divorce behaviour, such as class-specific mating or random mating, differential fertility, and labour market participation of spouses that influences the ability to save, are the main factors. The propensity to save may be influenced by the tax system and by the social protection system which covers social risks on a broader or smaller scale and with higher or lower benefits. Uncertainty about expected lifetime income and about the lifespan of the individuals, or of both spouses in the case of a couple, introduces the precautionary motive into considerations about wealth accumulation and decumulation. Finally, the bequest motive and the legal regulations on the division of estates among heirs, including the motive to invest in the children's education and support their start in life by gifts *inter vivo*,[20] may play a role, at least for couples with children or close relatives.[21]

Elaborated models that include most of these factors often yield inconclusive results as to the accumulation or decumulation of household wealth after retirement and the effects of bequests on the inequality of the wealth distribution. Davies and Shorrocks (2000, p. 616) state in their review, 'the broad consensus is that, after the first few years of retirement, private wealth . . . declines in retirement. What remains in considerable doubt is the speed at which dissaving takes place'. In the discussion that follows, we provide some empirical facts for Germany to verify whether or not they are in line with this view.

Figure 6.1 displays average levels of disposable wealth of various age groups of households[22] as a proportion of the overall average disposable wealth, for four sample years – 1983, 1988, 1993 and 1998.

The hump shape is well known. In every ICS sample, one middle-aged group has the highest relative wealth position. However, the respective age group is not the same. In the ICS of 1983, it is the group at ages 50 to 54 years; in the ICS of 1998, it is the group at ages 60 to 64 years. This difference points to a cohort effect.

Household size changes over the course of life. Therefore, it is interesting to check whether the familiar hump shape remains the same if we look at household disposable wealth per household member. To keep values comparable to the previous approach, all members of a household are classified according to the age of the head of household irrespective of their own age. Figure 6.2 shows much less of a hump; the peak shows now at about the same age in each cohort.

A decrease in relative average wealth holdings is only visible for the age group over 65, the mandatory retirement age in Germany. The ICS of 1993 presents an exception even here because there is no decrease at all.

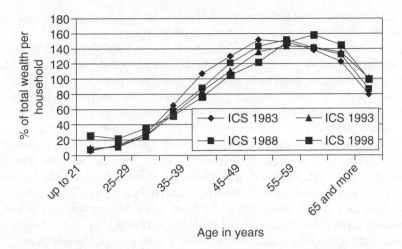

Figure 6.1   Relative wealth position of various age groups of households

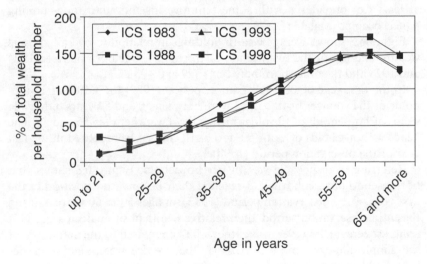

Figure 6.2   Relative wealth position of various age groups of household members in West Germany

Obviously, this flattening of the hump is the effect of changing household size, especially in old age, when one spouse dies and leaves most or all of its personal wealth to the surviving spouse. It seems obvious that, to improve the explanatory power of models of wealth accumulation and distribution, the bequest motive should not only be discussed with respect to children but also modelled with respect to surviving spouses.

In a time series of cross-sectional data, one cannot distinguish between the effects of economic development and changes in the institutional structure that influence each birth cohort at a different point in their life cycles and the life-cycle effects caused by the ageing of each individual member of a certain birth cohort. A long time series of cross-sectional data, however, makes it possible to construct pseudo birth cohorts that can be observed for a certain period of their life course. Such a pseudo birth cohort consists of as many annual birth cohorts as there are years between the various sample years, on condition that the time interval between the various samples remains constant. If the cross-sectional data came from a random sample, one could assume that different random samples of the same pseudo birth cohort were obtained at different points in their life course. The same is true of a quota sample like the ICS, though the results may be biased to some extent. This methodology is not a full substitute for real panel data with which one can observe the life course of each individual separately and aggregate life courses as desired. However, this methodology at least can provide us with some tentative insights until long-running panels become available.

Figure 6.3 shows average wealth holdings in relation to overall average wealth holdings of the two pseudo birth cohorts, one born between 1924 and 1928 and the other born between 1929 and 1933.

In the first year of our observation period (1983) the heads of households of the younger birth cohort were between 50 and 54 years old, while heads of households of the older birth cohort were between 55 and 59. The heads of households of both pseudo birth cohorts were retired in the last year of the observation period (1998).[23]

Referring to disposable wealth per household, Figure 6.3 shows that both pseudo birth cohorts had reached their best relative position in the first year of the observation period (1983), at ages 50 to 60 years. During the entire observation period, their relative wealth position decreased. This relative decrease, however, was rather small compared to the prediction of the simple life-cycle model. In 1998, the average wealth holdings per household of the older birth cohort was still around the overall average, and average wealth per household of the younger birth cohort was still far above the overall average. This points to the fact that, though these cohorts on average could not save as much as the average household to keep their relative position, there was no dissaving in monetary terms after retirement. Therefore, it is extremely implausible that both cohorts, on average, will run down their disposable wealth to almost zero during their lifetimes. On the contrary, several German studies predict high inheritances

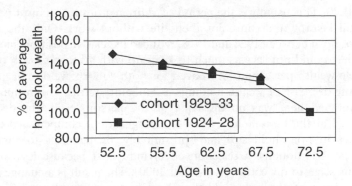

*Figure 6.3   Average wealth holdings per household of birth cohorts
1924–28 and 1929–33 in relation to overall wealth holdings of
household members in West Germany*

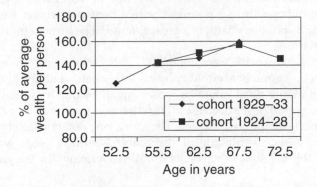

*Figure 6.4   Average wealth holdings per household member of birth
cohorts 1924–28 and 1929–33 in relation to overall wealth
holdings of household members in West Germany*

expected by the younger generation, which in public discussions is often
dubbed 'the generation of heirs' (see Hauser and Stein 2001, pp. 147–58;
Braun et al. 2002).

Is this picture the same if the relative position of the members of
these two birth cohorts is calculated on a per capita basis, while continuing
to classify all household members according to the age of the head of
household?

Looking at the relative wealth position from the perspective presented in
Figure 6.4, the younger cohort born between 1929 and 1933 did not fall
behind in their relative position at all but increased it until an age between

65 and 70. This usually is the period of retirement in which most persons are still healthy and can enjoy their life without work. Only the oldest cohort, born between 1924 and 1928, reduced its relative position, meaning that they could not save as much to keep up with average growth of disposable wealth per capita. Moreover, for both cohorts we do not find an absolute decrease of wealth holdings in monetary terms. This means that, on average, there was no dissaving at the person level. The decrease observed at the household level is to a large extent compensated for by changes in household size and, presumably, by bequests to surviving spouses. Additionally, a selection effect may exist because less wealthy persons seem to die earlier (Reil-Held 2000). The result is a change in the composition of the pseudo birth cohort in favour of the richer group which, in turn, causes an increase in average wealth holdings. This effect could only be controlled for by using data from a long-term panel. We can conclude, therefore, that in Germany, because of the rather well-developed public pension system and social insurance provisions for the cost of nursing in old age, there is no evidence that birth cohorts on average run down their disposable wealth to a great extent.[24] The bequest motive seems to be very strong.

If disposable wealth were completely self-accumulated from current income, young households would possess little wealth, and the distribution of wealth among them would be rather equal. Inequality would develop during the course of life decrease after retirement when wealth is run down to finance consumption in old age. Therefore, one can gain insight into the deviations if the distribution of disposable wealth is noted within age groups. Table 6.7 shows the results for West Germany for the years 1983 and 1998.

In all age groups the distribution of household disposable wealth at the household level is a little more unequal than at the individual level but displays the same pattern. In 1983 inequality was highest within the youngest age group, then it decreased until retirement age, and finally it increased again.[25] In 1998, inequality within age groups was considerably lower in every age group than in 1983, but the same pattern emerges. Inequality is highest among the young households, decreases until retirement age, and then increases again. This pattern is exactly the opposite of what might be expected. To explain this pattern one must take into account inheritances and gifts *inter vivo* that some members of the youngest age group have already received.

We can only hint at some facts known for West Germany. Based on data from the German Socio-Economic Panel (GSOEP), wave 1988, Schlomann estimates that 8.5 per cent of the households of the youngest age group had already received inheritances during their lifetime (Schlomann 1992,

Table 6.7   *Inequality of household disposable wealth within age groups at the household and at the individual level in West Germany, 1983 and 1998 (Gini coefficients in per cent)[a]*

Age groups according to the age of the head of household	1983[1]		1998[2]	
	Households	Persons	Households	Persons
All	70.1	66.2	64.0	62.4
18–29	85.1	82.7	79.9	74.8
30–44	65.8	63.4	65.1	61.0
45–64	62.6	59.6	56.3	54.5
65 and older	75.4	72.1	62.2	59.4

Notes: a. Calculations are based on various ICS. For details see appendix Tables 6A.1 and 6A.2. Gini coefficients were calculated by setting negative disposable wealth holdings of certain households to zero.

Sources:
1. Schlomann (1992), Tables 6.15 and 6.16, p. 164; figures are rounded. Household disposable wealth also comprises equity in private businesses.
2. Authors' calculations.

Table 8.1).[26] The proportion increases to 14.4 per cent of the age group between 30 and 44 years, 21.1 per cent of the age group between 45 and 64 years, and is lower again for the oldest cohort over 65 years. It must be noted, however, that the participants of the GSOEP were asked about inheritances they had received since 1960, that is, during the past 28 years. This would include all of the inheritances of the youngest age group and, to a lesser extent, those of the older age groups. Based on the ICS for 1998, Stein finds that, among the households of the top decile, about 27.5 per cent mention that houses or apartments they possess were inherited or given to them as a gift *inter vivo* (Stein 2004, Table 3.23). Among the entire population only 8.9 per cent of the households declare that they inherited houses or apartments. This is about a fifth of all homeowners. From this fragmentary information we can derive the tentative conclusion that inheritances and gifts *inter vivo* play an important role in overall inequality of disposable household wealth, especially among the youngest age group.[27] For a considerable group of the population, original accumulation (the accumulation of wealth by saving from one's own earned income) is hardly the only source of the wealth they hold in old age. This seems especially true for the top wealth holders.

INEQUALITY OF DISPOSABLE HOUSEHOLD WEALTH COMPARED BETWEEN EAST AND WEST GERMANY

In 1949 the Federal Republic of Germany (FRG) was founded on the territory occupied by American, British and French Allied Forces, and a so-called 'social market economy' was established. In contrast, the Soviet government, in collaboration with the German Communist Party, established the socialist German Democratic Republic (GDR) in the Soviet zone. Enterprises and farms were expropriated and transformed to large and highly integrated industrial complexes, so called *Kombinate*, and to agricultural co-operatives, so-called *Landwirtschaftliche Produktionsgenossenschaften*. Private property of means of production was no longer allowed. Larger houses that could be rented to tenants also became state property or the property of housing co-operatives. The GDR introduced the system of a planned economy run by state authorities and with its own nonconvertible currency (mark of the GDR, M). The economy was integrated into the Eastern bloc. Step-by-step border controls were tightened to stop a continuous flow of emigrants from the GDR to the FRG. In 1962 the Berlin Wall was erected to close the last loophole for emigration. Over the years the economy of the GDR lagged more and more behind the development in the Western world, and economic and political difficulties mounted in all the socialist states. It is up to the historians to gauge precisely the various factors that led to the breakdown of the socialist bloc. In Germany the Berlin Wall fell in November 1989 and within a few days all the border controls were removed. It took only a few months to elect a democratic parliament in the GDR, which then began the transformation of its economic and social system. In spring 1990 this parliament decided to reunite the GDR with the FRG. The governing bodies of the FRG and the Four Powers[28] accepted this decision. Within a few months a reunification treaty was concluded, detailing how the economic and social system of the GDR could be transformed to fit the Constitution of the Federal Republic of Germany (*Grundgesetz*) and its social order.

In July 1990, a monetary union was concluded, substituting the currency of the GDR with the Deutschmark (DM). Wages and other current incomes as well as prices were converted on a one-to-one basis. Monetary assets and liabilities were converted two-to-one, with the exception of savings of M 6000 per person, which were also converted one-to-one. Foreign debts of the GDR were to be paid back by united Germany.[29] State property of the production sector and of land was privatized by a new organization called the *Treuhandanstalt*. Contrary to expectations, this process resulted in a deficit of about DM 300 billion. Land, houses and companies that had been expropriated were restituted in kind. The West German legal system was introduced, including labour market regulations, the social protection system and the tax system. Special regulations guaranteed a minimum income in case of unemployment and retirement. Very generous early retirement regulations and special employment measures were also introduced. Despite the one-to-one conversion of the East German currency, the wage level amounted to a little less than 50 per cent of the West German average wage in 1991. East German pensions were tied to the East German wage level and, consequently, were also very low. Although both groups soon saw considerable increases of their incomes in monetary and in real terms, pensioners gained most from the change in the old-age protection system. During the first half of the 1990s, West German financial aid to East Germany increased from DM 100 billion in 1991 to DM 125 billion in 1995. In 1991, these transfers amounted to roughly 4 per cent of the West German gross domestic product (GDP) while amounting to almost 50 per cent of the East German GDP. These West–East transfers were channelled partly through the social security system and partly through direct transfers from West German to East German budgets. West–East transfers are still continuing on a large scale, which explains part of Germany's problems with budget deficits. The economy in the Eastern part of reunited Germany is still lagging far behind in productivity and income growth. It may take another 20 years before the discrepancy between the Eastern and the Western parts of Germany is reduced to a politically negligible difference.

It comes as no surprise that the transformation from the socialist system of the GDR to a social market economy in East Germany had serious consequences for the distribution of disposable household wealth, not only at the time of reunification but also for a long time thereafter.[30] As Table 6.1 indicates, disposable wealth per household in 1993 was 126 600 euros in West Germany compared to 38 400 euros in East Germany. From 1993 to 1998 the gap between West and East German households was somewhat reduced in relative terms. However, in 1998, the disposable wealth of West German households on average was still about 2.6 times that of East German households.

Table 6.8 compares the Gini coefficients for disposable wealth, disposable household income, and equivalent disposable income of persons between East and West Germany in 1993 and 1998.

We see again that inequality of the distribution of disposable net household wealth is much greater than inequality of household disposable incomes or equivalent disposable incomes of individuals. Surprisingly, the distribution of household disposable wealth is more unequal in East Germany than in West Germany, but the distribution of disposable

Table 6.8   Distribution of disposable wealth and disposable income across
households and household size-adjusted equivalent disposable
income compared for individuals in West and East Germany,
1993 and 1998 (Gini coefficients in per cent)[a]

| Resident population | East Germany | | West Germany | |
Year	1993	1998	1993	1998
Household disposable wealth[1]	69.4	67.6	62.2	64.0
Household disposable income[2]	22.8	30.2	33.3	33.5
Equivalent disposable income of persons[3]	19.9	21.8	26.9	27.2

Notes: a. Calculations are based on various ICS. For details see Appendix Tables 6A.1 and 6A.2. Gini coefficients were calculated by setting negative disposable wealth holdings of certain households to zero.

Sources:
1.   Hauser (2003), Table 7.1.
2.   Hauser (2003), Table A.1.
3.   Hauser (2003), Table A.1.

household incomes and of equivalent disposable incomes of persons is less unequal. While the inequality of disposable wealth decreased from 1993 to 1998 in East Germany, it increased in West Germany. Both household disposable incomes and equivalent disposable incomes became considerably more unequal in East Germany while inequality in West Germany increased only very little. On all counts, therefore, we can see a tendency toward convergence.

Table 6.9 presents the decile shares of household disposable wealth. In East Germany the top decile lost while the fifth to the ninth decile increased their shares. In West Germany only the three top deciles gained while all the lower deciles lost.

It is interesting to look at the distribution of the two main components of disposable net wealth: net financial wealth and net housing wealth. Table 6.10 shows that inequality of net financial wealth has increased more in East Germany than in West Germany, and that it has come close to the West German level. A much greater discrepancy exists with respect to net housing wealth, although there is also a slight tendency toward convergence. Differences in the distribution of net housing wealth seem to be the main reason for greater inequality of disposable household wealth in East Germany. This can be explained by a much lower proportion of

Table 6.9   Distribution of household disposable wealth in West and East Germany in 1993 and 1998 (decile shares in per cent)

Resident population	East Germany		West Germany	
	1993	1998	1993	1998
1st decile	−0.3	−0.5	−0.3	−0.4
2nd decile	0.6	0.2	0.3	0.1
3rd decile	1.2	0.9	0.7	0.6
4th decile	1.9	1.7	1.6	1.3
5th decile	2.6	2.9	3.3	3.0
6th decile	3.8	4.5	7.1	6.5
7th decile	5.8	7.3	11.2	10.7
8th decile	9.6	12.5	15.1	15.2
9th decile	22.2	22.5	20.2	21.1
10th decile	52.6	47.8	40.8	41.9
Total	100.0	100.0	100.0	100.0

Notes: Calculations are based on various ICS. For details see Appendix Tables A 6.1 and A 6.2.

Source: Hauser and Stein (2001), Table 5.3, p. 112.

Table 6.10   Distribution of net financial wealth and net housing wealth across households in West and East Germany in 1993 and 1998 (Gini coefficients in per cent)[a]

Resident population	East Germany		West Germany	
	1993	1998	1993	1998
Net financial wealth	51.6	62.0	60.6	65.3
Net housing wealth	85.9	82.5	69.1	70.4
Total disposable wealth	69.4	67.6	62.2	64.0

Notes: a. Calculations are based on various ICS. For details see Appendix Tables 6A.1 and 6A.2. Gini coefficients were calculated by setting negative disposable wealth holdings of certain households to zero.

Source: Hauser and Stein (2001), Table 5.8.

Table 6.11 *Inequality of household disposable wealth within age groups of households in East and West Germany, 1998 (Gini coefficients in per cent)*[a]

Resident population Age groups	East Germany		West Germany	
	1993	1998	1993	1998
All	69.3	67.6	62.2	64.0
18–29	75.3	83.3	75.2	79.9
30–44	71.3	66.6	62.9	65.1
45–64	63.3	62.7	54.0	56.3
65 and older	65.1	65.1	61.7	62.2

Notes: a. Calculations are based on various ICS. For details see appendix Tables 6A.1 and 6 A.2. Gini coefficients were calculated by setting negative disposable wealth holdings of certain households to zero.

Source: Authors' calculations.

homeowners and land owners in East Germany,[31] and a tremendous rise in land prices after unification when market prices were allowed to replace the low land and house prices fixed by the government.

Since ownership of means of production, especially equity in private businesses and large land holdings, were not allowed in the former GDR and, therefore, could not be inherited or received as gifts *inter vivo*, presumably the distribution of disposable wealth among age groups should be much closer to the life-cycle model than in West Germany. Table 6.11 shows that this hypothesis cannot be supported.

In East Germany inequality within all age groups is on a higher level than in West Germany but with a similar pattern. We find the highest inequality among the group of young households, decreasing with age until retirement age and then increasing again. From 1993 to 1998, inequality among the youngest age group even increased in both parts of Germany but more so in the East than in the West. For the older age groups one finds a convergence in inequality. One decade after unification, the East German pattern of household wealth distribution within and between age groups has mostly converged to that of West Germany. Obviously, a tendency of convergence between East and West Germany can be found not only at the macro level of GDP per capita, but also from various perspectives of inequality analysis. The consequence of narrowing the gap in per capita GDP is more inequality in distribution of incomes but less inequality of wealth.

CONCLUSIONS

The results presented show that the inequality of the distribution of household disposable wealth in Germany is somewhere in the middle of industrialized countries. Inequality decreased slightly from 1973 to 1993 and then increased again. The inequality of the distribution of disposable household wealth and of disposable household income in East Germany is converging to West German levels, although from different starting points. For united Germany we can expect an increase in the inequality of disposable household wealth for three reasons. First, a further retrenchment of the welfare state is under way and this will force the long-term unemployed, the prematurely disabled and early retirees to run down their household wealth for consumption during their working life, thus increasing the proportion of households with little or no wealth holdings. Second, it will become more difficult for those with reduced social transfers to accumulate wealth. Third, the inheritances due to come during the two decades will be much larger than in earlier years. Additionally, they will be distributed more unequally because each family has fewer heirs due to the decrease in birth rates. We can also expect that political decisions under discussion, like a reduction in the highest marginal tax rate, a permanent abolition of the former wealth tax, a further reduction in capital gains taxes, and a reduction of the inheritance tax will increase this trend to greater inequality of wealth in Germany.

NOTES

*   The authors wish to thank Jay Zagorsky, Ohio State University, who acted as a discussant, and all the participants of the Levy Wealth Conference for helpful comments.

1.   See specifically, pages 607 and 663.
2.   An earlier survey by Wolff (1991) drew similar conclusions.
3.   The paper by Burkhauser et al. (1997) is based on the German Socio-Economic Panel (GSOEP). There are methodological differences with respect to the analysis of the concentration of wealth between the Burkhauser et al. paper and our study. The two most important differences are as follows. (1) Burkhauser et al. use persons as the units of measurement. To derive Gini coefficients for the disposable wealth of individuals, household wealth is divided by the sum of the weights of the household members based on the original OECD equivalence scale. We use either the household or persons as units of measurement. If persons are used, household wealth is divided by the number of members without weighting. (2) Burkhauser et al. calculate the Gini coefficient and the quintile shares based on a ranking according to the net equivalent income of each person. Persons with zero or negative income are excluded. Our ranking is based on disposable wealth, and all households or persons with zero disposable wealth or negative disposable wealth are included when decile shares are computed. To calculate Gini coefficients, units with negative disposable wealth are set to zero. In general, the method used by Burkhauser et al. leads to lower values of the Gini coefficient, and to a much higher share of wealth of the lowest quintile.

4. Although there are some other data sources, a cross-sectional time series can be constructed from the ICS. A Scientific Use File of the ICS 2003 became available at the end of 2005. Furthermore, in 2002 GSOEP conducted a special high-income and wealth survey, the data of which are available for analysis (see Schupp and Wagner 2003). While the GSOEP data can be used anywhere by the international research community on a contractual basis, microdata of the German Federal Statistical Office can be analysed only within Germany due to legal restrictions. It is possible for foreigners to do research at the German Federal Statistical Office, Wiesbaden, as a guest. For a comparison of the GSOEP with the ICS see Becker et al. (2003).
5. Wolff (1991, p. 94) describes household disposable wealth as including: 'assets and liabilities that have a current market value and that are directly or indirectly marketable (fungible). A typical list of assets includes owner-occupied housing and other real estate; consumer durables and household inventories; cash checking and savings accounts; bonds, and other financial instruments; corporate stocks or shares; the equity in unincorporated businesses; trust funds; and the cash surrender value of life insurance policies and pension plans.'
    In this list liabilities are not specified although they have to be deducted. It must be noted, however, that the following results for Germany generally neglect consumer durables. Additionally, equity in private businesses is not included in most years. Traded stocks are included in financial assets at market value.
6. For details, see Appendix Tables 6A.1 and 6A.2.
7. The cut-off points referring to monthly net income of households were DM 15 000 in 1973, DM 20 000 in 1978, DM 25 000 in 1983 and 1988, and DM 35 000 DM in 1993 and 1998. As can be derived from Merz's analysis (Merz 2001), households with a monthly net income of more than DM 8000 based on income tax records are grossly underrepresented in the ICS. Merz found that about 270 000 'rich' households were missing from the grossed-up figures of the 1998 ICS. In the mid-1990s these amounted to about 0.75 per cent of all households in unified Germany. The income of approximately 37 000 of these households exceeded the cut-off line.
8. Billion is equal to one thousand million throughout the chapter.
9. The figures for 1973 are a special case because the authors Mierheim and Wicke (1978) adjusted their estimates derived from the ICS to national totals. We take these estimates at face value.
10. It should be noted that Burkhauser et al., who used the GSOEP, calculated a Gini coefficient of 69 per cent in 1988.
11. Mierheim and Wicke adjusted for missing households and missing assets only for 1973.
12. Stein (2004, sec. 3.1.4.3) estimates that the group of top wealth holders which are not covered owns about 5 per cent of total disposable wealth. If this group were included in the ranking it would increase the share of the top decile by about 4 to 5 percentage points.
13. For details, see Mierheim and Wicke (1978, pp. 21–30, 38–54).
14. The ICS contained the tax value of equity in private businesses only in 1973 and 1983. This tax value had to be converted to market prices by a roughly estimated multiplier.
15. During the 1980s and 1990s, Germany experienced considerable immigration, mostly from non-European Union countries. Net immigration between 1980 and 1990 amounted to about 800 000 persons. Between 1991 and 1997, another 1.5 million persons entered united Germany. The most important groups of immigrants were family members joining their already resident spouses who originally came into the country as 'guest-workers', repatriates from former socialist countries, refugees and asylum seekers. In general, these immigrants came with very little or no wealth. See Enquête-Kommission Demographischer Wandel (1998, Table 2, p. 738).
16. The Gini coefficients for West Germany, excluding foreign households, were 61.9 per cent (1993) and 63.5 per cent (1998).
17. Stein (2002, Table 4, p. 11 and Table 6, p. 12). The decrease in the ownership rate of housing wealth between 1993 and 1998 seems to be due to net immigration, as immigrants usually are not able to acquire housing wealth within a short period after immigration for lack of financial assets. Burkhauser et al. (1997, Table 5) compare the

ownership rates of houses and apartments between Germany and the US by age group and by gender. At the end of the 1980s the overall US rate is about one-third higher than the German rate.

18. We distinguish age groups (households or household members according to the age of the head of household) from birth cohorts (households or members of households with the same year of birth of the head of household).

19. Under the assumption of perfect capital markets with the possibility of borrowing on future earnings, initial wealth personal holdings at the beginning of working life would actually be negative and debts would be unequally distributed.

20. The Latin expression gifts 'inter vivo' means gifts 'between living persons'.

21. For an overview of the relevant factors see Davies and Shorrocks (2000, pp. 608–27).

22. The households are classified according to the age of the head of household.

23. Due to limitations of the data in the sample of 1998, the members of the oldest cohort include all households with a head older than 70 years with no upper age limit. If dis-saving with increasing age exists, this biases average wealth holdings of the 'true' birth cohort members downward.

24. Similar conclusions are drawn for the presently old cohorts by Börsch-Supan et al. (2003).

25. This picture would have to be modified, especially for the elderly, if capitalized pension wealth were included in our definition of household disposable wealth. Inequality within the youngest cohort, however, would not change very much.

26. A comparison of the GSOEP and the ICS can be found in Becker et al. (2003).

27. Davies and Shorrocks (2000, p. 655) after discussing the various contributions, give a rough estimate of the influence of bequests on wealth holdings to lie between 35 per cent and 45 per cent.

28. The Four Powers are the former allies of the Second World War: the United States, the United Kingdom, the Soviet Union and France.

29. For the period after reunification we use the terms East Germany and West Germany when we have to distinguish between the two parts of Germany.

30. In comparing East and West Germany one can look either at the population resident in the former GDR in 1989, irrespective of the residence at the time of the survey (principle of origin), or at the population resident on the territory of the former GDR (principle of territory). This makes a difference when there is considerable migration between the two parts of Germany, which is still the case. In what follows we stick to the principle of territory.

31. In 1993 the proportion of homeowner households in East Germany was only 27.4 per cent compared to 50.7 per cent in West Germany. By 1998 this proportion had increased to 33.9 per cent in East Germany, while falling to 49.1 per cent in West Germany. (Hauser and Stein 2001, p. 120). While in the former GDR it was very difficult to keep up houses, resulting in the deterioration of the buildings, land kept its value.

REFERENCES

Becker, I., J.R. Frick, M.M. Grabka, R. Hauser, P. Krause and G.G. Wagner (2003), 'A comparison of the main household income surveys for Germany: EVS and SOEP', in R. Hauser and I. Becker (eds), *Reporting on Income Distribution and Poverty. Perspectives from a German and a European Point of View*, Berlin, Heidelberg and New York: Springer, pp. 55–90.

Börsch-Supan, A. (1994), 'Savings in Germany, part 2: behavior', in James M. Poterba (ed.), *International Comparison of Household Saving*, Chicago, IL: University of Chicago Press, pp. 207–36.

Börsch-Supan, A., A. Reil-Held and R. Schnabel (2003), 'Household saving in Germany', in A. Börsch-Supan, (ed.), *Life Cycle Savings and Public Policy. A*

Cross-National Study of Six Countries, San Diego and London: Elsevier/ Academic Press, pp. 57–99.

Braun, R., F. Burger, M. Miegel, U. Pfeiffer and K. Schulte (2002), *Erben in Deutschland – Volumen, Psychologie und gesamtwirtschaftliche Auswirkungen*, edited by Deutsches Institut für Altersvorsorge, Cologne: published in-house.

Burkhauser, R.V., J.R. Frick and J. Schwarze (1997), 'A comparison of alternative measures of well-being for Germany and the United States', *Review of Income and Wealth*, **43**, 153–72.

Davies, J.B. and A.F. Shorrocks (2000), 'The distribution of wealth', in A.B. Atkinson, and F. Bourguignon (eds), *Handbook of Income Distribution*, vol. I, Amsterdam, Lausanne, New York, Oxford, Shannon, Singapore, Tokyo: North Holland, pp. 605–75.

Deutsche Bundesbank (1993), 'Zur Vermögenssituation der privaten Haushalte in Deutschland', *Monatsbericht* (October), 19–32.

Deutsche Bundesbank (1999), 'Zur Entwicklung der privaten Vermögenssituation seit Beginn der neunziger Jahre', *Monatsbericht* (January), 33–50.

Enquête-Kommission Demographischer Wandel (1998), *Herausforderungen unserer älter werdenden Gesellschaft an den einzelnen und die Politik*, edited by Deutscher Bundestag, Bonn, published in-house.

Hauser, R. (2003), 'The development of the distribution of income and wealth in Germany – an overview', in R. Hauser and I. Becker (eds), *Reporting on Income Distribution and Poverty. Perspectives from a German and a European Point of View*, Berlin, Heidelberg and New York: Springer, pp. 7–28.

Hauser, R. and H. Stein (2001), *Die Vermögensverteilung im vereinigten Deutschland*, Frankfurt a. M. and New York: Campus.

Merz, J. (2001), *Hohe Einkommen, ihre Struktur und Verteilung*, research report published by the Bundesministerium für Arbeit and Sozialordnung, Bonn.

Mierheim, H. and L. Wicke (1978), *Die personelle Vermögensverteilung in der Bundesrepublik Deutschland*, Tübingen: Mohr-Siebeck.

Reil-Held, A. (2000), 'Einkommen und Sterblichkeit in Deutschland: Leben Reiche länger?' in Beiträge zur angewandten Wirtschaftsforschung, Mannheim, working paper no. 580-00.

Ring, A.M. (2000), *Die Verteilung der Vermögen in der Bundesrepublik Deutschland, Analyse und politische Schlußfolgerungen*, Frankfurt a. M., Berlin, Bern, Brussels, New York, Vienna: Peter Lang.

Schlomann, H. (1992), *Vermögensverteilung und private Altersvorsorge*, Frankfurt a. Main and New York: Campus.

Schupp, J. and G.G. Wagner (2003), *Forschungsprojekt Repräsentative Analyse der Lebenslagen einkommensstarker Haushalte*, published by the Bundesministerium für Gesundheit und Soziale Sicherung, Bonn, published in-house.

Stein, H. (2002), 'The development of aggregate private wealth and its distribution in Germany since 1970', EVS-Project at the Chair of Economics and Social Policy, University of Frankfurt, working paper no. 30.

Stein, H. (2004), *Anatomie der Vermögensverteilung. Ergebnisse der Einkommens- und Verbrauchsstichproben 1983–1998*, Berlin, edition sigma.

Wolff, E.N. (1991), 'The distribution of household wealth: methodological issues, time trends, and cross-sectional comparisons', in L. Osberg (ed.), *Economic Inequality and Poverty. International Perspectives*, New York: Sharpe, pp. 92–133.

Wolff, E.N. (1996), 'International comparisons of wealth inequality', *Review of Income and Wealth*, **4**, 433–51.

APPENDIX

Table 6A.1 *General information on the Income and Consumption Surveys (ICS) (Einkommens- und Verbrauchsstichproben) of the German Federal Statistical Office (Statistisches Bundesamt)*[a]

Year	ICS 1983	ICS 1988	ICS 1993	ICS 1998
Type of survey	repeated cross-section (no panel)			
Sampling method	quota sample based on the mandatory random Micro Census (Micro Census = 1 per cent survey of all inhabitants)			
Household definition	income sharing unit			
Definition of household head	person with the highest income			
Sample size (households)	44 500	45 000	50 000	62 300
Willingness to participate	Less willing to participate are: (1) self-employed, farmers, workers (2) single-person households (3) households with very low or very high income			
Coverage of East Germany	no		yes	
Coverage of households with foreign heads	no		yes	
Grossed-up number of persons covered (in 1000)	52 648	53 229	80 758	79 775
Inhabitants	61 383	61 715	81 338	82 037
Weighting	Weights derived from marginal distributions of the obligatory and random Micro Census for each federal state based on household size, social status of head, and net household income			
Size of households covered (number of persons)	1–6	1–6	1–9	1–9 and more
Households or persons not covered	homeless institutionalized persons households with very high monthly net incomes			

Table 6A.1 (continued)

Year	ICS 1983	ICS 1988	ICS 1993	ICS 1998
Cut-off line for households with very high monthly net incomes	12 782 euro[b]		17 895 euro[b]	
Size of the sub-sample used for analysis (per cent of original sample)	98%		80%	
Size of subsample used for analysis (number of households)	42 752	43 730	40 230	49 720
Size of the subsample used for analysis (number of persons)	118 367	116 606	104 837	128 022

Notes:
a.   Anonymized versions of these surveys were made available by the German Federal Statistical Office to the Chair of Economics, Social Policy and Distribution Studies of the University of Frankfurt am Main. Calculations of the authors are based on these files if not otherwise mentioned.
b.   Figures are recalculated at the official exchange rate 1 euro = 1.95583 Deutschmarks.

Sources: Statistisches Bundesamt (1994), *Wirtschaftsrechnungen – Einkommens- und Verbrauchsstichprobe 1988, Aufgabe, Methode und Durchführung*, Fachserie 15, Heft 7, Stuttgart; Statistisches Bundesamt (1995), *Statistisches Jahrbuch 1995 für die Bundesrepublik Deutschland*, Wiesbaden; Statistisches Bundesamt (2000), *Datenreport 2002*. Herausgegeben vom Statistischen Bundesamt in Zusammenarbeit mit dem Wissenschaftszentrum Berlin für Sozialforschung und dem Zentrum für Umfragen, Methoden und Analysen, Mannheim, Wiesbaden.

Table 6A.2   Wealth components reported in the Income and Consumption Surveys of the German Federal Statistical Office

Year	ICS 1983	ICS 1988	ICS 1993	ICS 1998
Components of wealth	Gross property wealth (real estates and houses) + gross monetary wealth (including quoted shares) − liabilities (consumer debt and housing debts) = net total wealth			
Recorded monetary wealth	Savings and loans accounts Quoted shares Bonds Savings with other banks Other monetary wealth (investment funds, etc.)	Savings and loans accounts Quoted shares Bonds Savings with other banks Other monetary wealth (investment funds, etc.) Life insurance Current accounts		Savings and loans accounts Quoted shares Bonds Savings with other banks Other monetary wealth (investment funds, etc.) Life insurance
Estimated monetary wealth	Life insurance (by contract volume and age of the reference person) Current accounts (by income position, ownership of property wealth, age of the reference person)	not necessary		Current accounts (by income position, ownership of property wealth, age of the reference person
Consumer debt etc.		recorded		
Rateable value for taxation of property assets		recorded		
Market values of property assets	Calculation by means of a conversion factor on the basis of the rateable value for taxation of property assets. The aim is to adapt the taxation values of property assets to the market values		recorded (estimate by owner)	

Table 6A.2   (continued)

Year	ICS 1983	ICS 1988	ICS 1993	ICS 1998
Debts for housing construction		recorded		
Wealth components not recorded	Market value of equity in private businesses (except current value of quoted shares) Consumer durables Cash, jewellery, works of art agricultural assets of farmers			
Estimation of market value of wealth components only partly recorded	The ownership of wealth components is recorded in some cases, but not the market value. These values are estimated by income position, ownership of property wealth, age of reference person and number of persons living in the household		Not necessary	The ownership of wealth components is recorded in some cases, but not the market value. These values are estimated by income position, ownership of property wealth, age of reference person and number of persons living in the household

Sources: Statistisches Bundesamt (1994), *Wirtschaftsrechnungen – Einkommens- und Verbrauchsstichprobe 1988, Aufgabe, Methode und Durchführung*, Fachserie 15, Heft 7, Stuttgart.

7. Household wealth distribution in Italy in the 1990s

**Andrea Brandolini, Luigi Cannari,
Giovanni D'Alessio and Ivan Faiella***

INTRODUCTION

Like other major economies, in the second half of the 1990s Italy recorded an exceptional rise in share prices, which came after a decade of oscillations around a flattened trend (Figure 7.1). In March 2000 the Milan stock exchange share index (MIB) peaked at 3.2 times the value it had recorded at the end of 1996. Following this buoyant performance, in December 2000 the value of company shares and mutual funds held by Italian households exceeded 1000 billion[1] euros, or 40 per cent of their financial assets. Within

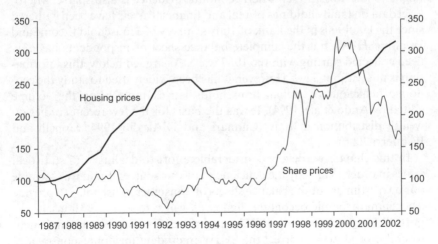

Source: Share prices: monthly averages of the MIB index from the Bank of Italy database. Housing prices: semi-annual series of the average price per square metre of new houses as estimated by Muzzicato et al. (2002).

Figure 7.1   Share and housing prices in Italy, 1987–2002 (index, average in 1987 = 100)

the next two years, however, share prices fell abruptly. The MIB index lost two-fifths of its value, and holdings of risky assets in households' portfolios decreased to 640 billion euros. Housing prices have moved differently. They more than doubled between 1987 and 1993. After a short-lived reduction, they exhibited little variation until mid-2000, when they reverted to a new phase of steep growth. These wide changes in relative asset prices may be assumed to have had considerable influence on the distribution of household wealth. Were the gains from the stock market boom of the late 1990s spread across many families, or were they concentrated in the hands of a few investors? What about the subsequent sharp contraction? What are the distributive implications of variations in housing prices?

In this chapter we address these questions by investigating the distribution of wealth among Italian households and its evolution from 1989 to 2000. A major difficulty we have to cope with is the quality of available data. However uninformative on distributive aspects, the aggregate balance sheets of the household sector would provide a natural starting point. Unfortunately, despite a centennial research tradition,[2] there are no estimates, official or unofficial, of the aggregate wealth of Italian households. Financial accounts have been published by the Bank of Italy since the early 1960s, albeit with discontinuities; tangible assets were only estimated in a few occasional studies (Tresoldi and Visco 1975; Banca d'Italia 1986; Pagliano and Rossi 1992). Microeconomic evidence is also sparse. Micro-level data on family holdings of real and financial assets have been gathered since the late 1960s in the Bank of Italy's Survey of Household Income and Wealth (SHIW), but the complete balance sheet of respondents has only been collected starting with the 1987 wave. As argued below, this information is not without flaws. However, it has been widely used to study the economic behaviour of Italian households, an example being the volume edited by Ando et al. (1994). It was the basis for the few recent studies on wealth distribution in Italy (Cannari and D'Alessio 1994; Jappelli and Pistaferri 2000).

In this chapter we devote considerable effort to dealing with statistical issues in order to remedy the deficiencies of our sources. First, we assemble our own estimates of the balance sheets of consumer households to provide a benchmark for microeconomic figures as well as to show how households' portfolios have changed over the last four decades.[3] Second, we implement several procedures to correct the SHIW microdata for nonresponse, non-reporting and under-reporting, and we present results for adjusted and unadjusted data alike. The consideration of both sets of results helps to verify the robustness of our conclusions.

The first section that follows describes the composition of households' portfolios according to aggregate data, followed by a section that examines the characteristics and quality of the SHIW microeconomic data. This section also illustrates the adjustment procedures, more precisely described in the Appendix, and their impact. We then report on microeconomic figures on household wealth and its relation to age, work status and region of residence, followed by a section on wealth inequality, and finally, our concluding section. Our main findings are that inequality of household net worth rose steadily during the 1990s and that it was especially the increased concentration of financial wealth that determined such a path.

THE COMPOSITION OF HOUSEHOLD NET WORTH IN MACRO ESTIMATES

In Italian macroeconomic statistics the 'household sector' has been typically broken down into the two sub-sectors 'sole proprietorships' and 'consumer households', purporting to separate the productive activity of small businesses from the accounts of households as consumption units. Here we follow this tradition by concentrating on consumer households. We estimated their balance sheets from two main sources, the Financial Accounts and the National Accounts, hence the label FANA used throughout the chapter (details regarding the methods of estimation are provided in Appendix A of Brandolini et al. 2004). It is important to bear in mind that there are significant discontinuities which only in some cases were we able to remedy. Our estimates are therefore to be taken with caution. They are meant to offer a broad view of the evolution of Italian households' wealth in the last 40 years as well as to provide an aggregate benchmark for the subsequent analysis based on individual data.

Household wealth is defined as the total market value of dwellings, consumer durable goods and financial assets, net of debts. Equities include unlisted shares and noncorporate equities, but not the value of small unincorporated businesses. The values of life insurance and private pension funds, and public pension rights are also not included. We estimate that the net worth of Italian households amounted to 6100 billion euros at the end of 2000,[4] or 5.2 times the gross domestic product. In 1965, the same ratio was 2.5. On the whole, between 1965 and 2000 household wealth went up by 5.8 per cent per year in real terms, that is, after deflating by the consumer price index in December of each year. Real net worth per capita increased by an average 5.5 per cent each year, from 16 400 to 105 400 euros at 2000 prices.

The largest part of household net worth is made up of dwellings. In the last 40 years, their share in total wealth has fluctuated between 51 and 66 per cent (Figure 7.2, top panel). The stock of durable goods has gradually

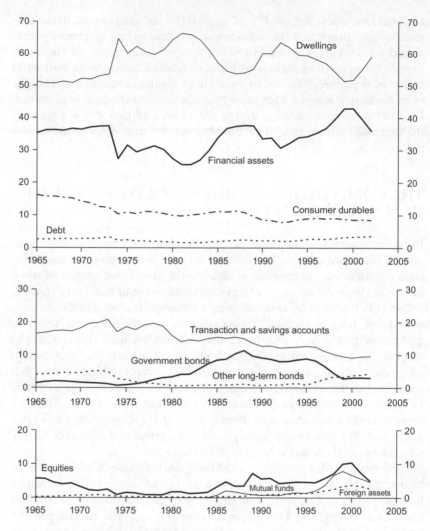

Source: Brandolini et al. (2004), Appendix A.

Figure 7.2   Composition of household net worth, 1965–2002 (percentage shares of net worth)

declined from 16 to less than 9 per cent of total net worth. The weight of tangible assets as a whole has shown a modest tendency to fall, to the benefit of financial assets: fitting a linear trend, the share of financial assets appears to have grown by about 1 percentage point every ten years. Lastly, financial liabilities have remained low for most of the period: they accounted for about 2 per cent of net worth until the mid-1990s. They subsequently increased to 3.6 per cent in 2002.

Important reallocations of households' portfolios towards financial assets took place during the last two economic expansions. The share of financial assets rose from 26 to 38 per cent between 1982 and 1989, and from 34 to 43 per cent between 1995 and 2000. The first increase was mainly associated with the spread of direct ownership of Italian government bonds and Treasury bills: from below 2 per cent up to 1977, their share grew to 4 per cent in 1982 and to a peak of 11 per cent in 1988; it then gradually diminished and has held steady at around 3 per cent since 1999 (Figure 7.2, middle panel). The second shift was instead driven by equities and mutual funds (Figure 7.2, bottom panel). The importance of equities in households' portfolios was already rising in the mid-1980s, but stock holdings doubled from 5 to 10 per cent of net worth between 1995 and 2000, in parallel with the stock market boom and the rapid privatization of state-owned corporations and public utilities. Over the same five years, the proportion of household wealth held in mutual funds rose from 1 to 7 per cent. In both episodes, however, the portfolio reallocations were not lasting, as they were followed by a quick, if incomplete, return to previous allocation between tangible and financial assets. The diversification into government bonds in the 1980s, and equities and mutual funds in the 1990s, had more permanent effects on the composition of the financial portfolio, since it overlapped with the long-run decline in the share of transaction and savings accounts in net worth, from 19 per cent in the late 1970s to below 10 in 2000–2002.

As a result of the recent evolution, 'in 1998 the portfolio of Italian households was much more strongly tilted toward risky assets than it had ever been in the past' (Guiso and Jappelli 2002, p. 253). Despite theses changes, the wealth composition of Italian households stands out in an international perspective for the high shares of tangible assets and cash and transactions accounts, for the low diffusion of life insurance and pension funds, and for the very modest level of indebtedness (Paiella 2004; Magri 2002; Faiella and Neri 2004).

Supply side factors have traditionally played an important role. In the early 1990s Guiso et al. (1994, p. 23) remarked that: 'regulations, high down payments for the purchase of durables and housing, wide interest rate spreads and limited competition make it considerably more difficult to obtain access to credit and insurance in Italy than in almost all other industrialized countries of comparable level of development'. This situation changed in the following years, when increased competition among financial intermediaries lowered entry costs, stimulated the diversification of assets and eased the access to credit, and the extensive privatization of state-owned companies helped the growth of the stock market (Guiso and Jappelli 2002). Other factors contribute. The prominence of residential housing in household portfolios reveals a strong preference for owner-occupation, which is only in part attributable to the imperfections of the rental market and the presence of borrowing constraints (Di Addario 2002; Paiella 2002).[5] The low level of consumer credit may reflect the smaller share of large retailers in commercial distribution than in other countries.

THE BANK OF ITALY'S SURVEY OF HOUSEHOLD INCOME AND WEALTH

The main source of information on household wealth at the micro level is the SHIW, conducted by the Bank of Italy yearly from 1965 to 1987 (except for 1985), every other year until 1995, and then in 1998 and 2000 (the reference is to the year for which, not in which, the survey is conducted). The SHIW gathers information on household microeconomic behaviour. Detailed data have been collected continually on the social and demographic characteristics of household members, their incomes and, since 1980, their consumption expenditure. Estimates of households' tangible assets are also available from the outset, whereas financial assets have been surveyed irregularly. The latter have been recorded on a regular basis since 1987, although their comparability over time is lessened by changes in the format of the questions. Records used in this chapter relate to 1989, 1991, 1993, 1995, 1998 and 2000 and are drawn from the Historical Archive (HA) of the survey (Version 2.1, released in January 2003).

The sample size is about 8000 units per year. The basic survey unit is the 'household', defined as a group of individuals linked by ties of blood, marriage or affection, sharing the same dwelling, and pooling all or part of their incomes. Institutional population is not included. Data are collected in personal interviews conducted by professionally trained interviewers. Participation is voluntary and not remunerated. As a result, nonresponse is high. In the last six waves, the response rate, net of units not found at the available address, ranged between a minimum 43.3 per cent in 2000 and a maximum 72.0 per cent in 1993. Thus, not only the level but also the variability of the response rate is a matter of some concern. It must be observed, however, that item nonresponse is relatively small, since interviewers are not paid for the questionnaires where answers to the main questions, among which wealth holdings, are missing.[6] Further methodological details on the SHIW are given in Banca d'Italia (2002a), Brandolini and Cannari (1994) and Brandolini (1999).

Wealth Data in the SHIW

We define household net worth from the SHIW as the total value of tangible assets (consumer durable goods, jewellery and other valuables, real estate, businesses) and financial assets (transaction and savings accounts, government bonds, equities and other assets), net of financial liabilities (mortgages and other debts). We do not include cash and currency, severance pay (*trattamento di fine rapporto*), social security wealth, and the cash values of life insurance and private retirement accounts because they are not recorded in the survey.[7] On the other hand, we include valuables and businesses which were not accounted for in aggregate estimates. Note that businesses cover firms, both incorporated and unincorporated, where respondents do some work. We stick to the standard practice of considering these businesses to be tangible assets because their value is closely linked to the work of the proprietors, while company shares held simply as a form of saving are classified among financial assets. Wealth components are recorded in the SHIW as follows.

Consumer durable goods, jewellery and other valuables

Respondents are asked to provide their best estimate of the monetary value at the end of the year preceding the interview for three categories of durable goods: precious objects (jewellery, old and gold coins, works of art, antiques), means of transport (cars, motorbikes, caravans, boats, bicycles) and furniture, furnishings, household appliances and sundry articles.

Real estate

Dwellings, nonresidential buildings and land are subjectively evaluated by respondents. For instance, all interviewees are asked the following question: 'In your opinion, what price could you ask for the dwelling in which you live (if sold unoccupied)? In other words, how much is it worth (including any cellar, garage or attic)?' For homeowners, the answer provides the value of their principal residence.[8] Similar questions are asked for every piece of real estate, considered separately, possessed by the household at the end of the previous year.

Businesses

The valuation of businesses is particularly delicate, since in Italy the percentage of self-employed labour is among the highest in OECD countries. The SHIW adopts two methods. Members of the professions, sole proprietors, freelancers and members of family businesses are asked how much their firm would be worth should they sell it. This value must include any equipment used, stocks and goodwill, and must exclude the value of buildings and land. Active shareholders and partners in incorporated firms are asked to indicate the market value, at the end of the previous year, of their own share in the firm. These values are those underlying our figures.[9]

Financial assets

The range of financial assets listed in the questionnaire expanded over the years, mostly driven by financial innovation and portfolio diversification. In the last wave, 25 different categories were specified. Moreover, the formulation of the questions varied over the years. In 1989, amounts were inferred indirectly by asking respondents the percentage composition of their household's total wealth, together with the amount held in checking accounts. In subsequent surveys, respondents were asked to choose, from among 15 brackets, the one corresponding to the amount held of each asset. In 1998 and 2000, they were also asked for point estimates. Whenever missing, we approximate the point estimate with the midpoint of the interval. We also include among financial assets credits *vis-à-vis* relatives or friends not living in the house and the trade credits towards customers of professionals, freelancers, sole proprietors and family businesses. All values refer to the end of the previous year.

Debts

Outstanding debts at the end of the year preceding the interview are recorded in the same manner since 1987. They include: debts serving to meet needs of the household, distinguished by type of purchase (buildings and restructuring, jewellery, motor vehicles, furniture and electrical appliances, and nondurable goods such as holidays); debts *vis-à-vis* relatives or friends not living in the house; debts connected with the business activity; and the trade credits of suppliers for professionals, freelancers, sole proprietors and family businesses.

All wealth components are basically valued on a 'realization' basis, or 'the value obtained in a sale on the open market at the date in question' (for this definition and a discussion of valuation criteria, see Atkinson and Harrison 1978, pp. 5–6). On the other hand, the calculation of total household wealth suffers from an inconsistency due to the format of the questions: real estate and unincorporated businesses are estimated at the time of the interview, whereas all other wealth components are valued at the end of the previous year. We do not correct for this inconsistency.

We take the household as the unit of observation. (In the SHIW individual ownership is known for real estate only.) The distributions of total wealth and its main components are computed by weighting each household by either the original or the adjusted sample weights (see below), without making any allowance for the household size or composition.

The Quality of the SHIW Wealth Data

Comparisons with external sources, such as the national accounts, show that the quality of income and expenditure estimates in the SHIW is comparable to that of similar surveys in other countries: for instance, underestimation of disposable income is valued at around 30 per cent (Brandolini 1999; Cannari and Violi 1995). Data on wealth, on the other hand, are typically less reliable and their accuracy tends to vary across different assets, misreporting being lower for tangible assets than financial assets.

The 13th General Population and Housing Census (Istat 1995) provides a useful benchmark to assess the coverage of houses in 1991. According to the SHIW, the total number of dwellings owned by households (inclusive of those occupied under a redemption agreement or in usufruct) is 16.9 million, about a quarter less than in the census (Table 7.1). The number of houses occupied by their owners slightly exceeds that recorded in the census, but this over-representation disappears after adjusting for non-response as discussed below. While respondents are ready to disclose the ownership of the house where they live, it appears that they are far more hesitant to unveil other possessions: less than 40 per cent of the dwellings which are not occupied by the owners are reported among the SHIW assets,[10] even after adjusting for nonresponse.

The SHIW total value of real estate falls short of the FANA aggregate by a proportion varying between 34 per cent in 1993 and 15 per cent in 2000 (Table 7.2, top panel). (Since the FANA aggregates include only dwellings while the SHIW figures also cover land and nonresidential buildings, the comparison understates the shortfall.) The evaluation for durable goods is about two-thirds of the aggregate figure in the 1990s. Taking tangible assets as a whole, in the six waves considered, the average discrepancy between the SHIW estimate and the corresponding FANA figure is 26 per cent. Problems are greater for financial assets. Transaction and savings accounts appear to be underestimated in the SHIW by an average of 64 per cent, government bonds by 70 per cent, and private bonds, company shares and investment shares by 85 per cent; worryingly, the underestimation varies considerably from one year to the other (see also Cannari et al. 1990; Cannari and D'Alessio 1994).

Several reasons can account for the differences between aggregate and survey figures.

- Survey data are well known to suffer from a tendency of interviewees, consciously or not, to under-report their wealth. The adjustments for these nonsampling errors explained in the next section allow us to reduce substantially these discrepancies. A further problem for

Table 7.1 Ownership of dwellings in 1991 (thousands and per cent)

Condition of dwellings	Census	SHIW unadjusted		SHIW adjusted for nonresponse		SHIW adjusted for nonresponse and nonreporting of dwellings not occupied by owners	
	Number	Number	Reporting rate	Number	Reporting rate	Number	Reporting rate
Occupied	17 757	15 171	85.4	14 960	84.2	–	–
Owner-occupied[a]	13 419	13 745	102.4	13 393	99.8	13 393	99.8
Rented[b]	3500	914	26.1	1028	29.4	–	–
Other use	838	512	61.1	539	64.3	–	–
Unoccupied	4571	1776	38.8	1843	40.3	–	–
Holiday homes[c]	–	1378	–	1441	–	–	–
Vacant or other use[d]	–	397	–	401	–	–	–
Total	22 328	16 947	75.9	16 802	75.3	22 940	102.7
of which: not owner-occupied	8909	3202	35.9	3409	38.3	9547	107.2

Notes:

a. Include dwellings occupied under a redemption agreement or in usufruct.
b. Dwellings rented all year to persons, households, firms and organizations.
c. Include dwellings rented part of the year to persons and households.
d. Include dwellings used for family business activity, rented part of the year to firms and organizations, and other unclassified dwellings.

Sources: Authors' calculations on data from the SHIW-HA (Version 2.1) and Istat (1995), Table 2.17, p. 96, Table 4.62, p. 453, Table 4.69, p. 461.

Table 7.2 Household net worth: reporting rate in the SHIW (percentage ratios to FANA figures)

Year	Total tangible assets	Consumer durables	Real estate	Total financial assets	Transaction and savings accounts	Government bonds	Private bonds, equities, mutual funds	Gross wealth	Debt	Net worth
SHIW: unadjusted										
1989	75	85	73	26	39	26	9	58	34	59
1991	67	68	67	21	28	23	10	53	46	54
1993	66	62	66	24	26	27	19	54	57	54
1995	75	62	77	25	26	30	17	60	47	60
1998	81	67	84	28	46	26	19	63	37	63
2000	83	67	85	27	51	46	15	62	36	62
Mean	74	69	75	25	36	30	15	58	43	59
SHIW: adjusted for nonresponse, nonreporting and under-reporting										
1989	105	87	108	59	77	67	27	89	34	91
1991	87	69	89	49	49	66	32	75	47	76
1993	81	63	84	52	44	72	47	73	57	73
1995	88	64	92	57	46	75	56	79	48	80
1998	96	70	100	75	89	88	65	89	38	90
2000	97	69	101	72	114	152	47	87	38	89
Mean	92	70	96	61	70	87	46	82	44	83

Source: Authors' calculations on data from the SHIW-HA (Version 2.1) and aggregate sources as described in Brandolini et al. (2004), Appendix A.

survey-based wealth estimates stems from the high concentration of wealth and the low probability of including the wealthiest households in the sample. Our adjustments can do little to correct for this under-representation. In the US Survey of Consumer Finances (SCF) and in the Canadian Survey of Financial Security, this problem is addressed in the survey design through the over-sampling of high-income households. (But the over-sampling of families of senior white-collar employees, businessmen and professionals in the SHIW for 1987 gave unsatisfactory results; see Brandolini and Cannari 1994, p. 381.)

● The aggregate figures themselves rest on many measurement hypotheses and are subject to errors and revisions. For instance, in the last methodological revision of the financial accounts, the value of equities held by households in 1995 was lowered by over 30 per cent, in part owing to the use of a more comprehensive source on the balance sheets of unlisted companies (see Banca d'Italia 2002b, p. 50). The aggregate financial balance sheet is especially uncertain for the household sector, whose holdings are often calculated 'residually' by deducting from the total the holdings of all other institutional sectors.

● Differences in sector boundaries and variable definitions prevent data from being fully comparable. Although we were able to separate out financial assets and liabilities of small unincorporated businesses, the financial statistics still include nonprofit organizations and institutional population (that is, persons living permanently in institutions like hostels, nursing homes for the elderly, residential schools, prisons, military bases) which are not covered by the SHIW. Moreover, the SHIW respondents may employ valuation criteria which differ from those underlying aggregate statistics: they might fail to include the interest on deposits accrued in the year, but not yet paid; they rate durable goods at their price in the second-hand market, or perhaps at their historical cost, whereas national accounts apply substitution prices to the real stock of durable goods computed with the perpetual inventory method; they value their house at a subjectively perceived realization price while national accounts would use actual market prices; and so forth.

To sum up, there are large differences between the estimates of household net worth obtained from aggregate sources on the one hand, and the SHIW on the other. These differences are due partly to irreconcilable diversities in classifications and definitions, and partly to shortcomings in both micro and macro sources. Divergence in both levels and time patterns is a matter of concern and makes it necessary to interpret the SHIW data with prudence, but it would be wrong to blame them alone for the discrepancies. Being aware of their deficiencies, we believe that a more complete and reliable analysis of the SHIW wealth data must explicitly account for underestimation. The discussion of the statistical techniques used to adjust the SHIW data is the object of the next section.

Corrections for Nonresponses, Nonreporting and Under-reporting

There is ample evidence that the probabilities of avoiding the interview (nonresponse), of being reticent about assets actually owned (nonreporting) and of undervaluing declared asset holdings (under-reporting) are typically not independent of wealth (see for the SHIW: Cannari and D'Alessio 1990, 1993; D'Alessio and Faiella 2002; for other surveys: Avery et al. 1988; Hayashi et al. 1988; Curtin et al. 1989; Kennickell 2000; Morissette et al., Chapter 5, in this volume. This observation brings us to discard a simple proportional adjustment to FANA aggregates by constant factors and to prefer methods that take advantage of all available information. We apply three procedures (see the Appendix for details).

1. The first procedure exploits the figures on the number of contacts needed in the 1998 survey to obtain an interview, as suggested by D'Alessio and Faiella (2002). Households requiring at least two visits before accepting the interview are assumed to be representative of nonresponding units. Under this assumption, the estimated probability of not participating in the survey at the first visit, conditional on being interviewed at a later visit, is a proxy for the unconditional probability of not participating at all, and can be used to recalculate weights adjusted for differential response rates across households with different characteristics (among which income and wealth). This correction can only partially remedy the under-representation in the sample of very rich households.
2. A model proposed by Cannari et al. (1990) and refined by Cannari and D'Alessio (1993) is applied to correct for nonreporting and under-reporting of financial assets. The method is based on the outcome of a statistical matching of the SHIW data for 1987 with the microdata from a survey carried out in the same year by the Banca Nazionale del Lavoro (BNLS) on a sample of its customers. It rests on the assumption that the BNLS information on respondents' financial behaviour is more reliable, owing to the trust that customers are likely to place in their own bank.
3. Borrowed from Cannari and D'Alessio (1990), the third procedure accounts for the nonreporting of dwellings not occupied by their

owners. The procedure is based on the assumptions that (a) the empirical distribution of the number of dwellings not used as principal residence recorded in the SHIW is a discrete Poisson distribution (conditional on certain household characteristics); and (b) the probability of the owners declaring such dwellings is a binomial distribution. Together, these assumptions imply that the probability of owning a dwelling other than one's own residence also follows a Poisson distribution. This distribution can be estimated and used to impute ownership.

These procedures significantly affect the SHIW evidence. With regard to dwellings, we have already noticed how the adjustment for nonresponse brings the number of owner-occupied houses perfectly into line with the census total, while it improves only marginally the estimate for the other dwellings. The latter discrepancy is adjusted through the third procedure, even if the stochastic nature of the correction leads to an overshooting of the census figure by around 7 per cent (Table 7.1).

Table 7.3 shows the cumulative impact of the various corrections. In 2000, the share of households without any financial assets falls from 19 to 16 per cent after correcting for nonresponse; it drops to 7 per cent after adjusting also for non- and under-reporting. Owing to these adjustments, the proportions of holders of transaction and saving accounts and of government debt rise on average by 15 and 13 percentage points respectively, while that of holders of private bonds, equities and mutual funds goes up by 5 percentage points.[11] The share of proprietors of dwellings increases by about 1 percentage point every year with the adjustment for nonresponses, and by a further 2 to 5 points with the adjustment for non- and under-reporting. The latter has declined steadily over time, thanks to better controls on the SHIW fieldwork, and a probable reduction in tax evasion, and hence household reticence, brought about by the introduction of the municipality tax on real estate. In general, the imputation affects mainly households in the lower tail of the wealth distribution. The older and the less educated the household's head, the higher is the size of the adjustment. The correction is larger for households headed by a female, or a self-employed or nonemployed person.

Taking the average over the six waves from 1989 to 2000, the adjustments increase the mean values of real estate and financial assets by 31 and 148 per cent, respectively (Table 7.3). The value of household debts is only affected by the adjustment for nonresponse and it is raised by 5 per cent (9 per cent in 2000). Overall, household net worth increases by 41 per cent. The shortfall with respect to FANA aggregates is reduced from 75 to 39 per cent for total financial assets, from 26 to 8 per cent for tangible assets, and

Table 7.3   Impact of the adjustments on the SHIW data (per cent and percentage ratios to unadjusted figures)

Year	Share of households holding the asset							Mean values (over the whole population)						
	Real estate			Financial assets				Real estate			Financial assets			
	At least one	Principal residence	Other real estate	At least one	Transaction and savings accounts	Government bonds	Private bonds, equities, mutual funds	Total	Principal residence	Other real estate	Total	Transaction and savings accounts	Government bonds	Private bonds, equities, mutual funds
Unadjusted														
1989	69	64	23	69	69	18	6	100	100	100	100	100	100	100
1991	70	66	25	81	81	23	8	100	100	100	100	100	100	100
1993	69	63	32	83	83	22	10	100	100	100	100	100	100	100
1995	71	66	33	84	83	26	11	100	100	100	100	100	100	100
1998	72	67	27	86	86	12	18	100	100	100	100	100	100	100
2000	74	69	25	81	80	12	21	100	100	100	100	100	100	100
Mean	71	66	27	81	80	19	12	100	100	100	100	100	100	100
Adjusted for nonresponse														
1989	69	65	24	73	73	20	7	106	104	110	112	111	115	111
1991	71	66	27	84	84	25	9	106	104	110	112	109	113	121
1993	70	64	33	85	85	24	11	106	104	109	109	106	108	115
1995	72	67	34	86	85	28	11	106	105	109	109	106	110	116
1998	73	68	28	88	88	12	20	108	106	113	118	111	111	128
2000	75	71	27	84	83	13	23	109	108	115	116	115	112	119
Mean	72	67	29	83	83	20	13	107	105	111	113	109	112	118

239

Table 7.3 (continued)

Year	Share of households holding the asset							Mean values (over the whole population)						
	Real estate			Financial assets				Real estate			Financial assets			
	At least one	Principal residence	Other real estate	At least one	Transaction and savings accounts	Government bonds	Private bonds, equities, mutual funds	Total	Principal residence	Other real estate	Total	Transaction and savings accounts	Government bonds	Private bonds, equities, mutual funds
Adjusted for nonresponse, nonreporting and under-reporting														
1989	74	65	42	96	96	34	12	152	104	283	236	206	267	326
1991	76	66	42	96	95	37	12	137	104	239	238	182	296	330
1993	74	64	45	94	94	35	14	129	104	187	222	176	272	247
1995	75	67	43	94	94	38	16	123	105	166	237	182	254	333
1998	75	68	38	95	95	25	23	123	106	173	278	201	343	352
2000	77	71	35	93	93	23	26	123	108	169	279	233	338	314
Mean	75	67	41	95	95	32	17	131	105	203	248	197	295	317

Source: Authors' calculations on data from the SHIW-HA (Version 2.1).

from 41 to 17 per cent for net worth (Table 7.2). In a few cases our procedures lead to estimates exceeding the FANA values. The corrections, and therefore the remaining discrepancies *vis-à-vis* aggregate figures, vary considerably from year to year: the adjusted SHIW data capture between a minimum of 73 per cent of the FANA net worth in 1993 and a maximum of 91 per cent in 1989.

In general, the adjustments bring the composition of household wealth closer into line with the aggregate evidence. If we compute the differences, in absolute value, between the SHIW and the aggregate shares in net worth, we find that they fall considerably, after the adjustments, in all waves and for every one of the six components reported in Table 7.2 except debt. By averaging it out across all waves, the sum of the absolute discrepancies diminishes from 38 per cent on unadjusted data to 22 per cent on adjusted data.

This summary of the more detailed figures reported in the tables shows the substantial impact of the correction procedures on the SHIW evidence. Our adjustments are meant to offer a more realistic description of the distribution of household wealth in Italy. However, our adjusted results might be regarded with some suspicion – because of an excess of manipulation. In the light of this consideration, in the following sections we focus on figures adjusted for nonresponse, nonreporting and under-reporting, but we also report and occasionally discuss unadjusted figures.

MICROECONOMIC EVIDENCE ON HOUSEHOLD NET WORTH

At the end of 2000, the adjusted average net worth of Italian households amounted to 270 000 euros, one-third more than in 1989 after correcting for changes in the consumer price index (Table 7.4).[12] Between 1989 and 2000, mean wealth has been growing in real terms by 2.7 per cent per year, while real disposable income has remained virtually unchanged. Apart from capital gains on some asset holdings, this sustained pace of wealth accumulation has been made possible by the high propensity to save of Italian households.

Tangible assets account for the largest, if falling, share of wealth: 73 per cent in 2000. The predominance of real assets is largely attributable to home-ownership, which in Italy is among the highest in the European Union.[13] In 2000, the principal residence was worth, across all households, an average of 101 600 euros, or 38 per cent of total wealth. Between 1989 and 2000, this value went up by 61 per cent in real terms as a result of an increase in home-ownership (from 65 to 71 per cent) and residence size (from 111 to 118 square metres) and above all, owing to an exceptional rise in housing prices which

Table 7.4　Household net worth in the SHIW

Wealth component	Mean values[a] €		Share in net worth %		Annualized growth rate
	1989	2000	1989	2000	1989–2000 %
Unadjusted					
Total tangible assets	115 300	164 200	87.7	87.1	3.3
Consumer durable goods	16 800	16 300	12.8	8.6	−0.3
Jewellery and other valuables	3500	3900	2.7	2.1	1.0
Principal residence	60 600	94 500	46.1	50.1	4.1
Other real estate	22 400	30 900	17.0	16.4	3.0
Businesses	12 100	18 500	9.2	9.8	3.9
Total financial assets	17 800	27 900	13.5	14.8	4.2
Transaction and savings accounts	10 800	13 100	8.2	6.9	1.8
Government bonds	5200	4000	4.0	2.1	−2.4
Private bonds, equities, mutual funds	1800	10 700	1.4	5.7	17.6
Gross wealth	133 100	192 000	101.2	101.8	3.4
Debt	1600	3400	1.2	1.8	7.1
Net worth	131 500	188 600	100.0	100.0	3.3
Disposable income[b]	26 000	26 400	–	–	0.1
Adjusted					
Total tangible assets	160 500	195 500	80.0	72.5	1.8
Consumer durable goods	17 700	17 300	8.8	6.4	−0.2
Jewellery and other valuables	3600	4300	1.8	1.6	1.6
Principal residence	63 000	101 600	31.4	37.7	4.4
Other real estate	63 300	52 400	31.5	19.4	−1.7
Businesses	12 800	19 900	6.4	7.4	4.1
Total financial assets	41 900	77 900	20.9	28.9	5.8
Transaction and savings accounts	22 300	30 600	11.1	11.4	2.9
Government bonds	13 800	13 500	6.9	5.0	−0.2
Private bonds, equities, mutual funds	5800	33 700	2.9	12.5	17.3
Gross wealth	202 400	273 400	100.8	101.4	2.8
Debt	1600	3700	0.8	1.4	7.9
Net worth	200 700	269 600	100.0	100.0	2.7
Disposable income[b]	29 700	29 800	–	–	0.0

Notes:
a.　Figures may not add up to totals because of rounding. Mean values are expressed at 2000 prices by using the consumer price index and are rounded to hundreds of euros.
b.　Total household income net of taxes and social security contributions.

Source:　Authors' calculations on data from the SHIW-HA (Version 2.1).

exceeded by 40 per cent that of consumer prices. The other real estate properties made up 19 per cent of net worth in 2000, much less than in 1989. As to the other tangible assets, businesses, consumer durable goods and valuables accounted for 7, 6 and 2 per cent of wealth, respectively.

From 1989 to 2000, total financial assets went up from 21 to 29 per cent of wealth, growing by 6 per cent per year in real terms. This increase was largely driven by investments in risky assets: the mean real value of private bonds, equities and mutual funds rose by 17 per cent per year, which caused their share in wealth to expand from 3 to 13 per cent. This substantial shift in household portfolios towards risky assets probably reflects both a true reallocation and the rocketing stock market prices of the late 1990s. Although household debt increased much more rapidly than gross wealth, its share of wealth appears to be low in comparison with the FANA statistics. All in all, the unadjusted figures do not contradict this basic picture. However, the share of tangible assets is constantly higher than in the adjusted data and, over the period, the shift towards financial assets looks substantially less pronounced; changes in the value of other real estate are rather different as well. On the other hand, the mean values of principal residence, businesses and private bonds, equities and mutual funds rise at very similar annual growth rate.

Asset holdings and wealth composition vary considerably across classes of the population ranked by wealth (Table 7.5). In the bottom fifth of the population, consumer durables account for the largest fraction of net worth, followed by transaction and savings accounts (43 and 29 per cent, respectively, in 2000). As much as 16 per cent of the poorest had no bank or postal account in 2000. In middle classes, an overwhelming proportion of wealth is held in the form of real estate, among which the principal residence represents the largest share. Businesses and risky financial assets are most frequent among the richest households. In 2000, 43 per cent of the most affluent twentieth of the population had businesses and 65 per cent possessed private bonds, equities or mutual funds. While the ownership of equities and mutual funds spread across all classes during the 1990s, their amount came to account for a large proportion of portfolios only among the very rich. In 2000, the top 5 per cent held over 20 per cent of net worth in these assets compared with 4 to 7 per cent in the middle classes and 2 per cent in the poorest fifth.

The cross-section age profile of wealth holdings exhibits the usual hump-shaped pattern. (Of course, as underlined by Shorrocks 1975, this pattern has no implications for the shape of the lifetime profile of wealth ownership. On the age–wealth pattern in the SHIW data, see also Jappelli and Pistaferri 2000.) We can make two observations, which parallel analogous comments for household incomes (Brandolini and D'Alessio 2003). First, some inter-generational redistribution substantially changed the

Table 7.5 Wealth holdings and composition, by population fractions (adjusted data)

Wealth component	1989							2000						
	Bottom 20%	Second 20%	Third 20%	Fourth 20%	Top 20%	Top 5%	All	Bottom 20%	Second 20%	Third 20%	Fourth 20%	Top 20%	Top 5%	All
Fraction of holders %														
Jewellery and other valuables	62.7	69.9	75.8	81.6	82.8	86.6	74.7	78.1	84.1	86.7	90.7	94.0	96.0	86.8
Principal residence	9.7	62.4	79.2	85.1	87.3	85.8	64.7	13.6	65.0	88.7	92.0	92.8	93.6	70.5
Other real estate	3.1	16.4	35.8	63.5	86.8	94.6	41.5	4.8	18.0	32.6	45.1	72.9	82.4	35.2
Businesses	3.6	11.3	17.9	28.5	39.6	56.4	21.0	2.1	9.2	10.7	19.2	28.5	42.7	14.7
Total financial assets	89.9	94.0	97.6	99.0	99.7	99.9	96.1	83.9	90.2	95.1	97.9	98.4	99.5	93.2
Transaction and savings accounts	89.7	94.0	97.6	98.9	99.7	99.9	96.0	83.8	90.0	94.8	97.4	98.3	99.4	92.9
Government bonds	16.0	26.1	35.0	39.9	50.8	61.0	34.1	7.3	19.2	23.3	31.9	31.8	34.3	22.8
Private bonds, equities, mutual funds	3.5	4.3	9.3	15.2	23.7	40.5	12.0	4.5	15.2	21.0	38.4	46.9	64.9	26.1
Debt	12.3	11.2	14.8	14.0	14.7	13.7	13.3	14.9	16.9	20.0	21.0	20.9	18.4	18.6
Share in net worth %														
Total tangible assets	62.7	75.8	80.5	82.0	83.2	76.7	79.9	68.7	77.3	84.1	82.2	79.9	58.1	72.5
Consumer durable goods	42.1	17.6	12.4	9.8	6.8	4.2	8.8	43.0	15.6	10.0	7.9	5.5	2.5	6.4
Jewellery and other valuables	6.3	2.5	1.6	1.5	1.2	2.3	1.8	6.5	2.6	1.7	1.5	1.4	1.5	1.6
Principal residence	10.6	44.4	46.7	38.3	30.2	18.9	31.4	16.3	49.6	60.3	53.6	39.9	20.3	37.7
Other real estate	1.9	7.4	15.7	26.5	38.7	42.2	31.5	2.0	6.7	10.2	15.2	26.0	22.0	19.4
Businesses	1.8	3.9	4.0	5.9	6.2	9.0	6.4	1.0	2.9	1.9	4.1	7.1	11.8	7.4

Total financial assets	42.9	26.1	21.0	19.0	17.3	23.6	20.9	37.3	26.7	18.1	19.6	21.3	42.5	28.9
Transaction and savings accounts	33.4	18.3	13.3	12.1	9.1	8.3	11.1	29.1	14.2	8.8	7.7	7.7	15.5	11.3
Government bonds	8.6	6.9	6.3	5.5	6.3	8.8	6.9	6.2	7.5	4.8	4.8	3.9	5.6	5.0
Private bonds, equities, mutual funds	1.0	0.9	1.5	1.4	1.8	6.5	2.9	1.9	5.0	4.4	7.1	9.7	21.3	12.5
Debt	5.6	1.9	1.5	0.9	0.4	0.3	0.8	6.0	3.9	2.2	1.8	1.2	0.5	1.4
Net worth	100.0	100.0	100.0	100.0	100.0	100.0	100.0	100.0	100.0	100.0	100.0	100.0	100.0	100.0

Source: Author's calculations on data from the SHIW-HA (Version 2.1).

relationship between 1989 and 2000: the net worth of households whose head is older than 65 increased from 81 to 114 per cent of the average, while that of those with younger heads fell from 90 to 67 per cent (Figure 7.3, left hand panel). This shift could be due to the ageing of cohorts whose wealth accumulation benefited from the high growth of the Italian economy in the 1950s and 1960s and the gradual advent of a relatively generous pension system. It also shows up in the improved condition of retired heads relative to salaried and self-employed heads (Figure 7.4, left-hand panel). The second observation is that the curvature of the age profile in Italy is much less pronounced than in Canada and the United States (Figure 7.3, right-hand panel). The smaller differences in wealth holdings across generations in Italy may follow from a generally lower degree of wealth concentration, or a more composite household structure, whereby the coexistence of several generations within the household makes the classification based on the head's age less significant than in the two North American countries.

With regard to regional differences, the average household wealth is higher in the North and the Centre than in the South and Islands, as a reflection of the different levels of economic development (Figure 7.4, right-hand panel; see also, Cannari and D'Alessio 2002). This gap is also likely to be influenced by the greater number of children in southern families. For instance, in 1989 household heads aged between 31 and 40 had on average two living sisters or brothers in the Centre-North compared with 2.8 in the South. The impact of the larger household size is twofold: it reduces resources available for the accumulation of wealth during life; it brings about a higher fragmentation of inheritance at the death of wealth holders. A significant change in the geographical distribution of net worth took place during the 1990s, as the North–South ratio widened from 1.4 in 1989 to 2.1 in 2000.

WEALTH INEQUALITY

The distribution of household wealth in Italy exhibits the highly asymmetric profile found in most countries (Figure 7.5). In 2000, median wealth was 143 000 euros, or 53.1 per cent of the mean (Table 7.6). The 95th percentile of the wealth distribution was 5.8 times the median, while the 95th percentile of the income distribution was 2.8 times. The share in total wealth of the bottom 40 per cent of Italian households, ranked in ascending order by net worth, was only 7 per cent, and that of the next 40 per cent was 29 per cent; the remaining 64 per cent was held by the most affluent fifth of the population. The richest 1 per cent of households possessed 17 per cent of total wealth.[14] The Gini index of concentration was 0.61, a much higher value than the 0.37 found for disposable income. The values of the Gini

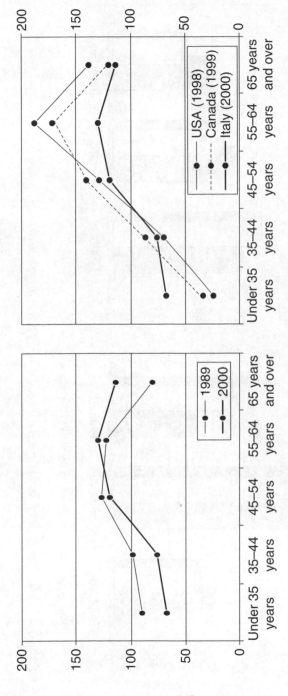

Sources: Authors' calculations on data from the SHIW-HA (Version 2.1) for Italy; Kennickell et al. (2000), Tables 1 and 3, pp. 5 and 7, for the United States; Morissette et al. Chapter 5, Table 5.8, for Canada.

Figure 7.3   Age profile of net worth (percentage ratio to total mean)

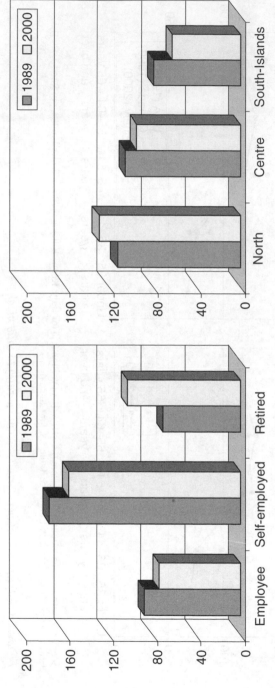

Source: Authors' calculations on data from the SHIW-HA (Version 2.1).

Figure 7.4 Net worth by work status and geographical area (percentage ratio to total mean)

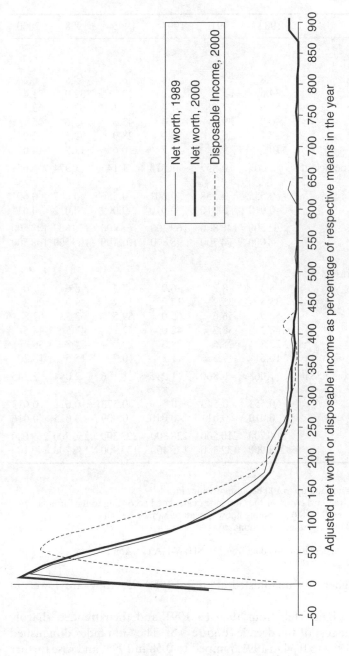

Sources: Author's calculations on data from the SHIW-HA (Version 2.1). Nonparametric estimation techniques implemented using STATA 7.0. Values bottom-coded at the 1st percentile and top-coded at the 99th percentile. Epanechnikov function is used as kernel and bandwidth is selected following a criterion that approximately minimizes the asymptotic mean integrated square error (AMISE). See Pagan and Ullah (1999, pp. 49–54).

Figure 7.5   Kernel density estimation of the distributions of household net worth and disposable income, 1989 and 2000

Table 7.6   Statistics of the distribution of household net worth

Statistic	1989	1991	1993	1995	1998	2000
Unadjusted						
Population share[a] %						
Bottom 40%	7.8	7.1	5.4	6.1	5.8	6.4
Next 40%	34.6	35.5	33.2	33.8	32.0	31.4
Top 20%	57.6	57.5	61.4	60.1	62.3	62.1
Top 10%	40.0	39.2	43.4	42.3	45.6	45.7
Top 5%	27.1	26.0	29.7	28.9	32.5	32.9
Top 1%	10.2	9.0	11.7	10.6	13.8	14.0
Half squared coefficient of variation	1.007	0.857	1.378	1.143	1.974	1.651
Gini index	0.555	0.558	0.601	0.586	0.607	0.601
s.e. [b]	0.010	0.010	0.010	0.009	0.012	0.011
Mean[c]	131 500	148 800	169 300	168 400	179 800	188 600
Median[c]	84 000	94 700	98 800	102 100	105 500	108 500
Adjusted						
Population share[a] %						
Bottom 40%	8.3	8.2	6.9	7.2	6.6	7.0
Next 40%	33.8	35.2	33.2	33.2	29.9	29.2
Top 20%	57.9	56.6	60.0	59.5	63.5	63.8
Top 10%	40.2	38.7	42.0	42.1	47.5	48.5
Top 5%	27.3	25.6	28.3	29.0	34.8	36.4
Top 1%	10.6	9.3	11.2	10.7	15.5	17.2
Half squared coefficient of variation	1.063	0.860	1.215	1.106	2.044	2.345
Gini index	0.553	0.543	0.579	0.573	0.611	0.613
s.e.[b]	0.010	0.011	0.010	0.009	0.015	0.016
Mean[c]	200 700	210 500	228 800	223 300	256 300	269 600
Median[c]	121 900	132 300	135 400	133 900	138 700	143 100

Notes:
a.   Figures may not add up to 100 because of rounding.
b.   Asymptotic standard errors of the Gini index calculated according to the formula derived by Cowell (1989), assuming known mean of sample weights.
c.   Euros at 2000 prices, rounded to hundreds.

Source: Authors' calculations on data from the SHIW-HA (Version 2.1).

index are higher for unadjusted data in 1989–95; they are lower in 1998–2000.[15]

Inequality slightly fell from 1989 to 1991 and then trended sharply upwards in the rest of the decade (Figure 7.6). The Gini index diminished from 0.55 in 1989 to 0.54 in 1991, jumped to 0.58 in 1993, and rose further

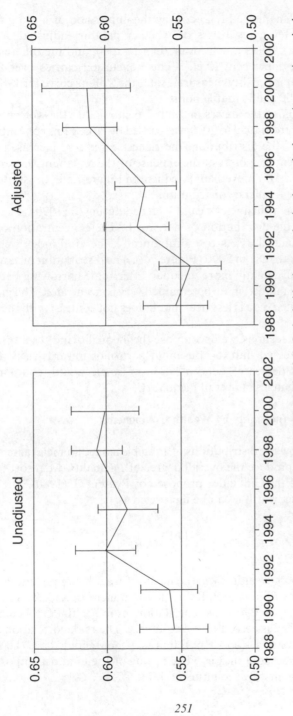

Source: Authors' calculations on data from the SHIW-HA (Version 2.1). On both sides, bars equal twice the standard error. Asymptotic standard errors are calculated according to the formula derived by Cowell (1989), assuming known mean of sample weights.

Figure 7.6   Gini index for household net worth, 1989–2000

to 0.61 in 1998. Unadjusted data convey the impression of a more stable distribution. However, regardless of whether data are adjusted or not, the Gini index in 1989 is much lower than in 2000, and the difference is significant at the 1 per cent level.[16] This conclusion carries over to all Lorenz-consistent inequality measures, since the Lorenz curve for 1989 lies above that for 2000 at all vingtile points.

The comparison of the shares in Table 7.6 shows that the worsening of wealth inequality from 1989 to 2000 was caused by large gains concentrated at the very top of the distribution: the richest 5 per cent increased their share by 9.1 percentage points at the expense of the remaining 95 per cent of the population. This movement is evident in Figure 7.5 in the stretching to the right of the frequency distribution.

The distribution of financial wealth widened during the 1990s at a much faster pace than the distribution of net worth. The concentration of the ownership of financial assets rose dramatically: the Gini index went up from 0.66 in 1991 to 0.81 in 2000 (Figure 7.7). The distribution of tangible assets became only slightly more unequal, after some narrowing between 1989 and 1991. Liabilities, in turn, remained very concentrated. The picture based on unadjusted data is less neat, but it does not contrast with that just described.

In the next two sections, we decompose the inequality indices to investigate how the observed shift in household portfolios towards risky assets and the different degree of concentration of single wealth components impinge on the changes in overall inequality.

Decomposition of Inequality by Wealth Components

To understand how the distributions of tangible assets, financial assets and debt combine to produce the overall degree of inequality, we resort to the decomposition of the Gini index proposed by Pyatt et al. (1980). The Gini coefficient G of net worth w can be factorized as:

$$G = \sum_{k=1}^{3} \left(\frac{\mu_k}{\mu}\right) G_k R, \tag{7.1}$$

where μ is the mean wealth, μ_k is the mean of wealth component k, with $\mu = \Sigma_k \mu_k$, G_k is the Gini index of wealth component k, and $R = \text{cov}[w_k, r(w)]/\text{cov}[w_k, r(w_k)]$ is the 'rank correlation ratio', with $r(x)$ being the ranking of households according to variable x. The rank correlation ratio is equal to unity only if $r(w) = r(w_k)$, that is, if households have the same ranking with respect to w and w_k. The results of the Gini decomposition are reported in the first five columns of Table 7.7.

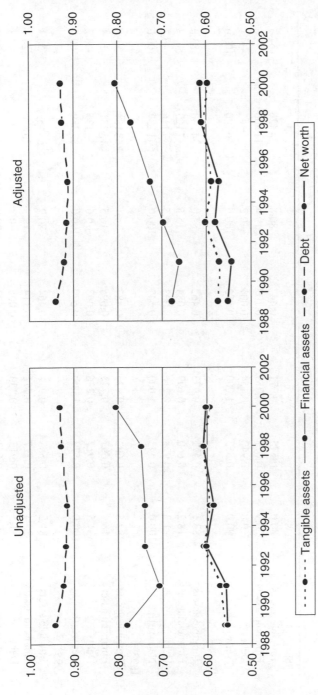

Source: Authors' calculations on data from the SHIW-HA (Version 2.1).

Figure 7.7   Gini index for household wealth components, 1989–2000

Table 7.7 Decomposition of the Gini index and the variance, by wealth components

Wealth component	% share in net worth	Decomposition of the Gini index				Variance decomposition	
		Gini index	Rank correlation ratio	Absolute contribution	% contribution	Absolute contribution[a]	% contribution
1989							
Tangible assets	80.0	0.575	0.971	0.447	80.8	24426	67.5
Financial assets	20.9	0.677	0.759	0.107	19.4	11806	32.6
Debt	−0.8	0.942	0.154	−0.001	−0.2	−42	−0.1
Net worth	100.0	0.553	1.000	0.553	100.0	36190	100.0
1991							
Tangible assets	83.1	0.571	0.973	0.462	85.0	34230	83.0
Financial assets	18.2	0.660	0.699	0.084	15.5	7123	17.3
Debt	−1.3	0.923	0.216	−0.003	−0.5	−116	−0.3
Net worth	100.0	0.543	1.000	0.543	100.0	41237	100.0
1993							
Tangible assets	82.8	0.602	0.976	0.487	84.1	68184	81.8
Financial assets	18.7	0.697	0.733	0.095	16.5	15331	18.4
Debt	−1.5	0.917	0.236	−0.003	−0.6	−135	−0.2
Net worth	100.0	0.579	1.000	0.579	100.0	83380	100.0
1995							
Tangible assets	81.2	0.588	0.971	0.464	80.9	66153	76.3
Financial assets	20.4	0.727	0.772	0.114	19.9	20890	24.1
Debt	−1.5	0.915	0.330	−0.005	−0.8	−300	−0.3
Net worth	100.0	0.573	1.000	0.573	100.0	86743	100.0

1998							
Tangible assets	73.9	0.607	0.965	0.433	70.8	156 465	63.3
Financial assets	27.3	0.772	0.859	0.181	29.7	91 310	36.9
Debt	−1.2	0.929	0.278	−0.003	−0.5	−571	−0.2
Net worth	100.0	0.611	1.000	0.611	100.0	247 204	100.0
2000							
Tangible assets	72.5	0.596	0.960	0.415	67.7	155 614	45.6
Financial assets	28.9	0.806	0.871	0.203	33.0	185 948	54.5
Debt	−1.4	0.932	0.326	−0.004	−0.7	−609	−0.2
Net worth	100.0	0.613	1.000	0.613	100.0	340 953	100.0

Note: a. Divided by 10^6.

Source: Authors' calculations on data from the SHIW-HA (Version 2.1). Figures may not add up to totals because of rounding.

In all years the rank correlation ratio for tangible assets is very close to one, suggesting that the ranking of households in terms of tangible wealth is very similar to that in terms of net worth. The proportion of total inequality accounted for by tangible assets fell from 81 per cent in 1989 to 68 per cent in 2000. Conversely, as a result of its increased weight in net worth and its much higher concentration, the contribution of financial assets grew from 19 to 33 per cent. *Ceteris paribus*, if the value of the Gini index of financial assets had been the same in 2000 as in 1989 (that is 0.677 instead of 0.806), the decomposition in Table 7.7 suggests that the Gini index of net worth would have been around 0.58, or 3 percentage points below its actual value. Alternatively, had the Gini index of tangible assets remained unchanged at 0.575 rather than increasing to 0.596, net worth would have shown a Gini index 1.5 points below its historical value. Lastly, keeping the wealth composition unchanged, the Gini index would fall by 1.2 points. This simple decomposition exercise confirms that it was chiefly the considerable increase in the concentration of financial wealth that imparted the inegalitarian twist to the overall distribution observed in the 1990s.

Shorrocks (1983) criticized this decomposition of the Gini index on the grounds that it is one of an infinite variety of potential rules and that it is then arbitrary to choose it over any other. To counter this objection, we have also reported in the last two columns of Table 7.7 the results from applying the unique decomposition rule proposed by Shorrocks, whereby the contribution of wealth component k to total inequality is equal to $\text{cov}(w, w_k)/\text{var}(w)$. The proportion of inequality attributed to financial assets is constantly higher with Shorrocks's rule than with the previous rule; the difference is especially marked in 1989 and 2000. However, the two inequality decompositions provide a consistent picture of the time pattern: they both point to a remarkable increase in the role of financial assets in explaining total wealth inequality – an increase which is even greater with the variance decomposition than the Gini decomposition.

Decomposition of Inequality by Population Subgroups

A second way to identify the factors behind changes in the size distribution of wealth is through the decomposition of inequality indices by homogeneous subgroups of the population. The aim of the decomposition is to distinguish the inequality within the groups from the inequality among the groups. In examining variations over time, we also have to consider the effect of changes in the relative size of the groups. Since the Gini index is not exactly decomposable by population subgroups, we turn to an index of the class of entropy measures characterized by Cowell (1980) and Shorrocks (1980), the half squared coefficient of variation:

$$E = \frac{1}{2}\left[\frac{1}{n}\sum_{i=1}^{n}\left(\frac{w_i}{\mu}\right)^2 - 1\right],$$ (7.2)

where w_i is the wealth of household i and n is the number of households. If households are partitioned into K groups according to some characteristic, the overall inequality index E can be exactly decomposed into within-groups, E^W, and between-groups, E^B, as follows:

$$E = E^W + E^B = \sum_{k=1}^{K} p_k \left(\frac{\mu_k}{\mu}\right)^2 E_k + \frac{1}{2}\left[\sum_{k=1}^{K} p_k \left(\frac{\mu_k}{\mu}\right)^2 - 1\right],$$ (7.3)

where subscript k now denotes a population subgroup and p_k, μ_k and E_k are the respective population share, average wealth, and half squared coefficient of variation. To isolate the impact of changes in population share, we rewrite (7.3) as:

$$E = E^{\overline{W}} + E^{\overline{B}} + E^P = \sum_{k=1}^{K} \bar{p}_k \left(\frac{\mu_k}{\mu}\right)^2 E_k + \frac{1}{2}\left[\sum_{k=1}^{K} \bar{p}_k \left(\frac{\mu_k}{\mu}\right)^2 - 1\right] + E^P,$$ (7.4)

where we fix the population weights at their values $\bar{p}_k$ in a base year and we recalculate the total mean at fixed weights as $\bar{\mu} = \Sigma_k \bar{p}_k \mu_k$. The within- and between-groups addenda in equation (7.4) are now net of variations in the relative group sizes, and the effect of a changing population structure is taken up in the residual term E^P. By construction, $E^P = 0$ in the base year.

Table 7.8 contains the results of decomposition (7.4). In the top panels we check the effect of sorting households by five demographic characteristics: household size, area of residence, sex, age and education of the household head. For all five characteristics, the overall inequality of net worth is almost entirely attributable to inequality within each group. As seen above, disparities in mean wealth among households residing in different parts of Italy are significant. Decomposition (7.4) shows, however, that these disparities explain little of the degree of wealth concentration in the country as a whole. What matters is the inequality inside each region. A similar conclusion is reached for the other groupings. For instance, in 2000 the mean wealth of households where the head had a university degree was 2.7 times the mean for households where the head had only completed elementary school. Yet, differences across groups classified by the head's education only account for 5 per cent of total inequality. On these bases, it is no surprise that the time pattern of total inequality largely tallies with that of the within-group components.

Table 7.8   Decomposition of half squared coefficient of variation, by population subgroups

Year	Within-groups at fixed weights		Between-groups at fixed weights		Group relative size effect		Total[c]
	Value[a]	Share[b]	Value[a]	Share[b]	Value[a]	Share[b]	
Household size							
1989	1.091	102.7	0.017	1.6	−0.045	−4.2	1.063
1991	0.866	100.7	0.011	1.2	−0.017	−1.9	0.860
1993	1.114	91.7	0.029	2.4	0.071	5.9	1.215
1995	1.045	94.5	0.030	2.8	0.030	2.8	1.106
1998	2.019	98.8	0.014	0.7	0.011	0.5	2.044
2000	2.335	99.6	0.010	0.4	–	–	2.345
Area of residence[d]							
1989	1.041	97.9	0.012	1.2	0.010	0.9	1.063
1991	0.837	97.3	0.014	1.7	0.009	1.0	0.860
1993	1.174	96.7	0.031	2.5	0.010	0.8	1.215
1995	1.064	96.2	0.033	3.0	0.010	0.9	1.106
1998	1.998	97.8	0.037	1.8	0.009	0.4	2.044
2000	2.297	98.0	0.048	2.0	–	–	2.345
Sex of household head							
1989	1.048	98.6	0.006	0.6	0.009	0.8	1.063
1991	0.853	99.1	0.006	0.7	0.002	0.2	0.860
1993	1.197	98.5	0.017	1.4	0.001	0.1	1.215
1995	1.107	100.1	0.010	0.9	−0.011	−1.0	1.106
1998	2.067	101.1	0.014	0.7	−0.037	−1.8	2.044
2000	2.335	99.6	0.010	0.4	–	–	2.345

Age of household head[e]

Year							
1989	1.007	94.7	0.032	3.0	0.024	2.3	1.063
1991	0.816	94.9	0.021	2.4	0.023	2.7	0.860
1993	1.161	95.6	0.032	2.6	0.021	1.8	1.215
1995	1.048	94.7	0.026	2.4	0.032	2.9	1.106
1998	1.973	96.5	0.012	0.6	0.058	2.9	2.044
2000	2.311	98.6	0.033	1.4	—	—	2.345

Education of household head[f]

Year							
1989	1.012	95.2	0.070	6.6	−0.020	−1.8	1.063
1991	0.841	97.7	0.069	8.0	−0.049	−5.7	0.860
1993	1.271	104.6	0.101	8.4	−0.158	−13.0	1.215
1995	1.110	100.3	0.119	10.7	−0.122	−11.1	1.106
1998	1.986	97.2	0.118	5.8	−0.060	−2.9	2.044
2000	2.228	95.0	0.117	5.0	—	—	2.345

Home ownership

Year							
1989	1.041	97.9	0.060	5.7	−0.038	−3.6	1.063
1991	0.810	94.1	0.068	8.0	−0.018	−2.1	0.860
1993	1.188	97.8	0.086	7.1	−0.060	−5.0	1.215
1995	1.047	94.7	0.092	8.3	−0.033	−3.0	1.106
1998	1.994	97.5	0.082	4.0	−0.032	−1.6	2.044
2000	2.251	96.0	0.094	4.0	—	—	2.345

Table 7.8 (continued)

Year	Within-groups at fixed weights		Between-groups at fixed weights		Group relative size effect		Total[c]
	Value[a]	Share[b]	Value[a]	Share[b]	Value[a]	Share[b]	
Stock holding[g]							
1989	1.423	133.8	0.100	9.4	−0.460	−43.3	1.063
1991	1.010	117.3	0.082	9.5	−0.231	−26.8	0.860
1993	1.457	119.9	0.129	10.6	−0.371	−30.6	1.215
1995	1.261	114.0	0.138	12.4	−0.292	−26.4	1.106
1998	2.008	98.2	0.182	8.9	−0.146	−7.1	2.044
2000	2.207	94.1	0.138	5.9	–	–	2.345

Notes:

a. Value refers to the absolute contribution of the component to the total index.

b. Share refers to the percentage ratio of the same contribution to the total index.

c. Figures may not add up to the total because of rounding.

d. The five areas of residence are: North-West, North-East, Center, South, and Islands.

e. Household heads are grouped by age in twelve classes: under 26 years, from 26 to 30 and then nine other classes of five years each, 76 and over.

f. The five levels of education of household heads are none, elementary school, middle school, high school, and university degree.

g. Stock holding refers to the possession of private bonds, equities or mutual funds.

Source: Authors' calculations on data from the SHIW-HA (Version 2.1).

The same decomposition method can be used to shed some light on the way home ownership and investment in risky assets determine total inequality (bottom two panels of Table 7.8). Even if the average net worth of homeowners was, in 2000, almost four times the average for nonhomeowners, this difference contributed only 4 per cent of total inequality. This contribution was somewhat higher in previous years, but not enough to affect the temporal trend of the overall index. The spreading of home ownership, from 65 to 71 per cent between 1989 and 2000, slightly reinforced the tendency of inequality to rise, as shown by the constantly negative sign of the relative size effect. This inegalitarian impact is very strong when households are grouped according to whether or not they possessed private bonds, equities or mutual funds. *Ceteris paribus*, the increase in inequality between 1989 and 2000 would have been about a third less than it actually was had the share of households holding the risky assets in 1989 been equal to that in 2000.[17] This classification also exhibits a greater inter-group inequality than any other of the groupings under consideration, but even in this case removing the full difference between group means would not alter the temporal pattern.

To sum up, the widening of the size distribution of net worth during the last decade was spread across all population groups and can be attributed only marginally to the demographic characteristic examined here. The same consideration carries over to the grouping of households by home ownership. The increase in the proportion of holders of risky assets, on the other hand, appears to have amplified, *ceteris paribus*, the tendency of inequality to grow.

CONCLUSIONS

This chapter was concerned with the size distribution of household wealth in Italy. We assembled aggregate data to sketch the evolution of household portfolios over the last 40 years and to provide a benchmark for the microeconomic evidence. This evidence was based on the Bank of Italy's Survey of Household Income and Wealth, a long-established sample survey which has gathered detailed and exhaustive information on the net worth of Italian households since 1987.

The limits of sample surveys for the study of wealth distribution are well-known, and have led some researchers to question their usefulness altogether. A more balanced view was taken by Atkinson and Harrison (1978) in their extensive investigation of the personal distribution of net worth in Britain:

> The experience to date suggests that sample surveys are unlikely by themselves to provide a fully satisfactory source of information about the size distribution

of wealth as a whole . . . Sample surveys may be a valuable supplement to the estate data, throwing light on the wealth not covered by the estate returns; they may also provide useful information about the holdings of certain types of asset (e.g. consumer durables). But in our view they cannot provide an alternative to the estate method as a source of evidence about wealth-holding at the top of the scale. (pp. 274–5)

Nevertheless, sample surveys are the primary source for wealth distribution in countries like Canada and the United States. In both countries, the under-representation of the wealthiest is brought under control by over-sampling high-income households.

Our SHIW data suffer from the problems of sample surveys and do not benefit from over-sampling. In this chapter, we documented nonresponse and misreporting in the SHIW and we observed large differences between the survey totals and the corresponding aggregate estimates. While being a matter of concern, these differences are not to be blamed wholly on the SHIW: they are due in part to irreconcilable diversities in classifications and definitions, in part to shortcomings in macro sources. We dealt with non-response, nonreporting and under-reporting in our data by performing several statistical adjustments. We believe that the adjusted data paint a more realistic portrait of the distribution of household net worth in Italy, but we also reported the evidence for unadjusted data in order to show the robustness of our conclusions and their sensitivity to these statistical adjustments. In spite of the corrections, the results still reflect the imprecise representation of the upper tail of the wealth distribution, and we reiterate the warning to interpret them with caution.

On the substantive side, the main results presented in the chapter are the following:

- The aggregate figures show that dwellings and, more generally, tangible assets are still the main components of household wealth. The share of total financial assets has fluctuated over the years, but has increased only modestly. The investment in risky assets grew considerably during the 1990s, in parallel with the stock market boom and the rapid privatization of state-owned corporations and public utilities. The portfolio composition has tilted again towards tangible assets in the last few years, with the fall in share prices and rise in house prices.
- According to the SHIW adjusted data, at the end of 2000 the average net worth of Italian households amounted to 270 000 euros. From 1989 to 2000, it grew in real terms by 2.7 per cent each year, while real disposable income remained unchanged. During the same period, households of the elderly, the retired and people living in the North experienced the highest increase in mean net worth.

- Asset holdings vary considerably across the wealth distribution. At the bottom, consumer durables account for the largest fraction of net worth. In middle classes, a very high proportion is held in real estate, particularly the principal residence. Businesses and risky financial assets are most frequent among the richest. While the ownership of equities and mutual funds spread across all classes during the 1990s, they accounted for a large proportion of portfolios only among the very wealthy.
- The distribution of wealth is much more unequal than the distribution of income. In 2000, the Gini index was 0.61 for net worth, compared with 0.37 for disposable income; it was 0.60 for tangible assets, and a much higher 0.81 for financial assets.
- Wealth inequality declined from 1989 to 1991 and then rose considerably in the rest of the 1990s. The increase was driven by large gains at the very top of the distribution.
- Our decompositions of inequality indices show that a great deal of the widening of household wealth distribution was due to financial assets, which have both augmented their weight in portfolios and become more heavily concentrated. This evidence suggests that the stock market boom of the 1990s was an important factor behind the recent growth of wealth inequality.

How does Italian wealth distribution compare with that of other countries? Let us consider the United States, and in particular the evidence of the SCF (Kennickell et al. 2000). On the basis of our adjusted data, in 1998 the mean Italian household was almost as rich as the mean US household (274 200 vs 282 500 US dollars, at average market exchange rate), whereas the median household was twice as rich as its American counterpart (148 400 vs. 71 600 US dollars). With unadjusted data, the mean household was poorer in Italy than in the United States by about a third, but the median household was still richer by almost 60 per cent. These results are rather surprising, especially in the light of the divergent performance of the two economies in the 1990s. Several factors can help to explain them. There are important differences in institutional settings, for instance, in the role of private pensions as well as in demography – the average family size is 2.6 persons in the SCF and 2.8 in the adjusted SHIW, while the shares of household heads older than 54 are 34.2 and 43.1 per cent, respectively. Moreover, the household saving rate has traditionally been far higher in Italy than in the United States, implying a stronger wealth accumulation even when American incomes grow faster.[18] On the other hand, differences in statistical methodology and definitions are so large that these figures can only be very rough approximations. At face value, however, these figures and, more generally, all available evidence, seem to suggest that the distribution of household wealth is much narrower in Italy than in the United States.[19] In-depth work to improve data comparability is necessary to ascertain whether these international differences are statistical artefacts, or true ones. This task is left for future research.[20]

NOTES

* This chapter is dedicated to the memory of Professor Albert Ando. We are indebted for very helpful comments to Riccardo De Bonis, Anders Klevmarken, Andrea Generale, Marco Magnani, Monica Paiella, Francesco Paternò, Luigi Federico Signorini and Jay Zagorsky and participants in the 27th General Conference of the International Association for Research in Income and Wealth (Djurhamn, Sweden, August 2002) and in the Conference on International Perspectives on Household Wealth at the Levy Institute of Economics (Annandale-on-Hudson, New York, United States, October 2003). In estimating aggregate statistics, we greatly benefited from the help and advice of Salvatore Muzzicato for tangible assets and Massimo Coletta for financial statistics. Christine Stone provided valuable editorial assistance. The views expressed herein are those of the authors and do not necessarily reflect those of the Bank of Italy.

1. 'Billion' is used to mean a thousand million.
2. Investigations were spurred by Pantaleoni's (1890) attempt to estimate the private wealth of Italy from information on estate duties. Alternative estimates were subsequently derived by direct inventory of assets and liabilities. Zamagni (1980) briefly reviews this literature and assembles the figures for the period 1874–1938. Goldsmith and Zecchini (1999) reconstruct the balance sheets for selected years between 1861 and 1973.
3. They draw on work conducted by one of the authors (AB) in collaboration with Salvatore Muzzicato.
4. All money values are reported in euros, using the irreversible parity of 1936.27 Italian lire to 1 euro. The terms 'wealth' and 'net worth' are used interchangeably throughout the chapter.
5. Borrowing constraints are correlated with the effectiveness of judicial procedures to recover the collateral of defaulting borrowers. In regions where such procedures are more efficient, the probability of rationing is found to be lower (Guiso and Jappelli 1991; Magri 2002; Fabbri and Padula 2004).
6. Nonresponse is a problem common to all sample surveys on household wealth, though it appears to be somewhat more pronounced in the SHIW. Kennickell et al. (2000, p. 28) report that in the Federal Reserve Board's Survey of Consumer Finances in both 1995 and 1998 the response rate was about 70 per cent in the basic sample and 35 per cent in the special section over-sampling the very rich; it fell to 10 per cent among the (likely) wealthiest families. In the wealth survey of Statistics Finland, the response rates were 72.5 per cent in 1987, 75.2 in 1994 and 64.9 in 1998 (see Jäntti, Chapter 9, Table 9.1 in this volume). In the Swedish household panel survey, Klevmarken (2004) notices that the share of imputed items increased from little less than 20 per cent in the 1980s to about 30 per cent in 1998.
7. In 2000, the proportions of Italian households holding life insurance and private pensions were 20 and 12 per cent, respectively. Imputing cash values on the SHIW information, Jappelli and Pistaferri (2000) estimate that in 1995 life insurance accounted for 10 per cent of household financial wealth (as defined in their study) and private pension funds for 4 per cent; the corresponding figures in 1989 were 5 and 2 per cent.
8. For recently built or renovated houses, prices per square metre implicit in the SHIW evaluations can be compared with the corresponding market prices as recorded in a survey of actual sales conducted among estate agents (for details on this source, see Muzzicato

et al. 2002). On average, the SHIW subjectively-perceived prices underestimate actual prices by 10 to 20 per cent. However, the comparison is not entirely homogeneous: actual prices refer to houses that were never occupied, whereas the SHIW evaluates mostly occupied houses. The SHIW and actual prices fall roughly in line when the latter are reduced by the discount factors reported in estate agent publications to allow for earlier occupation.

9. Alternatively, using the SHIW data, family businesses and firms of professionals, free-lancers and sole proprietors could be valued as expected proceeds from selling the activity, plus the value of buildings and land used in the activity, plus net trade credits less activity-related debts. With this definition, the household wealth total would not change, but its composition would be affected by the reclassification of some items: the value of buildings and land would be subtracted from other real estate, trade credits toward customers from financial assets, and debts and trade debits to suppliers from liabilities. This alternative definition is probably more consistent with the recommendations of the new system of national accounts, as quoted in the Inter-Secretariat Working Group on National Accounts (1993, p. 94):

> A balance sheet is also needed for the quasi-corporation showing the value of its fixed assets – land, buildings, machinery and equipment, and inventories – used in production, and also the financial assets and liabilities owned or incurred in the name of the enterprise – bank deposits, overdrafts, trade credit and debits, other receivables or payables, etc. It is assumed that the owner's net equity in a quasi-corporation is equal to the difference between the value of its assets and the value of its other liabilities so that the net worth of the quasi-corporation is always zero in practice.

10. As noted earlier by Cannari and D'Alessio (1990), estimating the number of rented dwellings owned by households from tenants' rather than owners' answers gives values much closer to the census figures (3.2 million in 1991).

11. The fact that the correction for nonreporting is based on data for 1987 may lead to an insufficient adjustment for equities and investment funds to the extent that their possession was less common in 1987 than in more recent years.

12. We focus on the comparison between 1989 and 2000 for both statistical and economic reasons. First, the discrepancy between the SHIW estimate for net worth and its aggregate counterpart was relatively low and similar in the two waves. Secondly, in both years the economic cycle was close to peak.

13. According to the Eurostat's European Community Household Panel (ECHP), in 1998 the proportion of households owning their house of residence was 71 per cent in Italy as compared with 69 in the United Kingdom, 59 in Sweden, 53 in France and 41 in Germany; the proportion was higher only in Greece and Ireland (74 per cent) and especially Spain (82 per cent). The ECHP fraction of homeowners is somewhat higher than in the SHIW because it includes houses occupied in usufruct.

14. Despite our adjustments, the share of the richest households is underestimated owing to their under-representation. To obtain some understanding, however imprecise, of the size of the wealth controlled by the wealthiest, we checked the world ranking published by *Forbes* of (known) billionaires in US dollars. In 2002, 13 Italian families appeared in *Forbes* (2002) for a total wealth estimated at 35 billion dollars, or 0.6 per cent of aggregate household net worth. This proportion compares to the 1.5 per cent owned by the 61 richest families in the United States and 2.6 per cent owned by the seven richest families in Canada.

15. The correction for nonresponse tends to increase concentration. On the contrary, correcting for non- and under-reporting has a mixed impact but predominantly in the direction of reducing dispersion. This pattern is the net outcome of two different effects (Cannari and D'Alessio 1993): (1) the adjustment for nonreporting tends to reduce inequality, because all wealthy households declare they hold bank deposits and, most of them, government bonds; (2) the correction for under-reporting leads to an increase in inequality, as the phenomenon matters more for those financial assets, such as private securities, investment fund shares and corporate equities – all held to a much greater extent by the wealthy.

16. The null hypothesis of equality of the two indices is tested by the asymptotically standard normal statistic $T_{ij}=(G_i-G_j)/(se_i^2+se_j^2)^{0.5}$, where G_i and se_i are the values of the Gini index and of its standard error in year i, respectively. Since this test applies only to independent samples, it is not appropriate for pair comparisons among figures referring to surveys that include a panel section like the SHIW. To the extent that the panel section leads to a positive correlation between estimates in subsequent years, the use of the statistic T_{ij} should make rejection of the null hypothesis less likely.
17. The counterfactual value of the index in 1989 is 1.523, that is the actual value less the relative size effect. The actual change of the index (1.282) therefore compares with a smaller counterfactual change (0.822).
18. A simple back-of-the-envelope calculation shows that an economy with a constant saving rate of 16 per cent and an annual real income growth of 1.3 per cent accumulates in ten years 80 per cent more than an economy where the saving rate equals 6 per cent and income grows at 1.9 per cent per year, assuming that the initial income of the first economy is 69 per cent of the income of the second economy (these values are the actual per capita values in the 1990s for Italy and the United States, respectively).
19. See Faiella and Neri (2004) for a direct comparison, and Wolff (1998) and Kennickell (2001) for further estimates for the United States. The problems of international comparisons of wealth inequality are discussed by Kessler and Wolff (1991), Wolff (1996) and Davies and Shorrocks (2000).
20. This is the aim of the Luxembourg Wealth Study (LWS), an international cooperative project launched in 2003 to create from existing data a database on household net worth comparable cross-nationally. The LWS project has currently the support of Canada, Cyprus, Finland, Germany, Italy, Norway, Sweden, the United Kingdom and the United States. For further information, see the website www.lisproject.org/lws.htm.

REFERENCES

Ando, A., L. Guiso and I. Visco (eds) (1994), *Saving and the Accumulation of Wealth. Essays on Italian Households and Government Saving Behaviour*, Cambridge: Cambridge University Press.

Atkinson, A.B. and A.J. Harrison (1978), *Distribution of Personal Wealth in Britain*, Cambridge: Cambridge University Press.

Avery, R.B., G.E. Elliehausen and A.B. Kennickell (1988), 'Measuring wealth with survey data: an evaluation of the 1983 Survey of Consumer Finances', *Review of Income and Wealth*, **34**(4), 339–69.

Banca d'Italia (1986), 'La ricchezza delle famiglie in Italia (1975–1985)', *Bollettino economico*, **7**, 11*–23*.

Banca d'Italia (2002a), 'Italian household budgets in 2000', in G. D'Alessio and I. Faiella (eds), *Supplements to the Statistical Bulletin*, **12** new series (6).

Banca d'Italia (2002b), *I conti finanziari dell'Italia*, Rome: Banca d'Italia.

Brandolini, A. (1999), 'The distribution of personal income in post-war Italy: source description, data quality, and the time pattern of income inequality', *Giornale degli Economisti e Annali di Economia*, **58**(2), 183–239.

Brandolini, A. and L. Cannari (1994), 'Methodological appendix: the Bank of Italy's Survey of Household Income and Wealth', in A. Ando, L. Guiso and I. Visco (eds), *Saving and the Accumulation of Wealth: Essays on Italian Households and Government Saving Behaviour*, Cambridge: Cambridge University Press, pp. 369–86.

Brandolini, A. and G. D'Alessio (2003), 'Household structure and income inequality in Italy. A comparative European perspective', in D. Del Boca and M. Repetto-Alaia (eds), *Women's Work, the Family and Social Policy. Focus on Italy in a European Perspective*, New York: Lang, pp. 148–91.

Brandolini, A., L. Cannari, G. D'Alessio and I. Faiella (2004), 'Household wealth distribution in Italy in the 1990s', Banca d'Italia, Temi di discussione, No. 530, October.

Cannari, L. and G. D'Alessio (1990), 'Housing assets in the Bank of Italy's Survey of Household Income and Wealth', in C. Dagum and M. Zenga (eds), *Income and Wealth Distribution, Inequality and Poverty*, Berlin: Springer-Verlag, pp. 326–34.

Cannari, L. and G. D'Alessio (1993), 'Non-reporting and under-reporting behavior in the Bank of Italy's Survey of Household Income and Wealth', in *Proceedings of the ISI 49th Session*, Florence: ISI, pp. 395–412.

Cannari, L. and G. D'Alessio (1994), 'Composizione e distribuzione della ricchezza delle famiglie', in N. Rossi (ed.), *La transizione equa, 1992–1993. Secondo rapporto CNEL sulla distribuzione e redistribuzione del reddito in Italia*, Bologna: Il Mulino, pp. 245–77.

Cannari, L. and G. D'Alessio (2002), 'La distribuzione del reddito e della ricchezza nelle regioni italiane', *Rivista economica del Mezzogiorno*, 16(4), 809–47.

Cannari, L. and R. Violi (1995), 'Reporting behaviour in the Bank of Italy's Survey of Italian Household Income and Wealth', in C. Dagum and A. Lemmi (eds), *Research on Economic Inequality*, vol. 6, Greenwich: JAI Press, pp. 117–30.

Cannari, L., G. D'Alessio, G. Raimondi and A.I. Rinaldi (1990), 'Le attività finanziarie delle famiglie italiane', Banca d'Italia, Temi di discussione, No. 135, July.

Cohen, S.B. and B.L. Carlson (1995), 'Characteristics of reluctant respondents in the National Medical Expenditure Survey', *Journal of Economic and Social Measurement*, 21(4), 269–96.

Cowell, F.A. (1980), 'On the structure of additive inequality measures', *Review of Economic Studies*, 47(3), 521–31.

Cowell, F.A. (1989), 'Sampling variance and decomposable inequality measures', *Journal of Econometrics*, 42(1), 27–41.

Curtin, R.T., F.T. Juster and J.N. Morgan (1989), 'Survey estimates of wealth: an assessment of quality', in R.E. Lipsey and H. Stone Tice (eds), *The Measurement of Saving, Investment and Wealth*, Chicago, IL: University of Chicago Press, pp. 473–548.

D'Alessio, G. and I. Faiella (2002), 'Non-response behaviour in the Bank of Italy's Survey of Household Income and Wealth', Banca d'Italia, Temi di discussione, No. 462, December.

Davies, J.B. and A.F. Shorrocks (2000), 'The distribution of wealth', in A.B. Atkinson and F. Bourguignon (eds), *Handbook of Income Distribution*, vol. 1, Amsterdam: North-Holland, pp. 605–75.

Di Addario, S. (2002), 'Italian household tenure choices and housing demand', Banca d'Italia, mimeographed.

Fabbri, D. and M. Padula (2004), 'Does poor legal enforcement make households credit-constrained?', *Journal of Banking and Finance*, 28(10), 2369–97.

Faiella, I. and A. Neri (2004), 'La ricchezza delle famiglie italiane e americane', Banca d'Italia, Temi di discussione, No. 501, June.

Forbes (2002), 'The world's richest people', issue 03.18.2002, available at www.forbes.com/billionaires.

Goldsmith, R.W. and S. Zecchini (1999), 'The national balance sheet of Italy (1861–1973)', *Rivista di storia economica*, **15** new series (1), 3–19.

Guiso, L. and T. Jappelli (1991), 'Intergenerational transfers and capital market imperfections. evidence from an Italian cross-section', *European Economic Review*, **35**(1), 103–20. Also in A. Ando, L. Guiso and I. Visco (eds) (1994), *Saving and the Accumulation of Wealth. Essays on Italian Households and Government Saving Behaviour*, Cambridge: Cambridge University Press, pp. 330–48.

Guiso, L. and T. Jappelli (2002), 'Household portfolios in Italy', in L. Guiso, M. Haliassos and T. Jappelli (eds), *Household Portfolios*, Cambridge, MA: MIT Press, pp. 251–87.

Guiso, L., T. Jappelli and D. Terlizzese (1994), 'Why is Italy's saving rate so high?', in A. Ando, L. Guiso and I. Visco (eds) (1994), *Saving and the Accumulation of Wealth. Essays on Italian Households and Government Saving Behaviour*, Cambridge: Cambridge University Press, pp. 23–69.

Hayashi, F., A. Ando and R. Ferris (1988), 'Life cycle and bequest savings', *Journal of the Japanese and International Economies*, **2**(4), 450–91.

Inter-Secretariat Working Group on National Accounts (1993), *System of National Accounts, 1993*, Brussels-Luxembourg, New York, Paris, Washington, DC: Commission of the European Communities-Eurostat, International Monetary Fund, Organization for Economic Cooperation and Development, United Nations, World Bank.

Istat (1995), *13° Censimento generale della popolazione e delle abitazioni, 20 ottobre 1991, Popolazione e Abitazioni*, Rome: Istat.

Jappelli, T. and L. Pistaferri (2000), 'The dynamics of household wealth accumulation in Italy', *Fiscal Studies*, **21**(2), 269–95.

Kennickell, A.B. (2000), 'Asymmetric information, interviewer behavior, and unit nonresponse', Board of Governors of the Federal Reserve System, mimeographed.

Kennickell, A.B. (2001), 'An examination of changes in the distribution of wealth from 1989 to 1998: evidence from the Survey of Consumer Finances', Board of Governors of the Federal Reserve System, mimeographed.

Kennickell, A.B., M. Starr-McCluer and B.J. Surette (2000), 'Recent changes in US family finances: results from the 1998 Survey of Consumer Finances', *Federal Reserve Bulletin*, **90**(1), 1–29.

Kessler, D. and E.N. Wolff (1991), 'A comparative analysis of household wealth patterns in France and the United States', *Review of Income and Wealth*, **37**(3), 249–66.

Klevmarken, N.A. (2004), 'On the wealth dynamics of Swedish families 1984–1998', *Review of Income and Wealth*, **50**(4), 469–92.

Little, R.J.A. and D.B. Rubin (1987), *Statistical Analysis with Missing Data*, New York: Wiley & Sons.

Madow, W.G., H. Nisselson and I. Olkin (1983), *Incomplete Data in Sample Surveys, Vol. 1 Report and Case Studies*, New York: Academic Press.

Magri, S. (2002), 'Italian households' debt: determinants of demand and supply', Banca d'Italia, Temi di discussione, No. 454, October.

Muzzicato, S., R. Sabbatini and F. Zollino (2002), 'I prezzi delle abitazioni in Italia: una rassegna di temi metodologici e la costruzione di un nuovo indice', Banca d'Italia, mimeographed.

Pagan, A. and A. Ullah (1999), *Nonparametric Econometrics*, Cambridge: Cambridge University Press.

Pagliano, P. and N. Rossi (1992), 'The Italian saving rate: 1951 to 1990 estimates', in G. Marotta, P. Pagliano and N. Rossi (eds), 'Income and Saving in Italy: a Reconstruction', Banca d'Italia, Temi di discussione, No. 169, June.

Paiella, M. (2002), 'Demand for housing, saving behavior and wealth allocation', Banca d'Italia, mimeographed.

Paiella, M. (2004), 'Does wealth affect consumption? Evidence for Italy', Banca d'Italia, Temi di discussione, No. 510, July. Forthcoming in *Journal of Macroeconomics*.

Pantaleoni, M. (1890), 'Dell'ammontare probabile della ricchezza privata in Italia dal 1872 al 1889', *Giornale degli economisti*, **1**, 2nd series (1), 139–76.

Pyatt, G., C.-N. Chen and J. Fei (1980), 'The distribution of income by factor components', *Quarterly Journal of Economics*, **95**(3), 451–73.

Shorrocks, A.F. (1975), 'The age–wealth relationship: a cross-section and cohort analysis', *Review of Economics and Statistics*, **57**(2), 155–63.

Shorrocks, A.F. (1980), 'The class of additively decomposable inequality measures', *Econometrica*, **48**(3), 613–25.

Shorrocks, A.F. (1983), 'The impact of income components on the distribution of family incomes', *Quarterly Journal of Economics*, **98**(2), 311–26.

Tresoldi, C. and I. Visco (1975), 'Un tentativo di stima della ricchezza delle famiglie (1963–1973)', *Rivista di diritto finanziario e scienza delle finanze*, **34**(4), 516–24.

Ulizzi, A. (1967), 'La reticenza degli intervistati nella rilevazione campionaria dei titoli', Banca d'Italia, Internal Report.

Wolff, E.N. (1996), 'International comparisons of wealth inequality', *Review of Income and Wealth*, **42**(4), 433–51.

Wolff, E.N. (1998), 'Recent trends in the size distribution of household wealth', *Journal of Economic Perspectives*, **12**(3), 131–50.

Zamagni, V. (1980), 'The rich in a late industrialiser: the case of Italy, 1800–1945', in W.D. Rubinstein (ed.), *Wealth and the Wealthy in the Modern World*, London: Croom Helm, pp. 122–66.

APPENDIX: ADJUSTMENT PROCEDURES

Adjustment for Nonresponse

Nonresponse is a problem in statistical surveys whenever it leads to samples where the less cooperative segments of the population are under-represented, thus generating biased estimates (Cohen and Carlson 1995). To limit these potentially distorting effects in the SHIW, particular attention is devoted in the fieldwork to elicit households' cooperation, although no money compensation is envisaged. When processing the data, the sample is post-stratified on the basis of certain characteristics of the house-hold head (sex, age and work status) to align the sampling distribution with distributions derived from external sources like the census or the labour force survey. Post-stratification permits correction for those differences in the households' propensity to participate which are ascribable to the char-acteristics considered in the post-stratification (Madow et al. 1983). However, standard post-stratification techniques cannot fully compensate for the bias induced by the lower propensity of richer households to take part in sample surveys, as wealth is typically not an available characteristic (D'Alessio and Faiella 2002).

D'Alessio and Faiella (2002) examine a few alternative models to esti-mate the *ex ante* probability of participating in the SHIW and find that they tend to produce similar results. The model that can be most easily replicated for the various surveys exploits the information on the number of contacts needed to obtain an interview. More precisely, it assumes that the house-holds requiring at least two visits before conceding the interview are repre-sentative of nonresponding units as a whole. Under this assumption, the unconditional probability of responding in the survey is taken to coincide with the estimated probability of responding at the first visit. Once such probability p_{ri} is available, an unbiased estimator of the population mean is (Little and Rubin 1987):

$$\bar{y} = \sum_{i=1}^{R} \left(\frac{1}{p_i p_{ri}} \right) y_i / \sum_{i=1}^{R} \left(\frac{1}{p_i p_{ri}} \right), \qquad (7A.1)$$

where p_i is the usual probability of selection and R is the number of responding households.

To obtain unbiased estimates, we borrow the procedure proposed by D'Alessio and Faiella (2002) and adjust the sampling weights as in equation (7A.1). The estimate of a logistic model on 1998 data reported in Table 7A.1 shows that the nonresponse probability rises with school

Table 7A.1   Estimated nonresponse probability, 1998

Variable	Parameter estimate	Standard error	Wald χ^2	Pr > χ^2	Standard estimate	Odds ratios
Intercept	0.317	0.383	0.682	0.409		
Poorly educated	−0.118*	0.064	3.422	0.064	−0.031	0.889
Highly educated	0.255**	0.101	6.336	0.012	0.041	1.290
North	0.604***	0.072	70.499	0.000	0.166	1.830
South	0.278***	0.082	11.573	0.001	0.069	1.320
Small municipality	0.628***	0.074	73.025	0.000	0.129	1.875
Age	−0.081***	0.010	70.965	0.000	−0.792	0.922
Age squared	0.001***	0.000	64.666	0.000	0.769	1.001
Household size	0.085***	0.024	12.722	0.000	0.060	1.089
Log of income	0.123***	0.032	14.838	0.000	0.072	1.131
Log of real wealth	0.004	0.006	0.452	0.502	0.010	1.004
Log of financial wealth	0.022***	0.007	10.419	0.001	0.054	1.022

Model Fitting Information and Testing Global Null Hypothesis BETA = 0

Criterion	Intercept only	Intercept and covariates	χ^2 for covariates
AIC	9147.864	8805.922	–
SC	9154.694	8887.885	–
−2 LOG L	9145.864	8781.922	363.942 with 11 DF (p = 0.0001)
Score	–	–	353.943 with 11 DF (p = 0.0001)

Note: * Significant at a 10 per cent confidence level; ** significant at a 5 per cent confidence level; *** significant at a 1 per cent confidence level.

Source: Authors' calculations on data from the SHIW-HA (Version 2.1).

attainment, household size, income and wealth; it is higher in the North and in smaller municipalities; it falls with the age of the household head up to the age of 60 and then it increases. These parameters are fitted to other surveys after re-scaling income and wealth by the ratio of each year average to the corresponding 1998 average, and calibrating the model intercept to allow for the different response rates in each survey. The adjusted sampling weights are finally post-stratified to re-establish the marginal distributions of components by sex, age group, type of job, geographical area and demographic size of the municipality of residence, as registered in population and labor force statistics.

Adjustment for Nonreporting and Under-reporting of Financial Assets

The adjustment builds on a method originally proposed by Cannari et al. (1990) based on the integration of the SHIW data for 1987 with the micro-data from a survey carried out in the same year by Banca Nazionale del Lavoro (BNLS) on a sample of its customers. The BNLS was not representative of the Italian population, but had the advantage of providing more reliable information on interviewees' financial behaviour, owing to the greater trust that customers are likely to place in their own bank. Indeed, after allowing for the different composition of the two samples, Cannari et al. (1990) found that SHIW figures fell short of the corresponding BNLS aggregates by about a half, under-reporting being higher for the households of the elderly, the less-educated and the self-employed. As adjustment for under-reporting proposed by Cannari et al. (1990) requires the availability of both the SHIW and the BNLS at the same time, and because no further BNLS has been carried out since 1987, we apply the updated and revised methodology developed by Cannari and D'Alessio (1993). The procedure works in three steps:

Imputation of bank and postal deposits
Assuming that there are no households reporting an asset without holding it, the probability of holding an asset conditional on not declaring it, $P_{h/nd}$, can be computed on the basis of marginal probabilities as:

$$P_{h/nd} = 1 - (1 - P_h) / (1 - P_d), \qquad (7A.2)$$

where P_h is the unconditional probability of holding an asset and P_d the unconditional probability of declaring it. While P_d can be estimated from the SHIW data as a function of household characteristics (such as the head's age and education, income, etc.), the estimate of P_h has to rely on external information. Let the asset be a bank deposit. Suppose that the logarithm of the probability of declaring a bank deposit is proportional to the logarithm of the probability of holding it and is independent of household characteristics:

$$\log P_d = k \log P_h \qquad (7A.3)$$

(in so far as $P_d \leq 1$, (7A.3) implies that $P_h \leq 1$ as well). Suppose also that the ratio P_d / P_h, that is the probability of reporting bank deposits conditional to holding at least one account, is equal, on average, to the ratio of the survey-based total of bank accounts to the corresponding figure derived from the statistics on the banking system, r:

$$E(P_d)/E(P_h)=r, \tag{7A.4}$$

where E stands for expected value. Together, equations (7A.3) and (7A.4) allow for the estimation of the parameter k, and then of the probability of holding bank deposits P_h. Equation (7A.2) is then used for imputation. This method has the desirable properties that P_d is always less than P_h and the two probabilities are positively correlated. As P_d increases with income, the latter feature prevents the imputation of bank deposits to the poorest households in the sample. For lack of better information, this method, including the estimated value for k, is also applied to postal deposits.

Imputation of financial assets, excluding bank and postal deposits
Under the assumption that they are not affected by nonreporting behaviour, the BNLS data allow us to compute P_h as a function of household characteristics. Equation (7A.2) can be used to impute the holding of an asset to nonreporting households. The amounts are subsequently imputed using standard imputation techniques. They are obviously under-reported to the same extent as nonimputed data.

Adjustment for under-reporting of financial assets
The logarithm of the true amount of financial assets w_i is assumed to be a linear function of characteristics x_i of household i:

$$\log w_i = b_0 + x_i b + u_i \tag{7A.5}$$

As above, the BNLS data are supposed to be unaffected by under-reporting and used to estimate (7A.5). Assuming that the true amount w_i is under-reported by a multiplicative factor related to household characteristics, the declared amount w_i^d is equal to $e^{a_0 + x_i a + v_i}$ times the true amount w_i. It follows that, after estimating the equation

$$\log w_i^d = b_0^d + x_i b^d + u_i^d \tag{7A.6}$$

on the SHIW data, the true amount can be recovered as

$$\hat{w}_i = e^{-\hat{a}_0 - x_i \hat{a}} w_i^d = e^{(\hat{b}_0 - \hat{b}_0^d) + x_i(\hat{b} - \hat{b}^d)} w_i^d. \tag{7A.7}$$

For further details and the full set of estimates see Cannari and D'Alessio (1993).

We use the estimates from 1987 data to correct for non- and under-reporting in subsequent years. Available data do not allow us to test the maintained assumption that households' reporting behaviour has not varied over the period. It is reassuring, however, to note that the extent of interviewees' reticence in 1987 was not very different from that found by Ulizzi (1967) 20 years earlier (Cannari and D'Alessio 1993, p. 400).

Adjustment for Nonreporting of Dwellings

We correct for the under-reporting of dwellings caused by nonsampling errors by adapting a method discussed by Cannari and D'Alessio (1990). The empirical distribution of the number of houses recorded in the SHIW, excluding those where the household lives, is well approximated by a discrete Poisson distribution, identified by the parameter $\lambda_d(x)$, where x is a vector of household characteristics (including sex, age and age squared of the household head, income, income squared, place of residence, municipality size, household size, home ownership, annual dummy). Lacking more precise information, we assume that all dwellings not used as principal residence are equally likely to be declared by the owners. The probability that one of these dwellings is declared in the SHIW can then be described by the binomial distribution

$$Pr(D = d \,|\, S = s) = \binom{s}{d} p^d (1 - p)^{(s-d)}, \tag{7A.8}$$

where s is the number of dwellings owned (excluding the household residence), $d \leq s$ is the number of those declared and p is the proportion of these dwellings recorded in the SHIW. Equation (7A.8) implies that the probability distribution of houses actually owned (excluding the household residence) is the same as that of declared houses or, more precisely, it is a Poisson distribution with parameter $\lambda_s(x) = \lambda_d(x)/p$. By computing $Pr(S = s \,|\, D = d)$, it is then possible to impute the ownership of nonreported dwellings. Characteristics and value are assigned by a hot-deck method controlling for geographical area and income brackets. For each year, the proportion p is computed as the ratio of the number of dwellings owned by the households (excluding the household residence) recorded in the SHIW, after the adjustment for nonresponse, to the corresponding 'true' figure. The latter figure is taken from the census for 1991 (so that $p = 0.383$; see Table 7.1); it is extrapolated on the basis of the average rate of growth of the number of family-owned dwellings as recorded in the censuses of 1981 and 1991 for other years.

Since respondents are requested to complete a separate sheet in the SHIW for each dwelling they own, not reporting certain assets is a way of saving time and reducing their answering burden. The method just described – seen as the equivalent of a proportional adjustment rule for a discrete variable – can account for such nonreporting behaviour, but relies on the crucial assumption that the degree of reticence of respondents is constant across socio-economic characteristics and, in particular, wealth classes. Some indirect evidence that the adjustment works satisfactorily is provided by the similarity of the distributions of rental incomes in the adjusted SHIW data and in tax returns, although it may still slightly under-estimate the under-reporting of the richest households.

8. On household wealth trends in Sweden over the 1990s

N. Anders Klevmarken*

INTRODUCTION

Sweden is known as a relatively wealthy country with an inequality of income and wealth that is low by international comparison. The public sector is large and includes rather generous transfers to private households, many of which are not means tested. Largest among these transfers are public pensions. Most Swedes who retire thus receive a major share of their pensions from the public. Until recently the incentives to accumulate private wealth for retirement have thus been less in Sweden than in countries with different pension systems. A relatively high taxation of the return to capital, on the stock of wealth and of gifts and bequests, have reduced these incentives even further.

It is possible to identify major changes in policy and markets at the end of the last century that have had an impact on wealth distribution. At the end of the 1980s the financial markets were deregulated, which resulted in a credit expansion and increased the demand for credit financed real estate and consumer durables. In the beginning of the 1990s a major tax reform was passed in the Swedish parliament that lowered marginal tax rates for labour incomes, introduced a flat tax rate of 30 per cent on capital incomes and broadened the tax base. Capital incomes were previously taxed at the high marginal rates of labour incomes, but the reform made taxation of labour and capital incomes more conformable.

Like many other countries Sweden also experienced volatile asset prices in the 1990s. In particular the prices of stocks and shares showed an exceptional increase until 1999, when the market turned down (see Figure 8.1). Compared to the price of these assets house prices were relatively stable during the whole period. But a closer look reveals that they decreased by almost 25 per cent from 1990 to 1993 and did not reach the 1990 level again until the end of 1999 or beginning of 2000. There were also regional differences in the movements of house prices. All these changes did not only inflate the average wealth of Swedish households but also increased wealth inequality.

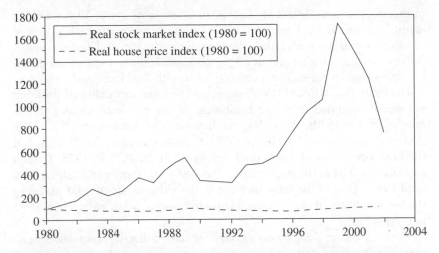

Note: Both price indices are relative to the CPI with the same base year.

Figure 8.1 Relative price indices for stocks and shares on the Stockholm Stock Exchange and for the prices on one- and two-family houses (1980 = 100)

It is also possible to trace effects from demographic changes on the distribution of wealth. In the 1990s the large baby-boom cohorts of the 1940s reached the age when people typically reach the peak of their wealth. They also started to retire at the end of the 1990s.

The plan of this chapter, first, is to give some background information about the level and inequality of household wealth in Sweden. Unfortunately there is no data source that measures the distribution of wealth consistently; we have to jump between different data sources and try to piece them together. Then follows a discussion of the changes mentioned above and their effects on the distribution of wealth. The chapter ends with a few concluding comments.

GENERAL FEATURES OF THE SWEDISH DISTRIBUTION OF WEALTH

Data Difficulties Dim a Longer Perspective

Using the estimates of Statistics Sweden, median household wealth was just above 80 000 crowns at the end of the 1970s (in 1997 prices).[1] This level reached a peak in 1990 at 115 000 and then stayed just above 100 000 crowns in this decade (see Table 8.1). This is an increase of about 30 per cent in about 20 years. Even if the year 1999 – with exceptionally high values of stocks and shares – is excluded, the increase in the top decile of the distribution was much higher, about 50 per cent, while the left tail of the distribution saw no increase. The inequality of wealth thus increased.

The estimates in Spånt (1987) suggested that the inequality of declared net wealth declined from the beginning of the previous century to the middle of the 1970s. According to Jansson and Johansson (1988), the decline then came to a halt in the 1970s. Statistics Sweden (2000) estimated the Gini coefficient of household net worth to be 0.78 in 1978. It then increased to 0.84 at the beginning of the 1990s and remained at about 0.86 until 1997.[2] Due to the large increase in the value of stocks and shares in the last few years of this decade, inequality probably increased even more in these years.

These estimates were based on register data collected from self-assessments for taxation and, in later years, also on reports directly to the tax authorities from banks, brokers and insurance companies. The quality of these data has thus increased, but they suffer from the constraints imposed by the taxation system; in particular this is true for the estimates before the second half of the 1990s. Certain assets, like most consumer durables, are not included because they were not taxed; others, such as bonds, condominiums and unlisted stocks and shares, are under-reported or their market value underestimated.[3] These circumstances very much influence both the estimates of levels and inequality. Compare the estimates from Statistics Sweden in the right panel of Table 8.1 with those of the left panel from the Swedish household panel surveys (HUS).[4] The latter estimates, mostly based on survey responses, show a much higher median level, a little more than 500 000 crowns in the 1980s, which increased to 676 000 in 1997. This is also an increase of about 30 per cent but for a five-year shorter period.

Table 8.1 also shows that the inequality of these survey data is smaller than that of register data. The right tail of the distribution has increased relative to the median but so has the left tail. There is an increase in inequality according to these estimates too but not as strong as in the estimates of Statistics Sweden. At first one might think that this is not totally unexpected. With survey data it is usually difficult to capture the extreme right tail of the wealth distribution, while register data do cover the very wealthy. But this is not the main explanation for the difference in inequality, which comes from the fact that data from Statistics Sweden use a household concept that originates from the taxation process and is not a concept suitable for economic analysis.

A household in HUS is a group of people that share the same dwelling and share meals, while the household concept used by Statistics Sweden depends

Table 8.1 Percentiles of net worth according to two different surveys, 1978–99 (1999 price level)

| | HUS survey[a] | | | | | Statistics Sweden HINK/HEK[a] | | | | | |
| | | | | | | Median in decile | | | | | |
Year	P10	P50	P90	P10/P50	P90/P50	1	5	10	P50	MD1/P50	MD10/P50
1978						−33	50	1271	83	−0.40	15.31
1983	6 *(9)*[b]	518 *(33)*	1407 *(104)*	0.012	2.716	−70	57	1155	90	−0.78	12.83
1985	36 *(6)*	516 *(13)*	1362 *(59)*	0.069	2.639	−88	64	1217	104	−0.85	11.70
1988						−138	75	1600	115	−1.20	13.91
1990						−154	70	1758	116	−1.33	15.16
1992	30 *(11)*	553 *(27)*	1692 *(74)*	0.055	3.058	−167	64	1494	101	−1.65	14.79
1995	55 *(10)*	624 *(15)*	1803 *(71)*	0.088	2.887						
1997	54 *(11)*	676 *(18)*	1972 *(59)*	0.080	2.916	−167	69	1900	109	−1.53	17.43
1999						−427	59	3815	106	−4.03	35.99

Notes:

a. The sample size of the HUS surveys ranges from 2619 to 4187 individuals, and the sample size of the HINK/HEK surveys from approximately 10 000 to 19 000 individuals. The two data sources differ in coverage and household definition (see text).

b. Italic numbers in parentheses are standard errors.

Sources: HUS: Klevmarken (2004) Table 1. HINK/HEK: Pålsson (2002) Table 2 and Statistics Sweden (2000).

on who might be considered for joint taxation. People who live together without being legally married and do not have common children are considered single; adult children who live with their parents as well as a single parent who lives with a child are also considered single. As a result Statistics Sweden gets too many one-person households compared to an economically meaningful definition, and most of them have very little wealth.

Table 8.2 compares HUS data with data from Statistics Sweden by type of asset. The fact that Statistics Sweden does not have any data on durables except for cars implies a major underestimate of this type of asset. However the HUS mean estimates of all assets and liabilities exceed those of Statistics Sweden. These differences in measures result primarily from the differences in household definitions, as well as because HUS data cover more assets and value them at market prices.

Another important difference between the two data sources is the age range covered. While Statistics Sweden covers the whole age range from the age of 16 without any upper limit, HUS starts at the age of 18 and has too few households above the age of 75 compared to the Swedish population.[5] This thinner coverage at both ends of the age distribution inflates the HUS mean and median estimates, and probably reduces measures of inequality.

Table 8.2   *Estimates of portfolio shares and mean wealth per household by type of asset and data source, 1985 and 1997 (1997 1000 SEK)*

	HUS		HINK/HEK	
	1000 SEK	%	1000 SEK	%
1985				
Real estate	492	52.2		59
Financial assets	156	16.6		33
Other assets (durables)	294	31.2		8
Gross total	942	100.0		100
Debts	268	28.4		39
Net total	674	71.6		61
1997				
Real estate	642	51.0	374	57.9
Financial assets	354	28.1	224	34.7
Other assets (durables)	264	20.9	48	7.4
Gross total	1259	100.0	646	100.0
Debts	276	21.9	179	27.8
Net total	983	78.1	467	72.2

Sources: Klevmarken et al. (2003), Statistics Sweden (2000) Table 6, Statistics Sweden (1990) Tables 2–4.

Who is Wealthy and Who is Poor?

Even if the wealth distribution in Sweden is less unequal than in most other countries and even if we disregard the extreme right tail of the distribution, there are large differences in wealth among ordinary people. Using relatively new data from Statistic Sweden,[6] Table 8.3 shows results from quantile regressions of net worth per adult equivalent in 1997 and 1999 on a number of socio-economic variables, including age, marital status, schooling, work, geographical region and type of housing.[7] In this analysis individual variables refer to the oldest member of the household. Table 8.3 includes slope estimates and standard errors in Swedish crowns for the 25th, 50th and 75th percentiles. The standard errors were obtained by bootstrapping.

The estimated marginal effect of an explanatory variable in general depends on the percentile of wealth distribution. Because the dependent variable is in Swedish crowns we find, for most variables, that the marginal effect is smallest in the left tail of the wealth distribution and largest in the right tail. Take, for instance, the case of being self-employed. For the self-employed, other than farmers, the first quantile is almost 14 000 crowns higher than it is for the employed, while the third quantile is about 76 000 crowns higher. As is pointed out below, this 'scale difference' does not always dominate. In some cases differences in motives to accumulate, or differences in exposure to market forces, show up in the estimates.

The relation between wealth and age – at the end of Table 8.3 – is not exactly the same as we are accustomed to seeing. Equivalized wealth first decreases to a minimum in the age bracket 30–34.[8] Then it increases, almost without any decrease, at the end of the life cycle. A small decrease can be noted only after the age of 75 and in the centre and right tail of the distribution. One might believe that this is a result of dividing through with the equivalence scale. In the beginning of the life cycle the family increases and at the end it decreases. However when the same model is estimated using just household net worth as a dependent variable, the same pattern remains. We thus have to seek other explanations. The initial decrease could be a result of households incurring debts when families are formed, children arrive, and families buy houses or condominiums. In the beginning of a working career, immediately after school, people experience uncertainty about future jobs and incomes and hesitate to take up loans but, after a few years, most have found good jobs and count on future increases in income. They then become more willing to borrow. At this age income uncertainty is also reduced by marriage or union formation. The probability that both spouses will lose their incomes is smaller than the possibility that one might. The larger incomes and the reduced uncertainty about the future thus make people more willing to borrow.

Table 8.3   *Quantile regressions of equivalized household net worth on selected socioeconomic variables, 1997 and 1999*

	Q25		Q50		Q75	
	slope	std	slope	std	slope	std
If married/cohabiting	1029	2141	−8336	2975	−24421	3722
If single woman	−12068	2461	−19003	2259	−26450	3143
If single man	0		0		0	
Work intensity	−15033	2333	−13099	2633	−1229	3084
If part-time old age pension	119230	21833	117688	25989	121792	65238
If other pension and <65	−6793	3149	−6155	3635	−7597	4571
If deducted pension investment	27679	2358	39046	2746	61743	3616
If immigrant from Nordic country	−14129	6761	−33487	6887	−45945	6244
If other immigrant	2725	4167	−7404	2363	−18841	4600
If self-employed	13914	5644	33374	6819	75750	14528
If farmer	494570	29275	824412	50409	1366749	73467
Unspecified education	5603	6741	−884	7358	−16799	7243
At most 9 years of schooling	20119	3980	−8285	4887	−43344	6082
Highschool or equivalent	27744	4218	8487	4049	−23474	6293
College/univ. < 3 yrs, technical	4683	7924	4817	6738	−1523	11093
College/univ. < 3 yrs, other	0		0		0	
College/univ. ≥ 3 yrs, technical	31687	8316	63361	10029	178872	27810
College/univ. ≥ 3 yrs, other	21841	5988	35122	4479	96066	12929
Own house in Stockholm	260220	8877	437279	15334	646975	31417
Own house in Gothenburg	199481	7274	279863	11340	397249	22034
Own house in Malmö	222833	13825	280910	22202	381307	24016
Own house in other cities	143270	4484	175066	5226	232010	11082
Own house in rural south	113325	5944	137681	5957	180636	11551
Own house in urban north	107610	5519	114004	6468	148941	19102
Own house in rural north	95213	6380	99229	7065	98925	10727
Co-op in Stockholm	165125	5110	232054	9634	421563	20091
Co-op in Gothenburg	90515	6673	80357	6735	93285	9322
Co-op in Malmö	70462	4982	59666	4276	67250	8848
Co-op in other s. cities	60021	4067	52265	2914	57570	5118

Table 8.3 (continued)

	Q25		Q50		Q75	
	slope	std	slope	std	slope	std
Co-op in rural south	53 589	5071	38 297	3655	36 281	4547
Co-op in urban north	67 333	7540	47 112	6773	42 638	15 675
Co-op in rural north	46 122	13 017	20 510	12 665	15 418	12 531
Rented in Stockholm	7005	3708	6228	2273	4565	2784
Rented in Gothenburg	−9005	4934	−7667	3613	271	3360
Rented in Malmö	−18 948	3897	−12 848	6946	−3832	4701
Rented in other s. cities	0		0		0	
Rented in rural south	6824	3448	7468	3307	22 268	3719
Rented in urban north	25 740	5148	18 433	5053	26 621	7282
Rented in rural north	27 144	4535	19 502	4566	31 818	11 194
Age 20–24	0		0		0	
Age 25–29	−48 674	3839	−21 501	1908	−13 661	3180
Age 30–34	−72 407	3441	−42 447	3440	−27 630	4227
Age 35–39	−62 229	4566	−38 444	3694	−22 466	2936
Age 40–44	−49 096	4195	−26 028	2998	−11 334	3101
Age 45–49	−24 291	3348	−1385	2764	38 998	8528
Age 50–54	8674	3759	52 148	7831	177 373	13 298
Age 55–59	35 411	4047	121 362	5493	319 101	15 263
Age 60–64	49 548	5521	161 888	9666	361 880	19 099
Age 65–69	73 089	5412	203 432	10 429	454 475	19 089
Age 70–74	74 043	7254	209 185	11 243	450 205	18 603
Age 75–79	91 491	8395	168 258	9700	385 251	16 520
Age 80–84	93 066	8690	175 362	8825	368 651	16 264
If 1997	7661	2263	−1411	1306	−18 728	2633
Intercept	−53 483	4938	5335	4488	73 406	6844
Pseudo R^2	0.098		0.160		0.200	

Note: The number of observations is 33 861.

The normally observed decrease in wealth among older people is, in this analysis, picked up by variables other than the age variable. The share of single women is high among old people, and single women are less wealthy than single men and married couples. We also find rather many elderly in rented apartments, and they are on average less wealthy than those who live in condominiums or owned houses. The variable work intensity – that is, a measure of the number of workers of a family – is also likely to pick up some of the age differences.[9] Most families with elderly members score zero on this variable, while younger and middle-aged families have positive scores. The estimates suggest that the higher the score, the lesser the wealth, in particular among the less wealthy. In the 75th percentile this variable is insignificant. Finally, due to an error in the coding of education, everyone above 74 got the code 'unspecified education', and this group has less wealth than most other educational groups. Population heterogeneity in other dimensions than age thus explains the hump-shaped age–wealth relation.

Though not included in the analysis above, one could add that bequests are likely to contribute to the cross-sectional hump shape too. About 30 per cent of Swedish households have received bequests. Although most bequests are small and the average bequest is smaller in Sweden than in the United States (compare the results of Klevmarken 2004 and Wolff 2002), they do contribute to the peak of the cross-sectional age–wealth profile because most bequests are given to middle-aged people. Although not conclusive, these results suggest that population heterogeneity and bequests rather than the life-cycle hypothesis explain the shape of the raw age–wealth relationship.

We also find that families with a head (oldest member) who had a part-time pension (before the age of 65) on average had about 120 000 more Swedish crowns in equivalized wealth than families in which the oldest member did not have this kind of pension. It thus takes some private wealth to cut down on market work before regular pension age. Interestingly, this effect is about the same in Swedish crowns in the entire wealth distribution. As a contrast, in families with a head who had a disability pension – in the table called 'If other pension and <65' – household wealth is somewhat lower than for otherwise comparable households.

Those who had claimed deductions for payments to a private pension policy in their self-assessment for income taxation on average owned 30 000–60 000 more than those who had no claims. Because the accumulated value of these pension policies were not included in the wealth concept used in this analysis, one might expect a negative effect. However, the current result is probably explained by wealthy people claiming a deduction more frequently than the less wealthy.

Immigrants were relatively less wealthy. The estimates suggest that immigrants from outside the Nordic countries do better than Nordic immigrants, a result that is somewhat unexpected. Self-employed people, in particular farmers, had much more wealth than employees. Median farm wealth exceeded median wealth by some 800 000 Swedish crowns, while the median wealth of the self-employed only exceeded that of the employed by about 30 000 Swedish crowns.

Schooling is a good predictor of wealth among the wealthy but not among the less wealthy. Having more than compulsory school does not increase the 25th percentile, while the difference in wealth at the 75th percentile between a graduate engineer and someone with only compulsory school is about 200 000 Swedish crowns.[10] Another interpretation of this result is that an academic education can lead to well-paid jobs that permit accumulation of wealth, while some academics end up in less well-paid jobs that give no advantage to higher education.

The area in which a family lives, and whether it has invested in a house, also become very important for its accumulated wealth. The trends in real estate prices depend on area, and price differences between them are large. Our results show that those who live in their own houses or condominiums are wealthier than those who live in rented apartments, depending on where the household lives. Median wealth is more than 400 000 Swedish crowns higher for a family that owns its home in Stockholm, compared to a family that rents a flat in a smaller city in central or south Sweden, while the relative advantage of owning a house in Gothenburg or Malmö is a little less than 300 000 Swedish crowns and, in the rural part of the country, about 100 000. The effect on the 75th percentile of having a house in one of the three big cities is even higher. The 75th percentile for those who own a house in Stockholm is about 650 000 Swedish crowns higher than for those who rent a flat in a smaller city. Geographical area is less important for those who have a co-op, with the exception of living in Stockholm. Median equivalized wealth of people with a co-op in Stockholm is almost 200 000 Swedish crowns higher than for families who live outside Stockholm and Gothenburg. The housing market in Stockholm has been a tighter market for a longer period than markets elsewhere in Sweden. There are no major differences in wealth among renters based on where in the country they live.[11]

The analysis above is limited to household private wealth. Wealth in the form of notional or real accounts in the public pension system and the system of negotiated group pensions are not included. Such wealth takes up a large share of the total wealth of Swedish households, as is discussed below in a section about public and occupational pensions.

THREE MAJOR CHANGES IN THE 1990S

The 1991 Tax Reform Changed the Portfolio Composition

At the end of the 1980s and at the beginning of the 1990s, major changes in the Swedish income tax system influenced household portfolios. Cuts in marginal tax rates, and limitations in the possibilities of deducting interest paid, were introduced in the second half of the 1980s; major tax reform followed in 1990–91. To recapitulate, this reform decreased the marginal income taxes, broadened the tax basis, and included major changes in the taxation of the returns from financial assets and real estate. The expected effects on the distribution of wealth were a decrease in the share of liabilities, real estate and consumer durables, and an increase in the share of financial assets, in particular, bank deposits and bonds. Table 8.2 confirms that most of these changes took place. Using HUS data the table shows that the ratio of debts relative to gross wealth decreased from 28 per cent to 22 per cent. The share of financial assets increased from 17 per cent to 28 per cent, while that of durables decreased from 31 per cent to 21 per cent. The share of real estate remained approximately the same.

Doubts about a Viable Public Pension System Offer Incentives to Increase Private Savings in Pension Policies

In the post-war period all Swedes above the age of 65 have been covered by a basic social security pension,[12] and in 1960 an income-related supplementary pension was introduced in the form of a pay-as-you-go system that covered all employees and many self-employed. Above a low-income threshold and below a ceiling, the income-related pensions were 60 per cent of the average income for the 15 best years. These pensions were indexed by the CPI. In the 1990s the viability of this system became a concern facing the large, ageing baby-boom cohorts, given the relatively low growth of the Swedish economy. In 1994 economic and political discussions of the future of the pension system and proposals for reforms resulted in a decision in parliament about a new pension system. It is less vulnerable to demographic and economic shocks, but it might also result in lower pensions than the previous system (see Klevmarken 2002).

In addition to the public social security pensions, most workers in Sweden are covered by negotiated group pensions (occupational pensions). Similar to the public pensions, some of them were of the defined benefit type. After the reform of the public system, however, most of them were changed in the direction of a defined contribution system. For most workers these pensions have a replacement rate of about 10 per cent after the age of 65; for workers with high wages – mostly white-collar workers – the replacement ratio is higher.[13]

Although an unfunded pension system like the (old) Swedish system does not have any funds except for buffer funds, those who have participated in the system face an implied liability. Workers have a claim on a future stream of pension payments that can be evaluated in the form of an implicit pension capital that can be attributed to everyone who is covered. For most Swedes this is a large amount compared to private wealth. The magnitude of the capital value of public pensions and negotiated group pensions was estimated in Andersson et al. (2002) using 1999 data from Statistics Sweden and assumptions about the future that are detailed in an appendix of that publication. Table 8.4 is obtained from two of the tables

Table 8.4 Private wealth and capital value of public pensions and negotiated group pensions, 1999 (medians in 1000 SEK computed at the individual level)

	Age 45–64				Age 65 and over
	Blue collar workers	White collar workers	Government employees	Local government employees	
Financial assets	70	121	119	80	114
Tangible assets	293	429	439	362	34
Debts	128	167	176	140	0
Old age pension	1117	1286	1278	1087	660
'Premiepension' (funded social security)	37	45	41	34	
Negotiated group pensions					76
Blue collar workers	204				
White collar workers ITP		245			
White collar workers ITPK		207			
Government employees STAT			232		
Government empl. STATF			129		
Local gov. empl. KOM				177	
Local gov. empl. KOMF				72	
Gross wealth	1690	2522	2362	1775	1238
Net wealth	1546	2354	2199	1634	1222

Note: This table was obtained using the individual and not the household as a unit.

Sources: Andersson et al. (2002) Tables 3.8 and 3.10. Computational details in Andersson et al. (2002) Appendix.

in Andersson et al. (2002). It compares, for two age groups and four major occupational groups, private wealth to the capital value of public old-age and negotiated group pensions. The table shows median assets, so it is not possible to add public and private assets and compare. However, it is still quite clear that the claims on the public pension system and on the negotiated group systems by far exceed private wealth. For blue-collar workers the value of the public old-age pensions exceeds 60 per cent of the median

Table 8.5   Estimates of mean wealth in private pension policies using alternative methods (1997 1000 SEK)

Year	% with policy	Overall mean	Mean if holding
HUS surveys (households)			
1985	14.4	13	89
1992	32.6	33	103
1997	24.9	30	120
Flood (2003) using LINDA (individuals)			
1999	30.3	31	104
2000	32.0	36	111

gross wealth (including pension wealth) and for white-collar workers it amounts to about half median gross wealth.

Reduced pensions would thus have a major impact on total wealth of an average Swedish household and the increased uncertainty about future pensions have increased private investments in pension policies. Table 8.5 illustrates this. In the middle of the 1980s less than 15 per cent of all households had private pension policies and the mean holding was rather small, about 90 000 crowns. At the end of the 1990s more than 30 per cent had this kind of asset and the average value had increased to an estimated 150 000 crowns per household. It is not possible to get more than an informed guess of the latter amount, because the first three rows of the table are based on survey data from HUS using the consumption-based household concept, while the last two rows of the table are estimates for individuals obtained from Flood (2003) that used register data from a longitudinal data base called LINDA.[14]

The Large Baby-boom Cohorts Retire Wealthy

The life-cycle hypothesis is a main vehicle in analysing wealth distribution, and its implications have been studied empirically in the previous literature. Most cross-sectional studies show a hump-shaped relation between wealth and age while studies based on panel data do not always confirm that households consume their wealth after retirement. Figure 8.2 displays cross-sectional profiles for equivalized household net worth for 1999. The age–wealth profile for the 90th percentile of the distribution shows a strong hump shape while it is much less pronounced for the median and has completely disappeared in the 10th percentile.

Those who are permanently in the left part of the distribution have very little they could liquidize for consumption when they retire. The wealth of

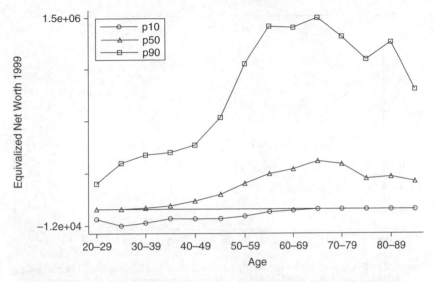

Source: Andersson et al. (2002), primary source HINK/HEK 1999 of Statistics Sweden.

Figure 8.2   *Age–wealth profiles for the 10th, 50th, and 90th percentile of net worth distribution, 1999 (equivalized household net worth, 1999 SEK)*

the large group in the middle of the wealth distribution primarily consists of owner-occupied houses and condominiums and many choose not to liquidize this asset when they grow old. They prefer to stay in their old home and they also seem reluctant to increase their mortgages. As a result we see only a weak hump shape. Only in the right upper part of the wealth distribution do we find households with financial wealth that is easier to use for consumption purposes. Is this the explanation for the hump shape of the 90th percentile? The wealth of many of these households generates a return that, jointly with pensions, is likely to maintain the consumption standard of these people when they grow old. Thus they might not need to reduce their wealth. So can we find an alternative explanation for the hump shape?

In the section 'Who is wealthy and who is poor?' above, age is associated with population heterogeneity that is able to pick up the hump in the age–wealth profile. We will now focus on one particular aspect of heterogeneity, namely that different birth cohorts have different experiences that influence their accumulated wealth. Figure 8.3 shows median age–net worth profiles for two years, 1983 and 1997. The shape of the profiles has changed. The peak is higher in 1997 than in 1983, and in the span of these 14 years, the age range moves from around 50 years to beyond the age of 60.

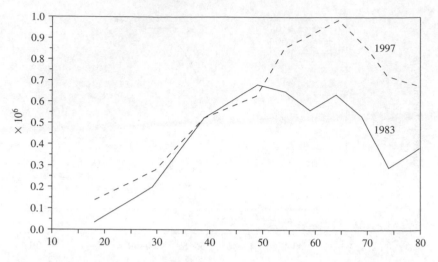

Note: The figure shows cross-sectionally estimated piecewise linear splines. Data originate from HUS surveys. Net worth does not include private pension policies and annuities.

Source: Klevmarken (2004) Table 2.

Figure 8.3   Median age-net worth profiles, 1983 and 1997 (1993 SEK)

The lack of stability in the age–wealth profiles suggests that there are other forces than stable life-cycle savings that determine the wealth distribution.

Andersson et al. (2002) and Klevmarken (2004) argued that most of the cross-sectional hump shape originated from cohort differences in wealth accumulation. In an attempt to separate birth cohort effects on wealth from the age effect, these studies showed that the cohorts of the 1940s and 1950s did better than older cohorts. They also did better than younger cohorts in the left tail of the distribution, while among those who were relatively wealthy, the cohorts of the 1960s and 1970s had succeeded better than any previous cohorts relative to their age. The latter observations might indicate a 'dot.com' effect that would have vanished if we had had access to more recent data covering the period after the recent stock market decrease. However the relative success of the large baby-boom cohorts is likely to have survived the stock market swings (Berg 2002). The cohorts of the 1940s could take advantage of the relatively prosperous 1960s and 1970s, periods of relatively high growth not disturbed by periods of high unemployment. These cohorts were able to get a job and keep it, buy a house or condominium and then surface on the price increases in the real estate and stock markets. Some of them also benefited from subsidies to those who invested in their own houses. Older generations had to carry on the heritage of the Depression in the 1930s and the wartime economy in the 1940s.

The age–wealth profiles' estimated net of these cohort effects showed almost no hump shape. Only the profile for the 90th percentile had a weak tendency to level off after the age of 70 (see Klevmarken 2004, Figure 7). The estimates in this age range were however rather uncertain because the number of observations of the oldest is small in the HUS surveys.

The implication of these findings is that there is relatively little private life-cycle saving in Sweden. Most of this kind of saving is done through the social security system and through the negotiated group pensions. Although Swedish households do accumulate wealth, active saving out of regular incomes is not the main explanation for changes in household private wealth, as pointed out by Pålsson (2002). More important are price changes in the asset markets and the ability of households to manage their portfolios.

CONCLUSIONS

At the end of the 1990s median household net wealth was about 700 000 Swedish crowns, while the mean was above 1 million. Compared to the United States, Swedish median wealth is somewhat higher, while the mean is only about half of that of the United States (see Klevmarken et al. 2003). Although the Swedish distribution of wealth is unequal, for instance compared to income distribution, it is much less unequal than that of the United States.

In the 1990s household median wealth in Sweden increased by about 30 per cent in real terms. Part of this increase came from increased savings after the tax reform at the beginning of the 1990s. The Swedish savings rate peaked at about 12–13 per cent in 1993–94 but dropped back down below 5 per cent in 1998–99. We have observed that savings in private pension policies have increased. However, it is hard to know to what extent this is new savings and to what extent it is a reallocation of portfolios. Part of the increase in wealth can also be attributed to the exceptional increase in the stock market, but its influence on median wealth is not as large as one might think because stocks and shares make up a large share of the portfolio only among the wealthy. However, the increase in the value of stocks and shares is the major explanation for the increase in inequality of wealth during this period.

More important for ordinary people than stock prices is the value of one- and two-family houses, which only increased by a modest 3 per cent in real terms in the 1990s. However the difference between peak and trough was larger, and there were large regional differences. Price increases were higher in the three big cities and in particular in Stockholm, which contributed to an increased regional inequality in wealth and probably also to the overall increase in inequality (see Berg 2001).

An important finding that has implications for the future is that the baby-boom cohorts have become relatively wealthy, both in terms of private wealth and in claims on the pension system. They are now retiring but still retain an influence in society, not only because of their size but also because of their wealth, although their wealth is more vulnerable to volatile prices in the financial markets than before, because the share of financial assets has increased and because the pension reforms have made future pensions more dependent on financial markets. There is also a political risk that the large baby-boom cohorts to an increasing extent will have to pay for the health services and care they will need in the future, services that now are financed through the general tax fund. If these forces do not erode the wealth of the baby boomers, which their children will inherit, bequests will then become more common than today and the amounts inherited will most likely increase. Most people think this will increase the inequality of the wealth distribution even further but, as demonstrated in Klevmarken (2004), that is not necessarily the case.

Finally this chapter has argued that private life-cycle saving is not so strong in Sweden, but that most of this kind of saving has been done through the public and collective pension systems. The 'savings boom' in the beginning of the 1990s should be seen as an exception, an adjustment to the change in the tax system. However the concern for the future viability of the pension systems, the change of these systems in the direction of funded systems, and the boom in the stock market have made Swedish households more aware of financial instruments like mutual funds, stocks and shares. Ownership of these assets have spread down the wealth distribution and this change, jointly with the increased savings in pension policies, might well signify a change in the savings behaviour of Swedish households towards more life-cycle savings.

NOTES

*   Useful comments from Lennart Berg, Daniel Hallberg, and Lars Osberg and other participants at the Levy Institute Conference on International Perspectives on Wealth in October 2003 are gratefully acknowledged.
1.   In the 1980s and 1990s the exchange rate between the USD and the SEK varied from 5 crowns per dollar to 8.50. In Klevmarken et al. (2003) we used the purchasing power parity 9.85.
2.   Statistics Sweden (2000), Table 16.
3.   Notional and real wealth in the form of public and negotiated group pensions are not included. These forms of wealth are not included in data from the HUS surveys either.

4. The Swedish household panel surveys (HUS) were originally designed using the US Panel Study of Income Dynamics (PSID) as a model. For a general description and details about survey design and variables included, see Klevmarken and Olovsson (1993), Flood et al. (1996), and the Internet home page of the HUS surveys, http://www.handels.gu.se/econ/econometrics/hus/husin.htm.
5. The sample of the first HUS wave in 1984 was limited to the age range 18–75. In later waves people have been followed even beyond the age of 75, but refreshment samples have been restricted to the ages 18–75.
6. These data originate from banks, brokers and insurance companies and not from self-assessment forms. Tax-assessed values of owner-occupied houses, secondary houses and condominiums have been replaced by estimates of market values. Also the market values of cars held by the household have been estimated. Private pension insurances and annuities are not included.
7. The choice of equivalence scale is somewhat arbitrary. In this case a scale recommended by the Swedish National Board of Health and Welfare was used: single, 1.16; married/cohabiting, 1.92; child aged 0–3, 0.56; child aged 4–10, 0.66; child aged 11–17, 0.76; and other adult, 0.96.
8. The age group 20–24 is the basis of comparison.
9. This variable takes the value 1 for one full-time worker, 2 for two full-time workers, 1.5 for one full-time and one half-time, and so on.
10. These estimates average out any cohort differences in schooling. The share of a birth cohort that goes on to higher education has increased in the period after the Second World War and the return to an additional year of schooling has decreased (Edin and Holmlund 1995, LeGrand et al. 2001).
11. Rent control has kept rents down in areas like Stockholm, while prices on co-ops and houses were not regulated.
12. Before 1976 the eligibility age was 67.
13. Depending on the group plan, occupational group pensions also allow for early retirement with more generous replacement rates.
14. Below a ceiling, investments in a private pension policy can be deducted against income in assessing taxable income. The tax authorities thus know when a taxpayer claims a deduction and the amount claimed is truncated by the ceiling. These data, available longitudinally in LINDA, have been used in Flood (2003) to estimate the current accumulated value of the investments of each individual in LINDA. It is encouraging to see that these two approaches to estimating investments in private pension policies give approximately comparable results.

REFERENCES

Andersson, B., L. Berg and A. Klevmarken (2002), 'Inkomst och förmögenhetsfördelningen för dagens och morgondagens äldre', in SOU 2002:29 Bilagedel B, *Riv ålderstrappan! Livslopp i förändring*, Fritzes Offentliga Publikationer, Erlanders Gotab AB, Stockholm. ISBN 91-38-21671-X ISSB 0375-250X.

Berg, L. (2001), *I slott och koja. De svenska hushållens förmögenhetsfördelning*, Ekonomiska sekretariatet, Nordbanken, Stockholm.

Berg, L. (2002), *Gungorna och karusellen. De svenska hushållens förmögenhetsfördelning*, Nordea, Stockholm.

Edin, P.-A. and B. Holmlund (1995), 'The swedish wage structure: the rise and fall of solidarity wage policy?', in R. Freeman and L. Katz (eds), *Differences and Changes in Wage Structures*, Chicago, IL: University of Chicago Press.

Flood, L. (2003), 'Formation of wealth, income of capital and cost of housing in SESIM', Report, Ministry of Finance, Stockholm, www.sesim.org.

Flood, L., N.A. Klevmarken and P. Olovsson (1996), *Household Market and Nonmarket Activities (HUS)*, Vols IV–VI, Uppsala: Department of Economics, Uppsala University.

Jansson, K. and S. Johansson (1988), *Förmögenhetsfördelningen 1975–1987 (The Distribution of Wealth 1975–1987)*, Stockholm: Statistics Sweden.

Klevmarken, N.A. (2002), 'Swedish pension reforms in the 1990s', Working Paper 2002:6, Uppsala: Department of Economics, Uppsala University.

Klevmarken, N.A. (2004), 'On the wealth dynamics of Swedish families 1984–1998', *Review of Income and Wealth*, **50**(4), December, 469–91.

Klevmarken, N.A., J.P. Lupton and F.P. Stafford (2003), 'Wealth dynamics in the 1980s and 1990s. Sweden and the United States', *Journal of Human Resources*, **38**(2), 322–53.

Klevmarken, N.A. and P. Olovsson (1993), *Household Market and Nonmarket Activities (HUS). Procedures and Codes 1984–1991*, Vols I–III, Stockholm: IUI/Almqvist & Wiksell International.

LeGrand, C., R. Szulkin and M. Tåhlin (2001), 'Lönestrukturens förändring i Sverige', in SOU 2001:53 *Välfärd och arbete i arbetslöshetens årtionde*, Fritzes Offentliga Publikationer, Erlanders Gotab AB, Stockholm.

Pålsson, A.-M. (2002), 'Myt och verklighet om de svenska hushållens förmögenheter', *Ekonomisk Debatt*, **30**(8), 679–91.

Spånt, R. (1987), 'The wealth distribution in Sweden 1920–1983', in E.N. Wolff (ed.), *International Comparisons of the Distribution of Household Wealth*, Oxford: Clarendon Press.

Statistics Sweden (1990), 'Förmögenhetsfördelningen 1975–1988. Urvalsbaserad statistik för hushåll på riksnivå', *Statistiska Meddelanden* Be21 SM9002. Statistics Sweden, Örebro.

Statistics Sweden (2000), *Förmögenhetsfördelningen i Sverige 1997 med en tillbakablick till 1975*, Report 2000:1, Örebro ISSN 1400-3147.

Wolff, E.N. (2002), 'Inheritances and wealth inequality, 1989–1998', *American Economic Association Papers and Proceedings*, **92**(2), 260–64.

9. Trends in the distribution of income and wealth: Finland, 1987–98

Markus Jäntti*

INTRODUCTION

Like many OECD countries, Finland experienced a surge in income inequality in the 1990s. Although its levels of income inequality are, by international standards, fairly moderate, inequality – as measured by the Gini coefficient of disposable income – has risen to levels last seen in the early 1970s (Figure 9.1). Factor income inequality increased substantially over the decades, but the increase decelerated in the second half of the 1990s, when disposable income inequality started to increase. This has led many to seek the reasons for increased inequality in changes in taxes and public sector transfers.

A somewhat different view of inequality trends emerges from studying changes in disposable income decile group means and their components, shown in Figure 9.2. The graphs are drawn on a log scale, so that changes in relative inequality can be visually assessed from the slopes of decile group mean incomes, shown in the upper left panel. If the slopes – that is, the growth rates of income in different parts of the distribution – are similar across all income groups, relative income inequality is unchanged. Higher (lower) growth at the top suggests widening (narrowing) income differences. The richest decile group saw its income increase considerably faster than the rest of the income distribution in the last years of the 1990s, whereas the two poorest groups had fairly anaemic income growth; that is, relative inequality increased, as would be expected based on the Gini coefficients in Figure 9.1.

Turning to selected components of disposable income – wage, self-employment and property income – the average of which, within each decile group, is shown in the remaining panels of Figure 9.2, suggests some differences to the series of Gini coefficients. The graph that stands out is that of property income in the richest decile group, shown in the lower right panel. The share of disposable income from property income increased for this group, rising from around 12 per cent in 1990 to more than 45 per cent

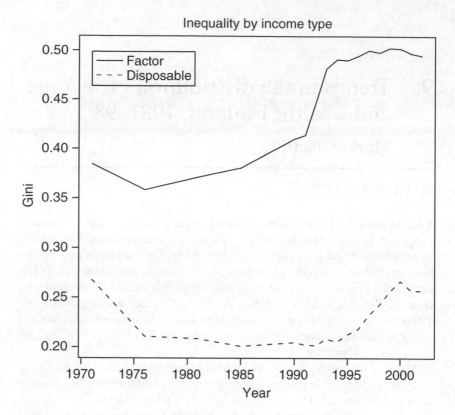

Source: Author's calculations from income distribution survey microdata.

Figure 9.1   Income inequality, Gini coefficients, 1971–99

in 2000. These figures suggest that at least part of the story of increased inequality is related to property income.

Increases in inequality that are driven by property income can be due to many factors, including increased returns to capital and increased concentration of wealth holdings. This chapter explores the role that wealth has played in increasing economic inequality in Finland and studies the bivariate distribution of income and (gross and net) wealth, using data from 1988, 1994 and 1998 wealth surveys gathered by Statistics Finland. While these surveys are irregularly and widely spaced, they do cover a period during which large changes in capital markets and overall economic conditions took place. Moreover, they cover the period during which income inequality increased substantially from historical lows to levels observed before 1976.

The chapter is structured as follows. The literature review section briefly examines earlier studies of the inequality of wealth and of income in Finland and contrasts these with studies in other countries. The data section describes the wealth surveys used for the analyses in this chapter. The trends in the inequality of income and wealth are presented in the section on distribution of income and wealth and the model-based results are discussed in the section on regression models for income, wealth and debts. The final section offers a few concluding comments.

LITERATURE REVIEW

The increase in inequality in Finland in the latter half of the 1990s is well documented (in English) by, among others, Riihelä et al. (2002), Riihelä et al. (2001) and Suoniemi (2000). The overall trends in inequality as shown in these studies are in line with the trends shown in Figure 9.1 and 9.2. Trends in the distribution of wealth have been studied less frequently, and most often in Finnish only. Contributions include Tuomala and Vilmunen (1985), Sinko (1991) and Virén (2002). Statistics Finland (2000), which describes the 1998 wealth survey, shows Lorenz curves and Gini coefficients for both gross and net wealth across all three surveys. These suggest a considerable increase in the inequality of wealth across the years.

Ilmanen and Keloharju (1999) and Karhunen and Keloharju (2001) examine patterns of share ownership in Finland, based on the stocks held in the Finnish Central Securities Depository (FCSD). FCSD holds mostly publicly traded shares, which, for the household population, accounted for about 5 per cent of gross wealth in 1998. The total market value at the end of the year of publicly traded companies increased from 19 billion euro (in 2001 prices) in 1987 to 37 billion in 1994 and 141 billion in 1998. However, the share of that financial wealth that was held by domestic individuals declined between 1987 and 1998, from 17 per cent to 7 per cent (Karhunen and Keloharju, 2001, p. 193). Thus, while the value of all shares increased by 281 per cent between 1994 and 1998 (assuming a 17 per cent share in 1994, as well), the value of publicly traded shares held by private individuals increased by 57 per cent. While this is a respectable increase in gross wealth during no more than four years, most of the increase in share values occurred among institutional and foreign investors.

In conclusion, then, the evidence suggests that, during the years covered by the wealth surveys, the inequality of wealth held by domestic individuals increased, as did the inequality of disposable income. This increase was not as great as the changes in stock market indices might lead one to believe,

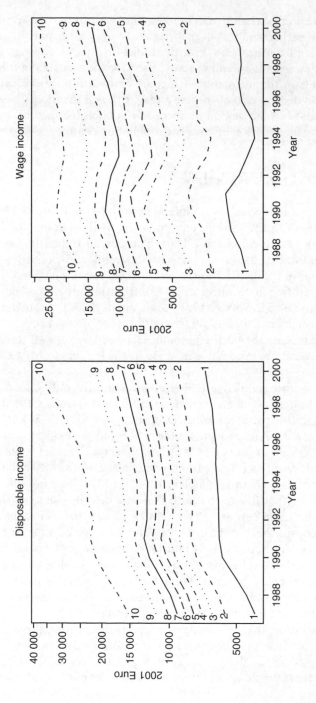

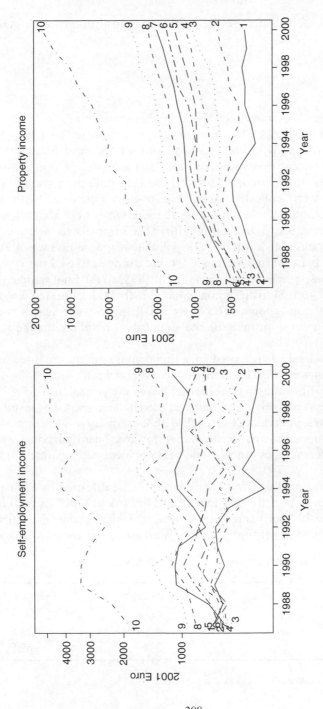

Source: Author's calculations from income distribution survey microdata.

Figure 9.2 Income inequality, disposable income decile groups means of various income factors of 1987–2000

because much of that increase occurred among institutional and foreign shareholders.

DATA

Statistics Finland conducted (by and large) comparable wealth surveys in 1987/88, 1994 and 1998.[1] The first survey was conducted as a two-year panel. While the study of changes in wealth for the same household is interesting, this was a one-off event and, as I am interested in changes across a longer time period, I discarded the 1988 data in this study. The wealth data were collected using face-to-face interviews with the sampled household member (however, the interviews were about household, rather than just individual, wealth). The sample sizes and overall nonresponse rates are shown in Table 9.1. The response rate was a little more than 70 per cent in 1987 and 1994, but dropped to 64.9 per cent in 1998. The gross sample was also smaller in 1998, so the final sample size is 3893 in that year. Statistics Finland has constructed calibrated weights to correct for nonresponse. The fairly small sample size places some restrictions on how meaningful the detailed population breakdowns might be.

Statistics Finland has prepared a file that contains all the cross-sections of the wealth surveys with harmonized income and wealth definitions. The concept of wealth is roughly comparable across the years, but the 1987/88 definition is less comprehensive than that used in later years. For instance, in 1994 and 1998, interviewees were asked about primary residences, as well as vacation homes and apartments owned for investment purposes, while in 1987/88 different types of real estate were not identified separately in the interviews.

An important omission from the concept of wealth used by Statistics Finland – with respect to what Davies and Shorrocks (2000, p. 607) call 'augmented wealth' – is that pension wealth, other than that in instruments purchased in private pension insurance markets, is not included. As the

Table 9.1 Sample size and nonresponse in the wealth survey

Year	Gross sample	Net sample	Response rate
1987	7677	5566	72.5
1994	6926	5210	75.2
1998	5937	3893	65.6

Source: Author's calculations from wealth survey microdata.

bulk of future pensions consists of legislated (therefore, compulsory) pensions that, for private sector employees, are paid by private pension insurance companies, a large fraction of holdings that will generate future income are not accounted for. The reason that neither legislated public nor private work-related pensions are included in the concept of wealth is that they lack many of the other characteristics of financial assets – rights to future work-related pensions cannot be sold or used as collateral or left as bequests. Since a large fraction of the population has acquired some work-related pensions, inclusion of these assets might have a large impact on distribution of wealth figures. A closer examination of this issue is on the agenda, but is not included in this chapter.

All monetary amounts are expressed in 1998 euros, unless otherwise indicated, using the cost of living index to inflate earlier years to the 1998 Finnish markka and the euro–markka exchange rate (5.946 FIM/EUR). In income distribution research, it has been standard practice – at least since Danziger and Taussig (1979) – to examine the distribution of equivalent income distributed across persons. It is not immediately clear what the most sensible practice for wealth is. But, since an objective of this chapter is to study the bivariate distribution of income and wealth, I do use an equivalence scale. Thus, I have equivalized all the economic resources (that is, the wealth and the income variables) using a so-called Citro-Michael equivalence scale, with parameter values that correspond to the OECD scale (National Research Council, 1995; Bradbury and Jäntti, 1999). I have used the calibrated sampling weights, which I have adjusted to sum to population size (that is, the original sample weights have been multiplied by household size). In the regression equations, in order to generate standard errors and diagnostic statistics that have sensible magnitudes, I have further modified the weights so that they sum to sample size.

THE DISTRIBUTION OF INCOME AND WEALTH

In this section, I examine the marginal distributions of disposable income, gross wealth, debts and net wealth. Table 9.2 shows some descriptive statistics for the main resources that I study, namely disposable income, gross wealth, debt and net wealth (gross wealth minus debt). Average income increased across all three surveys, but gross and net wealth (as well as debt) decreased from 1987 to 1994, only to increase again. Average net wealth increased between 1987 and 1998 from 34 538 euros to 41 362 euros – driven by the increase in average gross wealth. Almost all households have some assets; the proportion of those with zero wealth hovered around 1.5 per cent in all three surveys. The proportion with zero debt, however, increased

Table 9.2   Descriptive statistics on main economic resources

		Mean (euros)	Gini	Zeros (%)	N[a]
Disposable income	1987	12456	19.7	0.0	5566
	1994	13285	21.2	0.1	5210
	1998	15296	25.2	0.0	3893
Wealth	1987	42249	47.0	1.6	5566
	1994	39561	48.7	1.4	5210
	1998	49297	52.3	1.3	3893
Debt	1987	7711	66.3	26.8	5566
	1994	7458	69.9	34.9	5210
	1998	7935	70.9	39.3	3893
Net wealth	1987	34538	55.1	10.2	5566
	1994	32103	60.4	13.6	5210
	1998	41362	61.5	11.2	3893
Wealth subject to taxation, tax records	1987	15998	56.9	11.1	5566
	1994	22064	55.7	19.2	5210
	1998	23805	59.4	21.3	3893
Debt, tax records	1987	10592	66.8	25.3	5566
	1994	9975	71.6	38.4	5210
	1998	9242	70.3	34.3	3893
Net wealth, tax records	1987	5406	162.4	40.0	5566
	1994	12089	109.4	38.9	5210
	1998	14562	99.0	39.1	3893

Note: a. N is the number of households, but the statistics apply person weights.

Source: Author's calculations from wealth survey microdata.

by 12.5 percentage points, from 1987 to 1998, perhaps driven by the very high and volatile market interest rates (to which most new debt became tied after capital market liberalization in the late 1980s).

The estimated Gini coefficients suggest that all four variables have become more dispersed over time. The pattern of disposable income inequality is familiar from Figure 9.1. Its Gini coefficient increased by five percentage points, an increase of almost a quarter from the level in 1987. The Gini coefficients of gross wealth, debt and net wealth increased by similar magnitudes.

The estimated Lorenz curves for each variable are shown in Figure 9.3, and the differences between different data waves are shown in Figure 9.4. The Lorenz curves suggest that increases in relative inequality are most often unequivocal – the curves rarely cross. For income and gross wealth, the Lorenz curves for 1988 and 1994 lie very close to each other, while the curve for 1998 is clearly below these, suggesting that the increase in dispersion occurs in the late 1990s. The distribution of debt, on the other hand, becomes more dispersed in 1994. The Lorenz curve of net wealth, the only variable considered here that can take values on the whole real line, is below zero to around one-third of the population. The first three decile-group means of net wealth are negative in all three years. The inequality of net wealth in 1998 does not Lorenz dominate that in 1994. However, in this, as in all other cases, the 1998 Lorenz curve is everywhere below that in 1987.

Table 9.3 shows descriptive statistics for the main components of wealth and income in the different years. Average household earnings increased slightly after a substantial fall in 1994, while property income increased substantially, by more than a factor of three, from 742 euros to 2532 euros. Transfer income increased by almost one-half between 1987 and 1994 (driven, in part, by the substantial increase in unemployment) and decreased only slightly by 1998. Average taxes also increased over the years.

The U-shaped pattern in gross wealth is driven mainly by the housing and securities components of wealth. Securities declined between 1987 and 1994 and increased substantially in 1998. While the value of housing wealth did not decline between 1987 and 1994, it increased quite substantially between 1994 and 1998. The decline in debt is mostly due to a decrease in mortgages.

Recall, from Table 9.2 and Figure 9.3, that the inequality of the main economic resources increased across the wealth surveys. This is not uniformly true, or even mostly true, of their main components. The Gini coefficients of the components are for the whole population, rather than for those with positive amounts recorded. As the last three columns in Table 9.3 attest, the proportion of the population with zero resources often undergoes large changes across the years. The somewhat erratic changes in the Gini coefficients of particular components may be a result both of changes in the distribution of the component among those with positive amounts and in the proportion of those with zero amounts.[2]

The data in Karhunen and Keloharju (2001, p. 210) suggest that, between 1995 and 2000, the inequality of wealth in publicly traded shares, among those holding shares increased somewhat. The Lorenz curves drawn for those two years do not cross, and the Gini coefficient increased from 0.859 to 0.874. The point estimate based on the wealth survey for overall securities wealth among the whole population was 0.952 and 0.950 in 1994 and 1998, respectively (see Table 9.3). Karhunen and Keloharju (2001) provide the Gini coefficient for the whole population's holdings of publicly traded shares in June 2000, at which point they estimate a Gini coefficient of 0.983.

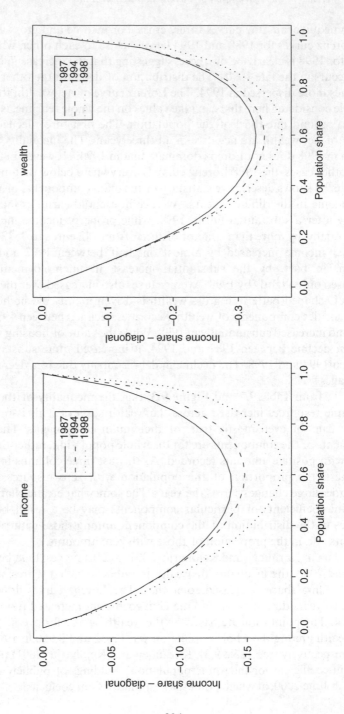

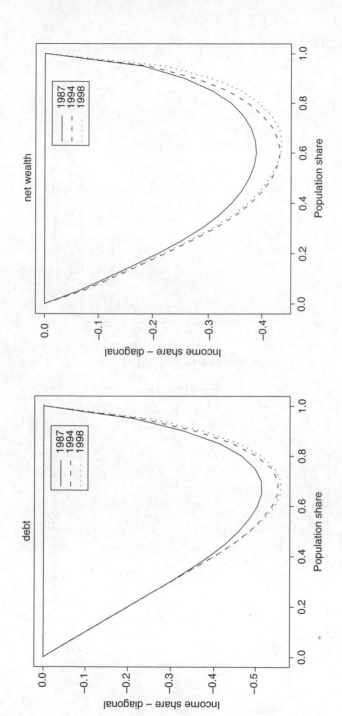

Source: Author's calculations from wealth survey microdata.

Figure 9.3 Lorenz curves of the main economic resources

305

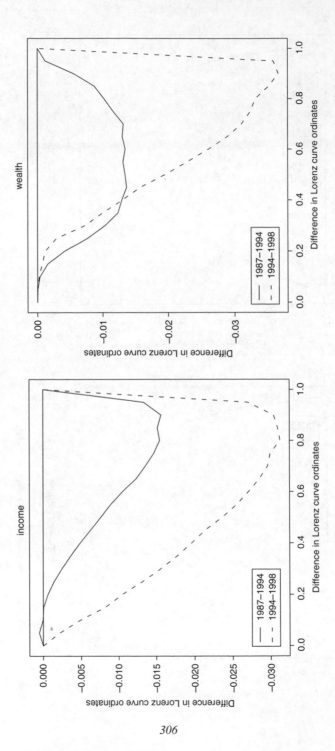

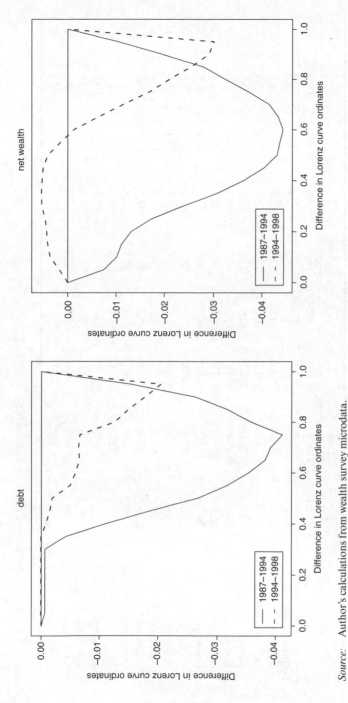

Source: Author's calculations from wealth survey microdata.

Figure 9.4   Differences across years in Lorenz curves of the main economic resources

Table 9.3 *Descriptive statistics on components of main economic resources*

	Mean			Gini			Zeros		
	1987	1994	1998	1987	1994	1998	1987	1994	1998
Disposable income	12 456	13 285	15 296	19.7	21.2	25.2	0.0	0.1	0.0
Earnings	12 616	1036	2990	40.0	49.4	48.7	7.5	16.0	17.7
Property income	742	1423	2532	78.8	73.8	74.6	22.9	25.9	23.8
Transfers	3384	5621	5362	62.0	48.4	52.8	8.6	5.9	7.2
Taxes	4287	4796	5588	43.9	44.2	46.3	3.6	1.8	1.8
Wealth	42 249	39 561	49 297	47.0	48.7	2.3	1.6	1.4	1.3
Housing	29 754	29 485	35 841	48.7	50.9	53.0	26.1	26.9	26.8
Leisure housing	3723	4366	4773	89.0	88.6	89.2	77.9	78.6	78.5
Transport equipment	3135	3220	4040	62.4	61.7	62.4	27.1	23.6	22.2
Bank deposits	3806	4132	4557	74.4	77.2	75.8	14.8	13.8	7.7
Securities	1463	1234	3263	94.3	94.5	93.5	52.2	69.7	61.1
Other financial assets	368	687	1291	90.3	87.4	91.2	65.6	38.3	53.3
Debt	7711	7458	7935	66.3	69.9	70.9	26.8	34.9	39.3
Mortgages	5770	5917	5821	74.9	77.0	78.4	53.3	60.0	62.1
Consumer loans	1038	947	981	79.8	85.8	86.8	54.8	59.0	71.1
Study loans	463	469	374	92.7	92.4	92.0	83.5	85.5	85.2
Other loans	439	125	759	93.7	99.3	97.1	85.4	97.8	92.4

Source: Author's calculations from wealth survey microdata.

308

Next, I examine the distributions using nonparametric methods. In particular, I have estimated the density functions, using local polynomial methods (Loader 1999) with adaptive bandwidths. Although pictures based on nonparametric density methods are informative, deriving such estimates is, in this context, not without its problems. In order to compare resulting estimates across time, much care needs to be exercised in estimating the densities for a resource variable in different years.

Nonparametric density estimates, by their nature, are suited for examining the properties of continuous variates while a substantial fraction of the population has zero income, wealth and/or debt. The lump at zero needs to be dealt with because a large lump causes serious problems for density estimation. The data are also very highly skewed, with very sparse data in the right tail of the distribution. This problem is even more pronounced for the distributions of wealth and debt than it is for the distribution of income. There are a number of ways to deal with this problem, including varying the bandwidth and transforming the data to be less widely dispersed. I resort to both methods, but this remains an issue. In particular, although taking the natural logarithm of the level data deals with the sparseness of the data in the right tail, it creates a new problem of sparseness in the left tail.

The estimated densities for all four economic resources in the three waves of data are shown in Figure 9.5. The differences in density estimates across consecutive waves of data are shown in Figure 9.6. The densities are estimated using local third-degree polynomial approximations of the density, using adaptive k-nearest neighbour bandwidths, with the fraction k chosen using a combination of likelihood cross-validation and least-squares cross-validation methods (see Loader, 1999, ch 11).[3]

The estimated densities are not very informative in themselves, and make it hard to see the changes in inequality that they generate. The differences in estimated densities allow a closer view of the changes that have taken place. The changes in the distribution of wealth between 1987 and 1994 occurred as a small shift of mass from two regions just under 100 000 euros, both to the left and to the right. The shift from 1994 to 1998 was dominated by a shift of mass, to the right, around 100 000 euros. The distribution of net wealth shifted in the same manner as gross wealth. The distribution of income also shifted to the right, but the range of income affected in the two periods was narrower than it was for wealth.

While density estimation has been used successfully to analyse sources of changes in inequality, it is less practical to use that procedure here.[4] Because the sample sizes are fairly small, interesting breakdowns, especially along several characteristics, will yield very small sample sizes. This is even more of a problem for me because I am, in part, interested in the bivariate distribution of income and wealth, where the sample size requirement is

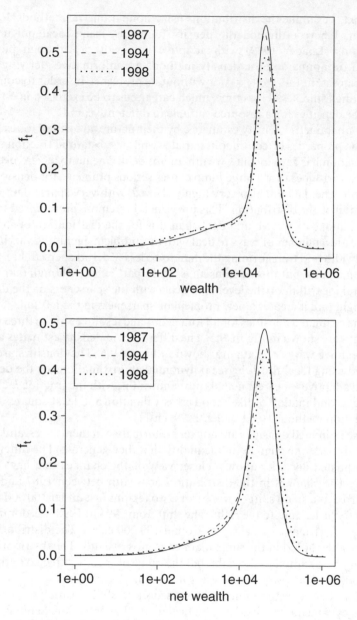

Source: Author's calculations from wealth survey microdata.

Figure 9.5   Estimated density functions

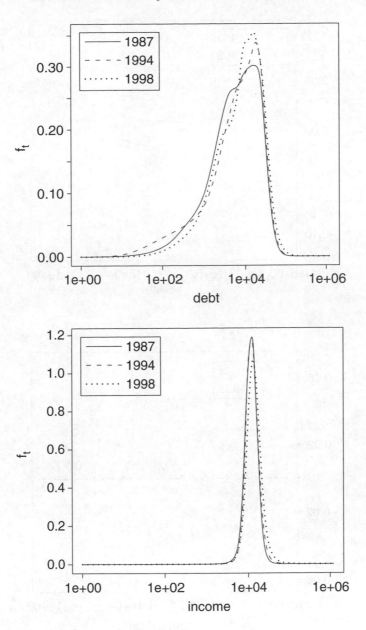

Figure 9.5   (continued)

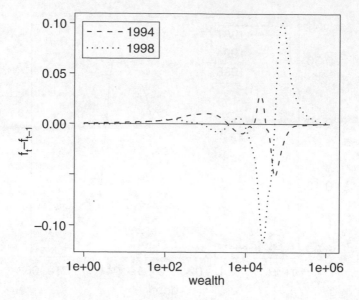

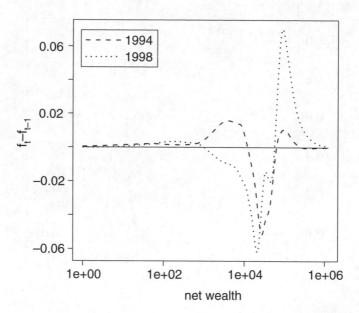

Source: Author's calculations from wealth survey microdata.

Figure 9.6   Differences in estimated density functions

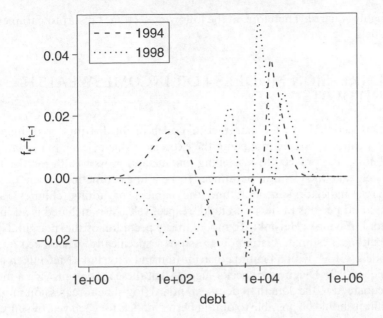

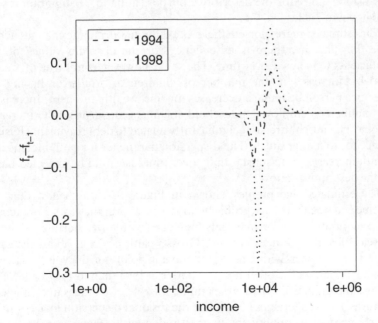

Figure 9.6   (continued)

roughly squared. Therefore, in the following section, I resort to parametric models.

REGRESSION MODELS FOR INCOME, WEALTH AND DEBTS

In this section, I consider parametric models of the distribution of income and wealth. I start by modelling the expected value of each marginal distribution and proceed to modelling income and gross wealth jointly. The models take the location parameter to be a linear function of age (seven interval indicators); gender; and the number of adults, children, and employed persons in the household, respectively. Also included is an indicator for living in Helsinki. To model the (expectation of the) marginal distributions, I estimate Gamma regressions – specifically, generalized linear models (GLM) with a Gamma distribution and a log link (McCullagh and Nelder 1989). Diagnostic checks suggest that these models provide a more adequate fit to the data than does a standard (log-)linear regression model. While it should be possible to obtain better models for each year/resource – in the sense that they give a better fit to the data – these estimated Gamma regressions suffice for the descriptive purpose at hand.[5] Estimation results are shown in Tables 9.4–9.6.

The estimated regression coefficients exhibit few dramatic changes across time. For income, there is a tendency for the absolute values of the coefficients to increase over time. The same, however, is not true of wealth or debt. Increases in the number of children or adults, or having the reference person be female, decreases income, wealth and debt. Increasing the number of employed household members, unsurprisingly, increases income. Having children is insignificantly related to debt. Living in Helsinki seems not to matter much. The dispersion parameter for both income and wealth increases quite substantially over time, as would be expected based on the descriptives above.

The estimated age profiles, shown in Figure 9.7, do suggest that, for income and wealth, the age profile became steeper over the years. For income, the peak now occurs at remarkably high ages, with lower starting values for 30-year-olds and younger persons. Gross wealth peaks at about the same point and is steeper, with a far lower starting point, for the young. The age profile of debt, on the other hand, is flatter in 1998 than in 1987 or 1994.

I use the estimated GLMs to examine the role of changes in coefficients ('returns'), characteristics ('X's') and the residual dispersion in accounting for changes in inequality in income and wealth. There is a large and growing literature on trying to sort out which factors give rise to what part

Table 9.4   Regression model – dependent variable: income

	1987	1994	1998
(Intercept)	9.337	9.251	9.246
	(0.018)	(0.023)	(0.041)
Age [30,40)	0.128	0.137	0.163
	(0.014)	(0.018)	(0.034)
Age [40,50)	0.204	0.198	0.260
	(0.014)	(0.018)	(0.034)
Age [50,60)	0.228	0.320	0.411
	(0.016)	(0.020)	(0.035)
Age [60,70)	0.208	0.393	0.526
	(0.019)	(0.024)	(0.042)
Age [70,80)	0.145	0.330	0.419
	(0.023)	(0.026)	(0.046)
Age [80,100]	0.150	0.272	0.551
	(0.036)	(0.038)	(0.061)
Female 1	−0.084	−0.085	−0.111
	(0.010)	(0.011)	(0.020)
Adults	−0.041	−0.036	−0.040
	(0.007)	(0.009)	(0.015)
Children	−0.081	−0.066	−0.067
	(0.004)	(0.005)	(0.008)
Employed	0.158	0.218	0.262
	(0.007)	(0.008)	(0.015)
Order (Helsinki)	−0.000	−0.000	−0.000
	(0.000)	(0.000)	(0.000)
Dispersion	0.10	0.14	0.32
n	5502.00	5152.00	3867.00
k	12.00	12.00	12.00
AIC	105 517.96	99 850.22	77 161.03

Note: Standard errors in parentheses.

Source: Author's calculations from wealth survey microdata.

of inequality.[6] I settle here for the following simple procedure based on the estimated Gamma regressions.

'Model-based' inequality is the inequality of predicted income, based on the regression model for the location parameter and the estimated dispersion parameter.[7] I estimate the inequality of model-based inequality by predicting (for each case) the value of the location parameter, based on the GLM estimates. I then use the predicted location parameter and the ML estimate of the dispersion parameter to draw (again for each case) a random number from

Table 9.5   Regression model – dependent variable: wealth

	1987	1994	1998
(Intercept)	10.221	9.559	9.569
	(0.053)	(0.058)	(0.086)
Age [30,40)	0.560	0.550	0.735
	(0.041)	(0.047)	(0.071)
Age [40,50)	0.759	0.863	1.007
	(0.042)	(0.046)	(0.071)
Age [50,60)	0.895	1.196	1.422
	(0.047)	(0.051)	(0.074)
Age [60,70)	1.025	1.651	1.843
	(0.056)	(0.060)	(0.087)
Age [70,80)	0.969	1.492	1.726
	(0.067)	(0.067)	(0.096)
Age [80,100]	0.987	1.448	1.829
	(0.106)	(0.097)	(0.129)
Female 1	−0.179	−0.185	−0.170
	(0.030)	(0.029)	(0.042)
Adults	−0.083	−0.057	−0.059
	(0.022)	(0.022)	(0.032)
Children	−0.072	−0.057	−0.078
	(0.012)	(0.013)	(0.017)
Employed	0.181	0.325	0.375
	(0.021)	(0.021)	(0.032)
Order (Helsinki)	−0.000	−0.000	−0.000
	(0.000)	(0.000)	(0.000)
Dispersion	0.90	0.92	1.42
n	5502.00	5152.00	3867.00
k	2.00	12.00	12.00
AIC	127 149.98	117 975.85	89 747.52

Note: Standard errors in parentheses.

Source: Author's calculations from wealth survey microdata.

the Gamma distribution. The Gini coefficient is calculated across all cases. To stabilize the estimates of model-based inequality, I repeat this procedure 20 times and take as its estimate the average value of the Gini coefficient.[8]

Consider, first, the distribution of income, for which the decomposition is shown in the upper panel of Table 9.7. The point of departure is inequality in the base year, say t_1, as measured by the Gini coefficient. This is shown, for the period 1987–94, on the first line in the first column. The calculation for 1987 is 0.219 (estimated without using sampling weights).

Table 9.6   Regression model – dependent variable: debt

	1987	1994	1998
(Intercept)	9.667	9.566	9.494
	(0.072)	(0.079)	(0.106)
Age [30,40)	0.159	0.135	0.134
	(0.052)	(0.059)	(0.080)
Age [40,50)	−0.059	−0.081	−0.102
	(0.054)	(0.059)	(0.081)
Age [50,60)	−0.285	−0.286	−0.091
	(0.066)	(0.072)	(0.090)
Age [60,70)	−0.292	−0.645	0.044
	(0.097)	(0.113)	(0.138)
Age [70,80)	−0.816	−0.414	−0.103
	(0.150)	(0.165)	(0.216)
Age [80,100]	−1.172	−1.144	0.477
	(0.535)	(0.590)	(0.694)
Female1	−0.162	−0.028	−0.099
	(0.042)	(0.042)	(0.053)
Adults	−0.252	−0.212	−0.276
	(0.031)	(0.032)	(0.041)
Children	−0.017	−0.008	0.027
	(0.015)	(0.016)	(0.018)
Employed	0.165	0.238	0.361
	(0.030)	(0.029)	(0.040)
Order (Helsinki)	−0.000	−0.000	−0.000
	(0.000)	(0.000)	(0.000)
Dispersion	1.24	1.19	1.30
n	3 775.00	3 245.00	2 266.00
k	12.001	2.00	12.00
AIC	82 347.84	69 317.01	48 931.02

Note: Standard errors in parentheses.

Source: Author's calculations from wealth survey microdata.

Contrast this with model-based inequality in t_2, shown in the second column as 0.2. Letting the GLM coefficients take their 1994 values increases the Gini coefficient to 0.209, while, in addition, letting the covariates take the 1994 values (but holding the dispersion at its 1987 value) lowers the Gini coefficient to 0.207. Furthermore, letting the dispersion parameter take its 1994 value (which is the inequality of income, based on the Gamma regression in 1994) pushes the Gini coefficient to 0.213, while the unweighted estimate, based on the data, is 0.222.

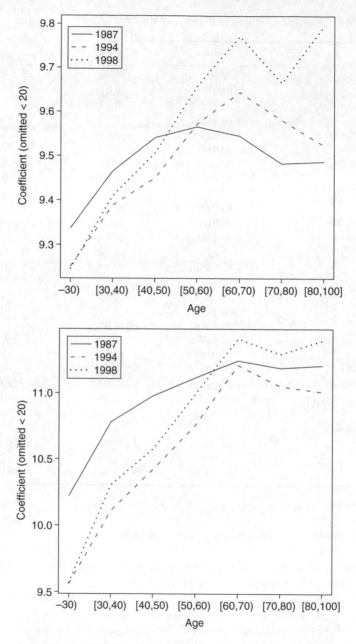

Source: Author's calculations from wealth survey microdata.

Figure 9.7 Estimated age profiles, Gamma regressions

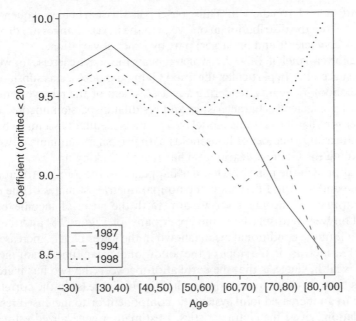

Figure 9.7   (continued)

Table 9.7   Counter-factual Gini coefficients for income and wealth

	Data in t_1	Model in t_1	Coef in t_2	+ Xs in t_2	+ Dispersion in t_2	Data in t_2
Income						
1987–94	0.219	0.200	0.209	0.207	0.213	0.222
1994–98	0.222	0.213	0.227	0.227	0.254	0.268
1987–98	0.219	0.200	0.226	0.221	0.254	0.268
Wealth						
1987–94	0.457	0.534	0.560	0.559	0.576	0.472
1994–98	0.472	0.576	0.587	0.587	0.596	0.493
1987–98	0.457	0.534	0.573	0.567	0.596	0.493

Note: Counter-factual Gini coefficients based on Gamma GLMs.

Source: Author's calculations from wealth survey microdata.

The numbers in the second row, for changes from 1994 to 1998, suggest that coefficients pushed inequality up and characteristics brought it back, in part. This is true for 1987 to 1998 as well. In 1998, however, the regression model in 1998 does not 'overshoot' inequality, as it does in 1994.

Instead, it underpredicts it. Thus, based on this particular sequence (of moving from the distribution in one year to the next), changes are driven in part by coefficients and in (larger) part by residual variation.

The lower panel of Table 9.7, which repeats the above exercise for wealth, is less successful. In particular, the fitted Gamma model seems substantially to overshoot inequality, rendering any assessment of the relative contributions of coefficients, characteristics and residual dispersion unconvincing. The reason that the Gamma model overpredicts inequality seems to be that there are a large number of households with very small amounts of wealth, something the Gamma distribution has trouble picking up.[9]

To approach the issue of what has happened to the joint distribution of income and wealth, I first show the nonparametric estimates of the mean and variance of income, given wealth. Both the mean of income, conditional on wealth (displayed in the upper panel of Figure 9.8) and the variance, about the conditional mean (shown in the lower panel), increase over time. The increase in the slope of the conditional mean function of income, given wealth, suggests that the correlation between the two has increased across time. In order to investigate whether this increase in the correlation is due to an increased joint systematic component or to increased residual correlation, given the characteristics, I estimate a generalized estimating equation (GEE) with a Gamma distribution and log link for gross wealth and income, jointly, in the three years (Zeger et al. 1988).[10]

The estimated coefficients, shown in Table 9.8, are fairly close to the estimates of the univariate GLMs. This is unsurprising, as GEE basically is bivariate GLM that is robust with respect to the correlation of the multiple measurements. What I would like to point out at this stage is the estimated residual correlation of income and wealth, shown near the bottom of Table 9.8. While this parameter is treated by GEE as a nuisance parameter, rather than as one of substantive interest, the increase in its value from 0.35 to 0.42 suggests that the correlation of the unsystematic part of income and wealth did increase across the years.[11]

The distributions (joint density and conditional mean curve) of the raw residuals from the GEE model for 1987 and 1994 are shown in Figure 9.9. The broken lines, showing the distribution in 1998, suggest that the dispersion increased, and that the mean curve of income, given wealth, also became steeper for the residuals. The increase in the correlation can be driven by many things. It is not, however, simply an 'increased returns to wealth' phenomenon. The correlation between property income and wealth, and between property income and security wealth, was higher in 1998 than in 1994. But the correlation was as high or higher in 1987. The nature of the increased residual correlation needs to be investigated further.

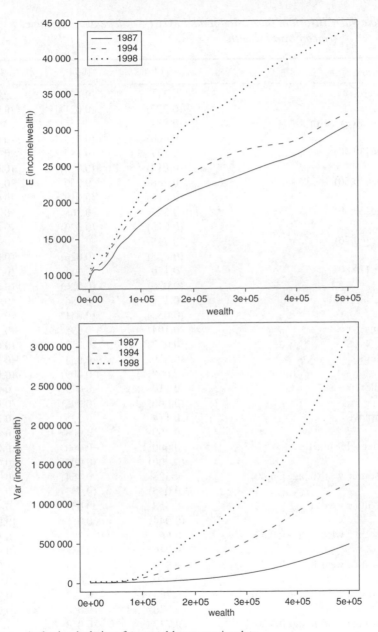

Source: Author's calculations from wealth survey microdata.

*Figure 9.8   Nonparametric estimates of mean and variance of income
given wealth*

Table 9.8 Bivariate regression model (GEE) – dependent variables:
income and wealth

	1987	1994	1998
(Intercept)	9.311	9.271	9.373
	(0.022)	(0.021)	(0.041)
ResourceWealth	0.881	0.357	0.550
	(0.060)	(0.059)	(0.087)
Age [30,40)	0.177	0.187	0.225
	(0.017)	(0.018)	(0.038)
Age [40,50)	0.260	0.250	0.310
	(0.016)	(0.019)	(0.037)
Age [50,60)	0.243	0.368	0.425
	(0.018)	(0.020)	(0.039)
Age [60,70)	0.215	0.420	0.480
	(0.025)	(0.026)	(0.054)
Age [70,80)	0.170	0.351	0.347
	(0.026)	(0.026)	(0.057)
Age [80,100]	0.179	0.284	0.471
	(0.052)	(0.041)	(0.123)
Female 1	−0.104	−0.095	−0.106
	(0.012)	(0.012)	(0.021)
Adults	−0.089	−0.053	−0.058
	(0.009)	(0.009)	(0.016)
Children	−0.110	−0.075	−0.091
	(0.006)	(0.006)	(0.009)
Employed	0.174	0.225	0.234
	(0.009)	(0.008)	(0.016)
Order (Helsinki)	0.000	−0.000	−0.000
	(0.000)	(0.000)	(0.000)
Resource wealth: age [30,40)	0.428	0.454	0.502
	(0.045)	(0.057)	(0.082)
Resource wealth: age [40,50)	0.558	0.659	0.664
	(0.044)	(0.055)	(0.078)
Resource wealth: age [50,60)	0.662	0.882	0.858
	(0.046)	(0.056)	(0.077)
Resource wealth: age [60,70)	0.737	1.234	1.027
	(0.050)	(0.061)	(0.088)
Resource wealth: age [70,80)	0.763	0.122	0.984
	(0.076)	(0.068)	(0.094)
Resource wealth: age [80,100]	0.772	0.072	1.020
	(0.122)	(0.104)	(0.177)
Resource wealth: female 1	−0.093	−0.082	−0.045
	(0.029)	(0.026)	(0.037)

Table 9.8   (continued)

	1987	1994	1998
Resource wealth: adults	−0.066	−0.028	−0.024
	(0.018)	(0.022)	(0.029)
Resource wealth: children	0.009	0.011	−0.024
	(0.011)	(0.012)	(0.015)
Resource wealth: employed	−0.008	0.090	0.043
	(0.015)	(0.020)	(0.026)
Resource wealth: order (Helsinki)	0.000	0.000	0.000
	(0.000)	(0.000)	(0.000)
Corr 1	0.35	0.31	0.42
Dispersion	0.54	0.56	0.84
n	5490.00	5140.00	3855.00
AIC	1800	1666	1427
	318.06	384.26	922.01

Note: Standard errors in parentheses.

Source: Author's calculations from wealth survey microdata.

CONCLUSIONS

The analysis in this chapter demonstrates that (1) the inequality of income has increased substantially in Finland from 1987 to 1998; (2) this increase was accompanied by an increase in the inequality of wealth (gross and net); and (3) these increases are only to a minor extent due to changes in observed population characteristics or the 'returns' to those characteristics. The joint distribution of income and wealth is characterized by a substantial increase in the residual correlation and conditional variance of wealth, given income.

This chapter has documented the trends in the inequality of income and wealth and has investigated the dimensions along which inequality has changed. The results suggest that population structure does not account for many of the changes, and that the increases in the inequality of income and wealth seem, at least in part, to be two sides of the same phenomenon (reflected in the increase in residual dependence). There are many possible explanations for this, including a substantial increase in either (the inequality of) property income (that is, returns to wealth). or in the holding of wealth that generates property income, or both. The estimated correlation coefficients between the wealth-related income components and wealth, however, have not increased between 1987 and 1998. And, while

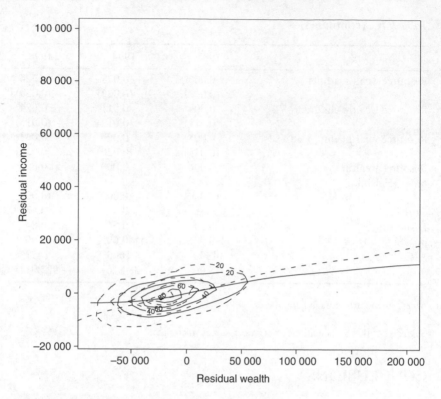

Source: Author's calculations from wealth survey microdata.

Figure 9.9   Residuals of income and wealth, GEE model in 1987 and 1998

financial wealth has increased over time, it is still a fairly small part of overall household wealth. Thus, a simple explanation that features the returns to property in the lead role is not sufficient to account for the observed changes in inequality.

The fact that at least part of the increase in income inequality is due to increases in property income does have some policy relevance. Income from financial assets is, in Finland, taxed at source, at a flat rate. As the share of property income has increased dramatically at the top of the income distribution, this has tended to bring down effective tax rates, reducing tax progressivity. Finland moved to taxing capital income only at source, rather than at both the source and recipient level, in 1994. If inequality reduction is a policy goal, then the shift away from the double taxation of property income (by taxing it only at source) may need to be reconsidered in light of the large changes in the inequality of income and wealth.

NOTES

* The author would like to thank Jan Otto Andersson, Leif Nordberg, Anders Klevmarken and Markku Säylä for helpful comments.
1. See Statistics Finland (1991), Statistics Finland (1997) and Statistics Finland (2000) for survey descriptions.
2. I have estimated Gini coefficients without first censoring the distributions at zero, which, for disposable income (in general) and net wealth (in particular) may lead to very large estimates that are not constrained to lie in the unit interval.
3. The algorithm uses a fraction k of the nearest neighbours at each evaluation point.
4. See, for example, DiNardo et al. (1996) or Burkhauser et al. (1996).
5. The models are estimated for observations with positive observations on the dependent variable. This matters little for income or for wealth, where the number of zeros is low, but it is of greater consequence for debt.
6. See, for example, Jenkins (1994), Juhn et al. (1993) and, for a recent overview, Shorrocks (1999).
7. The estimates of the dispersion parameters that I use are not the regular GLM ones, which are considered to be nuisance parameters, but maximum likelihood estimates of them (Venables and Ripley 1999). The MLEs tend to be a bit lower than the numbers reported in Tables 9.4–9.6.
8. This is a little like the multiple-imputation procedures that are recommended for use when missing values occur in the data. In that case, different imputation rules are implemented, resulting in multiple versions of the data with different imputed values in place of the missing values. The parameter of interest is estimated as the average across parameter estimates for each single imputation round.
9. I have also estimated 'regression' models for three parameter distributions, such as the Singh-Maddala (also known as the Burr distribution) with and without covariates, for income, wealth and debt. Most distributions, including the Singh-Maddala, fail to generate usable estimates for wealth or debt. Results for the three-parameter distributions are not reported in this chapter.
10. The use of the GEE approach here is related to the seemingly unrelated regression (SUR). If I used a gaussian error distribution, this would be very similar to SUR, with log income and log wealth as dependent variables.
11. Since the correlation is treated as a nuisance parameter, the standard GEE algorithms do not produce any estimate of its variance, which is why the change in point estimates needs to be treated with some caution.

REFERENCES

Bradbury, Bruce and Markus Jäntti (1999), 'Child poverty across industrialized countries', Innocenti Occasional paper 71, UNICEF, International Child Development Centre, Florence.

Burkhauser, Richard V., Amy D. Crews, Mary C. Daly and Stephen P. Jenkins (1996), 'Where in the world is the middle class? A cross-national comparison of the vanishing middle class using kernel density estimates', Working paper, ESRC Research Centre on Micro-social Change, University of Essex.

Danziger, Sheldon and Michael Taussig (1979), 'The income unit and the anatomy of income distribution', *Review of Income and Wealth*, **25**(4), 365–75.

Davies, James B. and Anthony F. Shorrocks (2000), 'The distribution of wealth', in Anthony B. Atkinson and François Bourguignon (eds), *Handbook of Income Distribution*, vol. 1, New York: North-Holland, pp. 605–75.

DiNardo, John, Nicole M. Fortin and Thomas Lemieux (1996), 'Labor market institutions and the distribution of wages, 1973–1992: a semi-parametric approach', *Econometrica*, **64**(5), 1001–46.
Ilmanen, Matti and Matti Keloharju (1999), 'Shareownership in Finland', *Liiketaloudellinen aikakauskirja*, **48**(2), 257–85.
Jenkins, Stephen P. (1994), 'Accounting for inequality trends: decomposition analyses for the UK 1971–1986', *Economica*, **61**(4), 1–35.
Juhn, Chinjui, Kevin Murphy and Brooks Pierce (1993), 'Wage inequality and the rise in returns to skill', *Journal of Political Economy*, **101**(3), 410–43.
Karhunen, Jussi and Matti Keloharju (2001), 'Shareownership in Finland', *Liiketaloudellinen aikakauskirja*, **50**(2), 188–226.
Loader, Clive (1999), *Local Regression and Likelihood*, New York: Springer-Verlag.
McCullagh, Peter and John A. Nelder (1989), *Generalized Linear Models*, 2nd edn, New York: Chapman & Hall.
National Research Council (1995), *Measuring Poverty: A New Approach*, Washington, DC: National Academy Press.
Riihelä, Marja, Risto Sullström and Matti Tuomala (2001), 'What lies behind the unprecedented increase in income inequality in Finland during the 1990s?', Discussion Paper 247, Government Institute for Economic Research, Helsinki.
Riihelä, Marja, Risto Sullström, Ilpo Suoniemi and Matti Tuomala (2002), 'Income inequality in Finland during the 1990s', in J. Kalela, J. Kiander, U. Kivikuru, H. Loikkanen and J. Simpura (eds), *Down from the Heavens, Up from the Ashes*, Government Institute for Economic Research, Helsinki, pp. 385–410.
Shorrocks, Antony F. (1999), 'Decomposition procedures for distributional analysis: a unified framework based on the shapley value', unpublished manuscript, University of Essex and Institute for Fiscal Studies.
Sinko, Pekka (1991), 'Varallisuus, pääomamarkkinat ja kotitalouksien kulutus – mihin katosi säästäminen?', VATT Keskustelualoitteita (VATT Discussion Paper) 1, Valtion taloudellinen tutkimuskeskus (Government Institute for Economic Research), Helsinki.
Statistics Finland (1991), *Household Saving 1988*, Income and Consumption 1991:3, Helsinki: Statistics Finland.
Statistics Finland (1997), *Household Wealth and Debt in Finland*, Income and Consumption 1997:17, Helsinki: Statistics Finland.
Statistics Finland (2000), *Household Wealth*, Income and Consumption 2000:26, Helsinki: Statistics Finland.
Suoniemi, Ilpo (2000), 'Decomposing the gini and the variation coefficients by income sources and income recipients', Working Paper 169, Labour Institute for Economic Research, Helsinki.
Tuomala, Matti and Jouko Vilmunen (1985), 'On the trends over time in the degree of concentration of wealth in Finland', University of Helsinki, Helsinki.
Venables, William N. and Brian D. Ripley (1999), *Modern Applied Statistics with S-Plus*, 3rd edn, New York: Springer-Verlag.
Virén, Matti (2002), 'Rahat vanhoille, velat nuorille', unpublished manuscript (in Finnish), University of Turku.
Zeger, Scott L., Kung-Yee Liang and Paul S. Albert (1988), 'Models for longitudinal data: a GEE approach', *Biometrics*, **44**, 1049–60.

PART III

Other Types of Wealth Inequality

10. Parental wealth effects on living standards and asset holdings: results from Chile

Florencia Torche and Seymour Spilerman*

INTRODUCTION

This chapter examines aspects of the replication of inequality across generations and attempts to assess the extent to which parental resources influence the life chances and living standards of adult children. We expect household wealth to be a critical matter, especially in a society in which there is a weak public safety net or in which the credit market is inefficient. In the first case, families need to self-insure – accumulate savings to smooth consumption expenditures over periods of income fluctuation, such as might result from illness or job loss. In the second case, financial wealth is necessary in order to finance large expenditure items (for example, a home, a new business) or to provide collateral in seeking a bank loan for such an expenditure.

These considerations can be especially relevant to the welfare of children and young adults. In the absence of public support programmes, poor families may have difficulty keeping children in school, especially teenage children, and forgoing the earnings that would otherwise be brought to the household. Such calculations, it is recognized, are responsible for the high drop-out rate from middle school, noted for less-developed countries (Moser 1998). Similarly, substantial costs are often involved in establishing a new household, which can pose a major burden for a young couple that has had little time in which to accumulate savings (Spilerman 2004). In each case, parental assets can play a critical role in advancing the life chances and economic well-being of the offspring.

If parental resources are important to the financial welfare and living standards of children, there remains a matter of the mechanics of the transmission process. This issue entails, first of all, a consideration of parental decision making regarding the amount to invest in a child's educational attainment versus providing assistance in the form of financial gifts (Becker

1981). A second consideration involves the pattern of allocation of direct transfers over the life course – both in terms of timing and purpose of the transfer: whether for the purchase of critical household items, or at times of financial crisis, or as regular ongoing assistance. There is also the related matter of the contribution of asset holdings to living standards. Indeed, we might have less interest in the wealth distribution of a country if most families can live reasonably well from earnings; if household wealth, for example, accounts for the disparity between driving a Chevrolet versus a BMW, rather than the gap between owning and not owning a vehicle.

A consideration of the impact of parental wealth on the living standards of offspring requires an examination of direct and indirect effects. Following Becker (1981), parental wealth can influence living standards through investments in children's education, permitting more years of attendance or enrolment in better-quality schools and consequently higher income, or through direct transfers of financial and material assets. Our focus in this chapter, however, departs from Becker's concern with parental decision making in that we seek to assess the contribution of the different modes of parental transfer (educational investments vs direct assistance) to aspects of a family's well-being. As a consequence, we are interested in which dimensions of the family's economic well-being are financed from their labour market income, and possibly reflect parental investments in education, and which are supported by direct transfers of parental resources.

These matters may have very different resolutions in developed and in less-developed countries, in nations with a comprehensive public welfare system and in countries with weak public service programmes, since patterns of parental assistance are deeply influenced by the availability of public support programmes as well as by other institutional arrangements (Kohli 2005; Attias-Donfut and Wolff 2000; Spilerman 2004). In the present chapter we examine the noted issues in Chile, a less-developed country, one that in recent years has experienced an extensive privatization of its public social service programmes (Raczynski 1994). Chile is of interest both as a case study in the organization of parental transfers in that reasonably good data are available on the topic, and as a setting in which considerable parental assistance is required for the successful establishment of the new generation.

In an earlier study (Spilerman and Torche 2004) parental resource effects were addressed from the perspective of living standard *potential*, essentially a consideration of the parental effects on measures of the household income and wealth stock of offspring. One finding was that parental wealth influences household income largely through its impact on educational attainment. The educational system in Chile is broadly inclusive, however, and was found not to be merely a conduit for the transmission of parental advantage. Indeed, the addition of the respondent's educational attainment to an earnings or a household income equation contributed substantially to the variance explained by the measures of parental wealth and parental background. This was not the case, however, with respect to the determination of household wealth. In this instance there was strong evidence of the importance of direct transfers, with little indication of a possibility that families in Chile that lack parental resources succeed in accumulating much in the way of a wealth stock from earnings alone.

In this chapter we continue to explore the relation between parental wealth and economic well-being, though we move from an analysis of living standard potential – a measure of capacity based on income and wealth – to an examination of *realized* living standards, as evidenced by the consumption behaviour of families. The chapter is divided into four sections. In the first, we describe the Chilean setting, compare it with the United States, and discuss the empirical association between parental wealth and different dimensions of adult children's economic well-being. Not surprisingly, we note that the rate of asset ownership tends to be lower in Chile and that there is a greater tendency to asset concentration at high income levels. There is one noteworthy exception: home ownership in Chile is rather evenly dispersed among the income deciles, a theme that is developed later in the chapter.

The second section addresses the impact of parental wealth on two broad dimensions of the economic well-being of adult children, namely living standard (as expressed by consumption level) and asset ownership. This analysis reveals a consistent pattern: parental wealth has a positive impact on each consumption measure, an effect that is net of other parental attributes. This effect is largely indirect, operating through the parental contribution to child's education and labour market earnings. In comparison, a similar analysis of the impact of parental wealth on the ownership of different asset types (with the exception of home residence) suggests a direct transmission of parental resources. Thus, in the main, these results are consistent with the findings in Spilerman and Torche (2004). The third section presents a structural equation model in which the two dimensions of economic well-being – consumption level and assets ownership – are formulated as unobserved constructs, with the prior measures now introduced as indicator variables. The use of latent constructs with multiple indicators mitigates the confounding of living standard (a hierarchical measure) with life-style choice (a mix of consumption expenditures).

The final empirical section examines the particular status of home ownership in Chile from the perspective of time to ownership and home value. Departing from the pattern noted for the other asset types – and in contrast with findings from the United States and Western Europe (for example, Engelhardt and Mayer 1994; Mulder and Smits 1999; Guiso and Jappelli 1999) – we find that parental resources have little impact on the waiting time from marriage to ownership. The explanation for this is found in the housing policy implemented by the Chilean government since the 1960s, which has largely detached access to residential ownership from family resources. Yet, while parental resources have little effect on the waiting time to ownership, they do retain a substantial impact on home value.

ASSET OWNERSHIP IN CHILE

Even though Chile has made significant economic progress in the last three decades, the level of economic well-being is far from that of most industrialized countries. Per capita income is $4890, which compares to $30 740 in the US (World Bank 2000a). Income inequality is extremely high, as indicated by the Gini coefficient, which reaches 56.5, compared to 40.8 in the US (World Bank 2000b). Furthermore, the pattern of Chilean inequality is characterized by a high concentration in the top decile and relatively less inequality across the rest of the income distribution (Torche 2005). There are no available estimates of the wealth distribution for Chile, but low per capita income and high income inequality suggest a high wealth concentration as well, which likely means that a large proportion of the population has very modest wealth holdings. In this context it is worth asking whether parental wealth has an impact on children's outcomes in the broad population, not merely among the wealthy. If even modest parental resources can be shown to be consequential for living standards, it becomes important to explore how the various transmission mechanisms – for example, direct financial assistance, investments in children's human capital – are used by parents to pass advantage to the next generation.

To put the wealth holdings of the Chilean population in context, we present in Table 10.1 information on the ownership of several asset types and the distribution of ownership by income level in both Chile and the US. The Chilean data come from the 2003 Survey of Intergenerational Financial Linkages in Chile (IFLC), a nationally representative household survey; the US data are from the 1998 Survey of Consumer Finances (SCF). The asset types are primary residence, financial assets, business equity, small residential property, commercial real estate and vehicle ownership. We lack estimates of the financial value of these assets in Chilean households or of the proportion of net worth accounted for by the assets; in the US according to the SCF they comprise 70.3 per cent of total family wealth[1] (Kennickell et al. 2000). We do, however, have data for the two

Table 10.1 Distribution of asset ownership by income group, Chile and US

	Financial assets[2]		Real estate[3]		Residential property[4]		Business		Vehicle		Housing status Chile			Housing Status US		
	Chile	US	Chile	US	Chile	US	Chile	US	Chile	US	Own	Rent	Other[5]	Own	Rent	Other[5]
Percentile of income[1]																
Less than 20	0.1	11.5	3.4	2.1	4.5	1.9	8.0	3.8	11.3	58.7	65.0	11.3	25.2	39.8	54.5	5.7
20–39.9	1.9	26.3	3.1	6.1	4.3	6.8	11.0	5.7	16.0	81.9	68.2	10.7	21.8	55.4	40.9	3.8
40–59.9	1.9	39.4	3.4	7.7	7.0	11.8	13.8	9.0	25.6	89.2	67.3	15.8	17.3	68.0	28.6	3.4
60–79.9	2.7	51.6	6.5	9.5	13.0	17.0	18.6	13.9	45.3	93.0	68.4	16.4	15.8	79.2	19.5	1.3
80–89.9	7.1	64.2	9.1	14.1	17.0	17.7	32.2	18.8	72.1	92.8	70.5	20.0	9.6	88.4	11.0	0.6
90–100	22.0	82.2	25.0	21.1	42.5	35.5	39.5	31.0	91.9	90.0	75.0	21.4	3.7	93.0	6.3	0.7
All households	3.6	40.0	6.4	8.6	11.0	12.8	17.0	11.5	35.0	82.8	67.5	14.9	17.6	66.3	30.7	3.0

Notes:

1. Percentiles for the Chilean Survey are as follows: (1) Less than 23; (2) 23–39.9; (3) 40–58; (4) 59–82; (5) 83–91; (6) 92–100. Table entries indicate percentiles for the US data.
2. Includes saving bonds, other bonds, publicly traded stocks, and mutual funds.
3. Comprises farm, land, commercial and rental property, and other types of nonresidential real estate.
4. Includes second home, vacation home, time shares, one- to four-family rental property, and other types of residential property.
5. 'Other' includes co-residence with parents, relatives or friends, housing as part of job compensation, temporary quarters, and other tenure arrangements. In Chile 58 per cent of this category consists of co-residence with parents or other relatives.

Sources: Survey of Intergenerational Financial Linkages in Chile, 2003. Survey of Consumer Finances, 1998 for the US. Both surveys were weighted to be nationally representative.

countries on the rate of ownership of each asset type and on their distributions by income level.

From Table 10.1 it is evident that financial holdings (stocks, bonds, mutual funds) are the most scarce asset in Chile, with ownership by only 3.6 per cent of households, as opposed to 40 per cent in the US. The ownership rate ranges from almost zero for the lowest income group in Chile to some 22 per cent in the highest category. Note that while the increase in the rate is fairly linear in the US, in Chile there is a sharp gap between the top decile and the rest of the income categories. This gap is consistent with the pattern of economic inequality in the country, which is characterized by high concentration in the very top percentiles (Torche 2005).

Real estate ownership (farm, land, commercial and rental property, and other types of nonresidential property) averages 6.4 per cent in the Chilean population, with the rate of ownership increasing from some 3 per cent to 25 per cent across the income range. The distribution is quite similar to that found in the US, a surprising finding given that Chile is poorer and more unequal. A possible explanation relates to the higher prevalence of land ownership in Chile, often consisting of small plots. The findings for residential property (second residence, vacation home, and so on) are also much the same in the two countries. Observe, however, that in the case of each of these asset types the gap between the highest decile and the immediately lower income category is considerably greater in Chile – further testimony to the concentration of economic resources.

With an ownership rate of 17 per cent in Chile and 12 per cent in the US, business equity is the one asset that is more prevalent in Chile. The distribution is relatively similar in the two countries, showing a monotonic, almost linear, increase across the income categories. While we cannot examine the value of business equity with the Chilean data, the high prevalence of small informal enterprises in Chile – peddler stands and homefront stores – suggests that the value of business equity is quite modest for most households that report this asset (Wormald and Rozas 1996).

In contrast, the rate of vehicle ownership is much lower in Chile – 35 per cent versus 83 per cent in the US. Moreover, the distributions across income groups are strikingly different, especially at the low end of the scale. In the US, there is little variation beyond the second quintile, suggesting that by this income level most families who wish to are able to purchase a vehicle; in short, the ownership decision is a life-style choice. In Chile, in contrast, the rate remains low until the highest quintile, suggesting a strong financial constraint on vehicle ownership.

The most interesting difference between the countries in pattern of asset ownership concerns primary residences. While the average rate is comparable in the two countries – 67.5 per cent in Chile, 66.3 per cent in the US – the distributions across income categories are quite disparate; indeed, they are the reverse of the vehicle ownership pattern. In the US, the trend is one of a linear increase with income level, beginning with an ownership rate of some 40 per cent for the lowest category. In comparison, in Chile, some 65 per cent in the bottom group are homeowners, with little change in the rate as one moves to higher categories.

The conspicuous difference between the two countries in the association of home ownership with income derives from the particular institutional arrangements in Chile. Since 1964, with the coming to power of a progressive Christian-Democratic government, a widespread redistribution programme was instituted to respond to the sharp inequalities in the country and the growing urban unrest as a consequence of migration from the countryside. One dimension of the redistributive programme was a policy of housing construction. This policy addressed the 'housing deficit' by providing home ownership access to the poor; however, the government's efforts were not enough to satisfy the growing demand of rural migrants, giving rise to illegal occupation of unused plots. As a consequence, a significant proportion of the poor became homeowners, either through the government programmes or by means of illegal occupation (Departamento de Estudios MINVU 2004). Access to home ownership through illegal occupation became more frequent during the subsequent Socialist administration, in power between 1970 and 1973.

The overthrow of the Socialist government and emergence of a military regime in 1973 radically redefined the state housing policy. Illegal access was eliminated (though many existing homes with questionable titles were legalized by the government), and a new market-based strategy was implemented. This strategy included deregulation of the land market, private participation in construction via contracting, and targeted demand-based housing subsidies – 'housing voucher programmes' (Pardo 2000, Rojas 1999). An important element of continuity was the focus on home ownership, as opposed to rental access, as a housing solution for the poor (Departamento de Estudios MINVU 2004).

Housing subsidies were significantly expanded during the 1990s, providing home ownership access for hundreds of thousands of lower- and middle-class families (Departamento de Estudios MINVU 2004). The provided residences tend to be located in the urban periphery, where land is cheaper, and of low market value. Most government subsidy programmes require a small contribution from the recipient and are explicitly targeted toward the poor and the working class. Selection is based on a point system keyed to an extensive list of family characteristics, including waiting time, family income and family size (Rojas 1999). As of the year 2000, more than 50 per cent of the households in the three lowest quintiles have become homeowners through the state programme (Mideplan 2000). An international comparison is illustrative: the urban home ownership rate in Chile is one of the highest in the world, with only Singapore, Mexico, Pakistan and Israel having higher rates (World Bank 1993; Spilerman 2004). Because the government strategy is to provide housing solutions to the poor through ownership instead of subsidized rentals, the average home price–income ratio for Chile is one of the lowest in the world. In contrast, the rent–income ratio is quite high, surpassed only by Korea, Mexico and Singapore (Cummings and Dipasquale 2002).

Because of these institutional arrangements most Chilean families can become homeowners if they queue for the state subsidy. This equalization in access to home ownership contrasts with a sharp segmentation by income class in the value of owned homes. Table 10.2 reports the value of primary residences by income group for Chile and the US. The first two columns present values in local currency (US dollars and Chilean pesos respectively); the two last columns report the figures as a percentage of home value in the lowest income category. In contrast with the flatness in

Table 10.2   Median value of primary residence for homeowners, by income category, Chile and US

Income percentile[1]	Home value		Home value, relative to low category	
	US (2001 US$)	Chile[2] (2003 pesos, in thousands)	US	Chile
Less than 20	59 900	10 600	1.0	1.0
20–39.9	81 600	12 300	1.4	1.2
40–59.9	92 500	14 400	1.5	1.4
60–79.9	119 700	21 300	2.0	2.0
80–89.9	149 100	30 000	2.5	2.8
90–100	244 900	58 500	4.1	5.5
All households	108 800	20 300		

Notes:
1. Percentiles for the Chilean Survey are as follows: (1) Less than 23; (2) 23–39.9; (3) 40–58; (4) 59–82; (5) 83–91; (6) 92–100. Table entries indicate percentiles for the US data.
2. Average exchange rate in 2003 was 691 Chilean pesos/US dollar.

Sources: Survey of Intergenerational Financial Linkages in Chile, 2003; Survey of Consumer Finances 1998, for US, adjusted to 2001 dollars. Both surveys are weighted to be nationally representative.

the response of the ownership rate to household income in Chile (Table 10.1), home *value* increases with income level, much as in the US, though with a sharp jump at the highest income group. Thus, even though access to home ownership is largely detached from family resources in Chile, this is hardly the case with respect to home value.

The tenancy pattern in Chile differs from the US in another way. In the US the clear alternative to home ownership is rental status (Table 10.1). In Chile, however, a greater proportion of the nonownership population resides with parents or relatives (the 'other' category in Table 10.1) than rents housing. The disparity is especially pronounced in the two lowest income quintiles – in which some 25 per cent of the population lives with a relative (or in a nonstandard tenure arrangement) versus 11 per cent that rent. Residing with a parent, which accounts for the majority in this category, is a form of parental assistance that is much less utilized in the US.

There are three conclusions from this section. First, as expected from the differences in level of economic development in the two countries, the proportion of households that own some of the noted assets is significantly lower in Chile for most asset categories; nonetheless, asset ownership in Chile is not limited to the elite. Second, the distribution of asset holdings across income groups is very unequal, characterized by a substantial gap between the top income decile and the prior categories, which parallels the high concentration of financial and material resources in the population. Third, the distribution of home ownership departs from the pattern of the other asset types and is strikingly different from the ownership pattern in the US, in that even the very poor have a high rate of access to residence ownership.

PARENTAL WEALTH AND CHILDREN'S OUTCOMES

Descriptive Statistics and Analytic Strategy

In this chapter we investigate the contribution of parental asset holdings to children's living standards, with particular consideration of the transmission mechanism – whether parental investments in education or direct transfers of financial and material resources. The data used in the study come from the 2003 Survey of Intergenerational Financial Linkages in Chile (IFLC), conducted by Spilerman and Torche. The IFLC survey employed a nationally representative, multistage stratified sample of 4408 Chilean households.[2] Respondents were male household heads or their wives or partners. Information was collected about household resources and income, respondent's background and work experience, and spouse or partner's background and work experience. Considerable detail was sought about the asset holdings of the respondent, of his or her parents, and of the spouse or partner's parents.

In Table 10.3 we present descriptive statistics of the association between parental wealth and several measures of the economic well-being of adult children. The measures in the table cover two broad dimensions of well-being: consumption level and asset ownership. 'Parental wealth' refers to the resource holdings of both sets of parents of the couple, measured when respondent and spouse or partner was each in his or her teen years. It is not possible to ask respondents about the value of parental holdings at that early stage, due to their limited knowledge about parental resources in past decades and to fluctuations in the inflation rate. Our strategy, consequently, was to inquire about the ownership of different kinds of parental assets: business equity, real estate, residential property and financial assets (stocks, bonds, mutual funds); an approach to wealth measurement whose validity is supported by Sahn and Stifel (2003). The parental wealth measure is formulated as the sum of Z-scores from a count of the different asset types, with the scores averaged from both sets of parents.

The entries reveal a strong association between the parental wealth measure and the economic well-being of adult children. The score for each consumption item increases substantially as one moves from low to high levels of parental wealth; the same is true for the ownership rate of each asset type. The only exception is the rate of home ownership (row 9), which is not responsive to parental wealth. This singular pattern is associated with the detachment of home ownership from financial resources, as detailed in the previous section. The three last rows of the table refer to several determinants of consumption level and asset ownership; in particular, respondent's education, occupational status and household earnings, which are presumed to function as intervening variables, transmitting the parental advantage. Not surprisingly, the measures are also responsive to parental wealth. With these results we turn to two related questions. First, whether the beneficial impact of parental advantage operates through children's human capital and income, or directly through transfers of resources. Second, how this general assessment of the path of parental transmission differs according to the particular aspect of economic well-being that is under consideration.

To address these questions, we undertake a multivariate analysis of the effects of parental wealth on the different facets of family economic status. One caveat with regard to the data: while the conceptual argument emphasizes the role of parental assistance and intergenerational transfers, our analysis is limited to the impact of parental assets, as summarized by the parental wealth measure. While a transfer process is presumed to account for the parental effects on economic well-being, the details of the transmission process are not delineated in this study.

Table 10.3   *Descriptive statistics relating couple's living standard to parental wealth, Chile 2003*

Measures of couple's economic well-being[1]	Parental wealth[2]					
	1 = Low	2	3	4	5 = High	N
Consumption level:						
Vehicle ownership[3]	0.30	0.40	0.40	0.50	0.61	3667
Domestic service[4]	0.04	0.08	0.11	0.14	0.31	3667
Number of household items[5]	−0.43	0.17	0.27	0.87	2.02	3648
Subjective standard of living[6]	−0.35	−0.03	0.17	0.27	0.85	3516
Asset ownership:						
Financial assets[7]	0.01	0.02	0.06	0.05	0.13	3656
Business ownership[8]	0.12	0.21	0.21	0.25	0.29	3667
Real estate ownership[9]	0.04	0.09	0.09	0.11	0.18	3660
Residential property[10]	0.08	0.12	0.12	0.18	0.23	3663
Home ownership[11]	0.66	0.65	0.65	0.66	0.63	3671
Human capital/household income:						
Education of husband[12]	9.04	9.89	10.28	10.83	12.87	3671
Occupational status of husband[13]	34.11	36.82	37.91	40.35	43.27	3586
Labor market income[14]	322.87	419.45	436.41	572.09	930.30	3596

Notes:
1. Entries are for married and cohabitating couples where male head is aged 25–69. All values are for year 2003.
2. Parental wealth is measured as the sum of Z-score from counts of ownership of business equity, real estate, residential property (excluding primary residence) and financial assets (stock, bonds, mutual funds). The measure combines wealth holdings of both sets of parents. Because a large proportion of parents had zero or near zero asset holdings the low wealth category contains 60 per cent of the sample; the remaining categories approximate wealth deciles: (2) 11.7 per cent; (3) 8.5 per cent; (4) 11.2 per cent; (5) 9.4 per cent.
3. Proportion of couples who own one or more vehicles.
4. Proportion of couples who use domestic service.
5. Sum of Z-scores from count of ownership of five common household items.
6. Subjective SOL by respondent is a five-point ordinal scale: 1 = Much below average; 5 = Much above average.
7. Proportion of couples who own financial assets (stock, bonds, mutual funds).
8. Proportion of couples who own a business (full or part ownership).
9. Proportion of couples who own real estate.
10. Proportion of couples who own residential property.
11. Proportion of couples who are homeowners.
12. Number of years of schooling completed.
13. Occupational status coded by International Socioeconomic Status Index scores (Ganzeboom et al. 1992).
14. Monthly labour market income of household in Chilean Pesos (thousands).

Source: Survey of Intergenerational Financial Linkages in Chile, 2003.

We distinguish between two dimensions of economic well-being: consumption level – a proxy for the couple's standard of living – and asset ownership, a household wealth indicator. The first is measured by the following items: vehicle ownership,[3] consumer durables ownership, use of domestic service, and a subjective standard-of-living indicator. The second dimension covers the following asset types: financial instruments (stocks, bonds, mutual funds), investment real estate, business equity and residential property (other than primary residence). The parental resource effects were estimated individually for each of the consumption and asset items as dependent variables, to ascertain whether the path of transmission varies with the outcome type.

The unit of analysis in the regression models is the married or cohabiting couple. The models include measures of three kinds of parental resources: father's years of schooling, father's occupational status, and parental wealth. Father's occupational status – a proxy for permanent income – is coded in terms of the International Socioeconomic Index (ISEI) (Ganzeboom et al. 1992). Parental wealth is measured as the sum of the standardized values of four dichotomous variables representing ownership of the different asset types: financial, land and investment real estate, residential property, and business equity. The parental resources terms were computed separately for each member of the couple to ascertain whether, possibly, there is a differential contribution from the holdings of parents of the male or the female partner. All parental resource terms refer to the period when respondent and partner were in their teen years.

Other variables included in the analysis are measures of the human capital of the couple (years of schooling by husband and wife) and monthly household income from labour market activity (in Chilean pesos). We emphasize labour market income, as distinct from total household income, because the latter includes income that derives from parental asset transfers, whereas our intent is to differentiate between parental effects linked to investments in human capital, and those tied to direct assistance. Controls were also introduced for age of husband at marriage or cohabitation, for number of years in current union, and an indicator term for whether either partner had a previous marriage or cohabitation. Husband's age at marriage or cohabitation and the term for duration of the union are indicators of two different processes: the accumulation of savings before marriage or cohabitation and subsequent savings by the couple; we expect each to be a function of the pertinent temporal variable and we view each as adding to a couple's capacity to finance its living standard expenditures. The impact of a prior marriage or cohabitation, in contrast, taps the possible depletion of resources associated with a marital rupture and should have a negative impact on asset ownership.

It is the case of that some of the parental variables have rates of missing data that approach 15 per cent (see Appendix Table 10A.1) and in a regression with several variables the proportion of observations with missing data can reach 25 per cent. Dropping cases with missing data is both inefficient and can lead to biased estimates. In order to retain these observations a multiple imputation procedure was used (Rubin 1987). Five complete data sets were created using the imputation software *Amelia* (Honaker et al. 2003). The analysis was replicated with each data set; the parameter estimates and standard errors were then combined. This approach provides unbiased estimates, assuming that the data are missing at random (MAR).

Our analytic strategy is the following. In order to assess the two paths of parental transmission – via investments in human capital and direct transfers of resources – we estimate two models of the impact of parental resources on each indicator of living standard and asset holdings. The first model reports the total effect of the parental resource terms, as measured by the coefficients in a reduced form model. The second adds the human capital terms for husband and wife, the couple's earnings,[4] and the control variables, and is intended to assess the extent to which the initial parental effects are diminished by these terms – an indication of indirect parental transmissions operating through investments in human capital.

Parental Wealth Effects on Consumption Behaviour

As noted, we have four consumption measures. The results for the first, vehicle ownership, are presented in Table 10.4. Vehicle ownership is formulated as a dichotomous variable, coded 1 if the couple owns one or more vehicles; hence the entries in Table 10.4 are estimates from a logistic regression model.

The first column presents total effects of the parental background measures on the log-odds of vehicle ownership. All the variables have positive effects, though parental education is significant only for the husband's father. Occupational status, a proxy for parental permanent income, is positive and significant for both sets of parents. Of particular consequence for this study, both parental wealth terms have significant impacts on ownership of this consumption item, effects that are net of the other parental terms – the parental resource variables that typically have been considered in the status attainment literature (for example, Blau and Duncan 1967; Duncan et al. 1972). To obtain a sense of the magnitude of the effects note that, for husband's father, a one standard deviation increase in educational attainment – approximately five years of schooling – would raise the odds of vehicle ownership by 20 per cent ($e^{[.038][4.81]}$),

Table 10.4   Parental resource effects on vehicle ownership, Chile 2003[1]

Explanatory variables	Model 1		Model 2	
Constant	−2.247***	(0.133)	−10.556***	(0.434)
Husband's father:				
Education[2]	0.038***	(0.011)	−0.002	(0.012)
Occupational status[3]	0.021***	(0.004)	0.006	(0.005)
Household wealth[4]	0.063***	(0.016)	0.016	(0.018)
Wife's father:				
Education[2]	0.011	(0.010)	−0.030*	(0.012)
Occupational status[3]	0.023***	(0.004)	0.009	(0.005)
Household wealth[4]	0.049**	(0.016)	−0.006	(0.018)
Husband's age at marriage[5]			0.013	(0.008)
Years of marriage[6]			0.030***	(0.004)
Husband or wife had				
previous marriage[7]			0.171	(0.122)
Husband's education[2]			0.050***	(0.015)
Wife's education[2]			0.029	(0.016)
Labour market income (ln)[8]			1.399***	(0.073)
Pseudo-R^2	0.092		0.249	
N	3811		3811	

Notes:
*p < 0.05, **p < 0.01, ***p < 0.001.
1. Unstandardized coefficients from logistic regression; standard errors in parentheses. Dependent variable coded 1 if household owns one or more vehicles; 0 otherwise. Results based on multiple imputation with five data sets.
2. Years of schooling completed.
3. Occupational status coded by ISEI status scores (Ganzeboom et al. 1992).
4. Estimate of parents' wealth holdings. See text for details.
5. Age of husband at time of marriage/cohabitation.
6. Years of marriage/cohabitation.
7. Indicator variable coded 1 if either husband or wife had a previous marriage or cohabitation.
8. Ln (household income from labour market activity, in Chilean pesos).

while a standard deviation shift in occupational status or in parental wealth translates, respectively, into changes of 33 per cent and 17 per cent in the odds of ownership.

The second model (column 2) adds terms for husband's and wife's educational attainments and for household labour market income, along with the controls. Not surprisingly, husband's education and household income have strong effects on vehicle ownership. Years of marriage also raises the odds; this term taps duration of resource accumulation, as well as the growth in husband's labour force experience.

A principal question for the study concerns whether the effects of the parental resources are direct or mediated by parental investments in the couple's human capital. This matter can be addressed by examining the change in the coefficients of the parental resource terms after respondent's and partner's human capital and the household income term are added to the model. From comparing models 2 and 1, it is evident that the changes are considerable; all the parental terms that previously were significant are reduced to insignificance. (We view the now significant, but negative, term for wife's father's education as a sampling anomaly.) We therefore conclude that the parental resource effects operate through educational attainment and labour market earnings, and reflect the ability of parents with more resources to provide better education to their offspring, which is translated into higher labour market income and a greater consumption capacity.

Finally, though peripheral to the current study, our findings permit a tentative observation about the educational system. Note that the McFadden's pseudo-R^2 in column 2 (0.249) is almost three times its size in column 1 (0.092). If the only avenue of access to education, better earnings, and a higher living standard (indexed here by vehicle ownership) were through parental resources, the change in R^2 from addition of the human capital and earnings terms would have been small. The observed, substantial increase indicates that education and labour market income not only serve as intervening variables, transmitting the parental resource effects, but have significant additional consequences; in short, access to schooling and income do not come solely from parental advantage. This finding suggests that government interventions in Chile over several decades to bolster educational attainment (see Spilerman and Torche 2004 for details), opening the possibility of schooling to poor families and encouraging enrolment by their children, may have served to weaken the linkage between parental resources and living standards, at least in regard to vehicle ownership.

Similar analyses were carried out with the other measures of children's living standard: use of domestic hired help, consumer durables ownership, and a subjective standard of living term. These variables were measured as follows. Domestic service is an ordinal variable and indexes whether the household had full-time hired domestic help, part-time help, or no domestic assistance. Consumer durables ownership was measured as the sum of the standardized scores of five common household items.[5] Finally, the subjective standard of living measure is an ordinal variable based on the following question: 'If you compare the living standard of this household with the average living standard in Chile, would you say that this household is: (1) much lower than average, (2) a bit below average, (3) about average, (4) a bit above average, or (5) much above average?'

The analysis of each standard of living measure (not shown, tables available from the authors) reveals a set of determinants that are similar to those found for vehicle ownership. In every case the parental wealth terms have positive, significant effects net of the other parental resource variables (column 1 models). Again, the effects of parental wealth become insignificant upon controlling for the couple's human capital and labour market income. Moreover, in every case, the explanatory power of the model, as judged by the R^2 coefficient, increases between two- and three-fold after adding terms for the children's human capital and income to the model, pointing to the presence in Chile of opportunities to acquire education and labour market income apart from the contribution of parental resources.

To summarize, with respect to the consumption measures, our findings show that parental wealth has a substantial impact on the living standards of adult children, but that the effect is largely indirect, operating through parental investments in education and earnings capacity. Also noteworthy, but hardly surprising, is the finding that duration of the union has a significant effect on the various indicators of the couple's living standard, consistent with a process of growth in human capital and earnings. Finally, our results suggest an observation about the workings of the education system and the labour market in Chile – namely that they appear to offer opportunity for upward mobility to children from poor households in which parental resources are insufficient to impart an advantageous starting point in life.

Parental Influences on Asset Ownership

This section examines the determinants of the second dimension of economic well-being, namely asset ownership. Whereas the utility of a consumption item is intimately tied to the use value of goods and services, the value of an asset item extends beyond any possible use value and relates primarily to the beneficial property of 'consumption storage' (Spilerman 2000). This feature is especially valuable in Latin America, where variations in the economic cycle can lead to unemployment and subemployment for large segments of the population and where public welfare coverage is limited, leaving many families unprotected and dependent on their own resources in the event of an economic crisis (Lustig 2001). In this context, even modest wealth holdings can be crucial to avoiding major discontinuities in consumption expenditures.

The parental resource effects are examined with respect to four asset types – real estate, financial assets (stock, bonds and mutual funds), business equity, and residential property (excluding primary residence);

ownership of each is a dichotomous outcome and logistic regression is utilized. (Due to the complex relationship between parental resources and home ownership, noted earlier, we analyse the home acquisition process separately in the next section.) Analogous to the examination of consumption level, we present a detailed analysis of one measure of the couple's asset ownership – real estate holdings – in the present section, followed by a summary of the findings from the other measures. Again, we estimate two models for each asset item. The first presents the total effects of the parental background variables; the second adds the human capital terms and the couple's labour market income to gauge the extent to which the parental resource variables operate indirectly, through returns to human capital investments.

One new consideration: it cannot be assumed that the respondent's *current* income affects the holdings of expensive assets, such as commercial real estate, which, to the extent they were financed by labour market income may have been purchased from savings over several years in the past. Ideally, to assess the extent to which asset holdings come from labour market income – and, indirectly, from parental resource effects through investments in children's education and earnings – we want a measure of the respondent's cumulative labour market income in the years prior to the purchase of the item. We lack such a measure and, instead, utilize a proxy based on life-course accumulations from labour market activity, formulated as the product of a couple's current labour market income and duration of marriage or cohabitation.[6]

Table 10.5 reports the contribution of the parental terms to real estate ownership. Model 1 reveals that the standard socio-economic measures of parental resources – father's education and occupational status – do not influence the couple's real estate holdings. Parental wealth, in contrast, has substantial effects, virtually identical in magnitude for the parents of each spouse or partner. The initial finding, then, is that parental wealth matters for real estate ownership, while the other parental resources are of little consequence.

Model 2 adds variables for the couple's human capital and for accumulated labour market income over the life course, along with the duration variables and the other controls. Observe first that the cumulative labour market income term is highly significant and has a large impact on the odds of real estate ownership; a doubling of cumulative income would raise the odds by 69 per cent. Husband's age at marriage also contributes to asset ownership; this measure taps career development and, possibly, savings that the husband brought to the marital union. Duration of marriage, in comparison, is not significant. This term was introduced as a proxy for savings over the marital course; however, its effect is fully offset by the

Table 10.5   Parental resource effects on real estate ownership, Chile 2003[1]

Explanatory variables	Model 1		Model 2	
Constant	−3.103***	(0.206)	−9.652***	(0.714)
Husband's father:				
Education[2]	0.042	(0.022)	0.036	(0.023)
Occupational status[3]	−0.000	(0.007)	−0.011	(0.008)
Household wealth	0.104***	(0.021)	0.087***	(0.022)
Wife's father:				
Education[2]	−0.000	(0.020)	−0.018	(0.022)
Occupational status[3]	0.006	(0.006)	−0.004	(0.007)
Household wealth[4]	0.104***	(0.021)	0.075***	(0.022)
Husband's age at marriage[5]			0.037**	(0.012)
Years of marriage[6]			0.004	(0.009)
Husband or wife had previous marriage[7]			−0.168	(0.209)
Husband's education[2]			0.018	(0.027)
Wife's education[2]			−0.002	(0.027)
Cumulative labour market income (ln)[8]			0.694***	(0.103)
Pseudo-R^2	0.061		0.122	
N	3811		3811	

Notes:
*$p < 0.05$, **$p < 0.01$, ***$p < 0.001$.
1. Unstandardized coefficients from logistic regression; standard errors in parentheses. Dependent variable coded 1 if the household owns farm, land, commercial/rental property, or other nonresidential real estate. Results based on multiple imputation with five data sets.
2. Years of schooling completed.
3. Occupational status coded by ISEI status scores (Ganzeboom et al. 1992).
4. Estimate of parents' wealth holdings. See text for details.
5. Age of husband at time of marriage/cohabitation.
6. Years of marriage/cohabitation.
7. Indicator variable coded 1 if either husband or wife had a previous marriage or cohabitation.
8. Estimate of household's cumulative labor market income since year of marriage/cohabitation. See text for details.

cumulative income variable, which also reflects duration of the union. This assessment was confirmed by replacing the latter with the term for current income; as expected the duration variable becomes significant and positive.

Of greater relevance is the consequence of the couple's educational attainment and labour market income for the parental wealth effects since these relate to the pathway of parental influence on respondent's asset holdings. The parental wealth terms remain highly significant with their magnitudes reduced in each case by some 20 per cent. It is evident that the bulk of the parental wealth effects on ownership of this particular asset are direct, indicative of parental financial and material transfers to offspring rather than a process of investment in education and subsequent earnings. At the same time the equation R^2 is much increased between models 1 and 2, suggesting that labour market income can be an independent means to asset accumulation in Chile, and that children from poor origins have sometimes used this route to build real estate holdings. We further emphasize that our estimate of the direct parental transmission is an upper bound, in that a more accurate measure of cumulative labour market income prior to asset acquisition would likely result in a reduction of the parental wealth coefficients in model 2.

Analyses of the couple's financial assets, business equity and residential property[7] confirm, first of all, that parental wealth is the primary parental resource that influences children's asset holdings, and, second, that direct transfers of resources are an important part of the acquisition process. Regarding the total parental effects (the equation [1] models), both parental wealth terms – for the parents of husband and wife – are significant for every asset type; in several instances one of the other parental resource terms is also significant though there is no consistent pattern to those effects. After controls are added for husband's education and cumulative household income (the equation 2 models), the net parental wealth effects are reduced, though both wealth terms remain significant for each asset type, with the sole exception of husband's parental wealth in the residential property equation; at the same time no other parental resource variable, neither father's education nor occupational status, achieves significance. Again, in the case of each asset type, the term for cumulative labour market income has a strong positive effect and the added R^2 from inclusion of this variable is considerable.

To summarize, we find evidence for two different patterns in the effects of parental resources on the economic well-being of children. With respect to the consumption items, it is the case that father's occupational status (a proxy for permanent income), father's education (an indicator of parental values since it is net of occupational status), and parental wealth all have substantial effects on the living standards of offspring. It is also the case that the parental resource terms operate through the child's education and, consequently, through labour market income. There is little evidence for direct financial transmission in the determination of the consumption items, probably because the costs associated with acquisition of these items are relatively small. In contrast, with regard to financial, business and investment assets, it is mainly parental wealth that matters and, further, much of the transmission appears to be direct. At the same time, our analysis suggests that part of the determination of consumption level and asset ownership in the Chilean population – a substantial portion in the case of the consumption items – comes about through schooling and income attainment in ways that are not derivative of parental resources.

STRUCTURAL EQUATION MODELS (SEM) OF LIVING STANDARD AND ASSET OWNERSHIP

As an alternative to examining the determination of each consumption and asset item separately, we consider a model of the parental effects on consumption level (living standard) and on asset ownership in which these two constructs are formulated as unobserved, latent variables, with the observed consumption and asset items serving as indicators. This formulation is introduced for two reasons. First, we have argued that the determination process is similar for the items in each construct, which suggests that each can be well represented by a summary underlying model. Second, the use of latent variables reduces the confounding between life-style choice (a preference for particular consumption items) and living standard (a hierarchical measure of well-being), in that what is now modelled is the shared variance in a family's consumption expenditures. Similarly, in the case of asset holdings, the SEM estimates tap the breadth of the wealth portfolio rather than ownership of a specific item.

For the examination of the consumption items, we use a MIMIC model (multiple indicators, multiple causes) in which a couple's parental resources, along with labour market income and the controls are viewed as influencing the living standard construct. This unobserved variable, in turn, is identified by its loadings on the several consumption items. The equations for the MIMIC model (Joreskog and Sorbom 1989, p. 173) are:

$$Y = \lambda \eta + \varepsilon \tag{10.1}$$
$$\eta = \gamma' X + \zeta \tag{10.2}$$

where Y is a vector of indicators of the latent variable η (living standard), λ is a vector of factor loadings relating the indicators to the latent variable, X is a vector of the exogenous 'causes' of η, and γ is a coefficient vector. The ε's and ζ's are assumed to be mutually uncorrelated.

The living standard construct is measured by the four consumption indicators: ownership of a vehicle, use of domestic service, ownership of consumer durables, and a subjective evaluation of one's standard of living. All the terms are categorical (with the exception of consumer durables, which is continuous, constructed as a sum of z-scores for ownership of five house-hold items). Because of the categorical nature of several of the indicators, estimation is by weighted least squares.

Our intent in this section is not one of building a full model of the parental effects on living standard or asset ownership, which would require a consideration of the determination of the several intervening processes – the fact, for example, that the couple's educational attainments and income mediate between parental resources and the outcome variables. Rather, our objective is to use SEM only to extend the formulations in Tables 10.4 and 10.5 by having the outcome variables represented by the common variance in the sets of indicator terms. Thus, we treat all the explanatory variables as exogenous and follow the structure of models 1 and 2 of the earlier tables, first estimating the total parental effects on a latent variable, then adding terms for the couple's human capital and labour market income along with the controls.

The results for the consumption items, viewed as indicators of a latent living standard construct, are presented in Table 10.6. The factor loadings of the indicators are reported in the first four rows; all have strong associ-ations with the latent variable (a standard error cannot be computed for the reference indicator, subjective SOL). Since the dependent variable is a stat-istical construct, to facilitate discussion of the relative effects of the explanatory variables, standardized coefficients are reported along with the unstandardized parameter estimates; the former appear in the third column of each model. The total effects of the parental terms (model 1) are con-sistent with the earlier discussion: all the parental resources, from both husband's and wife's families, contribute to the couple's living standard, though we now find more modest effects from the parental wealth terms, as indicated by the standardized estimates.

The full equation, which takes into account the couple's human capital and labour market income, is reported as model 2. Again, the results paral-lel the Table 10.4 findings; by far the largest contributions to living standard, as indicated by the standardized estimates, come from the couple's education and income variables. Net of these effects, while some of the parental terms – husband's father's education, wife's father's occupation – retain statistical significance, the effects are quite small relative to the couple's own resources. Moreover, since both parental wealth terms are insignificant, there is no evi-dence of direct financial transfers on behalf of the couple's living standard. In summary, the findings are fairly robust to specification, whether formu-lated in terms of the consumption components or a latent construct: there are strong parental effects, including parental wealth effects, on the living standard of offspring, but these transmissions operate almost entirely through parental investments in human capital and earnings capacity.

Table 10.6 Structural equation model of living standards, Chile 2003[1]

	Model 1			Model 2		
Factor loadings						
Subjective SOL[2]	1.000	–	0.747	1.000	–	0.756
Household items[3]	3.086***	(0.111)	0.765	2.508***	(0.095)	0.750
Domestic service[4]	1.198***	(0.048)	0.859	1.067***	(0.065)	0.884
Auto ownership[4]	1.045***	(0.033)	0.774	1.083***	(0.046)	0.790
Regressors						
Husband's father:						
Education	0.033***	(0.004)	0.183	0.011**	(0.004)	0.054
Occupational status[5]	0.010***	(0.002)	0.165	0.001	(0.002)	0.008
Household wealth[6]	0.029***	(0.006)	0.086	0.006	(0.005)	0.015
Wife's father:						
Education	0.018***	(0.004)	0.099	−0.005	(0.004)	−0.022
Occupational status[5]	0.013***	(0.001)	0.201	0.004**	(0.001)	0.046
Household wealth[6]	0.032***	(0.006)	0.095	0.001	(0.006)	0.004
Husband's age at marriage				0.007***	(0.002)	0.048
Years of marriage				0.020***	(0.001)	0.224
Husband or wife had a prior marriage[7]				−0.026	(0.037)	−0.010
Husband's education				0.044***	(0.005)	0.182
Wife's education				0.031***	(0.005)	0.126
Labour market income (ln)[8]				0.680***	(0.025)	0.614
R^2	0.345			0.754		
N	3811			3811		
Fit Indices:						
CFI	0.993			0.940		
RMSEA	0.017			0.034		

Notes:
*$p < 0.05$, **$p < 0.01$, ***$p < 0.001$.
1. Results based on multiple imputation with five data sets. For each model the column (1) entries are unstandardized coefficients, column (2) contains standard errors, and column (3) reports the standardized estimates.
2. Five category subjective scale.
3. Sum of z-scores for ownership of five common household durables.
4. Binary term for ownership of the item.
5. Occupational status coded by ISEI status scores.
6. Estimate of parents' wealth holdings. See text for details.
7. Dummy term, coded 1 if either partner had a prior marriage/cohabitation.
8. Ln (current household income from labour market activity, in Chilean pesos).

The comparable analysis for the determination of asset ownership is more complex. While our intent is only to extend the formulation of Table 10.5 by introducing a latent term for asset holdings, we cannot ignore the fact that one of the asset items – business ownership – can be a source of labour market income. Consequently, it is necessary to treat the cumulative income variable, along with asset holdings, as endogenous and introduce terms for the identification of each equation. For this purpose we add 'number of inheritances received' to the asset equation; this variable is assumed not to affect labour market income directly. Similarly, we add 'husband's occupational status' to the equation for cumulative labour market income, as any impact of this term on asset holdings would presumably come through the income variable. This more general SEM model is given by the equations

$$\mathbf{Y} = \lambda\eta + \varepsilon \tag{10.3}$$
$$\eta = \beta_1 Z + \gamma_1'\mathbf{X}_1 + \zeta_1 \tag{10.4}$$
$$Z = \beta_2\eta + \gamma_2'\mathbf{X}_2 + \zeta_2 \tag{10.5}$$

where equation (10.3) is the measurement model for the latent variable η (asset holdings), (10.4) is the structural equation for the determination of η, and (10.5) is the equation for the determination of Z, the endogenous variable for cumulative labour market income. In these equations, $\mathbf{Y}$ is a vector of indicators of the latent variable η; $\mathbf{X}_1$ and $\mathbf{X}_2$ are vectors of exogenous variables. The ε's and ζ's are assumed to be mutually uncorrelated.

The results from the SEM estimation of asset holdings are reported in Table 10.7. Since the model 1 specification contains only the parental resource terms, it is an immediate generalization of equation (1) of Table 10.5, with the single indicator model replaced by the factor analytic formulation of asset holdings. The findings with respect to the parental terms indicate that both occupational status (a proxy for income) and wealth contribute to the level of asset holdings, with the wealth terms having a greater effect, as suggested by the standardized estimates.

Adding terms for husband's and wife's educational attainment and cumulative income – our generalization of equation (2) of Table 10.5 – results in equations 2a and 2b for the two endogenous variables. While not central to our interests, we comment first on equation 2a. The findings for the determinants of cumulative labour market income conform to expectations: years of marriage has the greatest impact, followed by the human capital terms. Net of these variables, parental occupational status and wealth are significant, with standardized effects that are comparable in magnitude. Note also that there is no evidence of an effect of asset holdings on labour market income, though one of the asset indicators, for

Table 10.7 Structural equation model of asset holdings, Chile 2003[1]

	Model 1			Model 2a Cumulative income			Model 2b Asset holdings		
Factor loadings[2]									
Financial assets	1.000	–	0.566				1.000	–	0.507
Residential property	1.259***	(0.149)	0.699				1.315***	(0.170)	0.646
Real estate	1.395***	(0.165)	0.766				1.386***	(0.183)	0.676
Business ownership	0.701***	(0.098)	0.404				0.983***	(0.131)	0.498
Regressors									
Cumulative income[3]							0.319***	(0.051)	0.634
Asset holdings[4]				−0.025	(0.098)	−0.013			
Husband's father:									
Education	0.010	(0.005)	0.077	0.003	(0.004)	0.012	0.001	(0.005)	0.003
Occupational status[5]	0.005**	(0.002)	0.113	0.004**	(0.001)	0.047	−0.001	(0.002)	−0.019
Household wealth[6]	0.039***	(0.007)	0.166	0.023***	(0.006)	0.054	0.025***	(0.006)	0.118
Wife's father:									
Education	0.005	(0.005)	0.043	−0.001	(0.004)	−0.001	−0.003	(0.005)	−0.028
Occupational status[5]	0.005**	(0.002)	0.107	0.005***	(0.001)	0.063	−0.001	(0.001)	−0.014
Household wealth[6]	0.042***	(0.007)	0.174	0.023***	(0.005)	0.055	0.022***	(0.006)	0.103
Husband's age at marriage				0.008***	(0.002)	0.048	0.006*	(0.003)	0.071
Years of marriage				0.059***	(0.002)	0.636	−0.006*	(0.003)	−0.127
Husband or wife had prior marriage[7]				−0.080**	(0.030)	−0.029	0.041	(0.044)	0.029
Husband's education				0.042***	(0.004)	0.165	−0.001	(0.006)	−0.007

	(1)	(2)	(3)		(1)	(2)	(3)
Wife's education	0.055***	(0.005)	0.208		−0.001	(0.006)	−0.003
Husband's occup. status[5]	0.021***	(0.001)	0.285		0.284***	(0.051)	0.169
Inheritances[8]							
R² (Asset holdings)	0.207						
R² (Cumulative income)	0.632				0.464		
N	3811				3811		
Fit Indices:							
CFI	0.932				0.978		
RMSEA	0.022				0.025		

Notes:

*p < 0.05, **p < 0.01, ***p < 0.001.

1. Results based on multiple imputation with five data sets. For each model the column (1) entries are unstandardized coefficients; column (2) contains standard errors; and column (3) reports the standardized estimates.
2. Binary term for ownership of each asset item.
3. Estimate of household's cumulative labour market income since marriage (ln).
4. Latent variable.
5. Occupational status coded by ISEI status scores.
6. Estimate of parents' wealth holdings. See text for details.
7. Dummy term, coded 1 if either partner had a prior marriage/cohabitation.
8. Number of inheritances by both members of couple.

353

business equity, would presumably generate such income. Since business holdings is one of four indicators, its unique contribution to the income variable is diminished in this formulation. A more elabourate SEM model, in which business holdings is uncoupled from the other asset indicators, might well reveal an effect on labour market income, but such a formulation is beyond the intent of the present analysis.

Here, our principal interest is concerned with the determination of asset holdings (equation 2b of Table 10.7). By far the largest contribution, in the standardized metric, comes from cumulative labour market income (0.634). At the same time, from among the parental terms, only the wealth measures are significant, but their effects are sizeable (0.118; 0.103). Moreover, these coefficients underestimate the full contribution of parental wealth because the term for inheritance (0.169) also reflects a transfer of parental resources that is net of human capital investments. This part of the direct parental wealth transmission was introduced as a separate regressor in order for the income equation to be identified.

To summarize the findings from the SEM formulations: parental resources make a substantial contribution to both living standards and asset ownership in Chile. In the case of the former, all the parental terms have strong effects and they operate almost entirely through parental investments in the human capital of offspring. In the case of asset ownership, the landscape is radically different. Parental wealth is the dominant resource in terms of influencing respondent's asset ownership. Further, while a considerable portion of the parental effects comes through the labour market income of offspring, there are also strong direct parental transmissions, as evidenced by the sizes of the remaining parental wealth terms and the inheritance variable.

THE PARTICULAR STATUS OF HOME OWNERSHIP

What is the effect of parental resources on home ownership? Earlier, in the discussion of Table 10.1, we remarked that the ownership pattern for residences was strikingly different in Chile from either the possession of the other asset types or from home ownership in the US, in that there is only a modest sensitivity to household income. It was also apparent that the ownership rate in Chile bears little relation to parental wealth (row 9 of Table 10.3). We now return to this topic and examine in greater detail two aspects of residence ownership: the parental resource effects on the waiting time to ownership and on home value.

Waiting time to ownership is estimated using a Cox proportional hazard model (Wooldridge 2002, Chapter 20), with duration from marriage or cohabitation to the year of first owned home as the 'clock' of the process. The Cox model is specified by the equation

$$h(t,\mathbf{X}) = h_0(t)\exp(\boldsymbol{\beta}'\mathbf{X}) \tag{10.6}$$

where $\mathbf{X}$ is a column vector of parental and respondent characteristics, $\boldsymbol{\beta}$ is a parameter vector, $h_0(t)$ specifies the baseline hazard (which is not a function of the explanatory variables), and the left side term is the hazard of entering the state of ownership at time t by a respondent with covariate vector $\mathbf{X}$. Respondents who have never owned by the survey date are treated as right-censored observations.

Model 1a of Table 10.8 reports the total parental resource effects. Not unexpectedly in light of the above comments, they are weak; only one term, for the household wealth of wife's parents, has a positive effect and the impact of that variable is modest: a one standard deviation shift generates less than a 5 per cent change in the hazard rate ($e^{[.019*2.45]}$). We have, incidentally, no explanation for the negative effect of wife's father's education and doubt its significance in the full population. Thus, for the institutional reasons described earlier, the home ownership decision in Chile does not appear to be resource-constrained; at least, it is not the case that parental resources are brought to bear in a substantial way to reduce the waiting time to ownership.

We pursue the matter of the determinants of ownership in model 1b, in which terms have been added for the characteristics of husband and wife, along with a proxy for household income at the time of home acquisition. In regard to the latter, while we know the year of home acquisition, we do not have an income measure for that time point and, for many respondents, 'current household income' refers to a time many years after the acquisition of the first home. Since most first homes were obtained within a few years of marriage we base the respondent's income measure, instead, on questions that refer to the first three years of marriage or cohabitation. Specifically, two variables were introduced: a count of the number of members of the couple who were employed full-time during most of the first three years, and a term for husband's occupational status in that period, the latter serving as a proxy for early permanent income.[8]

With the inclusion of these terms there no longer is evidence of a direct parental effect on the hazard of ownership. There are, however, clear indications that the couple's own resources influence the ownership decision. Specifically, home ownership comes earlier for older husbands (presumably, their careers are more advanced and incomes are higher) and for ones who were in higher-status (and higher-income) occupations early in the marriage. Further, a prior marriage or cohabitation by either spouse

Table 10.8 *Parental resource effects on acquisition of first home and value of current home, Chile 2003[1]*

Explanatory variable	First home–hazard[2]		Value of current home[3]	
	Model 1a	Model 1b	Model 2a	Model 2b
Constant			15.807*** (0.062)	10.706*** (0.178)
Husband's father:				
Education[4]	0.007 (0.006)	0.004 (0.007)	0.033*** (0.006)	0.010** (0.004)
Occupation[5]	0.001 (0.002)	−0.002 (0.002)	0.008*** (0.002)	0.002 (0.001)
Household wealth[6]	0.001 (0.007)	−0.007 (0.007)	0.045*** (0.008)	0.014* (0.006)
Wife's father:				
Education[4]	−0.015** (0.005)	−0.019** (0.006)	0.039*** (0.006)	0.009* (0.004)
Occupation[5]	0.003 (0.002)	−0.001 (0.002)	0.007*** (0.002)	0.001 (0.001)
Household wealth[6]	0.019** (0.078)	0.012 (0.007)	0.029*** (0.007)	0.013* (0.005)
Husband – age at marriage[7]		0.014*** (0.003)		0.025*** (0.002)
Years of marriage[8]				0.013*** (0.002)
Previous marriage[9]		−0.239*** (0.038)		−0.055 (0.035)
Husband's education[3]		−0.008 (0.006)		0.026*** (0.004)
Wife's education[3]		0.001 (0.006)		0.026*** (0.004)
No. of spouses employed, early in marriage[10]		0.027 (0.065)		
Husband did not work, early in marriage[11]		−0.270* (0.133)		
Husband's occupation, early in marriage[5]		0.012*** (0.001)		
Cumulative labour market income[12]			−0.873*** (0.024)	0.440*** (0.019)
Lambda				0.112 (0.068)

LR Chi Sq. (N)	13.08 (6)	89.72 (13)	
Wald Chi Sq. (N)			786.2 (6)	2010.3 (12)
N	3688	3688	3811	3811

Notes:

*p < 0.05, **p < 0.01, ***p < 0.001.

1. Results based on multiple imputation with five data sets.
2. Cox proportional hazard model of duration from marriage/cohabitation to first home ownership. Residences acquired before, but within five years of the union were treated as acquired in first year of marriage/cohabitation. Observation was deleted if the residence was acquired more than five years before the union. Respondents who have not owned a home by the survey date are treated as right-censored observations.
3. Heckman Selection Model, estimated using Full Information Maximum Likelihood. Dependent variable is ln (home value in Chilean pesos). Probit selection equation for home ownership (not shown) includes community size variables for identification.
4. Years of schooling completed.
5. Occupational status coded by ISEI status scores (Ganzeboom et al. 1992).
6. Estimate of parents wealth holdings. See text for details.
7. Age of husband at time of marriage/cohabitation.
8. Years of marriage/cohabitation.
9. Indicator variable coded 1 if husband or wife had a previous marriage or cohabitation.
10. Number of spouses who worked full time during first three years of marriage/cohabitation.
11. Indicator variable coded 1 if husband not in labour force (full or part-time) during first three years of marriage/cohabitation.
12. Estimate of cumulative income from labour market activity since time of marriage/cohabitation, in Chilean pesos (ln).

lengthens the time to ownership, possibly because it may have resulted in a dilution of resources.

An observation worth making is that there is some contradiction between the findings of the two equations. Equation 1b makes clear that financial constraints do, in fact, impede the acquisition of a home. However, equation 1a provides only weak evidence that parents step up to the plate in this circumstance and contribute to the financing of a home purchase by their children. At this point we can provide no clear resolution to this contradiction; but the following material is suggestive. The Chilean survey inquired about respondent's views of the importance of assisting grown children with the purchase of a residence at the time of marriage; only 3 per cent replied that 'this was the responsibility of parents'. In an Israeli survey with an identical question, the comparable rate was 45 per cent (Spilerman 2004). Parental affection for children is unlikely to be different in the two countries, but the institutional arrangements are quite disparate and this may account for the differential response – and for differential rates of parental assistance in the two countries.[9]

Do the current *values* of acquired homes reflect parental resources? Equations 2a and 2b address this question using a Heckman selection model to correct for the fact that home value is observed only for the subset of respondents who are homeowners. Only the equations for home value are presented in Table 10.8, the probit selection equations for residence ownership are not shown since they largely replicate the hazard model results.[10] Model 2a makes clear that there are substantial parental effects on home value; children from higher economic origins are likely to own residences of greater monetary value. According to model 2b, however, the bulk of the parental transmission is through education and income[11] with the introduction of these terms the direct effects of parental wealth are reduced by some 60 to 70 per cent from their initial values. The implication, then, is fairly clear: parental resources do matter for home value, but their impact comes largely through parental investments in the human capital of offspring and only secondarily from financial assistance.

As noted in the introduction, the home acquisition process in Chile does not conform to what has been found for the US, Western Europe or Israel (for example, Hamnett et al. 1991; Engelhardt and Mayer 1994; Mulder and Smits 1999; Spilerman 2004), in that there is evidence in Chile of only modest direct parental assistance, either to facilitate an acquisition or permit offspring to purchase a residence of greater monetary value. Indeed, the results from the home value equations suggest parental effects that are more in line with the acquisition of consumption items than asset holdings, namely large total parental effects that mainly operate through investments in children's human capital. Clearly, a deeper understanding of the Chilean housing market will be necessary to better comprehend these somewhat counterintuitive findings.

CONCLUSIONS

Recent trends in Western countries point to a continued erosion in the availability of publicly funded social welfare programmes. This development will necessarily heighten the importance of private family resources, both as a protection against the financial consequences of crisis events such as illness or job loss, and to enhance a family's ability to finance household expenses at particular life stages, especially the retirement period and the years of raising children and facilitating their well-being.

The last matter speaks to issues in the replication of inequality across generations and the possible strengthening of the linkage between parental resources and the economic welfare of offspring. This is an issue of some import in capitalist countries because a basic tenet of fairness in this type of industrial regime is that the disparity in economic outcomes be linked to effort, education and hard work. To the extent that the determination of life chances is dominated, instead, by the initial conditions of parental resources, the equitable functioning of the system is called into doubt.

The degree of importance of parental resources is an empirical question and the assessment is likely to vary by country, reflecting the availability of public support programmes, ease of access to credit, as well as other institutional arrangements. In this chapter we have examined the issue of parental effects with data from Chile, a country with high inequality and a largely privatized social welfare system; in short, a setting in which parental resources would likely be consequential for children's outcomes. Our findings support this expectation, but the results are nuanced and vary with the dimension of children's well-being.

Parental resources have strong effects on both the living standard and asset holdings of adult children. Parental education and occupational status are most critical to living standard (as measured by consumption expenditures); parental wealth, in contrast, has the larger impact on the children's asset portfolio. Moreover, the pathway of transmission differs according to the outcome type under consideration: in the case of living standard, the parental effects are largely mediated by children's education and earnings; thus the avenue of transmission is via parental investments in education. With respect to the asset holdings of offspring, much of the transfer is direct and takes the form of parental financial assistance and inheritances.

At the same time, we find much to be sanguine about, in that there appears to be opportunity in Chile for the acquisition of consumption items and asset holdings apart from the influence of parental resources. This likely is a consequence of state investments over the years in primary and secondary education, as detailed in Spilerman and Torche (2004), which has made schooling accessible to children from poor families. A note of caution is necessary, however. The economic returns to primary and secondary education in Chile have declined significantly in recent decades. In contrast, the returns to tertiary education have grown rapidly, a pattern that helps explain the high concentration of income among the privileged, who have access to university education, and the high inequality in the country (Beyer 2000; Contreras 2002; Duryea and Pages 2002). Thus, unless further public investments are made to facilitate access by the poor to tertiary schooling, the equalizing role that the educational system has traditionally played in Chile might weaken.[12]

The findings with respect to home ownership are more complex. In contrast with the other indicators of asset holdings, the home acquisition process appears to be largely detached from parental resources. We have linked this finding to Chilean housing policy, which, beginning in the 1960s and with special vigour since the late 1980s, has provided subsidized access to home ownership, as opposed to rental solutions. The fact that the acquisition of a residence under this programme does not involve costs that are unbearable for young couples appears to have reduced the pressure for parental assistance.

If Chilean housing policy is a mediating factor between parental resources and home ownership, this is not the case with respect to home *value*, for which the parental effects are considerable. Interestingly, these parental resource effects appear to work mainly through children's education and occupational attainment, rather than taking the form of direct assistance, although the marginal significance of the parental wealth terms (Table 10.8, model 2b) provides weak evidence of direct transfers as well.

While the preceding analysis may be helpful to understanding the dynamics of intergenerational financial linkages in Chile, its full value will only emerge in comparisons with other country studies. It is through a comparative strategy that we can best comprehend the interactions between parental resources, institutional arrangements in a country, and the transmission of advantage, and proceed thereupon to develop efficient programmes to offset some of the disadvantages associated with poor family origins.

NOTES

*   This research was supported by Ford Foundation grant No. 1040-1239 to the Center for the Study of Wealth and Inequality, Columbia University. We would like to thank Mitali

Das for her advice on statistical issues. The conclusions are the sole responsibility of the authors.

1. Omitted from the wealth estimates are CDs, retirement accounts, the cash value of life insurance, managed assets, and other (nonspecified) financial and material assets. These categories are omitted from the US data because they lack a counterpart in the Chilean survey.

2. The sampling strategy included three stages. First, 87 primary sampling units (counties) were selected: Blocks within the PSUs were then selected, and finally households within blocks were chosen. Counties were stratified by size (less than 20 000; 20 000–100 000; 100 000–200 000; more than 200 000 inhabitants); and geographical zone (North, Centre, South). Optimal allocation was used to increase efficiency (Lohr 1999) by including all PSUs in the large-size stratum (more than 200 000 inhabitants) in the sample. The fieldwork was conducted between April and June 2003 and consisted of face-to-face interviews in the respondent's household.

3. Although the value of vehicles is a component of family wealth, our analytical formulation treats vehicles as a consumption item. The reason is that, unlike the other asset types, vehicles quickly depreciate in financial value though their 'use value' for a household can remain high (Wolff 2001).

4. Alternatively, we could have used husband's and wife's occupational status instead of the couple's current earnings in order to smooth earnings fluctuations and capture permanent labour market income. Analyses carried out using the occupational status terms show that the results are not sensitive to this change in specification.

5. They are refrigerator, washing machine, telephone, cable TV and computer.

6. The error from mismeasurement of this regressor would likely depress its effect on the dependent variable. Alternative measures of life course accumulation from labour market activity were considered, such as ones based on estimates of 'permanent income' – for example, the product of husband's occupational status and years of marriage or cohabitation. The substantive findings with such measures were identical to the results presented in the text.

7. The tables for these models are available from the authors.

8. Cases where husband did not have a status score because he was in school or otherwise did not work during the first three years of marriage or cohabitation were retained by means of the introduction of an indicator variable for 'husband not in the labour force'.

9. In Israel, where there is little co-residence with parents, home ownership is tightly linked to parental wealth and parental assistance. See Spilerman (2004) for details.

10. For identification purposes five dummy variables for community size were added to the probit equations. The rationale for their inclusion is that communities of different size have characteristically different home ownership rates. A likelihood ratio test for the added terms was highly significant.

11. Since home value is examined for *current* residence, the term for cumulative labour market income replaces the estimate of household income in the early marital period. Over the years respondents may have traded up in residence quality or made improvements to the structure, increasing its value. In this circumstance, the cumulative income term provides the appropriate estimate of the availability of funds from the couple's earnings to finance such additions to home value.

12. The trend to a widening wage gap between unskilled and skilled workers as a result of increased returns to knowledge is not a Chilean particularity, but a global trend (Heckman 2001; Mincer 1996). The strength and speed of the Chilean case is, however, remarkable.

REFERENCES

Attias-Donfut, C. and F.C. Wolff (2000), 'The redistributive effects of generational transfers', in S. Arber and C. Attias-Donfut (eds), *The Myth of Generational Conflict: Family and State in Ageing Societies*, London: Routledge, pp. 22–46.

Becker, G. (1981), *A Treatise on the Family*, Cambridge, MA: Harvard University Press.

Beyer, H. (2000), 'Educacion y Desigualdad de Ingresos: Hacia una Nueva Mirada' (Education and Earnings Inequality: Towards a New Approach), *Estudios Publicos*, **77**, 97–130.

Blau, P. and O.D. Duncan (1967), *The American Occupational Structure*, New York: Free Press.

Contreras, D. (2002), 'Explaining wage inequality in Chile: does education really matter?', Santiago: Department of Economics, Universidad de Chile.

Cummings, J. and D. Dipasquale (2002), 'The spatial implications of housing policy in Chile', in E. Glaeser and J. Meyer (eds), *Chile. Political Economy of Urban Development*, Cambridge, MA: JFK School of Government Harvard University, pp. 197–248.

Departamento de Estudios MINVU (Research Department, Ministry of Housing and Urban Development Chile) (2004), 'Panoramica de la Vivienda Social en Chile: Balance e Imagenes de un Siglo de Politicas Urbanas en Vivienda y Barrio', Santiago: MINVU.

Duncan, O.D., D. Featherman and B. Duncan (1972), *Socioeconomic Background and Achievement*, New York: Seminar Press.

Duryea, S. and C. Pages (2002), 'Achieving high labour productivity in Latin America: is education enough?', Washington, DC: Inter-American Development Bank, mimeographed document.

Englehardt, G. and C. Mayer (1994), 'Gift for home purchase and housing market behavior', *New England Economic Review*, May–June, 47–58.

Ganzeboom, H., P. de Graaf and D. Treiman (1992), 'A standard international socio-economic index of occupational status', *Social Science Research*, **21**, 1–56.

Guiso, L. and T. Jappelli (1999), 'Private transfers, borrowing constraints and the timing of homeownership', Center for Studies in Economics and Finance, University of Salerno, unpublished manuscript.

Hamnett, C., M. Harmer and P. Williams (1991), *Safe as Houses: Housing Inheritance in Britain*, London: Paul Chapman.

Heckman, J. (2001), 'Policies to foster human capital', Working Paper 2 N1, Joint Center for Poverty Research, Northwestern University/University of Chicago.

Honaker, J.A., J.G. King, K. Scheve and N. Singh (2003), 'Amelia: a program for missing data', software manual, Department of Government, Harvard University, http://gking.harvard.edu/stats.shtml.

Joreskog, K. and D. Sorbom (1989), *LISREL 7 Users Reference Guide*, Chicago, IL: Scientific Software International.

Kennickell, A., M. Starr-McCluer and B. Surette (2000), 'Recent changes in US family finances: results from the 1998 Survey of Consumer Finances', *Federal Reserve Bulletin*, **86** (January), 1–29.

Kohli, M. (2005), 'Intergenerational transfers and inheritance: a comparative view', in M. Silverstein, R. Giarruso and V.L. Bengtson (eds), *Intergenerational Relations across Time and Place*, New York: Springer.

Lohr, S. (1999), *Sampling: Design and Analysis*, Pacific Grove, CA: Duxbury Press.

Lustig, N. (ed.) (2001), *Shielding the Poor: Social Protection in the Developing World*, Washington, DC: Brookings Institution Press/IADB.

Mideplan (2000), *Situacion Habitacional en Chile* (Housing Situation in Chile), Documento de Trabajo 5, Santiago, Chile: Ministerio de Planificacion.

Mincer, J. (1996), 'Changes in wage inequality, 1970–1990', Working Paper 5823, National Bureau of Economic Research, New York, November.

Moser, C. (1998), 'The asset vulnerability framework: reassessing urban poverty reduction strategies', *World Development*, **26**(1), 1–19.

Mulder, C. and J. Smits (1999), 'First-time home ownership of couples: the effect of intergenerational transmission', *European Sociological Review*, **15**, 323–37.

Pardo, C. (2000), 'Housing finance in Chile: the experience in primary and secondary mortgage financing', Working Document, Best Practices Series, Sustainable Development Department Inter-American Development Bank, Washington, DC: IADB.

Raczynski, D. (1994), 'Social policies in Chile: origin, transformations and perspectives', Working Paper 4, Democracy and Social Policy Series, Notre Dame, IN: University of Notre Dame.

Rojas, E. (1999), 'The long road to housing sector reform: lessons from the Chilean housing experience', *Housing Studies*, **16**(4), 461–83.

Rubin, D. (1987), *Multiple Imputation for Nonresponse in Surveys*, New York: Wiley.

Sahn, D. and D. Stifel (2003), 'Exploring alternative measures of welfare in the absence of expenditure data', *Review of Income and Wealth*, **49**(4), 463–89.

Spilerman, S. (2000), 'Wealth and stratification process', *Annual Review of Sociology*, **26**, 497–524.

Spilerman, S. (2004), 'The impact of parental wealth on early living standards in Israel', *American Journal of Sociology*, **110** (July), 92–122.

Spilerman, S. and F. Torche (2004), 'Living standard potential and the transmission of advantage in Chile', in E. Wolff (ed.), *What Has Happened to the Quality of Life in the Advanced Industrial Nations*, Northampton, MA: Edward Elgar, pp. 214–53.

Torche, F. (2005), 'Unequal but fluid: social mobility in Chile in comparative perspective', *American Sociological Review*, **70**(3), 422–50.

Wolff, E. (2001), 'Recent trends in wealth ownership, from 1983 to 1998', in T. Shapiro and E. Wolff (eds), *Assets for the Poor: The Benefits of Spreading Asset Ownership*, New York: Russell Sage.

Wooldridge, Jeffrey (2002), *Econometric Analysis of Cross Section and Panel Data*, Cambridge: MIT Press.

World Bank (1993), *The Housing Indicators Programme*, vol. II: *Indicator Tables*, Washington, DC: World Bank.

World Bank (2000a), *Poverty and Policy in Latin America and the Caribbean*, World Bank Technical Paper no. 467, Washington, DC: World Bank.

World Bank (2000b), *World Development Indicators*, Washington, DC: World Bank.

Wormald, G. and J. Rozas (1996), 'Microenterprises and the informal sector in the Santiago metropolitan area', in V. Tokman and E. Klein (eds), *Regulation and the Informal Economy: Microenterprises in Chile, Ecuador, and Jamaica*, Boulder, CO: Lynne Rienner Publishers.

APPENDIX

Table 10A.1   Descriptive statistics for variables in the analysis, survey of intergenerational financial linkages, Chile 2003[1]

Variable	Mean	Standard Deviation	N
Husband's parents:			
Father's education	6.09	4.81	3223
Father's occupation[2]	32.11	13.59	3301
Parents' wealth[3]	−0.01	2.46	3730
Wife's parents:			
Father's education	6.29	4.70	3244
Father's occupation[2]	31.80	13.11	3326
Parents' wealth[3]	−0.04	2.45	3741
Couple:			
Age of husband at marriage	26.01	6.49	3737
Years of marriage	22.41	11.29	3804
Either member of couple had previous			
marriage/cohabitation	0.18	0.39	3807
Husband's years of schooling	9.88	4.13	3811
Wife's years of schooling	9.56	4.01	3806
Occupational status, husband, 2003[2]	37.05	14.13	3722
Ln (Labor Market Income)[4]	5.63	0.90	3701
Ln (cumulative labor market income)	8.59	1.05	3694
Ownership of durables[5]	0.13	3.34	3788
Vehicle ownership	0.38	0.48	3807
Use of domestic service	0.09	0.29	3807
Subjective SOL[6]	2.86	0.79	3808
Financial assets ownership	0.04	0.19	3794
Business ownership	0.17	0.38	3807
Real estate ownership	0.07	0.26	3800
Residential property ownership	0.11	0.32	3802
Home ownership	0.66	0.47	3811
Years from marriage to first home ownership	9.80	8.09	3550
Ln (home value)[7]	16.31	0.97	2477
No. spouses employed, early in marriage	1.23	0.54	3809
Husband's occupation, early in marriage[2]	35.99	14.39	3675

Notes:
1. Sample restricted to households with head aged 25–69 (N = 3811). Unweighted estimates reported.
2. ISEI status score (Ganzeboom et al. 1992).
3. Sum of Z-scores from count of ownership of financial assets, business equity, residential property (excluding primary residence) and real estate.
4. Household's monthly income from labour market activity, in Chilean pesos (ln).
5. Sum of Z-scores from count of ownership of the following household items: refrigerator, washing machine, telephone, cable TV and computer.
6. Five-point ordinal variable that compares household standard of living with average standard of living of Chilean households.
7. Estimate by respondent in Chilean pesos. Calculation is for homeowners.

11. Trends and turbulence: allocations and dynamics of American family portfolios, 1984–2001

Elena Gouskova, F. Thomas Juster and Frank P. Stafford

INTRODUCTION

Understanding household portfolio behaviour is important for a number of reasons. First, portfolio choice affects the rate of wealth accumulation, due to differential returns on asset types. The asset-specific risk also affects the distribution of wealth. Second, depending on portfolio composition, changes in macro variables, such as interest rates, stock prices, inflation and unemployment, may have different effects on household saving and consumption (Bertaut and Starr-McCluer 2002). Portfolio composition also determines the effects of public policies, such as the capital gains tax or social security reform, on personal saving (Poterba 2002). Knowledge of how households structure their assets is important in assessing the expanding role of defined contribution pension plans that shift the responsibility for decision making toward individuals; there may be room for policies aimed at raising the understanding of financial choices by households. Third, studying households' portfolio decisions may lead to better understanding of consumption and saving behaviour.

Empirical studies have been conducted on the evolution of household portfolios between 1983 and 1998 (Bertaut and Starr-McCluer 2002). Portfolios of the rich and elderly have been studied in Carroll (2002) and Hurd (2002). The effect of taxes on portfolio composition has been investigated in Poterba (2002), and King and Leape (1998). The effect of income and wealth on household portfolios (Uhler and Cragg 1971) and the demand for optimal holdings of financial assets (Perraudin and Sorensen 2000; Flavin and Yamashita 1998) have been explored.

While the Panel Study of Income Dynamics (PSID) has been used for studying household total wealth and household behaviour regarding some specific asset types, like housing (Flavin and Yamashita 1998) or business holdings (Hurst and Lusardi 2003), it has not, to the best of our knowledge, been employed for studying the full household portfolio choice. The majority of the studies on household portfolios were based on the Survey of Consumer Finances (SCF) (Bertaut and Starr-McCluer 2002; Carroll 2002; Hurd 2002; Katona et al. 1964; Poterba 2002). Analysis of data from the PSID, which is a true panel, allows the potential benefit of studying portfolio reallocation through time by individual households.

The main focus is on two aspects of household portfolio choice: portfolio span, defined as the number of asset types held; and portfolio composition. Using panel aspects of the data, we explore the possibility of a 'crowding-out' effect of stocks on other real estate (which excludes the primary residence).

Examination of the number of asset types held, which we refer to as portfolio span, shows large variability across demographic groups, with the race effect being particularly pronounced. Portfolio span is shown to be strongly associated with income, wealth and education variables. During the 1984–2001 period, we find an increase in the number of asset types held by households. However, when controls for age, wealth, income and education are introduced, the year difference becomes insignificant. Based on the evidence, we conclude that the observed increase in the number of portfolio components during these 17 years is more likely to be the result of changing demographic and socio-economic factors than increased financial sophistication of families.[1]

This chapter documents the extreme diversity of portfolio choices among households. The most popular portfolios held by households are identified. The top five portfolio types account for about 50 per cent of families, with the most common type – transaction account + owner occupied housing + transportation/vehicles – being held by 15 to 17 per cent of households. A substantial number of households hold no assets. The results of multivariate analysis indicate that life-cycle factors, income and wealth, as well as race and education, play important roles in the determination of portfolio choice. Over the 1984–2001 period, the main change in household portfolio composition is the substantial increase in stock ownership rates.

An interesting question regarding the growth of an 'equity culture' is how stocks have entered household portfolios and, in particular, whether equities have been replacing other assets. One possible candidate for substitution is other real estate, which excludes primary residence, as its ownership rate shows a decline during the period. If households consider stocks and real estate to be substitutes, one implication would be that while stocks were replacing real estate during the 1990s, the situation might have reversed after the stock market slump in 2001.[2] It is possible that when stocks became unattractive households tended to move their money into real estate, creating the upward pressure on real estate prices.

Given the opposite directions of real estate and equity in the time series on ownership rates, the proposition that they are substitutes in the household portfolio seems plausible. Our micropanel evidence shows that there is a significant relationship between the decision to buy/sell stocks and the decision to buy/sell real estate. So, with rising returns in equity markets coupled with decreasing costs of stock ownership during the period we may expect households to participate more in stocks and less in real estate. However, as the data indicate, the 'crowding-out' effect of stocks on real estate during the period was not particularly strong and, in addition, was lessened by the wealth effect from capital gains in the stock market.

The organization of the chapter is as follows. In the first section, we analyse the household portfolio span. The second section characterizes the distribution of portfolio types in the data. In the third section, we explore the question of whether stocks had been substituting for real estate in the household portfolio during the 1984–2001 period, followed by the chapter's conclusions.

HOUSEHOLD PORTFOLIO SPAN

We begin by examining the number of broad asset types held by a household, which we will refer to as portfolio span. The maximum portfolio span in our data set is seven, since PSID asks questions about seven different asset categories:[3]

1. equity in housing (primary residence) (H);
2. equity in real estate (second home, land, rental real estate, or money owed on a land contract) (R);
3. equity in business (also includes farm) (B);
4. equity in vehicle (cars, trucks, a motor home, a trailer or a boat) (T);
5. equity in stock[4] (includes shares of stock in publicly held corporations, mutual funds, and investment trusts) (SI);
6. transaction accounts (includes savings accounts, money market funds, certificates of deposit, government savings bonds, and treasury bills) (C);
7. other assets (includes bond funds, cash value in a life insurance policy, a valuable collection for investment purposes, and rights in a trust or estate) (V).

The Distribution of Portfolio Span

Figure 11.1 depicts the distributions of portfolio span for the years 1984 and 2001. (The other years show a very similar pattern.) The distributions are quite symmetric and unimodal with the mode at 3. About a quarter (25.3 per cent in 1984 and 24.3 per cent in 2001) of household portfolios are comprised of three asset types. The next most popular portfolio size is four (17.9 per cent in 1984 and 22.2 per cent in 2001). A considerable number of households hold no assets: 5.3 per cent in 1984 decreasing over the years to 3.7 per cent by 2001. Overall, Figure 11.1 underscores the fact that many households, close to half, have very simple portfolios that include no more than three elements (44.8 per cent in 1984 and 43 per cent in 2001).

Another interesting feature of Figure 11.1 is a shift away from the 'parsimonious portfolios' of zero, one or two elements, with growth in the share of families with four or more elements in their portfolios. Formal testing supports this impression. The difference between the distributions of number of components in 1984 and 2001 is statistically significant (the chi-square test statistic with 7 degrees of freedom is equal to 874.8, which corresponds to a

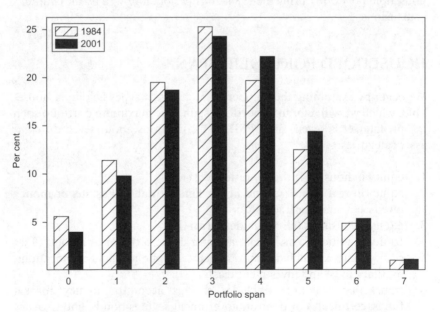

Note: The difference between the 1984 and 2001 distributions is statistically significant $(\chi^2(7) = 874.8)$.

Figure 11.1   Distribution of portfolio span, 1984 and 2001

p-value of less than 0.0001). In the multivariate analysis below we explore whether this shift is a reflection of changes in household behaviour or changing composition of households, with more households in life-cycle stages where additional assets are likely to be held (Campbell and Viceira 2002).

Distribution of Diversification Levels by Demographic Groups

The average span of household portfolios varies greatly across different demographic groups (Table 11.1). Portfolio span first increases for young and middle-aged householders and then decreases for families with a head aged 60 or older. The most frequent portfolio span in the group of those 18 to 30 years old is two (33 per cent), and for those in the 31–45 age range it is three (27 per cent). In 2001, four is the most frequent portfolio span for those in the 46–60 age group. Among householders aged 60 or older the four-element portfolio is still the most common; however, there is a reduction in the number of larger-size portfolios (five and larger). While the data indicate that the 'null' portfolio is more characteristic of younger households (6 per cent for those aged 18 to 30, in 2001), it also occurs among older households, albeit at a lower rate (2 per cent among 46- to 60-year-olds).

The disparity in portfolio span is particularly evident between white and African American households. Thus, the most popular portfolio among white families consists of three or four components, each with probabilities of 0.25 in 2001. The distribution of span for African American families shows the most common to be two (24 per cent), followed by one- and three-component portfolios (23 per cent and 21 per cent, respectively).

The probability of a null portfolio among African Americans is persistently about ten times that of white families (16.3 per cent for blacks and 1.7 per cent for whites in 2001; 24 per cent for blacks and 2.4 per cent for whites in 1984). This evidence certainly echoes the story of wealth and income inequalities between the racial groups, which is well documented in the literature. Since income and wealth are related to span, are there any remaining differences in the portfolio span once the effects of wealth, income and life-cycle position have been accounted for? During the period 1984–2001, similar to the overall distribution of portfolio size, conditional on race, the distribution exhibits a shift toward the upper end. A positive sign is the substantial drop in the likelihood of having null portfolios among African American families between 1984 and 2001 (from 24 per cent to 16 per cent).

Factors such as education, marital status and gender also appear to be associated with portfolio span. Thus, less-educated people, female-headed households and nonmarried people tend to hold less diversified portfolios.

As can be seen in Table 11.2 within each age, education and demographic group, median wealth is greater among those with a larger portfolio span.

Table 11.1   *Distribution of portfolio span, by characteristics of household head, 1984 and 2001*

		Portfolio span						
		0	1	2	3	4	5	6 or more
1984								
Total		5.3	11.1	19.4	25.4	20.0	12.6	6.2
Age of head	18 to 30	9.1	18.0	33.1	24.1	10.3	4.4	0.9
	31 to 45	4.4	8.6	16.7	26.5	22.3	14.6	7.0
	46 to 60	4.0	6.7	11.1	24.1	23.9	17.8	12.4
	60 or more	3.7	11.0	16.5	26.5	23.5	13.6	5.2
Race of head	White	2.4	9.3	18.5	26.6	22.0	14.1	7.0
	Black	24.1	22.9	25.5	17.5	6.7	2.3	0.9
Education of head	No high school degree	11.3	18.4	21.3	25.4	14.9	6.3	2.3
	High school degree	4.3	11.1	22.0	25.3	21.2	11.2	5.0
	Some college	2.8	6.4	17.1	30.8	21.0	13.1	8.9
	College degree or more	0.5	4.6	14.1	21.1	24.4	23.5	11.8
Sex of head	Male	2.5	6.9	16.8	26.1	23.5	16.0	8.2
	Female	11.4	20.2	25.2	24.0	12.3	4.9	1.9
Marital status	Married	1.0	4.4	13.9	27.2	26.1	18.1	9.4
	Not married	10.5	19.3	26.3	23.3	12.5	5.8	2.4
2001								
Total		3.7	8.9	17.3	24.6	22.9	15.3	7.3
Age of head	18 to 30	6.2	16.7	32.7	26.1	14.0	3.7	0.6
	31 to 45	4.7	9.8	17.8	27.4	22.1	12.9	5.4
	46 to 60	1.9	5.2	13.1	21.4	26.3	21.2	10.9
	60 or more	3.0	7.6	12.9	24.0	25.2	18.2	9.1
Race of head	White	1.7	6.6	16.3	25.0	25.0	17.1	8.2
	Black	16.3	23.1	24.1	21.6	9.4	4.2	1.2
Education of head	No high school degree	10.6	19.2	23.1	22.9	13.8	7.1	3.3
	High school degree	4.3	10.3	19.4	26.6	21.6	12.1	5.7
	Some college	2.5	7.3	16.9	27.4	23.5	15.9	6.6
	College degree or more	0.1	2.8	12.3	21.2	29.0	22.9	11.7
Sex of head	Male	1.9	6.2	13.7	25.4	25.2	18.4	9.1
	Female	7.9	15.1	25.7	22.6	17.5	8.2	2.9
Marital status	Married	0.6	2.8	9.8	25.7	28.2	22.0	10.9
	Not married	7.2	15.8	25.9	23.3	16.9	7.7	3.2

Note: Numbers represent percentages.

Table 11.2   *Median wealth, by portfolio span levels and by characteristics of household head, 1984 and 2001*

		Portfolio span						
		0	1	2	3	4	5	6 or more
1984								
Total		0	2	10	58	126	208	396
Age of head	18 to 30	0	1	5	19	51	84	158
	31 to 45	0	1	10	49	90	144	291
	46 to 60	0	3	22	87	153	237	511
	60 or more	0	8	29	95	203	250	523
Race of head	White	0	2	10	60	131	210	396
	Black	0	1	16	37	70	152	218
Education of head	No high school degree	0	2	19	58	129	236	352
	High school degree	0	2	10	58	120	206	343
	Some college	−1	1	5	49	116	157	416
	College degree or more	0	1	9	61	133	207	619
Sex of head	Male	0	1	11	59	127	211	407
	Female	0	2	10	53	126	167	235
Marital status	Married	0	2	14	64	133	214	440
	Not married	0	2	9	48	114	167	201
2001								
Total		0	1	7	56	151	309	552
Age of head	18 to 30	0	1	2	17	39	124	158
	31 to 45	0	1	6	41	119	220	408
	46 to 60	0	2	12	66	164	298	550
	60 or more	0	1	35	116	221	435	608
Race of head	White	0	1	6	62	158	309	566
	Black	0	1	13	38	64	282	543
Education of head	No high school degree	0	1	10	53	122	227	390
	High school degree	0	2	6	68	152	250	480
	Some college	0	1	8	49	129	290	542
	College degree or more	−18	−1	3	56	175	392	638
Sex of head	Male	0	2	8	57	154	341	552
	Female	0	1	6	54	134	191	530
Marital status	Married	0	2	11	61	164	345	581
	Not married	0	1	6	52	129	227	507

Note: Wealth is measured in thousands of dollars.

This result is in large part due to the fact that households with very diverse portfolios are apt to include holdings of investment real estate and business or farm equity, both of which tend to be characterized by large dollar amounts. The evidence suggests that greater wealth leads to more extensive portfolios, rather than just an increase in the dollar value of existing portfolio elements. Possibly, long-term wealth growth may be a primary factor behind the shift toward more diversified portfolios.

Multivariate Analysis of Portfolio Span

To disentangle various factors affecting household portfolio span, multivariate modelling is required. In this subsection we relate the variation in portfolio span to economic and demographic factors. Tables 11.1 and 11.2 indicate that factors such as wealth, age, race and education are likely to have an effect on the number of assets in household portfolios. Given the strong effect of race in the unconditional analysis, does the race effect on portfolio persist net of other factors? Additionally, multivariate modelling can provide some insight into the observed tendency toward larger portfolio sizes during the 1984–2001 period: are rising levels of diversification the result of a compositional change or are higher levels conditional on variables known to boost diversification, suggesting a broader shift toward higher levels of financial awareness?

Two approaches in modelling household portfolio size are used: linear regression and Poisson regression. Results are presented in Table 11.3. The regressions are estimated for the pooled data sample. Both models produce a good fit. The linear regression explains 48 per cent of the variation in portfolio span. Given the discrete nature of the dependent variable, the Poisson regression is probably the better model choice (Maddala 1997). The pseudo-R^2 of the Poisson regression is 43 per cent. It was calculated as the R^2 of the regression on predicted values obtained from the Poisson regression. The signs of the explanatory variables are as expected, and the effects are significant for most of the variables. Wealth and income have strong positive effects on portfolio span. Household diversification is quadratic in age: households in middle age have a greater portfolio span, but at older ages households tend to hold fewer asset types, possibly because they liquidate some. Using the estimated coefficients of age and age squared, the calculated age at which the quadratic function reaches its maximum is about 65 for the linear model and 58 for the Poisson regression.[5]

Being married and having more education have significant positive effects on portfolio diversification. The race effect is significant despite the

Table 11.3   *Regression of portfolio span*

	Linear regression		Poisson regression	
	Coefficient	t-value	Coefficient	Chi-square
Intercept	0.865***	15.7	0.1783***	35.0
Inc	0.0038***	31.5	0.0005***	248.0
Wealth1	2.00E-04***	23	0.00000***	86.8
Age of head	0.0821***	36.5	0.0345***	813.2
Age squared	−0.0006***	−28.5	−0.0003***	509.6
D_Black	−0.9917***	−67.1	−0.434***	2676.6
D_Other	−0.5919***	−19.1	−0.2031***	153.7
D_No high school degree	−1.0965***	−52.6	−0.4379***	1770.8
D_High school degree	−0.5219***	−27.7	−0.1663***	373.1
D_Some college	−0.2275***	−11.1	−0.0549***	35.2
D_Female	−0.1165***	−5.6	−0.0727***	35.7
Married dummy	0.7629***	34.8	0.3048***	665.0
Family size	−0.0132**	−2.6	−0.0044	2.5
D_year 1989	−0.0093	−0.5	−0.0011	0.0
D_year 1994	−0.0348*	−1.8	−0.0098	1.0
D_year 1999	0.0228	1.1	0.01	0.9
D_year 2001	0.0042	0.2	0.0063	0.4
N	35 813		35 813	
R^2	0.4797		0.4303	

Note: *** denotes significance at the 1% level; ** at the 5% level; * at the 10% level.

presence of wealth and income covariates. Based on the linear regression, controlling for all other covariates, an African American household has almost one full asset type less in its portfolio than a white household. This strongly significant result may imply some cultural or intergenerational aspects affecting household portfolio behaviour (Chiteji and Stafford 1999).

As we have noted before there is a significant shift between 1984 and 2001 toward greater portfolio span (see Figure 11.1). In the linear model the year dummy variables are nonsignificant with the exception of the 1994 coefficient, which is weakly significant. The results from the Poisson regression also suggest no time effects. Thus, the observed shift in portfolio size distribution seems to be more likely the result of an evolution of socio-economic factors rather than change in household behaviour conditioned on those factors. That is, as the population ages and becomes wealthier, and as the baby-boom cohort approaches retirement, we see more assets held.

PORTFOLIO COMPOSITION

In this section an alternative measure of household portfolios is explored, namely, the types of portfolios as specific combinations of asset types held. As with portfolio span, how do income, wealth, age, education, race and family composition affect choice among the different types of portfolios?

Participation

Between the 1980s and 2001 the main asset group to gain in popularity was stocks and IRAs (individual retirement accounts). In 1984 only 25 per cent of families reported holding stocks/IRAs based on stocks; this percentage rose steadily throughout the period and by 2001 was at 40 per cent of families.[6] The percentage of families with home equity rose from 60 per cent in 1984 to 65 per cent in 2001. Another distinct shift was away from holdings of other real estate, and there was some shift away from other valuable assets (a broad category including such assets as trusts, estates, cash surrender value of life insurance, and valuable collections). These shifts are presented in Figure 11.2.

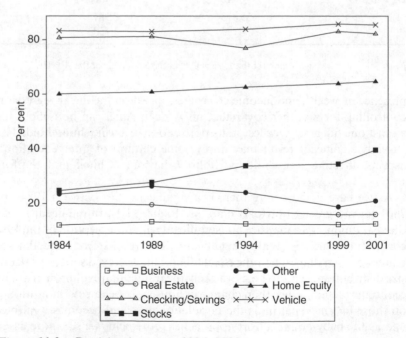

Figure 11.2   Participation rates, 1984–2001

Heterogeneity

Characterizing household portfolios on a multiple-asset basis is not straightforward. One approach is to categorize the asset types on the basis of risk and return and use these categories for the subsequent analysis. The benefit of such an approach is in specifying household portfolio in terms familiar to the mean-variance framework for portfolio choice in traditional economics. The shortcoming is that the grouping will be to some degree arbitrary because of variability in risks and returns within an asset type. Here the error may be large since the number of asset types is relatively small and asset types are broadly defined. Using the asset types as measured in the PSID, the variable of interest is a portfolio type, defined as a specific set of assets in the portfolio.

Even with seven asset types, the number of portfolio combinations becomes large (about 100 in our sample), with many of them held by very few families. The 'full portfolio', in which all asset types are present, is held by only 1 per cent of families. The top five most popular portfolio combinations were held by about half of the families in the 1984–2001 period. This is set out in Table 11.4, which lists the top ten most popular choices in each of the years. Figure 11.3 gives time series plots of frequency of occurrence for the eight portfolio types that are present among the top ten from 1984 to 2001. The top three portfolio types stay the same in all years. They are (1) transaction account + housing + transportation (C-H-T); (2) transaction account + transportation (C-T); and (3) transaction account + stock + housing + transportation (C-SI-H-T). Combined, they account for 33 per cent in 1984, 1989 and 1994, and about 38 per cent in 1999 and 2001 as shown in Table 11.4.

The most popular portfolio type, C-H-T (transaction account + housing + transportation), was held by 15 to 17 per cent of families between 1984 and 2001. The portfolio type C-SI-H-T (transaction account + stock + housing + transportation) was the third most frequently held in 1984 at 6 per cent, but became the second most popular combination by 2001, held by 12 per cent of families. This trend reflects the rising popularity of stocks in household portfolios over the last 20 years. While the frequency of the null portfolio, where no assets are reported, decreased during the 1984–2001 period, it still remains in the set of the seven most frequently occurring portfolio types.

Another large group of families with simple financial arrangements is composed of those who held either transportation only (T) or transaction accounts (C). In 1984 the proportion of transportation-only households was 5 per cent, the same as the proportion of those who held a transaction-only account. Combining the families with no wealth components and

Table 11.4 Distribution of the ten most popular portfolio types

Rank	1984		cum. %	1989		cum. %	1994		cum. %	1999		cum. %	2001		cum. %
	%		%	%		%	%		%	%		%	%		%
1	16	(C)(H)(T)	16	15	(C)(H)(T)	15	14	(C)(H)(T)	14	17	(C)(H)(T)	17	15	(C)(H)(T)	15
2	12	(C)(T)	28	11	(C)(SI)(H)(T)	26	10	(C)(SI)(H)(T)	24	12	(C)(T)	30	12	(C)(SI)(H)(T)	26
3	6	(C)(SI)(H)(T)	33	7	(C)(T)	33	9	(C)(T)	33	11	(C)(SI)(H)(T)	41	11	(C)(T)	38
4	6	NO ASSETS	39	6	NO ASSETS	39	6	NO ASSETS	40	5	(T)	46	5	(C)(SI)(V)(H)(T)	43
5	5	(C)(V)(H)(T)	44	5	(C)(V)(H)(T)	44	6	(T)	46	5	NO ASSETS	50	5	(T)	48
6	5	(T)	49	5	(T)	49	5	(C)(SI)(V)(H)(T)	51	4	(R)(C)(SI)(H)(T)	54	4	(H)(T)	52
7	5	(C)	54	4	(C)	53	4	(H)(T)	55	4	(C)(SI)(V)(H)(T)	58	4	NO ASSETS	56
8	4	(R)(C)(H)(T)	58	4	(C)(SI)(V)(H)(T)	57	4	(C)(V)(H)(T)	59	4	(C)	61	4	(R)(C)(SI)(H)(T)	60
9	4	(H)(T)	62	3	(R)(C)(H)(T)	60	3	(R)(C)(SI)(H)(T)	62	4	(C)(V)(H)(T)	65	4	(C)(SI)(T)	63
10	4	(C)(SI)(V)(H)(T)	65	3	(H)(T)	63	3	(C)	65	3	(H)(T)	68	3	(C)(V)(H)(T)	67

Notes: C = transaction account(s), SI = stocks (IRA accounts incl.), B = business, V = other assets, H = housing (primary residence), T = vehicle.

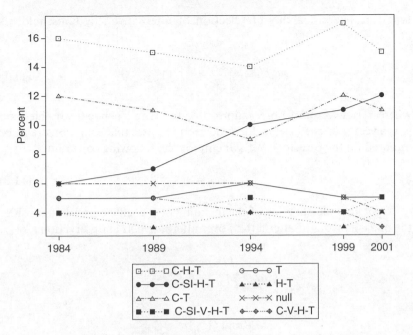

Figure 11.3   Trend of popularity types, 1984–2001

those with just a transaction account or a vehicle, about one-quarter of households (28 per cent in 1984, 24 per cent in 1994 and 26 per cent in 1999) seem to have kept their financial lives to the barest essentials.

Figure 11.3 shows how frequencies of different portfolio types vary over time. Some portfolio types, such as C-SI-H-T, gained popularity and others, such as C-V-H-T (transaction account, other valuable assets, housing and transportation), lost some ground.[7]

Modelling

Model

In this subsection we study the effect of income, wealth and demographic factors on the probability of holding a particular portfolio type. We will assume that a household views different portfolio types as independent alternatives. In order to model choice among several alternatives simultaneously we use a multinomial logistic model (Maddala 1997). In our choice of statistical model we follow Uhler and Cragg (1971), who also used the model to study the structure of asset portfolios of households. The model specifies that there are M mutually exclusive alternatives from which a choice is made. In our case a household chooses among different portfolio types, π. The probability of selection of alternative j by household i is given by:

$$P(\pi_{ij}) = \frac{e^{\beta_j x_i}}{\sum_{k=1}^{M} e^{\beta_k x_i}}, \quad j = 1, \ldots, M \tag{11.1}$$

where x_i is a vector of observations on a set of independent variables and β_j is a vector of coefficients. Identification requires that some constraint be imposed on the β vectors. We will employ the following constraint:

$$\beta_M = 0 \tag{11.2}$$

To get an understanding of the meaning of β coefficients, let us consider the odds in favour of alternative j over alternative M at observation i, Q_{jMi}:

$$Q_{jMi} = \frac{P(\pi_{ij})}{P(\pi_{Mi})} = e^{(\beta_j - \beta_M) x_i}$$

$$\frac{\partial(\log(Q_{jMi}))}{\partial x_i} = \beta_j$$

Thus, the coefficient β_j may be interpreted as the partial derivative of the logarithm of the odds in favour of alternative j over alternative M.

Estimation results

Using model (1) we investigated choice among the top household portfolio types. The parameter M was restricted to 5 to make the whole procedure manageable. The model was estimated in SAS for the 1999 and 2001 data. Table 11.5 gives the results for the 1999 data. The likelihood ratio test is equal to twice the positive difference between the log-likelihood for the fitted model and the log-likelihood for the saturated model (maximum log-likelihood achievable). The χ^2 statistic is not significant, suggesting a good fit.

In the regression for the 1999 data, the 'control' portfolio is the null portfolio. Thus, the odds we consider are the odds of having one of four types of portfolios – C-SI-H-T, C-H-T, C-T, or T – over the null portfolio. The coefficient estimates are mostly significant and the signs are as expected. The odds of having any type of portfolio over the null portfolio are increasing in income, wealth and education. The coefficients of income and wealth are increasing with portfolio complexity, suggesting that as income and/or wealth increase, the odds of having more a complex portfolio increases more rapidly than the odds of having a simpler portfolio type. Thus,

Table 11.5 *Multinomial logistic model, 1999*

	Portfolio: C-SI-H-T		Portfolio: C-H-T		Portfolio: C-T		Portfolio: T	
	Estim.	ChiSq	Estim.	ChiSq	Estim.	ChiSq	Estim.	ChiSq
Intercept	−9.4778***	124.0	−5.8171***	72.0	−1.8116***	9.3	−1.6294**	6.2
Wealth (1000)	0.0532***	201.8	0.0481***	166.3	0.0185***	26.6	0.0077**	5.2
Inc (1000)	0.0657***	98.0	0.0587***	81.6	0.0500***	61.7	0.0299***	19.8
Age of head	0.1083***	11.6	0.0719***	7.1	−0.0301	1.6	0.0301	1.2
Age squared	−0.0010***	10.4	−0.0006**	5.8	0.0002	0.7	−0.0005*	3.1
White (0/1)	2.7153***	79.8	1.7806***	72.1	1.7884***	88.6	0.7384***	14.7
Other (0/1)	1.4691***	14.0	0.7485***	7.2	1.3081***	27.1	0.2098	0.7
High school degree (0/1)	1.1877***	21.1	0.7704***	13.9	0.8530***	19.8	0.3265*	2.7
Some college (0/1)	2.2284***	50.3	1.3312***	24.5	1.9038***	59.4	0.1967	0.5
College degree or more (0/1)	3.1773***	47.1	1.6330***	13.9	2.4066***	32.9	0.6551	2.0
Female (0/1)	0.3501	1.9	0.7680***	12.5	0.3002	2.7	0.1479	0.6
Married (0/1)	1.8086***	40.6	2.3296***	82.9	0.9527***	16.1	1.2869***	26.9
N:	3508							

Notes:
*** denotes significance at the 1% level; ** at the 5% level; * at the 10% level.
The control is the 'null' portfolio. The χ² test statistic, 6929 on 104 degrees of freedom, is not statistically different from the saturated model.

increasing wealth by $10 000 increases the odds of having C-SI-H-T by 70 per cent, while the odds of having C-T are increased by only 20 per cent. Similarly, a $10 000 increase in income increases the odds of C-SI-H-T by 90 per cent and that of C-T by 70 per cent.

Strong effects on portfolio type choice are created by education and, in particular, by the variable 'college degree or more'. Thus, keeping all other covariates fixed, the odds of having a C-SI-H-T portfolio among college graduates is 24 times that of those with no high school diploma. The same factor for the C-T portfolio type is 11. The other educational levels have less-pronounced effects. For comparison with the above estimates, the odds of having a C-SI-H-T portfolio among high school graduates is 3.3 times that of those with no high school diploma. As with the portfolio diversification or span analysis, race is a strong predictor among the five portfolio types. With all other factors the same, the odds of having a C-SI-H-T portfolio among white families is more than 15 times greater than that among black families. The same factor for a C-H-T portfolio type is about 6. Single people are more likely to hold the null portfolio than married couples.

The logarithm of the odds is quadratic in age. Different signs of age and age-squared coefficients for different portfolios indicate that the odds for some portfolios are increasing in age and decreasing for others.

Simulation study

The estimated model can be used to obtain predicted probabilities of portfolio choice. Figure 11.4 illustrates how portfolio choice depends on age and income. It also highlights the differences in household portfolio allocation between black and white families.

The prediction is implemented for a married household with annual income equal to $45 000, net worth equal to $72 000, and where the head is a college graduate. The graphs on the left of Figure 11.4 are based on the householder's race being white while the graphs on the right show estimates for both white and black households. Figure 11.4 depicts probabilities among C-SI-H-T, C-H-T and C-T portfolio types. The null and transportation-only portfolios are excluded from the graph since their likelihood is very close to zero, which is not surprising given the household characteristics.

The probability of a simple transaction account + transportation portfolio type first decreases with age and then starts to increase around age 70 (see Figure 11.4, panel a). Consistent with the life-cycle allocation models (Campbell and Viceira 2002), the situation is reversed for the most complex portfolio type, which includes a transaction account, stocks, home equity and transportation (C-SI-H-T). The function increases early in life, reaches

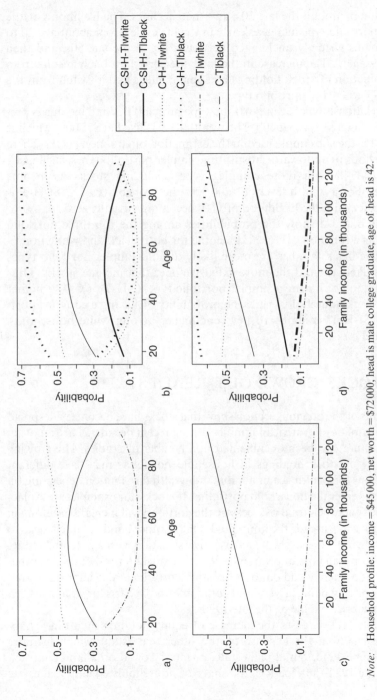

Note: Household profile: income = $45 000, net worth = $72 000, head is male college graduate, age of head is 42.

Figure 11.4   Predicted probabilities of portfolio choice

its maximum around the late 50s, and then declines. The likelihood of the C-H-T portfolio type increases early in the life cycle (from about age 20 to 30), remains virtually unchanged between 30 and the late 50s, and then increases again. The increase in the later life period probably results from the elimination of stock holdings by some families and a switch from the C-SI-H-T to C-H-T portfolio type.

The relationship between portfolio type probabilities and income is presented in Figure 11.4, panel b. The wealth level is fixed at $72 000, which is average for the subsample used in the estimation of equation (11.1). There is an obvious trend toward substituting simpler portfolio types, such as C-T and C-H-T, with more complex types including stocks as income increases. For a wealth level of $200 000, the probability of C-SI-H-T is even greater, with the likelihood of C-T becoming virtually zero.

Panels b and d show the probabilities among the top three portfolio choices as a function of age and income for both black and white households. The black families are more likely to hold simpler portfolio types and less likely to hold the more extensive ones that include stocks. Thus the likelihood of having a simpler portfolio type, C-H-T or C-T, is higher among black households while the probability of having a complex portfolio, C-SI-H-T, is about 10 per cent higher among white households. (See panel b.)

DO STOCKS 'CROWD OUT' REAL ESTATE?

The results of the previous section show that stocks have become widespread in the portfolios of American families during recent decades. The rise of an equity culture' has been documented in a number of studies. The growing popularity of stock holdings in household portfolios may have different implications for wealth accumulation and wealth distribution depending on how stocks enter the household portfolios. If stocks, for example, are replacing safer assets, then total riskiness of the portfolio will increase, resulting in higher risk exposure for the household. On the other hand, adding stocks to the existing mix of assets will increase diversification with a potential reduction in the overall portfolio variance. Whether stocks 'crowd out' some other asset types or merely add on to the existing portfolio is also important from the asset-pricing point of view and could inform the basis for what has been termed the price bubble of the late 1990s.

As Table 11.2 suggests, the increase of equity holdings might have happened partially at the expense of the other real estate, which includes second home, land, rental real estate, or money owed on a land contract. During the 1984–2001 period, the share of households owning real estate

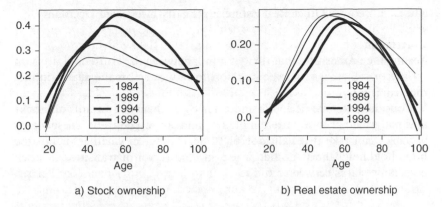

a) Stock ownership   b) Real estate ownership

Figure 11.5   The local regression estimates of ownership rates

fell from 20.1 per cent to 16.1 per cent. Since aggregated data may conceal some information, we estimated participation rates as a function of age using the micro data. The predicted stock and real estate ownership rates in 1984, 1989, 1994 and 1999 are given in Figure 11.5. The results show that overall during the period households were increasingly more likely to opt for stocks while real estate participation rates were decreasing. The degree of participation change, however, shows considerable variation with age. Thus the strongest increase in stock participation is seen among those older than 45, while the decrease in real estate participation rates is strong among those younger than 45.

The evidence suggests that substitution, if any, may have occurred in the following way. Developments in the equity market, notably the decrease in cost of access to well-diversified portfolios as well as strong returns, made equity an attractive portfolio element. Younger households, when adding portfolio elements, chose stocks over real estate, while older households, who may already have had real estate, simply added equities to their portfolios. Moreover, a stronger decline in the proportion of real estate holders in the later life period may not be observed because of the wealth effect: the capital gains realized in the stock market during the 1990s might have affected household decisions to hold on to their real estate, which, apart from investment purposes, can provide consumption services such as from a second or vacation home.

While it is tempting to suggest that the evidence in Figures 11.2 and 11.5 points to a substitution effect between stocks and real estate, this evidence is not enough, as the observed pattern may be spurious. In the next step, using micro-level panel data, we test the existence of a correlation between real estate and equity ownership transitions.

The Link Between Other Real Estate and Equity Investment Decisions

Correlation

Testing the proposition that there is a link between the household decision to buy or sell stocks and the decision to buy or sell real estate is implemented as follows.

Consider two time periods t and t' ($t > t'$). Ownership status of stocks and real estate at time t are denoted S_t and R_t, respectively. These status variables can take two values, 1 or 0, depending on whether or not the household holds the asset. Let $SS_{tt'}$ be a 1×2 vector of transition in stock ownership status between t and t'

$$SS_{tt'} = (s, s') \quad if \quad S_t = s \ and \ S_{t'} = s'$$

where $s \in (0, 1)$ and $s' \in (0, 1)$. $RR_{tt'}$ is defined analogously.

If stocks and real estate are substitutes in the household portfolio, then there should be dependence between the transition variables $SS_{tt'}$ and $RR_{tt'}$. On the other hand, if transitions in stocks and real estate are independent, then a household's decision regarding stocks is not related to the real estate decision. So, the null hypothesis to be tested is that $SS_{tt'}$ and $RR_{tt'}$ are independently distributed. Two variables are independent if their joint probability density is the product of marginal densities. In symbols, the null hypothesis can be written as:

$$H_0: P(SS_{tt'} = (s, s'), \ RR_{tt'} = (r, r') \ ) = P(SS_{tt'} = (s, s'))$$
$$\times P(RR_{tt'} = (r, r') \ ) \qquad (11.3)$$

where $(s, s') \in \{0, 1\} \times \{0, 1\}$ and $(r, r') \in \{0, 1\} \times \{0, 1\}$

We consider $SS_{tt'}$ and $RR_{tt'}$ as discrete factors with m levels. In our case, $m = 4$. Each observation is classified in one of the 16 possible cells in the cross-tabulation of $SS_{tt'}$ and $RR_{tt'}$. With independent observations, the joint distribution of counts in each cell follows the multinomial distribution. In this case the likelihood ratio test can be used for testing the hypothesis of independence equation (11.3). The test statistic is distributed as χ^2 with $(m-1)(m-1) = 9$ degrees of freedom.

Balanced panels of the PSID data were used to determine the transition variables $SS_{tt'}$ and $RR_{tt'}$ for various combinations of t and $t' \in \{1984, 1989, 1994, 1999, 2001\}$ where $t < t'$. Table 11.6 shows the results of testing equation (11.3) for some pairs of t and t'. All test statistics are highly significant. Therefore, the hypothesis that the transition in stock ownership and the transition in real estate ownership are independent is rejected.

Table 11.6   Test of independence of stocks and real estate transitions

Period	χ^2	$\text{Prob}(\chi^2)$
1984–89	453.67	<0.0001
1989–94	535.83	<0.0001
1994–99	471.36	<0.0001
1999–2001	519.13	<0.0001

Note: Degrees of freedom = 9.

Further investigation

Results showing a significant correlation between the decisions to invest in stocks and real estate and the evidence of movement in opposite directions in ownership rates during the 1984–2001 period seem to suggest that households considered these assets as substitutes. The whole period was characterized by the increasing importance and prevalence of equities in the family portfolio. We hypothesize that the effect of substitution was strongest among new investors, namely, those who had neither real estate nor stocks before. These households were increasingly more likely to invest in stocks and not in real estate. On the other hand, substitution where households rebalanced their portfolios by discarding real estate and adding stocks seems to have been less prevalent. We attempted to investigate one further possible substitution scenario. Given the overall decrease in real estate ownership, the rate should have declined still more among those who held or added stocks, because households who had money to invest increasingly chose stocks over real estate.

To explore this possibility we examine how, conditionally on stock ownership status, real estate ownership likelihood changes between two time periods, t_1 and t_2, $t_1 < t_2$. In particular, we would like to see if being a stockholder at time t_2 decreases the likelihood of owning real estate even more, as compared to the overall level. The issue is investigated with a logistic regression pooled over t_1 and t_2:

$$P(R=1) = F(X\beta + \gamma_1 S + \gamma_2 D_{t_2} + \gamma_3 (S \cdot D_{t_2})) \qquad (11.4)$$

where $F(\cdot)$ is the logistic cumulative distribution function; X is n_k matrix of observations on a set of variables including wealth, income, age, education, race and family size; β is a k_1 vector of parameters; and S and R are dummy variables for stock and real estate ownership status. The D_{t_2} is 1 if the observation is from the second time period and 0 if it is from the first period. The term $S \cdot D_{t_2}$ denotes the interaction between stock ownership status and time; it is equal to 1 if the observation belongs to t_2 and the household's portfolio includes equity. We expect the parameter γ_1 to be positive, as the probability of owning real estate among stock owners is generally higher than among those who hold no equity. Figures 11.2 and 11.5 suggest that γ_2 should be negative, as real estate participation rates were declining. Finally, if substitution happened because new investors increasingly chose stocks over real estate, then the proportion of real estate owners among stock owners should decline over the time period. This suggests a negative sign on γ_3.

Model (4) was estimated for two samples: one includes all households and the other is the sample of 'new investors', who had neither stocks nor real estate at time $t1$ and invested in at least one asset type, real estate or stocks, by t_2. Equation (11.4) was estimated for various pairs of $t1$ and t_2. Table 11.7 reports the results for the 1994–2001 period. (The results are broadly similar for other periods.) For brevity we report only estimates of γ_1, γ_2 and γ_3. As expected, a positive sign of γ_1 indicates an overall higher propensity to invest in real estate among the stockholders and a negative sign of γ_2 reflects the decrease in real estate participation rates between 1994 and 2001. The main focus is the parameter γ_3, which is statistically different from zero and negative for both samples. Thus, controlling for the

Table 11.7   Logistic regression of whether real estate, 1994–2001

	Sample A[a]		Sample B[b]	
	Coefficient	ChiSq	Coefficient	ChiSq
Whether stocks (0/1)	0.729***	93.2	0.68***	18.7
Year 2001 (0/1)	−0.113	2.4	−0.295**	5.3
(Year 2001)* (Whether stocks) (0/1)	−0.303***	8.4	−0.432*	3.2
N:	15 276		7465	
Likelihood ratio:				
ChiSq	2031.2		359.8	
DF	17		17	

Notes:
*** denotes significance at the 1% level; ** at the 5% level; * at the 10% level.
a.   All households.
b.   Those who had neither stocks nor real estate initially and invested in at least one asset by the end of the period.
Estimates of wealth, income, age, education, race, and family size covariates are omitted from the table.

overall decrease of real estate ownership, being a stock owner in 2001 further decreased the probability of owning real estate.

One limitation of the above analysis is possible bias of the estimates because of the endogeneity of S and R. However, given the correct signs for other variables, including X, we have reasonable confidence in the correctness of the γ_3 sign, which is enough for our purpose. Generally, more definite support for the proposition of substitution can be obtained with the simultaneous modelling of the household demand for all assets. This is, however, beyond the scope of the present chapter.

Long-run Distribution

The panel data allow us a glimpse at what the long-run implication of the interaction between equities and real estate might be for the distribution of asset ownership. In particular, what will happen to the distribution if the dynamics of ownership transition remain the same as observed in the 1984–2001 period? Will we observe crowding out of real estate by stocks?

Consider two time periods, t and t'. Assume that households keep adjusting their holdings of stocks and real estate from t' onward in the same way as between t and t'. Additionally, we will assume that the process of stock and real estate ownership follows a stationary Markov process. Observing household choices between t and t', the Markov transition matrix can be constructed. Calculating the limiting distribution of asset ownership implied by the matrix produces the results given in Table 11.8 for t and t'. Depending on the choice of t and t' there are some differences in the estimates of transition matrix and the limiting distributions. However, the main pattern is the same. While there is strong growth in stock ownership rates, real estate ownership rates stay virtually unchanged as the marginal distributions show.

The joint distribution indicates that most of the increase in stock ownership comes from the group that initially had neither stocks nor real estate. There is a substantial decrease in the proportion of the group of those holding neither who would buy stocks and thus increase the proportion of those with stocks and no real estate. The proportion of real estate-only holders shows a slightly negative trend while the likelihood of those who hold both assets increases. What does this projected limited distribution say about crowding out of real estate in household portfolios? Overall, there seems to be little evidence that the dynamics of real estate and stock ownership transition during the 1984–2001 period, if continued, would lead to a significant decrease in the real estate ownership rate. However, the data show that stocks have become the number one option for investment compared to real estate. Fewer households choose to hold real estate without equities in their portfolios. This should not necessarily lead to an overall decrease in the

Table 11.8 *End of period and limiting distribution of stocks and real estate ownership rates*

Period		P(R = 0, S = 0)	P(R = 0, S = 1)	P(R = 1, S = 0)	P(R = 1, S = 1)	P(S = 1)	P(R = 1)
1989–99	1999 dist.	0.513	0.283	0.07	0.133	0.416	0.204
	Limit dist.	0.462	0.328	0.059	0.151	0.479	0.21
1984–2001	2001 dist.	0.449	0.332	0.07	0.149	0.481	0.219
	Limit dist.	0.357	0.4	0.066	0.177	0.577	0.243

proportion of real estate holders. More people with stocks also hold real estate, possibly because of a wealth effect, since other real estate includes both purely commercial holdings and second or vacation homes.

It is important to note that the results based on the limiting distribution should only be taken as suggestive. They are valid only for this particular sample of households had they lived forever and acted according to the assumed stationary process. The important reality this ignores is the entrance of young households and the exit of older households, and the different preferences each group may have. The changing investment environment – interest rates, return and variability of assets – also affects household investment decisions, and was also ignored.

To summarize, in this section we conclude that stocks came to play a more important role as an investment option for households compared to other real estate. This change probably reflects the decrease in costs associated with stock ownership as well as the high returns of the 1990s, which led to the broadening of the investor base, as happened in the early 1960s. The data suggest that households might have considered stocks and real estate as substitutes. In this case, the development in the equity market induced some crowding out effect on real estate in household portfolios. The evidence suggests this effect not to be particularly strong, however. Furthermore, it appears to have been somewhat offset by the wealth effect created by capital gains in the equity market.

SUMMARY

This chapter studies the household portfolio, using PSID data from the 1984, 1989, 1994, 1999 and 2001 survey years. We consider two aspects of household portfolios: the span or number of asset types held and the composition of the household portfolio. We also investigate the possibility of the 'crowding-out' effect of stocks on real estate during the last 17 years, which were marked by a strong expansion of equities in household portfolios.

There is great variability in household portfolio span across demographic and life-cycle groups, with the race effect being particularly pronounced. Portfolio span was shown to be strongly associated with income, wealth and education. The observed increase in the number of portfolio components from 1984 to 2001 is more likely to have arisen from changing demographic and socio-economic factors rather than a general increase in the financial sophistication of families.

The data show portfolio composition to be extremely heterogeneous. Five identified portfolio types account for about 50 per cent of families, with the most common type, transaction account + housing + transportation, being held by 15 to 17 per cent of households. There are a substantial number of households with a null portfolio. The results of multivariate analyses indicate that choice of portfolio type is strongly associated with income, race and education. The results also seem to support some implications of life-cycle asset allocation models. Over the period 1984–2001, the main change in household portfolio composition is due to increased stock ownership rates.

Finally, we explored whether stocks were taking some of the place of real estate in household portfolios during the period. Our analysis revealed, first, that during the period households were increasingly more likely to invest in equities while the likelihood of investing in real estate was decreasing. Second, there is a correlation between the decision to buy/sell real estate and the decision to buy/sell equities. These two facts together support the proposition that households may consider these two assets as substitutes. We looked at the limiting distribution of asset ownership based on the Markov process to gauge the long-run implication of the interaction between equities and real estate. The results suggest that while the proportion of those who have real estate and no stock equities would decrease, the 'crowding-out' effect during the period was not strong enough to cause any significant reduction in the real estate ownership rate in the long run. This may be partially due to the fact that wealth gains from the equity market in the late 1990s were used by some households to diversify into real estate.

NOTES

1. A caveat is that the services by a specific asset type may have increased. To illustrate, in 2001 a mortgage arrangement is more likely to provide transaction services from a home equity line of credit.
2. Note that 95 per cent of the 2001 data were collected prior to 11 September 2001 and less than 5 per cent were collected after the stock market was closed for a two-week period following 11 September 2001.
3. For a brief description one can read Hurst et al. (1998), Appendix A, or go to the PSID Data Center website, http://simba.isr.umich.edu/, and select 'Wealth', then a year, then a wealth component. Then use the magnifying glass icon to discover the variable definition and codes for the selected component.
4. Note that prior to 1999 questions on stock and transaction account holdings were formulated to include holdings of IRAs. Starting in 1999 a new set of questions about assets held in IRA accounts was introduced; questions about stocks and transaction accounts had been reformulated to exclude IRA holdings. In our analysis we needed comparable variables across the years 1984–2001. Using the question about the proportion of stocks in an IRA account ('Are they mostly in stocks, mostly in interest earning assets, split between the two, or what?'), we created the new variable $Stock_t^*$ for $t = 1999, 2001$ as follows:

$$Stock_t^* = Stock_i + \alpha\_IRAt$$

where α is equal to 1 if the answer to the allocation question was 'mostly in stocks', 0.5 if 'split between the two', and 0 if the response was 'mostly in interest-earning assets'.

5. In our analysis we assume no cohort effect. Some studies, however, have shown that cohort effect might be nontrivial in households' demand for assets (see Poterba and Samwick (1997) and Ameriks and Zeldes (2001)).
6. During the strong stock market of the 1960s the percentage of families holding equities rose form 16 per cent in 1962 to 21 per cent in 1963 and 1964 (Katona et al. 1964).
7. We investigated the effect of portfolio type characteristics on change in popularity rank during the period 1984–2001. By a portfolio characteristic we mean presence or absence of a particular asset type. In other words, how did different asset types contribute to the change in the portfolio type rank? The results indicated that portfolios with stocks and housing have became more popular. There is also some evidence, not always statistically significant however, that portfolios with other real estate have declined in popularity.

REFERENCES

Ameriks, J. and S.P. Zeldes (2001), 'How do household portfolio shares vary with age?', http://www.gsb.columbia.edu/faculty/szeldes/Research.
Bertaut, C.C. and M. Starr-McCluer (2002), 'Household portfolios in the United States', in L. Guiso, M. Haliassas and T. Jappelli (eds), *Household Portfolios*, Cambridge, MA: MIT Press, pp. 181–217.
Campbell, J.Y. and L.M. Viceira (2002), *Strategic Asset Allocation: Portfolio Choice for Long-Term Investors*, New York: Oxford University Press.
Carroll, C.D. (2002), 'Portfolios of the rich', in L. Guiso, M. Haliassas and T. Jappelli (eds), *Household Portfolios*, Cambridge, MA: MIT Press, pp. 389–429.
Chiteji, N.S. and F.P. Stafford (1999), 'Portfolio choices of parents and their children as young adults: asset accumulation by African-American families', *American Economic Review*, **89**, 377–80.
Flavin, M. and T. Yamashita (1998), 'Owner occupied housing and the composition of household portfolio over the life cycle', NBER Working Paper No. w6389.
Hurd, M.D. (2002), 'Portfolio holdings of the elderly', in L. Guiso, M. Haliassas and T. Jappelli (eds), *Household Portfolios*, Cambridge, MA: MIT Press, pp. 431–72.
Hurst, E. and A. Lusardi (2004), 'Liquidity Constraints, Household Wealth and Entrepreneurship', *Journal of Political Economy*, **112**(2), 319–47.
Hurst, E., M.C. Luoh and F.P. Stafford (1998), 'Wealth dynamics of American families, 1984–1994', *Brooking Papers on Economic Activity*, **98**(1), 267–338.
Katona, G., C. Lininger and E. Mueller (1964), *Survey of Consumer Finances*, Research Center Monograph 39, Institute for Social Research, Ann Arbor, Michigan.
King, M.A. and J.I. Leape (1998), 'Wealth and portfolio composition: theory and evidence', *Journal of Public Economics*, **69**(2), 155–93.
Maddala, G.S. (1997), *Limited-Dependent and Qualitative Variables in Econometrics*, Cambridge, UK: Cambridge University Press.
Perraudin, W.R. and B.E. Sorensen (2000), 'The demand for risky assets: sample selection and household portfolios', *Journal of Econometrics*, **1**, 117–44.
Poterba, J.M. (2002), 'Taxation and portfolio structure: issues and implications', in L. Guiso, M. Haliassas and T. Jappelli (eds), *Household Portfolios*, Cambridge, MA: MIT Press, pp. 103–42.
Poterba, J.M. and A.A. Samwick (1997), 'Household portfolio allocation over the life cycle', NBER Working Paper No. w6185.
Uhler, R.S. and J.G. Cragg (1971), 'The structure of the asset portfolios of households', *Review of Economic Studies*, **38**, 341–57.

APPENDIX

Grants from the National Institute on Aging (NIA) made possible an important Panel Study of Income Dynamics (PSID) supplemental module on wealth, first implemented in 1984 and later expanded in the 1989, 1994, 1999 and 2001 questionnaires. For the most part, the wealth questions in 1999 and 2001 are included in 1984–94. Additional questions in 1989 and beyond provide information on active investments, so capital gains can be derived as a residual as well as wealth brought into or taken out of the household by entering or departing family members within each five-year period. When combined with information on the holdings of wealth, these additional questions provide data on household saving over each five-year and two-year period. The content included in the wealth supplements for each wave is summarized below.

Summary of Contents in the NIA-funded PSID Wealth Supplements 1984, 1989, 1994, 1999, 2001

1. Net value of real estate other than main home.
2. Net value of vehicles.
3. Net value of farm or business assets.
4. Value of shares of stock in publicly held corporations, mutual funds or investment trusts, including stocks in IRAs (in 1999 and 2001, the IRAs are separated out).
5. Value of checking and savings accounts, money market funds, certificates of deposit, savings bonds, Treasury bills, IRAs (in 1999 and 2001, the IRAs are separated out).
6. Value of other investments in trusts or estates, bond funds, life insurance policies, special collections.
7. Value and years of accumulations of pensions.
8. Value of debts other than mortgages, such as credit cards, student loans, medical or legal bills, personal loans.
9. Inheritance of money or property, year and value at time of inheritance.
10. Expected value of probable inheritances within next ten years of money or property (1984 only).

For on-line viewing of the verbatim wealth question text go to: http://www.psidonline.isr.umich.edu/, select 'Data and Documentation', then 'Packaged Core Data, Documentation, and Questionnaires'; in the 'Family File by Year' table, click on 1989, 1994, 1999 or 2001 Questionnaire 'HTML' link and scroll to Section W.

Summary of Contents in the PSID Active Saving Module 1989, 1994, 1999, 2001

1. Amount of money put aside in private annuities in past five years.
2. Value of pensions or annuities cashed in past five years.
3. Amount of money invested in any real estate other than main home in past five years.
4. Value of additions or improvements worth $10 000 or more to main home or other real estate in past five years.
5. Amount of money invested in a business or farm in past five years.
6. Amount of money from sale of farm or business assets in past five years.
7. Amounts and net value of any bought and sold stocks in publicly held corporations, mutual funds, or investment trusts, in past five years.
8. Value of assets over $5000 removed from family holdings by departure of family member in past five years.
9. Value of assets over $5000 added to family holdings by someone joining the family in past five years.
10. Value of any gifts or inheritance of money or property worth $10 000 or more in past five years.
11. Expected per cent of preretirement earnings replaced by pensions and social security when retired (for working head, wife, cohabiting partner age 45 or older).

12. Is wealth becoming more polarized in the United States?

Conchita D'Ambrosio and Edward N. Wolff*

INTRODUCTION

Recent work has documented a rising degree of wealth and income inequality in the United States during the 1980s and the 1990s. Regarding the distribution of income, some have reported that the increasing dispersion was due to the shrinkage of the middle class. In particular, Burkhauser et al. (1999) report that the effect of the business cycle during the 1980s was such that while economic growth benefited all groups, the gains were not evenly distributed and the great majority of the vanishing middle class became richer. In contrast, Blank and Card (1993) report an increase in the mass in the lower tail of the distribution with increasing poverty rates. The aim of this chapter is to investigate changes in the entire distribution of wealth and, at the same time, to look at another dimension of the distribution, polarization. Using techniques developed by Esteban and Ray (1994) and further extended by D'Ambrosio (2001), we examine whether rising wealth inequality is mirrored in an increase in polarization over the two decades.

Polarization refers to the formation of clusters around local poles. The distribution of wealth of the entire population is first decomposed into the distribution of wealth for different homogeneous groups within the population. We then examine the following issues: (1) Are the groups different so as to actually constitute poles with regard to wealth levels? (2) How great are these differences? (3) How persistent are these differences over time? (4) What are the causes of the observed changes? The emergence of clusters in a distribution has political relevance, since it may lead to political conflict within a society (see, for example, Esteban and Ray 1999).

The concept of polarization is used to compare the homogeneity of groups with the overall heterogeneity of a population. If the distribution of a variable such as wealth is very compressed within groups within a population (such as the racial groups of blacks and whites) but very diverse between groups, then we consider wealth 'polarized' between the groups.

Polarization is fundamentally different from inequality and thus cannot be measured by a Lorenz-consistent index. Suppose, for example, that the distribution of household wealth within a country is uniform over wealth levels 0 to 1000. Now imagine a transformation that causes the wealth of all the households with wealth between 0 and 500 to converge to 250, and the wealth of all the households in the interval 500 and 1000 to converge to 750. Any Lorenz-consistent inequality measure will register an unambiguous decline of inequality from this transformation. Nevertheless, clustering has increased. This society loses its middle class and polarizes to the two-point distribution at 250 and at 750.

Similarly, polarization cannot be additively decomposed into within- and between-group components using classical techniques. A new decomposition method is applied here. The method provides an index that can be used both to calculate the distance between social groups classified according to household characteristics and to track changes over time. The new method also reveals the factors that are reshaping the wealth distribution and allows us to identify precisely where these effects are having their greatest impact.

We examine polarization patterns and their change over time with regard to a number of household dimensions. The first is between home owners and renters; the second is by race and ethnicity, between non-Hispanic whites versus other groups; the third is by age class; the fourth is by family type – married couples, single males and single females; the fifth is by household income class; and the last is by educational class. The polarization indices are computed for total household wealth. We also look at polarization patterns for stock ownership.

The estimates of the wealth distribution and of its evolution through time, for the whole population and for its subgroups, are obtained by applying the kernel density estimation method. The same method is used to estimate counterfactual densities, that is, what the density of wealth would have been in one year if household characteristics (between-group component) or the distribution of wealth among households with the same characteristics (within-group component) had remained at the level of the previous year.

We find that wealth polarization followed different patterns, depending on the household dimension. In particular, polarization between home owners and tenants, as well as between different educational groups, continuously increased from 1983 to 1998, while polarization by income classes groups continuously decreased. In contrast, polarization by racial group first increased from 1983 to 1989 and then declined from 1989 to 1998, while polarization by age groups followed the opposite pattern.

The main finding of the decomposition method used to explain the observed changes in the wealth distribution is that changes in household characteristics did not have a large influence on the evolution of the wealth density during the period under examination. Instead, most of the observed variation in the overall wealth schedule can be attributed to the (dramatic) changes of the within-group wealth densities.

The rest of the chapter is organized as follows. The next two sections introduce the method used to estimate the wealth densities and the indices used to summarize the observed movements in the densities of wealth. The third section contains a description of the data sources. The application of the method to US data on household wealth is treated in the fourth section, followed by our conclusions.

THE ESTIMATION METHOD

The estimated distributions are derived from a generalization of the kernel density estimator to take into account the sample weights attached to each observation. The estimate of the density function $\hat{f}(y)$, is determined directly from the data of the sample, $y_1, y_2, \ldots, y_N$, without assuming its functional form a priori. The only assumption made is that there exists a density function $f(y)$ from which the sample is extracted. In detail:

$$\hat{f}(y_j) = \sum_{i=1}^{N} \frac{\theta_i}{h_N} K\left(\frac{y_j - y_i}{h_N}\right) \qquad \forall y_j \tag{12.1}$$

where N is the number of observations of the sample, h_N is the bandwidth parameter, $K(.)$ is the kernel function.[1] The sample weights are normalized to sum to 1,

$$\sum_i \theta_i = 1.$$

The counterfactual densities are obtained by applying the kernel method to appropriate samples. This technique has been derived from the one proposed by DiNardo et al. (1996).

Each observation is actually a vector $(y, z \mid t_y, t_z)$, composed of wealth y, a vector z of household characteristics and a date t at which respectively wealth and characteristics are observed, belonging to a joint distribution $F(y, z \mid t_y, t_z)$. The marginal density of wealth at one point in time, $f^t(y)$, can be obtained by integrating the density of wealth conditional on a set of household characteristics and on a date t, $f(y \mid z, t_y, t_z)$, over the distribution of household characteristics $F(z \mid t_y, t_z)$ at the date t:

$$f^i(y) = \int_{z \in \Omega_z} dF(y,z \mid t_y = t, t_z = t)$$

$$= \int_{z \in \Omega_z} f(y \mid z, t_y = t, t_z = t)\, dF(z \mid t_y = t, t_z = t) \qquad (12.2)$$

$$\equiv f(y \mid t_y = t, t_z = t)$$

where Ω_z is the domain of definition of household characteristics.

If all the variables are observed at two different times, for example, t_1 and t_2, then two counterfactual densities can be obtained from (12.2): the counterfactual density of wealth at t_1 and characteristics at t_2, represented by $f(y \mid t_y = t_1, t_z = t_2)$:

$$f(y \mid t_y = t_1, t_z = t_2)$$

$$= \int_{z \in \Omega_z} dF(y,z \mid t_y = t_1, t_z = t_2) \qquad (12.3)$$

$$= \int_{z \in \Omega_z} f(y \mid z, t_y = t_1, t_z = t_2)\, dF(z \mid t_y = t_1, t_z = t_2)$$

and analogously the counterfactual density of wealth t_2 and characteristics at t_1.

Under the assumption that the structure of wealth conditional on the distribution of household characteristics does not depend on the time of the household characteristics:

$$f(y \mid z, t_y = t_1, t_z = t_2) = f(y \mid z, t_y = t_1, t_z = t_1) \qquad (12.4)$$

and under the assumption that the distribution of household characteristics conditional on the time of the characteristics does not depend on the date when wealth is observed:

$$F(z \mid t_z = t_2, t_y = t_1) = F(z \mid t_z = t_2, t_y = t_2) \qquad (12.5)$$

then the counterfactual density of wealth at t_1 and characteristics at t_2 is:

$$f(y \mid t_y = t_1, t_z = t_2) = \int_{z \in \Omega_z} f(y \mid z, t_y = t_1)\, dF(z \mid t_z = t_2) \qquad (12.6)$$

This counterfactual density indicates the density that would have prevailed if household characteristics had remained at their t_2 level and if the household wealth distribution had been the one observed in t_1 for households with those characteristics. General equilibrium effects are, indeed, excluded from the analysis, as the effects of changes in the distribution of z on the structure of wealth are not taken into account. What we estimate is the effect of movements between groups on the total density of wealth under the assumption that the distributions within each group do not change over time.

Assuming instead that:

$$f(y|z, t_y = t_2, t_z = t_1) = f(y|z, t_y = t_2, t_z = t_2)$$

$$F(z|t_z = t_1, t_y = t_1) = F(z|t_z = t_1, t_y = t_2) \tag{12.7}$$

the counterfactual density of wealth at t_2 and characteristics at t_1 is:

$$f(y|t_y = t_2, t_z = t_1) = \int_{z \in \Omega_z} f(y|z, t_y = t_2)\, dF(z|t_z = t_1) \tag{12.8}$$

This counterfactual density focuses on the within-group component of the observed movements by estimating the effect of changes in the distribution of wealth among households with the same characteristic on the distribution of wealth for the whole population, assuming that the household characteristics do not change over time.

The difference between the actual and the counterfactual density represents the effects, on the one hand, of changes in the distribution of the characteristics of the households (between-group component) and, on the other, of changes in the wealth structure of households with given characteristics (within-group component). In particular, for simplicity, we can rewrite equation (12.2) with z as a discrete random variable:

$$f^t(y) = \int_{z \in \Omega_z} dF(y, z|t_y = t, t_z = t) = \sum_z \pi_z^t(y) f_z^t(y) \tag{12.9}$$

where $\pi_z^t(y) = F(z|t_y = t; t_z = t)$, the proportion of households in each group, and $f_z^t(y) = f(y|z, t_y = t; t_z = t)$, the density of wealth within each group. The total density of wealth, $f^t(y)$, can change over time both because there is a movement of households between groups, that is, the value of $\pi_z^t(y)$'s changes, and because the structure of wealth within each group changes, that is, the value of $f_z^t(y)$'s vary. Hence the variation in $f(y)$ going from t_1 to t_2 is approximately given by:

$$f^{t_2} - f^{t_1}$$

$$\simeq \sum_z [\alpha_z(t_2) - \alpha_z(t_1)] f_z(t) \mid_{t=t_1} + \sum_z \alpha_z(t) [f_z(t_2) - f_z(t_1)] \mid_{t=t_1}$$

$$= \underbrace{\left\{ \sum_z [\alpha_z(t_2) f_z(t_1)] - \sum_z [\alpha_z(t_1) f_z(t_1)] \right\}}_{between\ group} + \quad (12.10)$$

$$\underbrace{\left\{ \sum_z [\alpha_z(t_1) f_z(t_2)] - \sum_z [\alpha_z(t_1) f_z(t_1)] \right\}}_{within\ group}$$

It is clear from equations (12.6) and (12.8) that the counterfactual densities can be obtained by estimating[2] the component densities non-parametrically:

- $f(y \mid z, t_y = t_i)$ is estimated by applying the kernel method to the appropriate sample in year t_i;
- $F(z \mid t_z = t_i)$ is estimated non-parametrically as the proportion of households with given characteristics in year t_i.

SUMMARY INDICES

To summarize the observed movements, we use two kinds of indices: First, an index that takes into account the changes in the density of a given group over time, the coefficients of distance, that is, an index that summarizes how much any two given densities differ. Second, an index that takes into account the existing 'distance' between given groups in which a society can be partitioned at one point in time, the polarization index, that is, an index that tracks the moving apart of some densities classified according to some characteristic of the household.

Several coefficients have been suggested in the statistical literature for measuring distances between probability distributions.[3] In this work we use the Kolmogorov measure of distance, namely:

$$Ko = \frac{1}{2} \int \left(\sqrt{f_2(y)} - \sqrt{f_1(y)} \right)^2 dy \quad (12.11)$$

and the Kolmogorov measure of variation distance:

$$Kov = \frac{1}{2} \int |f_2(y) - f_1(y)| \, dy \quad (12.12)$$

The Kolmogorov measures of distance and of variation distance are measures of the lack of overlapping between groups. In particular, regarding the latter, $Kov = 0$ if the densities coincide for all values of y; it reaches the maximum, $Kov = 1$, if the densities do not overlap. The distance is sensitive to changes of the distributions only when both take positive values, being insensitive to changes whenever one of them is zero. It will not change if the distributions move apart, provided either that there is no overlapping between them or that the overlapping part remains unchanged.

For the second type of index, the index of polarization,[4] we use that suggested by Esteban and Ray (1994) as well as a modification that D'Ambrosio (2001) proposed.

The intuition behind the polarization index is the following. Take agents i and j, who own different levels of wealth in the society being analysed. i feels different from j, actually he is alienated from j, and from all the j's that exist in the society: $S(i) = \Sigma_{j=1}^{N} |y_i - y_j| \pi_j$ represents the separation that i feels from j, where y_i is the wealth owned by agent i and π_i is the relative frequency of group i. The effective separation, however, depends on how many agents similar to i are in the society. $E(i) = S(i)\pi_i^\alpha$ is the effective separation and α is the importance that we give to this phenomenon. Polarization in the society is the sum, over all the agents, of the effective separation that they are feeling:

$$P = \sum_{i=1}^{N} E(i)\pi_i = \sum_{i=1}^{N} \sum_{j=1}^{N} \pi_i^{1+\alpha}\pi_j |y_i - y_j|.^5$$

Esteban and Ray introduce a model of individual attitudes in a society to formalize the above intuitions and use some axioms to narrow down the set of allowable measures. In particular, Esteban and Ray suppose that each individual is subject to two forces: on the one hand, he identifies with those he considers to be members of his own group, $I : R_+ \rightarrow R_+$ represents the identification function; and on the other hand, he feels alienated from those he considers to be members of other groups, $a : R_+ \rightarrow R_+$ is the alienation function. An individual with wealth y_i feels alienated to a degree of $a(\delta(y_i, y_j))$ from an individual with wealth y_j. $\delta(y_i, y_j)$ is a measure of distance between the two wealth levels. For Esteban and Ray, this is simply the absolute distance $|y_i - y_j|$. The joint effect of the two forces is given by the effective antagonism function, $T(I, a)$, and total polarization in the society is postulated to be the sum of all the effective antagonisms:

$$ER(\eta, y) = \sum_{i=1}^{N} \sum_{j=1}^{N} \eta_i^{1+\alpha}\eta_j T(I(\eta_i), a(\delta(y_i, y_j))) \tag{12.13}$$

where η_i represents the population associated with y_i. The measure that satisfies the axioms introduced by Esteban and Ray has the following expression:

$$ER(\eta,y) = k\sum_{i=1}^{N}\sum_{j=1}^{N}\eta_i^{1+\alpha}\eta_j\delta(y_i,y_j) = k\sum_{i=1}^{N}\sum_{j=1}^{N}\eta_i^{1+\alpha}\eta_j|y_i - y_j| \quad (12.14)$$

for some constants $k > 0$ and $\alpha \in [1, 1.6]$ that indicates the degree of sensitivity to polarization.

This index of polarization is computed empirically as follows:

$$ER(\alpha) = \sum_{i=1}^{N}\sum_{j=1}^{N}\pi_i^{1+\alpha}\pi_j|\mu_i - \mu_j| \quad (12.15)$$

π_i and μ_i represent respectively the relative frequency[6] and the conditional mean in group i for a density of the logarithm of wealth $f(y)$, namely:

$$\pi_i = \int_{y_{i-1}}^{y_i} f(y)\, dy$$

$$(12.16)$$

$$\mu_i = \frac{1}{\pi_i}\int_{y_{i-1}}^{y_i} yf(y)\, dy$$

In other words, what is computed empirically is the degree of polarization in a society, where it is assumed that everyone in each given group possesses a wealth equal to the mean of the group.[7]

Following D'Ambrosio (2001), we can use the proposed modification[8] of *ER* to compute the level of polarization within a given society without assuming that everybody in each group has a wealth equal to the mean, and at the same time we can consider a characteristic, other than wealth, to generate the group partition, for example, race, age or education. Wealth polarization is hence thought to be linked to specific characteristics of the population. The idea behind the modification is a direct application of the method previously described. The total density of wealth, $f^t(y)$, at any point in time, is given by the sum of the densities of each group, weighted by the relative frequency of each group:

$$f^t(y) = \int_{z\in\Omega_z} dF(y, z\,|\,t_{y,z} = t)$$

$$= \int_{z\in\Omega_z} f(y\,|\,z, t_y = t)\, dF(z\,|\,t_z = t) \quad (12.19)$$

The polarization index has to register the moving apart of the densities classified according to some characteristics of the household that forms the groups and differences in the frequencies between the groups. Each individual identifies with those of his own group and feels alienated from those he considers to be members of other groups, as Esteban and Ray noted, but now the groups are identified by these other characteristics and not by levels of wealth. The index of polarization that Esteban and Ray proposed is modified in order to take into account the distance between the distributions of wealth of each group. The measure of distance between two distributions suggested is the Kolmogorov measure of variation distance and the following polarization index obtained from (12.14) can be computed:

$$EK(\alpha) = \sum_{i=1}^{N} \sum_{j=1}^{N} \pi_i^{1+\alpha} \pi_j Kov_{ij}$$

(12.20)

EK ranges between 0 and $(1/2)^{1+\alpha}$. The maximum is achieved when there are only two groups of the same size with no overlapping. The index can be normalized to take values between [0, 1] by multiplying it by $2^{1+\alpha}$.

DATA SOURCES

The data sources used for this study are the 1983, 1989, 1992, 1995 and 1998 Survey of Consumer Finances (SCF) conducted by the Federal Reserve Board. Each survey consists of a core representative sample combined with a high-income supplement. The supplement is drawn from the Internal Revenue Service's Statistics of Income data file. For the 1983 SCF, for example, an income cut-off of $100 000 of adjusted gross income is used as the criterion for inclusion in the supplemental sample. Individuals were randomly selected for the sample within predesignated income strata. The advantage of the high-income supplement is that it provides a much 'richer' sample of high income and therefore potentially very wealthy families. The presence of a high-income supplement creates some complications, however, because weights must be constructed to meld the high-income supplement with the core sample.[9]

The SCF also supplies alternative sets of weights. For the 1983 SCF, we have used the so-called 'Full Sample 1983 Composite Weights' because this set of weights provides the closest correspondence between the national balance sheet totals derived from the sample and those in the Federal Reserve Board Flow of Funds. For the same reason, results for the 1989 SCF are based on the average of SRC-Design-S1 series (X40131 in the database itself) and the SRC design-based weights (X40125); and results for the 1992, 1995 and 1998 SCF rely on the design-based weights (X42000) – a partially design-based weight constructed on the basis of original selection probabilities and frame information and adjusted for nonresponse.[10] In the case of the 1992 SCF, this set of weights produced major anomalies in the size distribution of income for 1991. As a result, the weights have been modified somewhat to conform to the size distribution of income as reported in the Internal Revenue Service's Statistics of Income (see Wolff, 1996, for details on the adjustments).

The Federal Reserve Board imputes information for missing items in the SCF. Despite this procedure, discrepancies remain for several assets between the total balance sheet value computed from the survey sample and the Flow of Funds data. Consequently, the results presented below are based on Wolff's adjustments to the original asset and liability values in the surveys. This takes the form of the alignment of asset and liability totals from the survey data to the corresponding national balance sheet totals. In most cases, this entails a proportional adjustment of reported values of balance sheet items in the survey data (see Wolff, 1987, 1994, 1996 and 1998 for details).[11]

The principal wealth concept used here is marketable wealth (or net worth), which is defined as the current value of all marketable or fungible assets, less the current value of debts. Net worth is thus the difference in value between total assets and total liabilities or debt. Total assets are defined as the sum of: (1) the gross value of owner-occupied housing; (2) other real estate owned by the household; (3) cash and demand deposits; (4) time and savings deposits, certificates of deposit and money market accounts; (5) government bonds, corporate bonds, foreign bonds and other financial securities; (6) the cash surrender value of life insurance plans; (7) the cash surrender value of pension plans, including IRA, Keogh and 401(k) plans; (8) corporate stock and mutual funds; (9) net equity in unincorporated businesses; and (10) equity in trust funds. Total liabilities are the sum of: (1) mortgage debt; (2) consumer debt, including auto loans; and (3) other debt.

This measure reflects wealth as a store of value and therefore a source of potential consumption. We believe that this is the concept that best reflects the level of well-being associated with a family's holdings. Thus, only assets that can be readily converted to cash (that is, fungible ones) are included. As a result, consumer durables such as automobiles, televisions, furniture, household appliances and the like, are excluded here, since these items are not easily marketed or their resale value typically far understates the value of their consumption services to the household. Also excluded is the value of future social security benefits the family may receive upon retirement (usually referred to as 'social security wealth'), as well as the value of retirement benefits from private pension plans ('pension wealth'). Even though these funds are a source of future income to families, they are not in their direct control and cannot be marketed.[12]

THE RESULTS

Several studies have already analysed the US distribution of wealth. The importance of monitoring its evolution through time and tracking where different groups of the population are located on the wealth scale is well recognized (Wolff, 1994, 1996, 1998, 1999).

The calculations, drawn from Wolff (2003) and contained in Table 12.1, show that wealth inequality, after rising steeply between 1983 and 1989, increased at a slower pace from 1989 to 1998. The share of wealth held by the top 1 per cent rose by 3.6 percentage points from 1983 to 1989 and the Gini coefficient (a measure of overall inequality) increased from 0.80 to 0.83. Between 1989 and 1998, the share of the top percentile grew by a more moderate 0.7 percentage points but the share of the next 9 percentiles fell by 0.4 percentage points and that of the bottom two quintiles grew by 0.9 percentage points, so that overall, the Gini coefficient fell from 0.83 to 0.82.

The addendum to Table 12.1 shows the absolute changes in wealth between 1983 and 1998. The results are even more striking. Over this period, the largest gains, in relative terms, were made by the wealthiest households. The top 1 per cent saw their average wealth (in 1998 dollars) rise by \$3.0 million, or by 42 per cent. The remaining part of the top quintile, as well as the second quintile, experienced increases from 21 to 24 per cent. While the middle quintile gained 10 per cent, the poorest 40 per cent lost 76 per cent. By 1998, their average wealth had fallen to \$1100.

The reason for additional research on this topic is to investigate in detail the increasing dispersion in the aggregate distribution of wealth observed from 1983 to 1989 and from 1989 to 1998. In particular, we look at another dimension of the distribution, polarization. We examine whether a pattern similar to what has been observed regarding inequality exists for trends in wealth polarization over this period. The questions we are addressing are the following. Are the distributions of wealth of different racial, age, family type, income class, educational groups behaving in the same way over time? Have the densities of these groups the same shape and, if not, are the differences increasing or decreasing over time? Our aim is, furthermore, to understand what determined the changes observed at the aggregate level. In particular, we want to determine if the increasing dispersion of the aggregate distribution is due to changes in household characteristics or to changes in the distribution of wealth within households with the same characteristics.

We examine polarization patterns and their change over time with regard to a number of household dimensions: (1) home owner status (home owners and renters); (2) race (non-Hispanic whites versus other groups); (3) age (head of the household is under 45 years old, between 45 and 69, older than 70); (4) family type (married couples, single males, single

Table 12.1   The size distribution of net worth, 1983–98

Year	Gini Coeff	Percentage share of wealth held by:								
		Top 1.0%	Next 4.0%	Next 5.0%	Next 10.0%	Top 20.0%	2nd 20.0%	3rd 20.0%	Bottom 40.0%	All
1983	0.80	33.8	22.3	12.1	13.1	81.3	12.6	5.2	0.9	100.0
1989	0.83	37.4	21.6	11.6	13.0	83.5	12.3	4.8	−0.7	100.0
1992	0.82	37.2	22.8	11.8	12.0	83.8	11.5	4.4	0.4	100.0
1995	0.83	38.5	21.8	11.5	12.1	83.9	11.4	4.5	0.2	100.0
1998	0.82	38.1	21.3	11.5	12.5	83.4	11.9	4.5	0.2	100.0
Addendum: mean values by quantile (in thousands, 1998 dollars)										
1983		7175	1187	516.2	278.7	864.5	133.6	55.5	4.7	212.6
1998		10204	1441	623.5	344.9	1126.7	161.3	61.0	1.1	270.3
% Change		42.2	21.4	20.8	23.7	30.3	20.7	10.0	−76.3	27.1

Source: Authors' calculations from the 1983, 1989 and 1998 Survey of Consumer Finances.

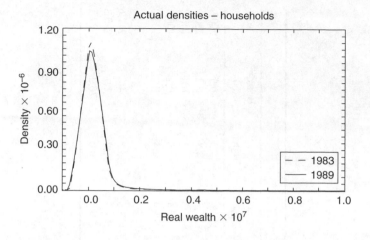

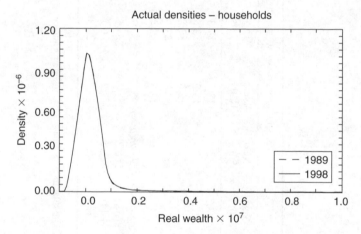

Figure 12.1   Distribution of household wealth, 1983–98

females); (5) income class (household income is under $25 000, between $25 000 and $74 999, over $75 000); (6) education (head of the household has under 16 years of education, 16 or above years of education); (7) stock and mutuals owner status (household owns stock and mutuals or does not).

The distribution of household wealth is characterized by a continuous increase in the dispersion over the years of analysis even if at a decreasing pace, as shown in Figure 12.1 where the estimated densities and the differences among them are plotted. In particular, the movement of mass from the center of the distribution towards the tails is dramatic for the period 1983–89 and not so sharp for the years 1989–98.

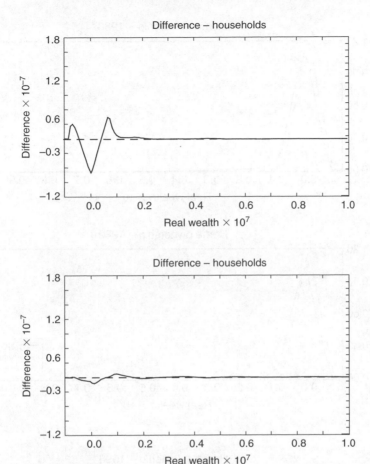

Figure 12.1 (continued)

By looking at the groups in which the total population can be partitioned according to household characteristics, we notice that wealth is not distributed in the same way at the same point in time, nor are the changes registered over time common among different groups (Figures 12.2–12.5).

Household wealth by home owner status, racial/ethnic group, educational group and stock ownership was distributed very differently between the groups in all the years analysed. In particular, the wealth density of renters, blacks and Hispanics, family heads with less than a college degree, and households not owning stock lay to the left (toward lower levels of wealth) compared to home owners, non-Hispanic whites, family heads with a college degree, and stock owners, respectively. The differences rose over time between home owners and renters, between college graduates and

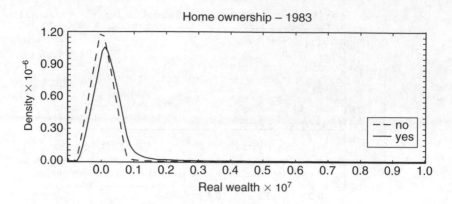

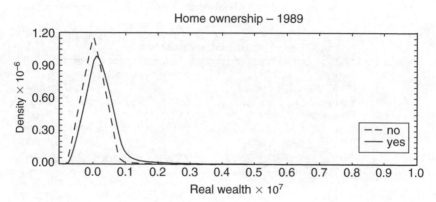

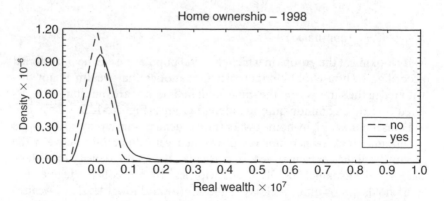

Figure 12.2 Distribution of household wealth by home ownership status and racial groups

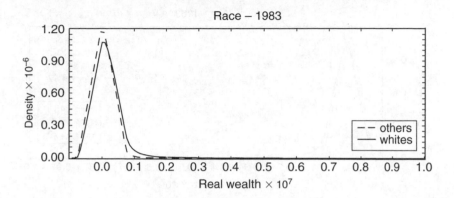

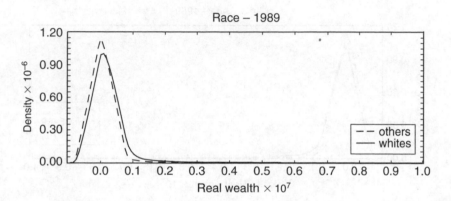

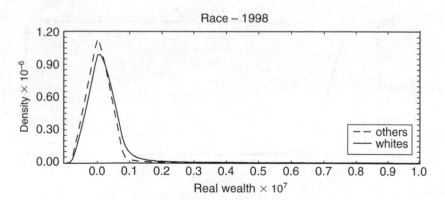

Figure 12.2   (continued)

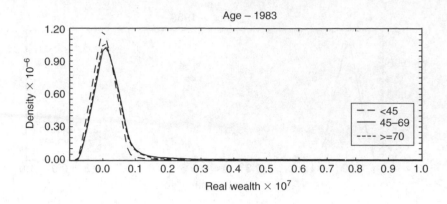

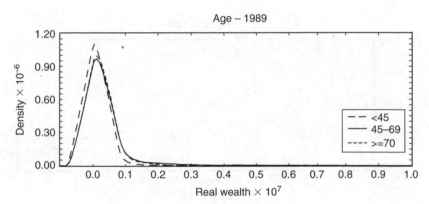

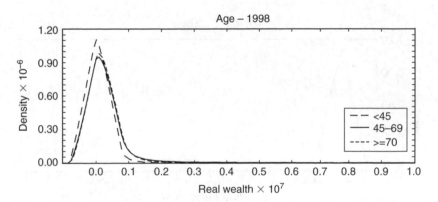

Figure 12.3   Distribution of household wealth by age and family-type group

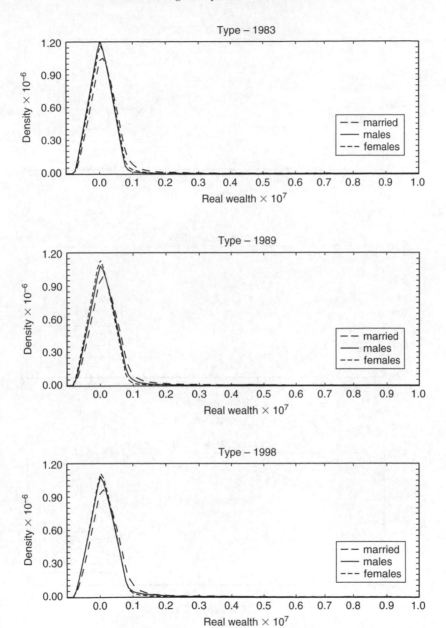

Figure 12.3 (continued)

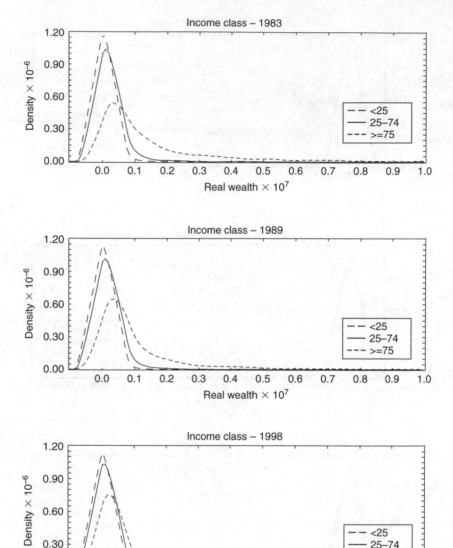

Figure 12.4   *Distribution of household wealth by income class and educational group*

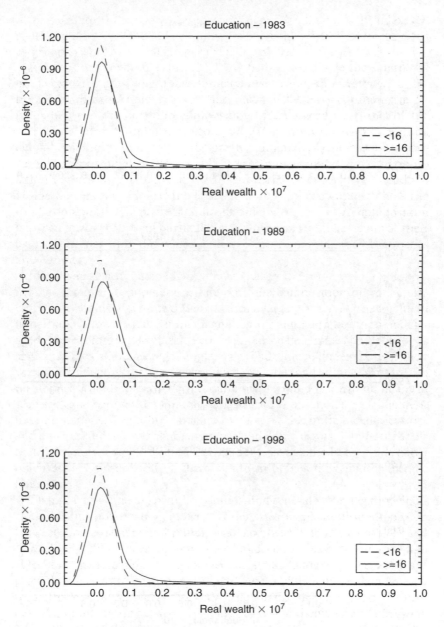

Figure 12.4 (continued)

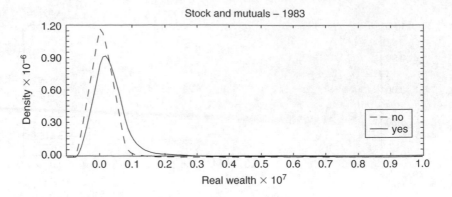

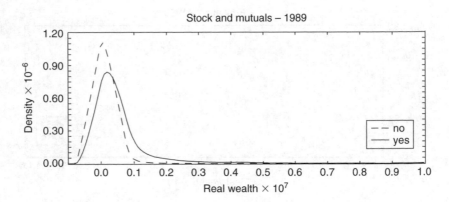

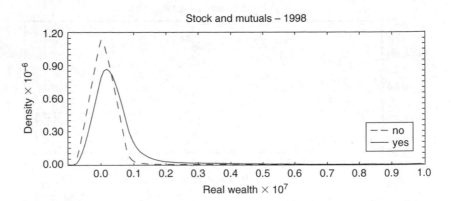

Figure 12.5   Distribution of household wealth by stock ownership group

non-college graduates, and between stock owners and nonowners, due to an increased mass of the wealth density at high levels of wealth for home owners, college graduates and stock owners, respectively. The polarization indices partially confirm these observations (Tables 12.2 and 12.3). In particular, the *EK* index shows a continuous increase over time by home owner, education, and stock ownership status. On the other hand, according to the *ER* index, polarization by educational and stock ownership status increased over time, while polarization by home ownership status declined from 1983 to 1989 and increased from 1989 to 1998, since this index captures only the differences in the means and not changes in the whole distributions.

Regarding racial groups (Figure 12.2), the difference in wealth densities first increased and then decreased. Between 1983 and 1989 the wealth owned by non-Hispanic whites increased, causing more density to shift toward higher wealth levels, while the wealth density of non-Hispanic

Table 12.2   Esteban and Ray polarization index among the distributions of 1983, 1989 and 1998

ER	alfa=1	alfa=1.3	alfa=1.6
Homeownership (1983)	0.2505	0.2064	0.1710
Homeownership (1989)	0.2321	0.1909	0.1580
Homeownership (1998)	0.2510	0.2081	0.1741
Race (1983)	0.1667	0.1460	0.1306
Race (1989)	0.1861	0.1587	0.1377
Race (1998)	0.1943	0.1676	0.1474
Age (1983)	0.2176	0.1689	0.1318
Age (1989)	0.1765	0.1363	0.1058
Age (1998)	0.1814	0.1387	0.1066
Family type (1983)	0.1514	0.1225	0.1002
Family type (1989)	0.1605	0.1242	0.0974
Family type (1998)	0.1440	0.1140	0.0915
Income class (1983)	0.3030	0.2439	0.1998
Income class (1989)	0.2872	0.2191	0.1700
Income class (1998)	0.2814	0.2048	0.1511
Education (1983)	0.2474	0.2144	0.1897
Education (1989)	0.2610	0.2285	0.2043
Education (1998)	0.2784	0.2348	0.2008
Stock and mutuals (1983)	0.3255	0.2828	0.2509
Stock and mutuals (1989)	0.3250	0.2835	0.2525
Stock and mutuals (1998)	0.3670	0.3091	0.2638

Source: Authors' calculations from the 1983, 1989 and 1998 Survey of Consumer Finances.

*Table 12.3   Esteban and Ray modified polarization index (normalized)
among the distributions of 1983, 1989 and 1998*

EK	alfa=1	alfa=1.3	alfa=1.6
Home ownership (1983)	0.1570	0.1592	0.1625
Home ownership (1989)	0.1620	0.1640	0.1671
Home ownership (1998)	0.1636	0.1670	0.1719
Race (1983)	0.0639	0.0689	0.0759
Race (1989)	0.0849	0.0892	0.0953
Race (1998)	0.0741	0.0787	0.0852
Age (1983)	0.1036	0.0991	0.0952
Age (1989)	0.0922	0.0876	0.0838
Age (1998)	0.1022	0.0961	0.0908
Family type (1983)	0.0749	0.0745	0.0749
Family type (1989)	0.0835	0.0794	0.0766
Family type (1998)	0.0825	0.0805	0.0796
Income class (1983)	0.1536	0.1532	0.1546
Income class (1989)	0.1552	0.1480	0.1427
Income class (1998)	0.1411	0.1280	0.1174
Education (1983)	0.0869	0.0928	0.1010
Education (1989)	0.1088	0.1172	0.1291
Education (1998)	0.1233	0.1281	0.1349
Stock and mutuals (1983)	0.1418	0.1514	0.1649
Stock and mutuals (1989)	0.1504	0.1621	0.1784
Stock and mutuals (1998)	0.1886	0.1959	0.2063

Source: Authors' calculations from the 1983 1989 and 1998 Survey of Consumer Finances.

whites shifted upward during the 1989–98 period. Polarization according to the *EK* index (Table 12.3) increased from 1983 to 1989 and then declined from 1989 to 1998, while according to the *ER* index, polarization (Table 12.2) increased continuously over the three years.

The differences in the wealth ownership by age group (Figure 12.3) first declined, between 1983 and 1989, and then increased, between 1989 and 1998, as a consequence of shifts in the wealth density of the oldest age group. The density of the oldest age group shifted toward that of the middle age group between 1983 and 1989, causing a decline in the level of polarization. Between 1989 and 1998, the wealth density of the oldest age group shifted away from that of the youngest, resulting in a rise in polarization.

With regard to family type, the results on polarization are sensitive to the index used. The modified Esteban and Ray index, *EK*, primarily shows an increase in polarization between households. From Figure 12.3, we can see that this result is due to the fact that the wealth densities of single male and single female households almost overlap, while the wealth density of married couples has put increasing distance between itself and the other two types of family groups over time.

The wealth densities by income group show a close correspondence between income levels and wealth. The distances among the income groups decreased over time, as did the *EK* and *ER* polarization indices.

To determine if the flattening of the aggregate wealth distribution over time is due to changes in household characteristics or to changes in the distribution of wealth within households with the same characteristics we use the decomposition method described above. The results are shown in Figures 12.6 to 12.11.

In the left-hand side of the figures are plotted the distances among the estimated density of the first year and the counterfactual densities of the second year obtained by using the estimated densities of each group of the second year and the relative frequencies of the first year (between-group decomposition). In the right-hand side of the figures are plotted the distances among the estimated density of the first year and the counterfactual densities of the second year obtained by using the estimated densities of each group of the first year and the relative frequencies of the second year (within-group decomposition). The main finding of the decomposition method is that changes in household characteristics did not have a large influence on the evolution of the US wealth density between 1983 and 1998. Instead, most of the observed variation can be attributed to shifts in the within-group wealth schedules, which underwent dramatic changes. During the 1983–89 period, within-group shifts of the wealth densities by home ownership status, age, family type, race and educational groups account for most of the change in the overall wealth density over the period. During the 1989–98 period, the same results are found by race, age and family income group. These results are confirmed by the measures of divergence and distance reported from Tables 12.4 to 12.10: decreasing values for all the within-group components in both periods except by income classes and stock ownership.

Portfolio Differences

The last part of the analysis considers portfolio differences among the various groups. In particular, we are interested in whether changes in the degree of polarization among groups are also reflected in changes in the degree of correspondence in wealth composition by group. For this purpose, we divide household assets into five groups: (1) owner-occupied housing; (2) other real estate and unincorporated business equity; (3) liquid

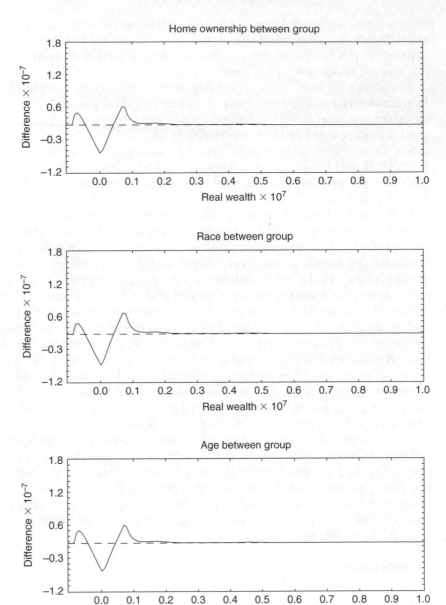

*Figure 12.6   Distance among the 1983 estimated density and 1989
counterfactual densities obtained applying the between- and
within-group decomposition*

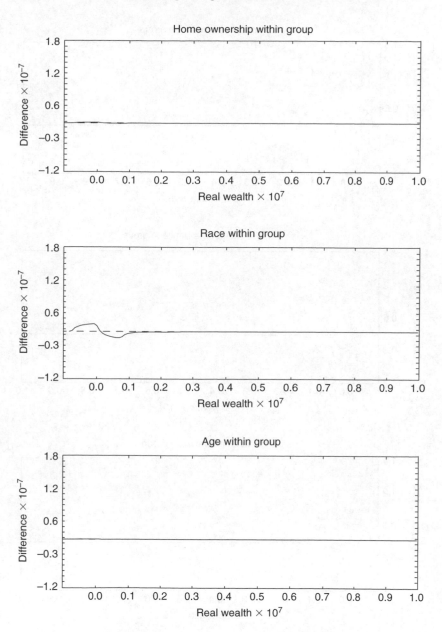

Figure 12.6 (continued)

Other types of wealth inequality

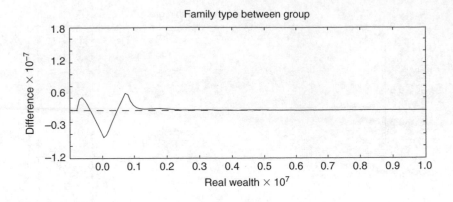

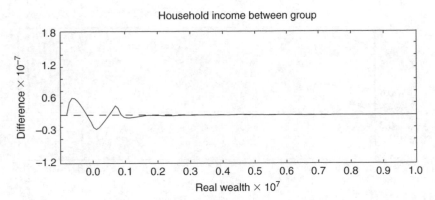

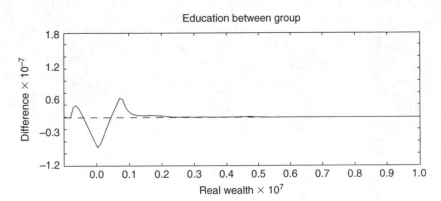

Figure 12.7   Distance among the 1983 estimated density and 1989 counterfactual densities obtained applying the between- and within-group decomposition

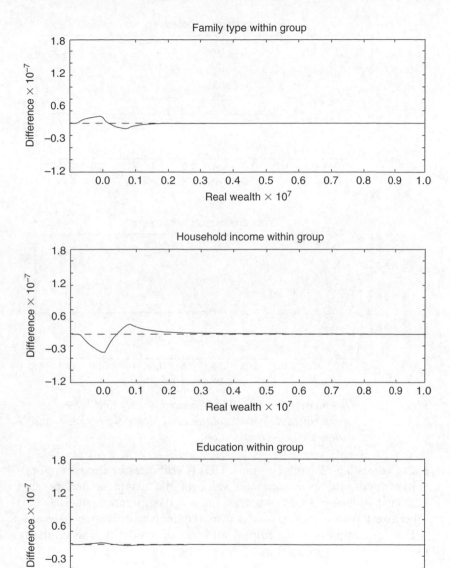

Figure 12.7   (continued)

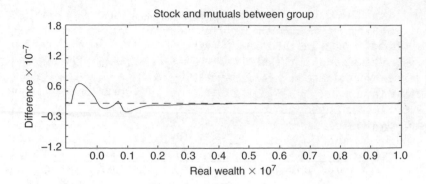

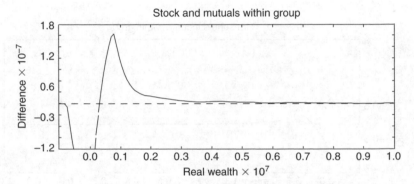

*Figure 12.8   Distance among the 1983 estimated density and 1989
                counterfactual densities obtained applying the between- and
                within-group decomposition*

assets, consisting of bank accounts, CDs (Certificates of deposit), money
market funds, the cash surrender value of life insurance and pension
accounts; (4) financial securities, trust funds and corporate equities; and (5)
other assets. We also include total debt as a component of household wealth.

For this comparison, we employ an index of similarity. The similarity
index between two groups 1 and 2 is given by:

$$SI = \frac{\sum_i m_i^1 m_i^2}{\left[\sum_i (m_i^1)^2 \sum_i (m_i^2)^2 \right]^{\frac{1}{2}}}$$

where m_i is the share of asset i in total assets. The index SI is the cosine
between the two vectors m_1 and m_2 and varies from 0: the two vectors are

orthogonal, to 1: the two vectors are identical. The dissimilarity index, DI, is defined as: $DI = 1 - SI$. The more dissimilar the portfolio compositions of groups 1 and 2 are, the greater the value of DI.

Results are shown in Table 12.11. As before, we divide the sample by home-owner status, age, race/ethnicity, age group, family type, educational group, stockholder status, and income class. We compute the DI index between the portfolio composition of each group and that of the total population. Moreover, we compute DI in two ways, with household debt and without. In all years, the greatest difference in portfolio composition was (not surprisingly) found between renters and the overall population (values of DI between 0.207 and 0.220 when debt is excluded). Home owners had almost the exact same portfolio composition as the total population. There are significant differences in wealth composition between racial groups. In particular, nonwhites had a higher share of their assets in homes than did whites and a lower share in financial securities and equities.

Middle-aged households had almost exactly the same wealth composition as the overall population. The portfolio composition of young and older households was quite different, with a larger share of their wealth in homes and a lower share in financial securities and equities than middle-aged households. While married couples and single females had portfolios similar to the overall average, single males had a much larger share of their wealth in both liquid assets and financial securities and equities. The wealth of more educated households was more tilted toward homes and financial securities and equities than that of less educated households. Stockholders, not surprisingly, had a higher share of their wealth in financial securities and equities and a lower share in homes and liquid assets than households that did not own stock. Both lower- and higher-income households had a much greater proportion of their wealth in homes than middle-income households.

Changes over time in portfolio composition generally parallel those indicated by the polarization indices. Differences in portfolio composition between home owners and renters widened over time between 1983 and 1998. Racial differences, on the other hand, narrowed between 1983 and 1989 and then remained unchanged in 1998. Differences between age groups also narrowed between 1983 and 1989 and then increased modestly from 1989 to 1998. There was very little change in portfolio differences between family types between 1983 and 1989 and then a sharp narrowing from 1989 to 1998, as the portfolios of single males became more similar to that of the overall population. Differences by schooling level widened dramatically from 1983 to 1989 and then narrowed somewhat over the 1990s. There was relatively little change in portfolio differences between

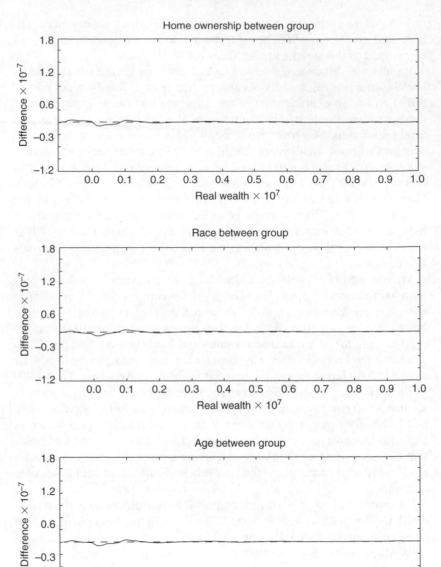

Figure 12.9   Distance among the 1989 estimated density and 1998 counterfactual densities obtained applying the between- and within-group decomposition

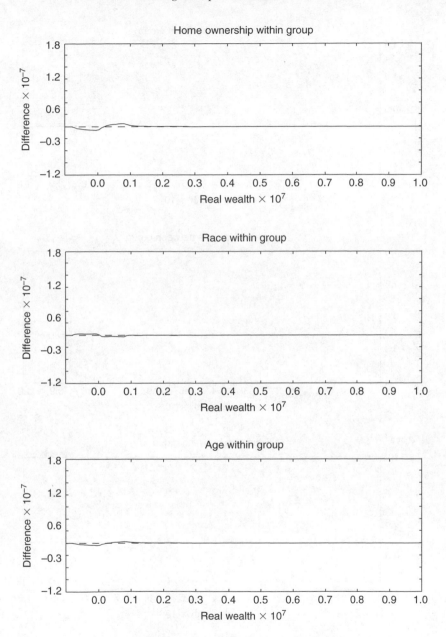

Figure 12.9 (continued)

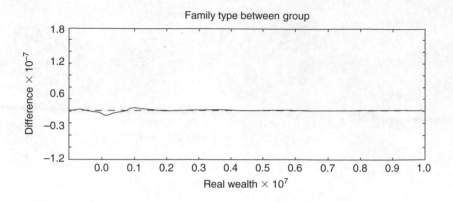

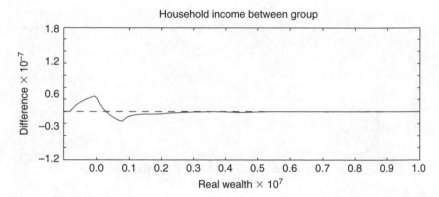

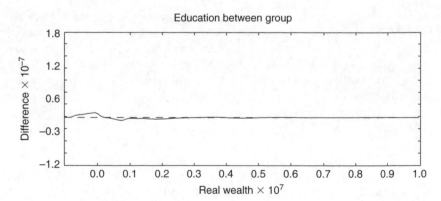

Figure 12.10   Distance among the 1989 estimated density and 1998 counterfactual densities obtained applying the between- and within-group decomposition

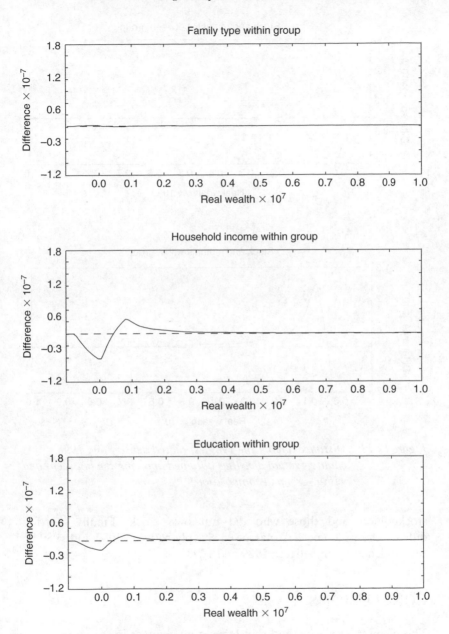

Figure 12.10   (continued)

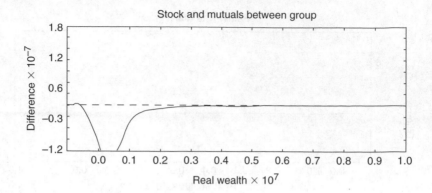

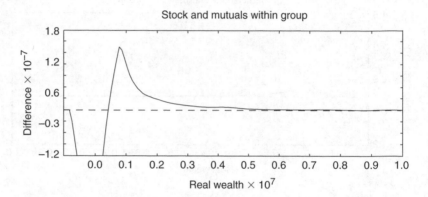

*Figure 12.11   Distance among the 1989 estimated density and 1998
                counterfactual densities obtained applying the between- and
                within-group decomposition*

stockholders and those who did not own stock. Finally, portfolio
differences by income class narrowed sharply between 1983 and 1989 and
then widened again between 1989 and 1998.

CONCLUSIONS

This chapter uses a method that focuses on changes in the entire wealth
distribution of the United States over the period from 1983 to 1998. We
find, first, on the basis of the decomposition analysis, that changes in
household characteristics had a minimal effect on the evolution of the

Table 12.4   Summary indices computed between the actual distribution of 1983 and the home ownership counterfactuals distributions

Home ownership	Kolmogorov distance	Kolmogorov variation distance
1983–89	0.0000	0.0011
within	(−99.9380)	(−96.6273)
1989–98	0.0000	0.0060
within	(−94.9386)	(−31.0677)
1983–89	0.0018	0.0318
between	(+1.5948)	(+2.1175)
1989–98	0.0006	0.0079
between	(−10.0644)	(−9.7833)

Source: Authors' calculations from the 1983, 1989 and 1998 Survey of Consumer Finances.

Table 12.5   Summary indices computed between the actual distribution of 1983 and the race counterfactual distributions

Race	Kolmogorov distance	Kolmogorov variation distance
1983–89	0.0001	0.0121
within	(−92.2421)	(−61.2548)
1989–98	0.0000	0.0030
within	(−97.7607)	(−65.4437)
1983–89	0.0020	0.0356
between	(+13.5814)	(+14.0644)
1989–98	0.0006	0.0071
between	(−7.2379)	(−18.0430)

Source: Authors' calculations from the 1983, 1989 and 1998 Survey of Consumer Finances.

overall wealth density between 1983 and 1998. Instead, most of the observed variation over time is attributable to shifts in within-group wealth schedules.

We find, second, that polarization between homeowners and tenants increased continuously from 1983 to 1998. This finding is somewhat consistent with the results reported in Table 12.12, which show that the ratio of median wealth between tenants and home owners declined continuously over the three years. However, the ratio of mean wealth between the two groups first rose between 1983 and 1989 and then declined from 1989 to 1998. By 1998, the gap in mean wealth between home owners and tenants was greater than in 1983. The increasing wealth polarization between home owners and renters also appears to be consistent with previous studies that

Table 12.6   Summary indices computed between the actual distribution of 1983 and the age counterfactual distributions

Age	Kolmogorov distance	Kolmogorov variation distance
1983–89	0.0000	0.0003
within	(−99.9572)	(−98.9063)
1989–98	0.0000	0.0036
within	(−97.6537)	(−58.5463)
1983–89	0.0017	0.0313
between	(+0.6049)	(+0.2554)
1989–98	0.0006	0.0068
between	(−8.4850)	(−22.0644)

Source: Authors' calculations from the 1983, 1989 and 1998 Survey of Consumer Finances.

Table 12.7   Summary indices computed between the actual distribution of 1983 and the family-type counterfactuals distributions

Family type	Kolmogorov distance	Kolmogorov variation distance
1983–89	0.0001	0.0108
within	(−92.7618)	(−65.5048)
1989–98	0.0000	0.0015
within	(−98.3791)	(−82.8675)
1983–89	0.0017	0.0309
between	(+0.9233)	(−0.9839)
1989–98	0.0006	0.0084
between	(−2.3740)	(−3.6220)

Source: Authors' calculations from the 1983, 1989 and 1998 Survey of Consumer Finances.

have emphasized the importance of home ownership as a vehicle for wealth accumulation in general (see, for example, Oliver and Shapiro 1997). Besides providing forced savings (through the amortization of mortgage debt), owning a home may also facilitate access to greater financial information and create a psychological disposition towards saving for the future.

Second, polarization between college graduates and nongraduates also increased continuously over the 1983–98 period. The pattern is somewhat different than that reported in Table 12.12. Between 1983 and 1989, the ratio of mean net worth between the two groups rose from 3.85 to 4.12 but then declined to 3.87 in 1998. Likewise, the ratio of median wealth between the two groups, after rising from 3.26 in 1983 to 4.09 in 1989 fell off to 3.58 in 1998. The finding of enhanced wealth polarization between the college

Table 12.8   *Summary indices computed between the actual distribution of 1983 and the income-class counterfactuals distributions*

Income class	Kolmogorov distance	Kolmogorov variation distance
1983–89	0.0014	0.0292
within	(−20.3469)	(−6.2786)
1989–98	0.0025	0.0433
within	(+290.9630)	(+396.0372)
1983–89	0.0015	0.0225
between	(−14.4303)	(−27.9846)
1989–98	0.0014	0.0253
between	(+113.4153)	(+189.6472)

Source: Authors' calculations from the 1983, 1989 and 1998 Survey of Consumer Finances.

Table 12.9   *Summary indices computed between the actual distribution of 1983 and the education counterfactuals distributions*

Education	Kolmogorov distance	Kolmogorov variation distance
1983–89	0.0000	0.0026
within	(−99.2663)	(−91.5612)
1989–98	0.0003	0.0156
within	(−46.4220)	(+78.6130)
1983–89	0.0019	0.0341
between	(+11.0982)	(+9.2447)
1989–98	0.0006	0.0091
between	(−13.4091)	(+4.6699)

Source: Authors' calculations from the 1983, 1989 and 1998 Survey of Consumer Finances.

educated and less educated groups is consistent with numerous studies of the labour market which have found a rising return to a college education over the period in question (see, for example, Levy and Murnane 1992).

Third, polarization by groups of income classes continuously decreased over the same period. This finding reflects, in part, the fact that the relative wealth position of the top income class, in terms of both means and medians, declined over the period from 1983 to 1998 (see Table 12.12). However, the relative wealth holdings of the lowest income class also deteriorated over these years.

Fourth, polarization by racial group first increased from 1983 to 1989 and then declined from 1989 to 1998. It is also true that the ratio of median wealth between nonwhites and non-Hispanic whites first declined from

Table 12.10   Summary indices computed between the actual distribution of 1983 and the stock and mutuals counterfactuals distributions

Stock mutuals	Kolmogorov distance	Kolmogorov variation distance
1983–89	0.0000	0.0017
within	(−99.7756)	(−94.6250)
1989–98	0.0006	0.0210
within	(−10.1995)	(+140.6749)
1983–89	0.0471	0.2933
between	(+2620.7987)	(+840.8016)
1989–98	0.0407	0.3015
between	(+6204.1112)	(+3357.2995)

Source: Authors' calculations from the 1983, 1989 and 1998 Survey of Consumer Finances.

0.09 in 1983 to 0.05 in 1989 and then rose to 0.12 in 1998. However, the ratio of mean wealth between the two racial groups actually increased from 0.24 in 1983 to 0.31 in 1989 before falling off a bit to 0.29 in 1998. The decreased racial polarization of the 1990s may partly reflect the rise of a black (and Hispanic) middle class in the United States (see, for example, Oliver and Shapiro 1997).

Fifth, polarization by age groups declined from 1983 to 1989 and then rebounded in the 1990s. This pattern may reflect the fact that the average wealth of the poorest age group, those households headed by a person under 45 years of age, relative to the overall mean first rose from 1983 to 1989 and then declined in 1998. However, the median wealth of the under-45 age group relative to the overall median declined continuously over the three years.

Sixth, the time trends in polarization by family type were sensitive to the index used. The results of Table 12.12 show that the relative wealth position of households headed by an unmarried female deteriorated over the period from 1983 to 1998 while the relative net worth position of single males improved. Female-headed households consist of both divorced and widowed women and those never married. The relative decline in the wealth of female-headed households as a group probably reflects the dramatic rise in the number of never-married women with children.

Seventh, polarization between households that own and those that do not own stock or mutual funds, after changing very little between 1983 and 1989, skyrocketed in the 1990s. This pattern is also reflected in Table 12.12. The ratio of mean wealth between stock owners and those who do not hold stock fell somewhat from 5.7 in 1983 to 5.5 in 1989 and then climbed to 6.2 in 1998, while the ratio of median net worth rose continuously, from 5.6 in

Table 12.11 *Portfolio composition by demographic and economic group and the DI index, 1983–98 (as a percentage of total assets)*

	Home	Other real estate plus business equity	Liquid assets	Financial securities plus equities	Other assets	Total debt	Total assets	DI index value[b]	
								Excl. debt	Incl. debt
1983									
All households	30.1	33.8	18.9	15.9	1.3	13.1	100.0	0.000	0.000
Home owner status									
Home owner	32.3	33.3	17.7	15.7	1.0	12.9	100.0	0.001	0.001
Renter	0.0	40.1	35.1	18.9	5.9	15.8	100.0	0.207	0.193
Race/ethnicity									
Non-Hisp. whites	29.0	34.1	18.9	16.6	1.3	12.6	100.0	0.000	0.000
Other races/ ethnicity	44.2	29.4	17.6	6.7	2.1	29.9	100.0	0.048	0.070
Age group									
Under 45	47.3	28.4	18.7	3.7	1.9	21.2	100.0	0.071	0.069
45–69	29.0	34.1	18.9	16.6	1.3	12.6	100.0	0.000	0.000
70 and over	44.2	29.4	17.6	6.7	2.1	29.9	100.0	0.048	0.070
Family type									
Married couples	25.8	37.9	17.8	17.3	1.2	8.8	100.0	0.007	0.010
Single males	23.7	23.0	26.2	26.5	0.7	1.7	100.0	0.063	0.084
Single females	29.4	35.6	17.6	16.3	1.1	13.0	100.0	0.001	0.001
Education									
Less than 16 years	29.9	29.6	26.4	10.7	3.3	17.2	100.0	0.020	0.021
16 years or more	33.7	24.8	24.5	14.6	2.4	13.2	100.0	0.024	0.023

Table 12.11   (continued)

	Home	Other real estate plus business equity	Liquid assets	Financial securities plus equities	Other assets	Total debt	Total assets	DI index value[b]	
								Excl. debt	Incl. deb
Stock holder									
Stock holder	21.8	37.6	16.5	22.9	1.3	12.7	100.0	0.026	0.025
Not a stock holder	38.7	29.8	21.4	8.7	1.4	13.6	100.0	0.025	0.024
Income group[a]									
<$25 000	43.8	31.6	20.6	2.8	1.3	18.3	100.0	0.055	0.052
25 000–$74 999	19.9	35.4	17.7	25.7	1.4	9.2	100.0	0.039	0.039
$75 000 or more	48.9	22.5	22.1	4.3	2.3	11.2	100.0	0.096	0.093
1989									
All households	30.2	31.2	20.4	13.3	4.9	15.0	100.0	0.000	0.000
Home owner status									
Home owner	33.5	29.1	19.9	13.1	4.3	15.3	100.0	0.003	0.003
Renter	0.0	49.9	24.5	15.2	10.5	12.5	100.0	0.212	0.201
Race/ethnicity									
Non-Hisp. whites	28.9	30.7	21.0	14.5	4.9	14.1	100.0	0.001	0.001
Other races/ ethnicity	39.4	30.4	16.4	8.0	5.8	30.2	100.0	0.022	0.044
Age group									
Under 45	41.6	35.6	14.8	3.0	5.0	22.8	100.0	0.042	0.041
45–69	28.9	30.7	21.0	14.5	4.9	14.1	100.0	0.001	0.001
70 and over	39.4	30.4	16.4	8.0	5.8	30.2	100.0	0.022	0.044
Family type									
Married couples	26.7	35.1	20.5	12.8	4.8	10.4	100.0	0.005	0.009
Single males	25.0	19.8	27.0	24.5	3.6	2.4	100.0	0.067	0.093
Single females	29.2	32.4	19.8	13.9	4.8	15.4	100.0	0.001	0.001

Education									
Less than 16 years	28.9	30.4	21.6	13.2	6.0	11.8	100.0	0.001	0.003
16 years or more	47.5	17.5	24.6	5.9	4.6	18.9	100.0	0.091	0.083
Stock holder									
Stock holder	23.7	35.5	18.4	17.1	5.3	16.2	100.0	0.016	0.015
Not a stock holder	36.7	26.9	22.3	9.5	4.5	13.8	100.0	0.015	0.014
Income group[a]									
< $25 000	41.6	29.7	20.2	4.0	4.6	18.4	100.0	0.035	0.032
$25 000–$74 999	21.2	32.3	20.5	20.7	5.2	12.4	100.0	0.028	0.027
$75 000 or more	43.2	23.5	24.2	5.3	3.9	9.1	100.0	0.051	0.056
1998									
All households	29.0	27.7	21.1	20.4	1.8	15.0	100.0	0.000	0.000
Home owner status									
Home owner	30.4	27.6	20.1	20.3	1.6	14.8	100.0	0.001	0.001
Renter	0.0	29.9	41.7	23.3	5.1	18.6	100.0	0.220	0.200
Race/ethnicity									
Non-Hisp. Whites	27.8	28.1	20.7	21.5	1.9	14.0	100.0	0.001	0.001
Other races/ethnicity	37.9	25.2	21.5	13.8	1.7	29.9	100.0	0.024	0.046
Age group									
Less than 45	41.5	23.2	25.5	9.0	0.8	24.6	100.0	0.056	0.057
45–69	27.8	28.1	20.7	21.5	1.9	14.0	100.0	0.001	0.001
70 and over	37.9	25.2	21.5	13.8	1.7	29.9	100.0	0.024	0.046
Family type									
Married couples	25.5	30.3	21.4	20.8	1.9	12.0	100.0	0.004	0.005
Single males	27.3	22.9	19.8	28.6	1.5	3.3	100.0	0.019	0.044
Single females	28.6	29.3	21.1	19.4	1.7	15.2	100.0	0.001	0.001
Education									
Less than 16 years	22.5	32.1	21.5	21.5	2.4	14.8	100.0	0.013	0.012
16 years or more	36.5	13.4	21.4	26.6	2.1	13.5	100.0	0.057	0.054

435

Table 12.11 (continued)

	Home	Other real estate plus business equity	Liquid assets	Financial securities plus equities	Other assets	Total debt	Total assets	DI index value[b]	
								Excl. debt	Incl. deb
Stock holder									
Stock holder	22.7	29.2	21.8	24.4	1.9	12.9	100.0	0.012	0.012
Not a stock holder	37.9	25.5	20.2	14.8	1.6	17.9	100.0	0.021	0.020
Income group[a]									
<$25 000	44.9	25.3	24.1	4.0	1.7	23.8	100.0	0.086	0.081
$25 000–$74 999	21.4	28.8	19.7	28.2	1.8	10.8	100.0	0.024	0.026
$75 000 or more	47.9	17.4	20.3	12.5	1.9	14.9	100.0	0.086	0.081

Notes:
a. Income in 1998 dollars.
b. DI index for portfolio composition of group in comparison to that of all households.

Source: Authors' calculations from the 1983, 1989 and 1998 Survey of Consumer Finances.

Table 12.12   *Ratio of group mean (median) net worth to the overall mean
(median) by household characteristic*

Group	Mean net worth			Median net worth		
	1983	1989	1998	1983	1989	1998
Home owner status						
Home owner	1.47	1.43	1.44	1.96	2.09	1.96
Renter	0.18	0.27	0.14	0.02	0.01	0.00
Race						
Non-Hispanic whites	1.17	1.21	1.19	1.29	1.44	1.35
Other races	0.29	0.37	0.35	0.12	0.07	0.17
Age						
Under 45	0.40	0.49	0.45	0.38	0.33	0.26
45–69	1.73	1.58	1.56	1.92	1.86	1.75
70 and over	1.21	1.32	1.30	1.51	1.89	2.08
Family type						
Married couples	1.34	1.42	1.34	1.46	1.70	1.51
Single males	0.34	0.63	0.67	0.15	0.56	0.35
Single females	0.50	0.29	0.44	0.45	0.36	0.42
Income class [1998$]						
Less than $25 000	0.28	0.26	0.24	0.22	0.12	0.13
$25 000–$74 999	0.65	0.65	0.60	1.26	1.29	1.20
$75 000 or more	4.79	4.15	3.91	5.50	5.55	5.19
Education						
Less than College graduate	0.62	0.63	0.55	0.76	0.78	0.68
College graduate	2.40	2.58	2.14	2.49	3.20	2.43
Stock ownership						
Owns stocks or mutual funds	2.89	2.90	2.49	3.57	4.11	3.85
Nonowner	0.51	0.53	0.40	0.64	0.62	0.42

Source: Authors' calculations from the 1983, 1989 and 1998 Survey of Consumer Finances.

1983 to 6.6 in 1989 and then to 9.1 in 1998. These results reflect, in part, the
rapid rise of stock prices during the 1990s. They may also be attributable
to greater access among stock owners to other financial instruments and
financing possibilities.

The analysis of portfolio differences among various groups highlights the
fact that changes in the degree of polarization among groups are also
reflected in changes in the degree of correspondence in wealth composition
by group.

On a final note, it is apparent that the polarization indices are a much
more complex measure of group homogeneity relative to population-wide
heterogeneity than a simple comparison of group means and medians

would suggest. Though trends in relative means and median generally parallel trends in the polarization indices, in several incidences the two sets are at variance.

NOTES

* We would like to thank Claudio Lucifora and the participants of the ESPE 2001 conference and of the conference on Saving, Intergenerational Transfers, and the Distribution of Wealth at the Levy Economics Institute of Bard College, 2000.
1. In this chapter, the kernel function used is the triangular, and the bandwidth parameter is chosen in order to match the sample value of the Gini coefficient.
2. An alternative estimation method for the counterfactual density of income at t_1 and characteristics at t_2 is proposed by DiNardo et al. (1996).
3. For a detailed survey, see, among others, Ali and Silvey (1966).
4. Wolfson's measure of polarization (1994) does not apply, as it is a measure of bipolarization and we are interested here in monitoring the movements of the distributions of all numbers of groups.
5. A similar interpretation can be given to the Gini coefficient, but in Gini the number of agents similar to the one under analysis does not matter; in other words, in the Gini coefficient the separation and the effective separation coincide. Hence the proportionality between P and Gini (Gini defined over the logs) when $\alpha = 0$.
6. The population weights η_i, $i = 1, \ldots, N$ are replaced by the population frequencies. The constant K is hence set to $k = [\Sigma_{i=1}^{N} \eta_i]^{-(2+\alpha)}$.
7. The Esteban and Ray index involves some previous grouping since it assumes that the society is partitioned into a small number of significantly sized groups, and groups of insignificant size (for example, isolated individuals) carry little weight (Esteban and Ray 1994, p. 824).
8. Esteban et al. (1999) have proposed an alternative modification of ER (α) to correct for not having included in the analysis the inequality within each group and the overlapping of the groups that has the effect of overestimating the level of observed polarization. In particular:

$$P(\alpha, \beta) = ER(\alpha) - \beta\varepsilon \qquad (12.17)$$

where:

$$\varepsilon = G(f) - G(\mu) \qquad (12.18)$$

the difference between the Gini coefficient computed on the ungrouped, $G(f)$, and grouped data, $G(\mu)$. β is the parameter that indicates the importance given to the approximation error.
9. Three studies conducted by the Federal Reserve Board – Kennickell and Woodburn (1992) for the 1989 SCF; Kennickell et al. (1996) for the 1992 SCF; and Kennickell and Woodburn (1999) for the 1995 SCF – discuss some of the issues involved in developing these weights.
10. The 1998 weights are actually partially design-based weights (X42001), which account for the systematic deviation from the CPS estimates of homeownership rates by racial and ethnic groups.
11. The adjustment factors by asset type and year are as follows:

Table 12.13 Adjustment factors by asset type and year

	1983 SCF	1989 SCF	1992 SCF	1995 SCF
Checking accounts	1.68			
Savings and time deposits	1.50			
All deposits		1.37	1.32	
Financial securities	1.20			
Stocks and mutual funds	1.06			
Trusts		1.66	1.41	1.45
Stocks and bonds				1.23
Nonmortgage debt	1.16			

Note: No adjustments were made to other asset and debt components.

It should be noted that the alignment has very little effect on the measurement of wealth inequality – both the Gini coefficient and the quantile shares. However, it is important to make these adjustments when comparing changes in mean wealth both overall and by asset type.

12. See Burkhauser and Weathers (2000) for recent estimates of social security and pension wealth.

REFERENCES

Ali, S.M. and S.D. Silvey (1966), 'A general class of coefficients of divergence of one distribution from another', *Journal of the Royal Statistical Society*, **A**(1), 131–42.

Blank, R.M. and D. Card (1993), 'Poverty, income distribution, and growth: are they still connected?', *Brooking Papers on Economic Activity*, **2**, 285–339.

Burkhauser, R. and R. Weathers (2000), 'Retirement, annuities, and bequests', in T.M. Shaprio and E.N. Wolff (eds), *Benefits and Mechanisms for Spreading Asset Ownership in the United States*, New York: Russell Sage Press.

Burkhauser, R., A. Crews, M.C. Daly and S.P. Jenkins (1999), 'Testing the significance of income distribution changes over the 1980s business cycle: a cross-national comparison', *Journal of Applied Econometrics*, **14**, 253–72.

D'Ambrosio, C. (2001), 'Household characteristics and the distribution of income in Italy: an application of social distance measures', *Review of Income and Wealth*, **47**(1), 43–64.

DiNardo, J., N.M. Fortin and T. Lemieux (1996), 'Labor market institutions and the distribution of wages, 1973–1993: a semiparametric approach', *Econometrica*, **64**(5), 1001–44.

Esteban, J.M. and D. Ray (1994), 'On the measurement of polarization', *Econometrica*, **62**(4), 819–51.

Esteban, J.M. and D. Ray (1999), 'Conflict and distribution', *Journal of Economic Theory*, **87**, 379–415.

Esteban, J.M., C. Gradin and D. Ray (1999), 'Extensions of a measure of polarization, with an application to income distribution of five OECD countries', Working Paper n.24, Institute de Estudios Económicos de Galicia, Fundación Pedro Barrié de la Maza, A Coruña, Spain. Also: Luxembourg Income Study

Working Paper Series, 218, Maxwell School of Citizenship and Public Affairs, Syracuse University, Syracuse, New York.

Kennickell, A.B. and R.L. Woodburn (1992), 'Estimation of household net worth using model-based and design-based weights: evidence from the 1989 Survey of Consumer Finances', Federal Reserve Board, mimeo.

Kennickell, A.B. and R.L. Woodburn (1999), 'Consistent weight design for the 1989, 1992, and 1995 SCFs, and the distribution of wealth', *Review of Income and Wealth*, **45**(2), 193–215.

Kennickell, A.B., D.A. McManus and R.L. Woodburn (1996), 'Weighting design for the 1992 Survey of Consumer Finances', Federal Reserve Board, mimeo.

Levy, Frank and Richard Murnane (1992), 'US earnings levels and earnings inequality: a review of recent trends and proposed explanations', *Journal of Economic Literature*, **30**(3), 1333–81.

Oliver, M.L. and T.M. Shapiro (1997), *Black Wealth, White Wealth*, New York: Routledge Press.

Wolff, E.N. (1987), 'Estimates of household wealth inequality in the United States, 1962–83', *Review of Income and Wealth*, **33**(3), 231–56.

Wolff, E.N. (1994), 'Trends in household wealth in the United States, 1962–1983 and 1983–1989', *Review of Income and Wealth*, **40**(2), 143–74.

Wolff, E.N. (1996), *Top Heavy: A Study of Increasing Inequality of Wealth in America*, updated and expanded edition, New York: New Press.

Wolff, E.N. (1998), 'Recent trends in the size distribution of household wealth', *Journal of Economic Perspectives*, **12**(3), 131–50.

Wolff, E.N. (1999), 'The size distribution of wealth in the United States: a comparison among recent household surveys', in James P. Smith and Robert J. Willis (eds), *Wealth, Work and Health: Innovations in Measurement in the Social Sciences*, Ann Arbor, MI: Universtity of Michigan Press, pp. 209–32.

Wolff, E.N. (2003), 'Recent trends in wealth ownership', in T.M. Shapiro and E.N. Wolff (eds), *Benefits and Mechanisms for Spreading Asset Ownership in the United States*, New York: Russell Sage Press.

Wolfson, M.C. (1994), 'When inequality diverge', *American Economic Review Papers and Proceedings*, **84**, 353–8.

Index